ACCESS:
AGING CURRICULUM CONTENT
FOR EDUCATION IN THE
SOCIAL-BEHAVIORAL SCIENCES

ACCESS:
AGING CURRICULUM CONTENT FOR EDUCATION IN THE SOCIAL-BEHAVIORAL SCIENCES

Iris A. Parham, Ph.D.
Leonard W. Poon, Ph.D.
Ilene C. Siegler, Ph.D., M.P.H.

Editors

SPRINGER PUBLISHING COMPANY
New York

Springer Publishing Company, Inc.
536 Broadway
New York, NY 10012

90 91 92 93 94 / 5 4 3 2 1

Library of Congress Cataloging-in-Publication Data

Aging curriculum content for education in the social sciences / Iris
    Parham, Leonard Poon, Ilene Siegler, editors.
        p.   cm.
    Bibliography: p.
    ISBN 0-8261-6070-0
    1. Aging—Psychological aspects—Outlines, syllabi, etc. 2. Aged—
Psychology—Outlines, syllabi, etc. I. Parham, Iris A. II. Poon,
Leonard W., 1942-   III. Siegler, Ilene C.
    BF724.8.A35   1989
    155.67—dc19   89-11351
                                                                    CIP

Printed in the United States of America

Contents

Preface

The Conference Report of the 1981 "Older Boulder" Conference on Training Psychologists for Work in Aging's (Santos & Vandenbos, 1982) recommended "brief 4–6 page modules outlining objectives, readings and illustrative materials . . ." (p. 24); this provided the official starting point for the present volume. As Storandt (1982, pp. 12–13) points out: The Older Boulder Conference began in the Education Committee of Division 20 of APA (Adult Development and Aging) in 1975–76 and continued as a Division-sponsored enterprise for the next 10 years.

In the summer of 1985, on behalf of Division 20, we (IAP, LWP, ICS) signed a contract with Springer Publishing Company to publish the much expanded/elaborated modules here. The process of completion proved to take longer than anticipated.

Throughout this process many individuals, but particularly Diana Woodruff-Pak and Susan Krauss Whitbourne, who developed previous prospecti, contributed to the fulfillment of Division 20's original aim of providing useful materials to increase the probability that aging content is taught in introductory psychology and graduate level courses whenever appropriate.

The high quality of modules in this volume speak most eloquently to the fine contributions of our authors.

IRIS A. PARHAM
LEONARD W. POON
ILENE C. SIEGLER
Richmond, VA

Editors' Guide to the Modules

PURPOSE AND SCOPE

Because of the diversity of the courses available which may contain aging content and the varied backgrounds of the students taking these courses, a versatile modular curriculum was designed. Each module could be used for undergraduate courses, graduate courses, and for "Independent Study" by both faculty and students. We also envision that the modules can serve as an introduction to a major area for single course development or research program design.

The individual modules are constructed in such a way that they can be selected independently for study or combined with other modules in order to accommodate the needs of undergraduate/graduate psychology curricula and those of interested individuals. Each module includes a variety of components designed to facilitate both teaching and learning of the instructional material. Most of the components can be used independently of the others, and it is expected that students and faculty will select for use the individual modular components most suited to their personal needs and objectives.

Again, the individual modules may be utilized in at least two ways: (a) for lecture preparation, or (b) for student course outline or self-paced independent study. First, modules may be used as resource materials in the preparation of approximately two to three hours of classroom lecture. A variety of suggestions for bibliographic and audiovisual references, classroom activities and assignments, test questions, and (in some cases) handouts are provided as tools for instructors in lecture preparation. Additionally, students and instructors may examine modules independent of structured classroom time on a self-paced, self-instructional basis. When modules are approached in this way, some of the suggested class activities, particularly those requiring group interaction, will need to be omitted; however, the remaining modular material should prove useful to the student or instructor interested in self-paced mastery of psychology of aging content. In either case, it is intended that, upon completion of a given module, instructors or students with no or limited previous knowledge in that area will gain a satisfactory level of comprehension of the topic.

Following are brief descriptions of each module as well as a generic outline of module content and an example/explanation of the Annotated Bibliography sections.

BRIEF DESCRIPTION OF MODULES

1. *Teaching Courses on the Psychology of Adult Development and Aging*, Irene Hulicka and Susan Whitbourne. This module includes almost every consideration in designing and teaching a course in aging. The authors discuss at length such questions as scope, audience diversity, specific topics, prerequisites, recommended textbooks and supplementary materials, and they offer an informative section on "Do's and Dont's" for teaching in this area which cuts to the heart of the matter.

2. *Methodological Constraints—So You Want To Do Research in Aging*, K. Warner Schaie. As stated by Dr. Schaie, this module presents material on research methodology in the psychology of aging that would not ordinarily have been presented in the traditional courses in research design and statistics. The module focuses on special research problems in this area, offers simple, clear basic designs which can be employed, and includes discussion of the limitations of these designs in terms of threats to internal and external validity. Schaie also includes an intriguing brief discussion of ethical issues involved in reporting aging studies research results (see his *American Psychologist*, 1988 article).

3. *Longevity*, Diana S. Woodruff-Pak and Mary Winn. The topic of longevity as covered in this module includes discussion of many issues in the psychology of aging: health, personality characteristics, lifestyle, stress, and adaptation. Included as well is a good grounding on other influencing factors such as heredity and race. Woodruff adds to the readability of her module by giving very practical suggestions to enhance longevity (after Woodruff, 1979).

4. *The Psychology of Health: Issues in the Field with Special Focus on the Older Person*, Barbara Felton and Tracey Revenson. This module covers the topic of health psychology as encompassed in studies of the role of social and psychological factors in the onset of illness, the psychological experiences of illness, the course of recovery, the direction and intensity of chronic episodes, and preparation for illness. Special attention is paid to social and psychological factors as they are both antecedents and moderators of psychological adjustment to illness.

5. *Mental Health and Aging*, Stephen H. Zarit and Diana Spore. This module describes the prevalence and kinds of psychological disorders/problems which may accompany aging as well as assessment and treatment issues across the second half of the life span. The strength of this module is in its comprehensiveness and attention to detail for a topic area which has a large and disparate empirical base.

6. *Sexuality and Aging*, Jodi L. Teitelman. This module offers a comprehensive overview of sexuality and aging, the psychological as well as physical changes which occur that impact on frequency and enjoyment of sexual activity in late life. Teitelman pays particular attention to the need for empirical studies in the area while offering a large sampling of supplemental materials: movies, exercises, and handouts to heighten the awareness of the complexity of late life sexual experience.

7. *Ageism*, Dean Rodeheaver. This module offers a comprehensive view of contemporary ageism, its evolution and impact, and the complexity of the interaction of ageism with sexism and racism. Rodeheaver also presents supplementary materials which clearly focus on the serious implications of active ageism as well as strategies for change.

8. *Aging, Work and Retirement*. Harvey L. Sterns, Ralph Alexander, Gerald Barrett, Lisa Schwartz, and Nancy Kebits. This module covers demographic issues, career planning, social policy and legal issues, performance factors, and leisure aspects relating to work and retirement. The issues presented are particularly timely as our society wrestles with the challenges of career change, early/late retirement, and leisure planning. The need for practitioners/teachers/students to have a good knowledge base in this area is obvious.

MODULE CONTENT

1. *Introduction*. The opening section consists of referenced narrative discussing the current state-of-the-art in research and clinical work for the major issues as well as addressing predominant stereotypes peculiar to each module topic. The perspective of the authors, the experienced teachers, are also included in this introductory section.

2. *Module Outline*. Topics covered in the module are summarized in outline form.

3. *Annotated Bibliography*. Most journal and book references included in the Introduction and Content Outline are listed individually and alphabetically. Each reference is briefly (approximately 1 paragraph) summarized and, when appropriate, critiqued methodologically. Each reference is assessed as to kind, recommendation, readability, and audience.

4. *Supplementary Material*. Depending on appropriateness to topic and availability, this section includes recommended handouts, class activities and/or audiovisuals. Handout materials were designed to concisely summarize and/or descriptively supplement didactic information included in the module. Classroom activities where appropriate are included to enhance the learning experiences of students. These include such activities as field site visits, classroom case study exercises, communication skill exercises, role playing, in-

class psychometric diagnostic demonstrations (e.g., stress inventories), and other experiential exercises. And finally, for some modules audiovisuals considered appropriate for supplementing didactic information are described. Name, date of production, length of presentations, and acquisition information available are included when possible for each audiovisual reference. When possible, audiovisuals are previewed and critiqued; otherwise, descriptive material concerning each medium are included when available.

ANNOTATED BIBLIOGRAPHY SECTIONS

Example 1

Reference with authors	Postscripts			
	Kind	Recommendation	Readability	Audience
Poon, L. W., Aging in the 1980s	HB	***	2–3	AG

Postscript meanings[1]

Kind	Recommendation	Readability	Audience
1. Textbook-*TB* or Textbook (chapter)	Classic-***	Beginner-1	General Public-GP
2. Handbook-*HB* Book B	Should be read to be educated-**	Moderate-2	Service providers-SP
3. Empirical Articles-*E* or *EA*	Don't Bother-*	Technical-3	Academic audience-AU or AG (AU-undergraduate; + AG graduate and above)
4. Clinical Article- Clinical[2]			(In Felton/Revenson *G-Graduate, *U-undergraduate)
5. Review Chapter-*RC* Review article-*RA*			
6. Theoretical Chapter-*TC* Theoretical Article-*TA*			

[1]There is some variability across modules and in some cases the kind of articles is spelled out [2], e.g., Teitelman, and Rodeheaver, and in other cases, Felton and Revenson, postscripts are modified (see specific postscript meanings on page 139).

Module Editors/Contributors

EDITORS

Iris Parham, Ph.D., is Associate Professor of Gerontology, Psychology, and Geriatric Medicine; Chair, Gerontology Department and Executive Director, Geriatric Education Center at Virginia Commonwealth University. She is co-author of two volumes of modules in geriatrics (Health Sciences Consortium); *Crisis Intervention with the Elderly: Theory, Practical Issues, and Training Procedures, 1988; Fundamentals in Geriatrics for Health Professionals: An Annotated Bibliography 1989.* Dr. Parham is a member of the Editorial Board, *Journal of Applied Gerontology; Journal of Genetic Psychology.* She has been a member of the Governor's Advisory Board on Alzheimer's Disease and Related Disorders; Treasurer, Southern Gerontological Society, 1984–1987; and member of the SGS, Board of Directors, 1987–1988.

Leonard W. Poon, Ph.D., is Professor of Psychology, Director, Gerontology Center, and Chair, Faculty of Gerontology, University of Georgia. He is a past president of Division 20 of APA (1983–84), a Fellow of Divisions 1, 3, and 20 APA and the Gerontological Society of America. Among his edited volumes are *Aging in the 1980s: Psychological Issues, Handbook of Clinical Memory Assessment of Older Adults.* Dr. Poon was also co-editor of the *Encyclopedia of Aging.*

Ilene C. Siegler, Ph.D., M.P.H., is Associate Professor of Medical Psychology in the Department of Psychiatry at the Duke University School of Medicine. She is affiliated with the Duke University Behavioral Medicine Research Center where she is Director of the UNC Alumni Heart Study. Dr. Siegler is a past president of Division 20 of APA (1984–85), and a fellow of APA and the Gerontological Society of America. Dr. Siegler has written over 75 publications. She co-authored, with Charles Edelman, *Federal Age Discrimination in Employment Law* (1978) and co-edited the first volume of *Clinical Psychology of Aging.* She was one of the Associate Editors of the *Encyclopedia of Aging* (1987).

CONTRIBUTORS

Ralph A. Alexander, Ph.D., is Professor of Psychology and Senior Fellow of the Institute for Life-Span Development and Gerontology. Research interests include selection, task performance, job evaluation, cognitive information processing, human/environment interfaces, statistical application and research methodology, and psychometrics and the psychology of measurement. His research has appeared in leading journals and he is on the editorial boards of *Personnel Psychology* and the *Journal of Applied Psychology.*

Gerald V. Barrett, Ph.D., J.D. has research interests which include personnel selection, law and personnel psychology, job evaluation, and information processing. His numerous publications have appared in many leading Industrial/Organizational journals, and he is also the author and co-author of a number of textbooks in the Industrial/Organizational area.

Barbara Felton, Ph.D., is Associate Professor, Department of Psychology, New York University and is a Fellow of the Gerontological Society of America. Her most recent work is in the area of gerontology and studying health care for the aged. Dr. Felton is a member of the editorial board of the *International Journal of Aging and Human Development.*

Irene F. Hulicka, Ph.D., is Distinguished Professor, State University at Buffalo, New York. Dr. Hulicka is a past president of Division 20 of APA (1981–1982) and a past chairperson, Behavioral and Social Science Section, Gerontological Society of America (1985–1986). She was a Fulbright Scholar in the USSR in 1981.

Tracey Revenson, Ph.D., is Assistant Professor, Department of Psychology, The Graduate School and University Center, City University of New York.

Dean Rodeheaver, Ph.D., is Assistant Professor of Human Development, University of Wisconsin, Green Bay. His research interests include social and personality development and gender roles.

K. Warner Schaie, Ph.D., is Evan Pugh Professor of Human Development and Psychology and Director, Gerontology Center, The Pennsylvania State University. Dr. Schaie is the 1988 Editor, *Journal of Gerontology: Psychological Sciences Section,* recipient of the 1987 Kleemeier Award from the Gerontological Society of America and recipient of the 1982 Distinguished Contribution Award from APA.

Diana L. Spore, M.G.S., is a doctoral candidate, Department of Individual and Family Studies, The Pennsylvania State University.

Harvey L. Sterns, Ph.D., is Professor of Psychology, Director, and Senior Fellow of the Institute for Life-Span Development and Gerontology at The University of Akron and Research Professor of Gerontology and Co-Director, Western Reserve Geriatric Education Center, Northeastern Ohio Universities College of Medicine. He has served on the editorial boards of *Psychology and Aging, The Gerontologist,* and *Human Development* and serves on the editorial boards of *Research on Aging,* and *Journal of Women and Aging.*

Jodi L. Teitelman, Ph.D., is Assistant Professor of Gerontology and Training Director of the Geriatric Education Center at Virginia Commonwealth University, Richmond, Virginia. Dr. Teitelman is co-author (with L. Dougherty) of the forthcoming handbook, *Psychosocial Aspects of Sexual Function and Dysfunction in the Elderly.* Additional co-authored books include *Crisis Intervention in the Elderly, Fundamentals in Geriatrics for Health Professionals* and the two-volume modular *Gerontology Curriculum for Health Professionals.*

Susan Krauss Whitbourne, Ph.D., is Associate Professor of Psychology, University of Massachusetts at Amherst. Dr. Whitbourne is a Fellow of Division 20 of APA and the Gerontological Society of America. She has authored the following books: *The Me I Know: The Study of Adult Identity,* and *The Aging Body and Adult Development,* 2nd Edition.

Mary B. Winn, B.A., is a second year graduate student in the Life Span Development Program at Temple University.

Diana S. Woodruff-Pak, Ph.D., is Professor of Psychology, Department of Psychology, Temple University, Philadelphia, Pennsylvania. Dr. Woodruff-Pak is a Fellow of Division 20 of APA and the Gerontological Society of America and is the author of *Psychology & Aging: Can You Live To Be 100?* and *Developmental Psychology: A Life Span Approach* (with James E. Birren, Dennis Kinney, and K. Warner Schaie).

Steven Zarit, Ph.D., is Professor of Human Development and Assistant Director for Research at the Gerontology Center, The Pennsylvania State University. He is member of the editorial board of *The Gerontologist* and is co-author of *Hidden Victims of Alzheimer's Disease: Families Under Stress* (with Nancy K. Orr and Judy M. Zarit).

1
Teaching Courses on the Psychology of Adult Development and Aging

Irene M. Hulicka, Ph.D
and Susan Krauss Whitbourne, Ph.D

Teaching a course or courses on the psychology of adult development and aging can be a marvelously challenging, interesting, and rewarding experience. Most students who take a course on the psychology of adult development and aging report intellectual growth and attitudinal change. Many students carry an interest in the topic into their future careers, whether those careers are in psychology, social work, medicine, pharmacology, or administrative work in health care settings. Further, after they are introduced to the study of adult development and aging, many students subsequently seek other educational experiences to expand their expertise.

To a considerable extent, the joy to be derived from offering a course on the psychology of adult development and aging and the value of the educational experience to students depend on careful planning of every aspect of the course. The planning must include content, topic coverage, emphasis, and goals of the course and its relationship to the total educational experience of the students.

We begin this module by identifying and subsequently discussing some of the related questions and issues to be covered in the course, sequence of courses, or other educational experiences that professors may be planning.

Drs. Hulicka and Whitbourne coauthored *Teaching Undergraduate Courses in Adult Development and Aging* (Copyright © 1979, Beech Hill Enterprises, Mount Desert, ME 04660). Inevitably there is some slight overlap between the content of the 1979 book and this module. Appreciation is expressed to Beech Hill Enterprises for its encouragement, for the preparation of this module, and for permission to use materials covered under a copyright.

PRELIMINARY QUESTIONS

Among basic preliminary questions, some of which need little or no discussion, are the following:

1. What is the scope of the course; that is, life span, adulthood and aging, adulthood, or aging?
2. Is the course designed primarily to provide liberal arts education or to provide career training at the preprofessional or professional levels?
3. What should be the relative emphasis within the course on informational content, skill acquisition, scientific acumen, attitudinal values, and practicum experiences?
4. For what level of students is the course to be offered; that is, lower or upper division undergraduate students or students at the master's, predoctoral, or postdoctoral level?
5. Will students taking the course represent considerable disciplinary homogeneity or diversity? For example, will they be primarily undergraduate psychology majors versus undergraduate students from a variety of programs including liberal arts disciplines and career training programs, or only psychology graduate students versus graduate students from several disciplines who take the course as a requirement or elective within a gerontology certificate program?
6. What major topics should be included in the course? What should be covered in every course on adult development and aging, and what topics would be especially appropriate for this particular group of students and the objectives of this particular course? How can topical coverage be adapted to take into account diverse student interests and educational goals?
7. Is the course under consideration the only course on adult development and aging offered by the department or is it the initial course in a planned sequence? Are optional related courses available in the psychology department curriculum or from other academic departments?
8. What are some of the crucial logistic considerations related to the design and conduct of the class? For example: What is the anticipated enrollment? How much time can the professor devote to course-related activities? What assistance will be available for activities such as review of written assignments and supervision of practicum experiences?

Since these questions are clearly interrelated, no attempt will be made to treat them as discrete items in the discussion that follows.

SCOPE OF THE COURSE

A rather straightforward question pertains to the scope of the course: What segments of the life span are to be studied? Table 1 summarizes the options relevant to answering this question. Listed along with each option are brief recommendations concerning the potential life span emphasis, degree of depth in each area covered, and linkage considerations with other courses.

It is strongly recommended that all courses on the psychology of adult development and aging, whether designed to reflect a liberal education or a career preparation emphasis, and whether at the lower division undergraduate or advanced graduate level, should be presented within the framework of processes of life span development. The last years of life are continuous with and inextricably linked with the events and processes of earlier life. All students should understand fully the concept that human development, including development beyond adolescence, is an ongoing and continuous process. The life of an individual cannot be neatly segmented into discrete, unrelated phases. It is for this reason that we specifically advise against teaching students a "passages" type of approach to development in adulthood and old age.

A second point to be emphasized is that factors other than age, including birth cohort, contemporary social conditions, and physical health, may account for differences among people of different ages. Not all students should be expected to develop the advanced research skills needed to appreciate this concept fully. All students can, however, acquire a basic understanding of the conceptual and practical limitations

TABLE 1 Scope of the Course

Scope	Degree of life span emphasis	Depth within each area	Linkage considerations
Human development	High	Low	Allow sufficient time to cover adulthood and late life adequately. Provide linkage between earlier and later life.
Adulthood and aging	Moderate	Moderate	Provide bridge with childhood and adolescence.
Adulthood	Low	High	Provide bridge with childhood, adolescence, and late life.
Late life	Low	High	Provide bridge with childhood, adolescence, and adulthood.

of age as a variable in research. Once they are sensitized to the importance of this issue, even those students being trained for relatively low level careers in service delivery can think about alternative explanations of phenomena (such as loss of memory organizational skills or increased psychological "interiority") in terms of competing variables other than age.

GOALS OF THE COURSE

Unlike many traditional courses in psychology, a course on the psychology of adult development and aging can serve a variety of goals. Before writing down a single course topic on the syllabus, the professor must consider his or her goals in teaching the course. Often, the course goals are dictated by programmatic concerns over which the professor has no control. In this case, it is essential that the professor be sure to have a clear understanding of the departmental priorities for the course, and the expectations of the students as they enter the course. The professor must compare these goals with his or her own personal goals in teaching the course. The goals that are eventually adopted should certainly fulfill the department's requirements, but they can also incorporate some of the professor's own preferences. In this section, we will describe some of the general considerations that the professor should keep in mind when engaging in this critical step of the course-planning process.

Liberal Arts Education and Career Training

Courses on the psychology of adult development and aging may be viewed as vehicles of liberal arts education that are intended to stimulate the intellectual and emotional growth of students. There are a number of ways this goal can be accomplished. The psychology department may decide to offer a course on adult development and aging as part of its elective sequence in human development. Such a course would most likely be organized in terms of the traditional topics in psychology, such as sensation, perception, intelligence, personality, abnormal behavior, and social psychology. Another approach is to offer a course on adulthood and aging in the psychology department that is intended to serve students fulfilling educational requirements in such core areas as cultural diversity, law and government, human services, the social sciences, the humanities, or cognitive science. Courses in this group would emphasize topics consistent with the area within which the course falls (such as aging in literature in a course offered within the humanities). In either case, the course's goals are going to be very different from the goals of a course offered as a unit within a training program specifically geared toward a profession that serves the elderly.

The liberal arts course can range from a smorgasbord type of exposure to the controversies in the field, to intense philosophical discussions of topics that college students are particularly interested in, to focused survey-type coverage of the main areas within the discipline. Emphasis can be placed on conceptualization, analysis, and critical evaluation. Such a course can bridge divisions between biology, social sciences, and the humanities. Through involvement in this course, the student can develop an appreciation of the complex causal interrelationships involved in the aging process. In the process of learning about these relationships and their effects on aging individuals, the student gains not only content, but critical thinking, organizing, and writing skills. Whatever the particular content of the course, its overall goal is to educate, rather than train.

In contrast, the professor of a career preparation course has the responsibility of ensuring that students acquire specific and useful career-related skills. The future speech therapist profits by exploring existential issues related to human aging and the meaning of life, or by being exposed to conceptual issues in the psychology of aging. More urgently, though, such a student needs to know about language functioning in the elderly, how language competency is affected by stroke, and the effects of decrements in linguistic functioning on the individual's self-concept. This student will be applying knowledge gained in the course on a day-to-day basis and must be prepared to put that knowledge into practice.

Given these considerations, there still is ample opportunity for bridging gaps between liberal arts and career training courses. The professor of a liberal arts course who feels committed to orienting students to the practical dilemmas faced by psychologists who work in the area of aging can pose a variety of intriguing questions of considerable applied significance. Students can be asked to assess the effects of specific variations in the physical environment on the measurable behavior of people in designated settings such as housing complexes for the elderly or nursing homes. Students can be given actual experiential involvement by designing a study and going into the field to collect data. In the process of conducting this kind of research, the student will invariably acquire information about the conditions in which elderly people live, as well as personal contact with a variety of older individuals. Students will also gain greater refinement of their observational and analytical skills than they would have achieved through involvement in a more abstract and perhaps "lifeless" assignment in the psychology department laboratory.

Along the same lines, the professor of a career training course who is eager to communicate his or her interest in philosophical, conceptual, and otherwise abstract concerns in the area of human aging need not be limited to teaching only a descriptive, factual account of the aging process with a practical orientation. Students can be involved in discussions about ethical and philosophical dilemmas concerning the rights of elderly patients, the responsibilities of family members to care for their aging relatives, society's obligations to subsidize care for the elderly, and euthanasia for the terminally ill elderly who wish to die. A variety of other approaches can stimulate the kind of critical thinking that is the goal of a liberal arts course. Advanced students can be engaged in activities such as comparing critically two approaches to cognitive assessment or psychotherapy. At a lower level, they can amass and evaluate information about generational differences in attitudes toward specific practices. Students in this kind of course can even be engaged in research, perhaps of a descriptive or survey-type nature. By taking on the role of the "researcher," the student can adopt a perspective that may prove invaluable in later work as a "practitioner." The enthusiasm of the "trainee" for "scholarship" in the broad sense of the word is likely to be greatly enhanced if instead of merely being given information to memorize and use, or instead of simply being taught how to perform a particular task, there is genuine student involvement in the best liberal tradition of self-education. Although external demands based on reality may require a very strong emphasis on either career training or liberal education, the astute professor of the psychology of aging course should be able to combine some elements of the two sets of goals. The content of the course naturally lends itself to a number of issues that cross not only diciplinary lines but also the demarcation between theory and practice.

Relative Emphasis on Informational Content, Scientific Approach, Career Skills, Attitudinal Values, and Experiential Involvement

Related to the potential division between and/or overlap of liberal education and career training goals are issues pertaining to the relative emphasis within psychology of adult development and aging courses on informational content, scientific acumen, career skills, attitudes, and experiential involvement. In some respects, more seems to be asked in terms of types of educational end products from psychology of aging courses than most other academic courses, including courses offered by the psychology department. Consider the following. Almost all discussions of the goals of geropsychology[1] classes identify sensitivity to attitu-

---

[1]Courses on the psychology of aging with particular emphasis on late adulthood.

dinal factors as a significant goal. Further, practicum-type experiences are widely regarded as being particularly useful for materializing attitudinal goals as well as for skill acquisition. Virtually all psychology of adult development and aging courses are expected to have a strong informational base. That is, professors and students alike are oriented to accumulating as many "facts" about the aging process as possible. At the same time, most professors in the field also want students to learn to examine these "facts" from a critical, scientific point of view. Although not all students in these courses are expected to develop the methodological sophistication necessary to design significant research, all are expected to develop sufficient scientific acumen to be acutely aware of possible errors in the conclusions of research studies. Such errors include those based on limited observations of nonrandom samples, probably involving different cohorts, different health statuses, and different living arrangements.

Decisions about the above requirements constitute a heavy agenda in the course-planning process. However, each requirement must be addressed in some fashion, even if it is to be treated in a relatively cursory manner. Thus, the relative emphasis must be set by the professor on how much the course will be oriented toward dispensing information, stimulating scientific acumen, teaching career skills, communicating attitudinal values, and providing experiential opportunities. Each of these decisions for a given course should vary with the liberal education versus career training goals of the course. The academic levels and backgrounds of the students must also be taken into account. In Table 2 the various options are laid out for considering each of these factors.

Some apparent discrepancies in the recommendations are intentional. For example, persons who elect to earn a master's degree after having had extensive work experience in settings serving older adults may particularly benefit from strong emphasis on factual information, increased sensitivity to the need for scientific objectivity in the collection and interpretation of information, and the dangers of overgeneralizing on the basis of limited observations of a biased sample. These students have the necessary knowledge from their own experiences about what older people are like and what the settings are like in which they live and are treated. What they need to learn about are the conceptual and methodological perspectives that their prior experiences have lacked. When taught this new information, these students can "plug in" their relevant experiences, and indeed gain new insights into what they have encountered in their work settings. In some cases, what they learn in the course will directly counter misperceptions and misconceptions gained in their work. For instance, a former nurse's aide who has seen only severely ill older people may be surprised to learn that the majority of older adults are able to live independently in the community. Similarly, it would challenge a social worker's estimation of the coping skills of middle-aged adults to learn that studies of personality rigidity show strong cohort

TABLE 2 Relative Emphasis in Course Orientation

Students' level and eduational program	Factual information	Scientific acumen	Career skills and applications	Attitudinal awareness	Experiential involvement
Under-graduate: liberal arts	High	High	Moderate	Moderate	Moderate
Under-graduate: preprofessional	High	Moderate	High	High	High
Master's with relevant employment experience serving older adults	Very high	High	Low	Low to moderate	Low
Applied master's with little or no relevant prior experiences	High	Moderate	Moderate	Moderate	High
Doctoral/ academic research	High	Moderate	High	Moderate	High
Doctoral/ applied, e.g., clinical	High	High	High	Moderate	High
Postdoctoral/ applied	High	Moderate	High	Moderate	High
Postdoctoral/ research	High	High	Low	Moderate	Low

effects. It is also likely that compared to the information they need to acquire, these experienced students need little educational emphasis on attitudes, career skills and applications, or supervised experience.

Conversely, persons who move directly into an applied master's program after earning an undergraduate degree are less likely to know what older adults are like. They are also less likely to have acquired erroneous information through overgeneralization from limited work-based observations and hence may need less remedial education. Furthermore, their career choice suggests that these students probably do not have predominantly negative attitudes toward older adults (although this assumption should be checked out carefully at the beginning of the course). Heavy emphasis on the acquisition of basic factual information and career skills is recommended for these students. They should also, however, have extensive supervised experiential involvement as a medium for learning.

It is tempting to consider education and training at the advanced predoctoral and postdoctoral levels as involving comparable issues and goals. However, it should be stressed that whereas there may be considerable commonality of educational needs and goals among several advanced graduate students developing specialization in different aspects of the psychology of aging, postdoctoral fellows have already developed substantial qualifications and may have widely different expertise and goals. Accordingly, postdoctoral education and training must be almost completely individualized to take into account the fellow's unique background and career aspirations. For scholars at both the pre- and postdoctoral levels, the preferred approach should be carefully targeted and individually planned educational experiences. At the predoctoral level, though, some formal courses and seminars can well serve certain educational goals.

In most educational experiences designed for persons at the advanced pre- or postdoctoral level, emphasis on scientific acumen can be moderate to low. It is not that scientific astuteness is unimportant for such scholars, but that they should already have well-honed scientific skills and sensitivity. Of course, they may be required to develop specific research techniques relevant to their unique interests and goals. Further, it might be helpful to direct their attention to some of the practical issues involved in doing research with elderly participants. For example, in reviewing research proposals for national funding agencies, we have on occasion found it necessary to suggest that the hypotheses might not be testable unless mundane changes are made in the research plan (e.g., shorter testing sessions, increasing the size or visibility of stimulus objects).

Obviously, development of informational expertise is of the utmost importance for all persons at the pre- and postdoctoral levels. Generally, at the upper echelons of the educational ladder, the function of the academic or professional mentor is to help identify such areas within the field that should be studied, to suggest relevant sources of information, and to support and perhaps occasionally even reinforce enthusiasm for subject matter mastery. Further, high emphasis on career skills, applications, and experiential involvement is strongly recommended. Perhaps one of the major needs of education in the psychology of adult development and aging is involvement in service areas of scientifically astute high-level professionals, who because of extensive experiential involvement with adults including elderly people may be very sensitive to applied issues and problems such as validity of assessment approaches and the need to evaluate the weaknesses as well as the strengths of treatment or intervention programs.

Disciplinary Homogeneity or Diversity of Students

An undergraduate course on the psychology of adulthood and aging may have stringent prerequisites, such as completion of a sequence in psychological statistics and experimental methodology. If this is the case, it is unlikely that many students other than advanced psychology majors would qualify. The professor can teach the course at a relatively high level, using one of the texts with a heavy emphasis on quantitative data collected through experimental and other rigorous methods. Students can be assigned original articles to critique in class, and be given a semester project that places them in the field or allows them to explore a topic in depth through library research. In many schools, though, practical exigencies of student enrollment will dictate that the course be opened up to students who have not had prior methods, statistics, and perhaps even introductory psychology courses. The adult development and aging course then serves as an optional course within the psychology major, a general education elective for students from most majors, and a required course for students in some preprofessional programs such as social work, nursing, or physical therapy. Faced with this heterogeneous collection of students, the professor will have to shift radically from the luxury of teaching junior and senior psychology majors. The professor will, moreover, probably be put in the position of having to review basic concepts of psychology and methods (such as methods of intelligence testing and principles of experimental design) before getting on to the business of discussing adult development and aging.

Likewise, a psychology of aging course in an applied gerontology master's program or a graduate level certificate in gerontology program might enroll students with diverse backgrounds, including some who have had very limited course work in psychology but perhaps have considerable expertise in applied disciplines such as education or nursing. Some of these students will be nonmatriculated returning students, continuing education students, and professionals interested in brushing up their academic expertise. These nontraditional students can be expected to place considerable demands on the professor to help them understand the psychology content of the course.

As a general rule, it behooves the professor to ensure that the major subject matter content and experiential emphasis in a psychology course is psychology, not social work, physiology, or history. However, any time there is a mixture of students from areas outside of psychology, whether they are undergraduate college students or adult continuing education students, the professor runs into a complicated Catch 22 situation. Students from different majors and professional disciplines each have their own particular biases. Social workers are interested in group processes; nurses are interested in physiology; education students are interested in cognitive processes. At the same time, these students lack the psychology background that majors and graduate students specializing in the field come equipped with. This leads the professor into the simultaneous risk of boring the psychology students with excessive review of prior concepts ("Do we have to learn about control groups again?") and losing the nonpsychology students in the morass of sequential designs, methods of personality assessment, and principles of environmental psychology. How is the professor to negotiate between these difficult alternatives?

In the first place, there is no point denying that the problem exists. The students will probably not tolerate the professor's ignoring their questions or complaints. The nonpsychology students will have their hands in the air almost constantly as the professor tries to proceed through the lecture on developmental research designs. The psychology students will groan when they hear about the stages of Piaget's theory for what is probably at least the fifth time in their undergraduate career. There are several ways to handle the dilemma of teaching the same course material to a multifaceted group of students.

One set of strategies involves subdividing the course in some way into smaller groups. Students with similar interests and knowledge of psychology can form study groups in which they help each other master concepts assigned them by the professor that are tailored to their particular needs. Another strategy is to take advantage of the multiple talents, ages, and levels of experience represented in a diverse student group. The senior psychology major can "instruct" the 45-year-old adult day care worker on some basic principles of experimental design. On other occasions, the day care worker will have valuable insights to offer the psychology student based on observations of elderly people in that setting. An even more radical approach would be to divide class meeting times according to student level and area of interest. The class might be "tracked" in some logical fashion for part or all of the semester.

Short of adopting one of these subdivision approaches, the professor can address the problem of student diversity by building into the course multiple levels of coverage. Common areas that will be new and of interest to almost all the students can be identified that form the centerpiece of the course syllabus. Areas can be added requiring special knowledge or experience according to the composition of the class. When review of basic psychology concepts becomes unavoidable, the professor can point out to more advanced students that there is always something to be gained from an extra review of basic statistics or concepts of learning. When psychology students need to learn from applied examples to clarify a point, the "practitioner" students can be called on to supply examples (this also helps the professor collect a storehouse of useful illustrations over the years). The main point is that the professor maintain a flexible approach, adapting the way the course is taught to the needs (and talents) of the class membership.

With respect to diversity of major fields and areas of interest represented in a class composed of students from a variety of disciplines, the
professor can take advantage of the fact that the study of aging not only
allows for but requires use of information derived from disciplines other
than psychology. These disciplines include biological and medical sciences, social sciences, and the humanities. In addition to mastering the
basic and assigned core of psychological materials, assignments may be
tailored or modified to correspond to the interests, career goals, and/or
expertise of the students. For example, a prelaw student may be permitted to study independently and perhaps to report back to the class on
issues pertaining to psychological measures and legal definitions of competency, legal actions that can be taken to have an individual declared
competent or incompetent, potential or measured psychological consequences of being declared incompetent, and so on. An education major
may be permitted or encouraged to study various memory-training programs and to design research to assess their effectiveness for certain
categories of people, or people with certain manifestations of memory
problems. A sociology major interested in racial or ethnic differences
could study similarities and differences among members of specific
groups in coping with changes such as retirement, widowhood, divorce,
or the death of a child, and the relative effectiveness of the coping
techniques in relation to some measures of psychological well-being.

In short, with a little ingenuity and flexibility on the part of both the
professor and the students, a course on adult development and aging
can focus on psychological topics and processes and, at the same time,
be enriched and vitalized if students are given the opportunity to use
their unique expertise to address questions particularly relevant to their
career goals and/or intellectual interests. Indeed, students can contribute
to the quality of the course substantially by providing material that goes
beyond what is provided by classroom instruction alone.

TOPICAL COVERAGE

There are some topics that probably must be included for study in all
basic courses on the psychology of adult development and aging. Some
of the major topics, with nonexhaustive examples of subtopics that
should also be given considerable priority, are summarized in Table 3.

Obviously, no single course can cover all important topical areas. It is
suggested that content selection among the list of recommended topics
in Table 3 (and additional topics at the end of the table) be influenced
somewhat by the professor's unique interests and expertise, as well as
the interests and needs of the class. Ordinarily, a professor is most

TABLE 3 Recommendations for Basic Topical Coverage

Topics to be included	Comments
Methods Types of designs used to study aging.	Make sure students acquire basic concepts of age, cohort, and time of measurement and can distinguish between age differences and age changes. Required methodological sophistication varies with level and career goals of students.
Physical functioning Age changes in the major organ systems of the body (body structure and appearance, muscles, heart, lungs, digestion, nervous system, endocrine, reproductive). Age changes in body's adaptability to the physical environment. Effects of changes in the body on self-concept. Compensation through exercise and other adaptive strategies.	Sensitize students to cohort differences in health, education, and nutrition that could contribute to observed differences between age groups. Emphasize the difference between normal aging and disease. Give sufficient emphasis to changes in early and middle adulthood as well as old age. Emphasize cohort differences in health habits as contributors to age differences.
Sensation and Perception Age effects on sensory systems, including sight, hearing, smell, taste, balance, touch, temperature, pain. Age effects on information processing and on complex perceptual processes such as illusions and depth perception. Slowing with age of reaction time; trade-off between speed and accuracy. Effect of "set" on reaction time.	Use classroom activities to simulate the effects of age on sensation. Discuss whether a fast reaction time is really an important asset for a person to have, and whether slowing with age of reaction interferes with work productivity in adulthood.
Memory and Learning Research findings on age differences in memory and their relation to current theories of the aging of cognitive processes. Effects of noncognitive variables on learning and memory efficiency, e.g., sensory acuity, speed, motivation.	Contrast between episodic and semantic memory in terms of age effects. Effects of age on rigidity, response set, and cautiousness. Discuss difference between normal age-related memory loss and senile dementia. Show how memory training techniques can be used to enhance memory functioning. Discuss relationship between memory and personality in terms

(Continued)

TABLE 3 Recommendations for Basic Topical Coverage (Continued)

Topics to be included	Comments
	of effects of anxiety and cautiousness on memory, effects of memory on everyday life, factors that influence complaints of memory loss. Discuss relation between personality rigidity and inflexibility in learning.
Intelligence	
Types of intellectual functioning and relationship to age in adulthood.	Ask students to consider the relevance of measured intelligence to a person's everyday functioning.
Sequential research designs in the study of age and intelligence. Effects of health and life-style on intellectual functioning.	Design training strategies to enhance intellectual functioning of adults of various ages.
Personality	
Data on the personality stability vs. change issue.	Relevance of personality theories to adulthood and old age. Personality assessment of adults and the elderly.
Descriptive research on "stages" of adult life.	Major forms of psychopathology as related to age. Look for ways to integrate the stability vs. change positions regarding personality development.
Effects of socialization on measured personality characteristics.	Discuss different kinds of roles and how they affect personality in adulthood. Critique personality theories in terms of their contributions to understanding development in adulthood. Discuss the difficulty of separating organic and cognitive changes in older people.
Social Psychology	
Attitudes toward the aged and their effect on intergenerational relationships.	Adults as consumers; marketing strategies and their effectiveness in persuading adults to change their buying habits.
Effects of role changes on personal identity in adulthood.	Have students take an attitudes-toward-aging questionnaire in class and discuss (or review) their answers.
The dynamics of intergenerational families.	
Processes of institutionalization.	Have students fill out a "Who Am I?" list of roles as they are now and as they expect to be in 20, 30, 40 years. Discuss how much of

TABLE 3 Recommendations for Basic Topical Coverage (Continued)

Topics to be included	Comments
	one's identity is influenced by social roles. Analyze family interactions among adult children and parents. Add sections, depending on student interest and relevance to the rest of the course, on widowhood, retirement, divorce, and grandparenthood.
Industrial/Organizational	
Changes in worker motivation and satisfaction with age.	Human factors engineering as applied to the aged in design of work equipment, cars, and appliances.
Changes in work productivity in adulthood.	Evidence bearing on question of technical obsolescence in older workers.
	Examine students' biases toward what is considered high productivity in a worker. Have students design special kinds of equipment taking into account needs of older workers.
	Discuss ways that managers can deal sensitively with problems of older workers.
Successful Aging	
Definitions of successful aging.	Discuss difficulties in developing a generalizable definition of successful aging.
Measurement of successful aging.	Consider limitations of life satisfaction and morale measures of successful aging.
Identification of factors that correlate with objective or subjective measurement of successful aging.	Consider actions under personal control that might contribute to successful aging.
Additional Topics	
Advocacy for the elderly. Death and dying. Minority aging. Women and aging. Methods of psychotherapy and their use in the elderly. Environmental psychology and design of living environments for the elderly. Psychopathology of aging, e.g., Alzheimer's disease and other causes of dementia.	Leave extra time in the syllabus to include topics that students identify as important. Have additional readings at hand as well as classroom exercises. Events reported in the local media can also be used to stimulate class discussion (e.g., elder abuse) as can anecdotes about family life from advice columns and popular TV shows that deal with aging.

effective at teaching what he or she knows best and feels most enthusiastic toward. Much of the job in teaching a course on the psychology of adult development and aging is communicating to students the message that this is an exciting and important field. The professor should not hope to teach everything about the topic but instead set a more realistic and ultimately more important goal of stimulating a desire to learn more among the students.

Within the list of topics outlined in Table 3, the professor will want to make choices that also take into account the educational levels of the students and their educational and career goals. For example, a course on adult development and aging within a doctoral level clinical psychology program must appropriately include considerable applied emphasis on effective coping strategies in early and late adulthood, approaches to assessment, and intervention techniques. A more experimentally oriented course would focus on research on human and animal learning, motivation, information processing, and physical functioning. A course emphasizing social and cultural processes would focus on topics listed in the area of social psychology as well as the special topics of minority aging and women and aging. For courses that are oriented toward career preparation in a given area, the professor could give greater attention to topics relevant to that particular specialty (e.g., physiology for nursing students, cognitive functioning for education students, etc.). This basic "menu" of topics gives the professor virtually infinite flexibility for adapting a course to meet the specialized needs and interests of any particular group of students at any given level.

CHOICE OF TEXT AND REFERENCES

The choice of a text for a course depends largely on the level of the students, goals of the course, desired topical coverage, and emphasis. The author's writing style, the availability of supplementary materials, and the text's currency are also important considerations in choosing a text. Only two decades ago, there was a tremendous paucity of texts for professors to choose from, and as a result most professors had to adapt their course to suit the text or else assign a great deal of reading from the library or from handouts. These awkward adjustments and compromises no longer need to be made. Currently there are available many texts appropriate for use in basic undergraduate courses. It is possible, at last, for the professor to choose the text that best fits the course's needs. There are also many other books in the current market that could be appropriate as texts or recommended reading for courses on specialized topics within the psychology of adult development and aging at either the undergraduate or graduate level. We have provided a sampling of some of the available selections of texts and specialized readings in Tables 4 through 7. These are *partial* lists only, constructed for the purpose of illustrating the wealth and variety of material currently available, and to provide a starting point for professors putting together libraries in the area of adult development and aging. It would be inappropriate and impossible for us to attempt to list all the books that a professor might want to review as potential texts, for recommended reading, or as source books for lecture preparation. The professor who wishes to conduct a more exhaustive search should contact a variety of publishers and ask for their publications in gerontology. Many of these publishers will send complementary desk copies or examination copies that the professor can then review in detail.

Table 4 lists a large number of texts appropriate for use in undergraduate basic courses in the psychology of adult development and aging, along with an indication of the text's emphasis, probable audience, and difficulty level. Table 5 provides the same information for a few books of readings and handbooks, including handbooks that would be valued as texts or references for graduate level courses. Table 6 provides a sample of books on clinical and applied gerontology, and Table 7 lists a number of special interest books, either dealing with prescribed populations such as elderly minorities or women or on defined topics such as cognitive functioning. Many of the books in Table 7 would be appropriate for segments of graduate level or undergraduate courses or as references for projects undertaken by students.

PLANNING COURSE ACTIVITIES AND ASSIGNMENTS

Suggestions for Activities and Assignments

The first stages of course planning can and should be as freewheeling and creative as is within the professor's capability. There is such a richness of content in this area that a course on adult development and aging has the potential to be a positive, memorable experience for all involved. The number of potential activities that accompany classroom instruction is almost limitless. The experiential element of the course alone can occupy most of the semester's activities, above and beyond the academic content of the course. This can include practicum activity at a field placement site, student research projects conducted on off-campus locations, interviews of adults selected because of some special attribute, and naturalistic observations of settings that have relevance to adult development and aging. Study groups, group projects, and the viewing of special films on pertinent topics are other potentially rewarding activities to add to classroom instruction. The professor will probably also

TABLE 4 Examples of Undergraduate Texts in the Psychology of Adult Development and Aging

Author(s)	Title	Publisher and date	Coverage or emphasis[a]	Audience and readability[b]
Atchley	Aging: Continuity and Change	Wadsworth, 1983	Social gerontology	AU,SP 2
Baum & Baum	Growing Old	Prentice Hall, 1980	Societal perspective; psychology, social, and biological development	AU 2
Belsky	The Psychology of Aging	Wadsworth, 1984	Theory, research and practice	AU,SP 2
Botwinick	We Are Aging	Springer, 1981	Social and psychological aging	AU 2
Hendricks & Hendricks	Aging in Mass Society	Little, Brown, 1986	Broad interdisciplinary coverage	AU,G 2
Hultsch & Deutsch	Adult Development and Aging	McGraw-Hill, 1981	Research based	AU 2
Kart	The Realities of Aging	Allyn & Bacon, 1981	Overview	AU 2
Neuhaus & Neuhaus	Successful Aging	Wiley, 1982	Social and physical aging	AU,SP 2
Newman & Newman	Understanding Adulthood	Holt, Rinehart & Winston, 1983	Social	AU 1
Perlmutter & Hall	Adult Development and Aging	Wiley, 1985	Psychological, social, physical	AU 2
Rice	Adult Development and Aging	Allyn & Bacon, 1986	Psychological, social, physical	AU 2

Author	Title	Publisher, Year	Description	Audience[a] Readability[b]
Santrock	*Adult Development and Aging*	Wm. C. Brown, 1985	Psychological, biological, social	AU 2
Schaie & Willis	*Adult Development and Aging*	Little, Brown, 1986	Overview with cognitive emphasis	AU 2
Stevens-Long	*Adult Life*	Mayfield, 1984	Social development	AU 2
Troll	*Continuations: Adult Development and Aging*	Brooks-Cole, 1982	Strong research base	AU 2
Turner & Helm	*Contemporary Adulthood*	Holt, Rinehart & Winston, 1986	Social development	AU 2
Ward	*The Aging Experience*	Harper & Row, 1984	Social gerontology	AU 2
Whitbourne & Weinstock	*Adult Development*	Praeger, 1986	Psychosocial, cognitive	AU,AG 2

[a]Audience: GP—General public; SP—Service providers; AU—Undergraduate; AG—Graduate or above.
[b]Readability: 1—Beginner; 2—Moderate; 3—Technical.

TABLE 5 Handbooks and Books of Readings on Adult Development and Aging

Author(s) or editor(s)	Title	Publisher and date	Coverage or emphasis[a]	Audience and readability[b]
Allman & Jaffe	Readings in Adult Psychology	Harper & Row, 1982	Development throughout adult life cycle	AU,GP 2
Binstock & Shanas	Handbook of Aging and the Social Sciences	Van Nostrand Reinhold, 1985	Research, theory, practice	AG 3
Birren & Schaie	Handbook of the Psychology of Aging	Van Nostrand Reinhold, 1985	Research, theory, practice	AG 3
Cox	Aging	Dushkin, 1987	Articles on timely topics	AU,SP,GP 2
Poon	Aging in the 1980s	APA, 1980	Theoretical and research issues	AG 3
Zarit	Readings in Aging and Death	Harper & Row, 1982	Diverse topics	AU,SP 2

[a]Audience: GP—General public; SP—Service providers; AU—Undergraduate; AG—Graduate or above.
[b]Readability: 1—Beginner; 2—Moderate; 3—Technical.

want to add supplemental readings to whatever text is chosen. These may include novels dealing with adult development and aging as well as particularly interesting and well-conducted research monographs on specific content areas. Written assignments can be made on the basis of any of these activities. Some suggested activities and assignments, experiential and academic, are described here. These suggestions are not meant to be an exhaustive list; the variety of offerings the professor makes available in these categories is only as limited as the professor's imagination and resources.

Experiential: Outside the Classroom

1. Visiting an elderly person once a week for an hour or so in that person's home or institution. Connections between students and elderly people can be made through local agencies on aging, nutrition sites, religious and other volunteer organizations, and institutions that have or want to have some connection to the school.

2. Making naturalistic observations at sites that serve some defined group of adults and older people. These can include:

Day care centers (for the young or the old) where family interactions can be observed at drop-off and pickup times.

Shopping malls or other public areas where older persons sometimes gather to spend the afternoon (in downtown areas these might include homeless people or people living in single room hotels). Students might make friends with some of the "regulars" there. Shopping malls (in the suburbs especially) are also excellent places to watch unobtrusively interactions among families of all ages and compositions.

Singles bars, where seeing the plight of lonely young adults trying to make friends and sexual contacts can provide important insights into the stresses of this period of life.

Grocery stores, where students can observe how elderly people with sensory or physical deficits manage to complete an important and sometimes difficult task of daily living.

Bingo games, dances, and other social activities frequented by older adults.

3. Conducting informal research in settings that serve a defined population. These settings can include any of the above if an appropriate set of variables can be identified. More-controlled settings would be needed for experimental studies; in this case, the choice of setting depends on the purpose of the research. The professor may want to

TABLE 6 Examples of Books on Clinical Aging and Applied Gerontology

Author(s) or editor(s)	Title	Publisher and date	Coverage or emphasis[a]	Audience and readability[b]
Abrahams & Crooks	*Geriatric Mental Health*	Grune & Stratton, 1984	Designed for clinicians working with elderly patients	AG,SP 2
Awad, Durost, Meir & McCormick	*Disturbed Behavior in the Elderly*	Pergamon, 1987	Practical clinical approaches to diagnosis and treatment	AU,AG,SP 2
Brink	*Clinical Gerontology*	Haworth, 1986	Assessment and intervention	AG,SP 2
Burnside	*Working with the Elderly*	Wadsworth, 1984	Group processes and techniques	AU,SP 2
Ernst	*Psychogeriatrics*	Vantage, 1987	Diagnosis and treatment	AU,AG,SP; GP 2
Hanley & Gilhooly	*Psychological Therapies for the Elderly*	New York University Press, 1986	Variety of therapeutic approaches	AU,SP 2
Hussian	*Geriatric Psychology*	Van Nostrand Reinhold, 1981	Behavioral approaches	AG 3
Janicki & Wisniewski	*Aging and Developmental Disabilities*	Paul H. Brooks, 1985	Mental retardation	AU,SP 2
Kane & Kane	*Assessing the Elderly*	Heath, 1981	Review of assessment instruments and approaches	AG,SP 2
Lewinsohn & Teri	*Clinical Geropsychology*	Pergamon, 1983	Clinical assessment and treatment of problematic behavior	AU,AG,SP 2
Mace & Rabins	*The 36-Hour Day*	Johns Hopkins University Press, 1981	Guide to families caring for Alzheimer's patients	GP,SP 1

Sadavoy & Leszcz	Treating the Elderly with Psycho-therapy	International Universities Press, 1987	Psychoanalytic approaches to therapy	AG,SP 3
Storandt	Counseling and Therapy with Older Adults	Little, Brown, 1983		AG,SP 2
Teri & Lewin-sohn	Geropsychological Assessment and Treatment	Springer, 1986	Behavioral approaches to specific problems	AG,SP 3
Wattis & Church	Practical Psychiatry of Old Age	New York University Press, 1986	Covers major diagnostic categories	AG,SP 2
Weiner, Brok, & Snadowsky	Working with the Aged		Social approaches to treatment	AU,SP, GP 1
Zarit, Orr, & Zarit	Hidden Victims of Alzheimer's Disease	New York University Press, 1985	Families under stress	AU,AG,SP, GP 1

[a]Audience: GP—General public; SP—Service providers; AU—Undergraduate; AG—Graduate or above.
[b]Readability: 1—Beginner; 2—Moderate; 3—Technical.

TABLE 7 Examples of Special Interest Books in the Psychology of Adult Development and Aging

Author(s) or editor(s)	Title	Publisher and date	Coverage or emphasis[a]	Audience and readability[b]
Botwinick	*Aging and Behavior*	Springer, 1984	Cognition, personality, motivation	AG,AU 2
Butler & Lewis	*Love and Sex after 40*	Harper & Row, 1986	Physiological, psychological, and social concerns	AG,SP,GP 2
Charness	*Aging and Human Performance*	Wiley, 1985	Cognitive and motor performance, research	AU,AG 2
Cole & Gadow	*What Does It Mean to Grow Old?*	Duke University Press, 1986	Reflections on aging from the humanities	AU,AG 2
Corso	*Aging Sensory Systems and Perception*	Praeger, 1981	Detailed analysis of research	AU,AG 3
DeSpelder & Strickland	*The Last Dance*	Mayfield, 1987	Encountering death and dying	AU,SP,GP 2
Erikson	*The Life Cycle Completed*	Norton, 1982	Psychosocial development	AU,AG 2
Fries & Crapo	*Vitality and Aging: Implications of the Rectangular Curve*	W. H. Freeman, 1981	Implications of rectangular population curve	AG 2
George	*Role Transitions in Later Life*	Brooks-Cole, 1980	Change and adaptation	AU 2
Hareven & Adams	*Aging and Life Course Transitions*	Guilford Press, 1982	Interdisciplinary perspective	AU,AG 2
Jackson	*Minorities and Aging*	Wadsworth, 1980	Impact of ethnicity and gender on aging	AU,AG,SP 2
Katchadourian	*Fifty: Mid-Life in Perspective*	W. H. Freeman, 1987	Physiological and psychological changes at midlife	AU,SP,GP 2
Kaufman	*The Ageless Self*	University of Wisconsin Press, 1986	Naturalistic observations and interviews	AU,GP 2

Author	Title	Publisher, Year	Description	Codes
Kertzner & Keith	*Age and Anthropological Theory*	Cornell University Press, 1984	Anthropological approaches to study of aging	AU,AG 2
Lawton	*Environment and Aging*	Brooks-Cole, 1980	Research, theory, practice	AU,AG,SP 2
Lyell	*Middle Age, Old Age*	Harcourt Brace Jovanovich, 1980	Poems, short stories, and plays on aging	AU,AG,GP, SP 2
Markson	*Older Women: Issues and Prospects*	Heath, 1983	Biological, psychological, and social issues	AU,AG 2
Meacham	*Family and Individual Development*	Karger, 1985	Family relations and development	AU,AG 2
Mines & Kitchner	*Adult Cognitive Development: Methods and Models*	Praeger, 1985	Material for seminar topics	AU,AG 2
Nahemow, McClusker-Fawcett, & McGhee	*Humor and Aging*	Academic Press, 1986	Empirical and theoretical	AU 2
Rabin & Stockton	*Long-Term Care for the Elderly*	Oxford University Press, 1987	Facts about income, care costs, etc.	AU,AG 2
Rybash, Hoyer, & Roodin	*Adult Cognition and Aging*	Pergamon, 1986	Processes of "knowing and thinking"	AG 3
Salthouse	*Adult Cognition*	Springer-Verlag, 1981	Reaction time, memory, information processing	AG 3
Saul	*Aging: An Album of People Growing Old*	Wiley, 1983	Literary, humanistic descriptions of aging people and processes	AU,GP 1
Schaie	*Longitudinal Studies of Adult Psychological Development*	Guilford	Methodology, cognition, personality	AU,AG 2
Shock	*Normal Human Aging: The Baltimore Longitudinal Study*	U.S. Dept. of Health and Human Services, 1984	Summarizes 23 years of Baltimore Longitudinal Study	AU,AG 2

(Continued)

TABLE 7 Examples of Special Interest Books in the Psychology of Adult Development and Aging (Continued)

Author(s) or editor(s)	Title	Publisher and date	Coverage or emphasis[a]	Audience and readability[b]
Smelser & Erikson	*Themes of Work and Love in Adulthood*	Harvard University Press, 1980	Exploratory probes into dimensions of human development	AU,AG,GP 2
Special Committee on Aging, U.S. Senate	*Developments in Aging: 1986*, Vol. 1	U.S. Government Printing Office, 1986	Source of information on demography, income, etc.	AU,AG,SP, GP 2
Vesperi	*City of Green Benches*	Cornell University Press, 1985	Study of elderly in Saint Petersburg	AU,GP 1
Whitbourne	*The Aging Body*	Springer-Verlag, 1985	Physiological changes and psychological consequences	AU,AG 2
Whitbourne	*The Me I Know: A Study of Adult Identity*	Springer-Verlag, 1986	Interview study of psychosocial processes	AU,AG 2
Woodward & Schwartz	*Memory and Desire: Aging-Literature-Humanities*	Indiana University Press, 1986	Psychoanalytic and literary approach to aging	AG 2

[a]Audience: GP—General public; AU—Undergraduate; AG—Graduate or above; SP—Service providers.
[b]Readability: 1—Beginner; 2—Moderate; 3—Technical.

consider training one group of students in the class in methods of data collection being used in a current research project taking place at an off-campus location (e.g., a room off the social hall in a nutrition site where the professor is collecting data on memory functioning in the aged). In the process of collecting data, students also gain exposure to a large number of elderly persons and have the chance to observe the setting itself.

4. Interviewing representatives of categories of adults and older people who fit a particular student's interest. These might include single parents, the teenage children of single parents, physically or mentally handicapped adults, female executives, family members of mentally disturbed adults, men in midlife (to ask about their experience, if any, of a "crisis"), workers in a particular field such as engineering or assembly line production, retired people, rural families, grandparents. (The possibilities here really are endless; the limiting factor will be the ingenuity of the student and professor in finding and getting the cooperation of potential interviewees.)

Experiential: Inside the Classroom

1. Guest speakers from any of the groups or settings described above who are willing to talk briefly to the class about their personal experiences and participate in a question-and-answer session.

2. Guest speakers with expertise in an area that the professor does not have. These speakers may be visiting scholars who are coming to campus anyway, other faculty from within the campus who specialize in a particularly interesting topic (such as neuropsychology of aging), and/or practitioners from the community who work with a defined population of adults (speech therapists, geriatric physicians, family counselors). Students should also be encouraged to attend public lectures given by visiting or local experts on aging.

3. Films that explore in depth an interesting and important area of adult development and aging. With home video recorders, video rental clubs, and portable video units to take to class, professors have an unprecedented opportunity to bring the media into class. Special showings can be assigned in the evening if it is impractical to show these films in class. The professor may also want to create his or her own video materials, such as commercials depicting older people, clips from the local or national news dealing with topics of relevance to the course, and visual montages that depict a variety of adults in a variety of settings. Some suggested films to show include the following (all are available in home video rental clubs or have been shown on television):

Harold and Maude
Do You Rember Love?
On Golden Pond
Harry and Tonto
Atlantic City
Wild Strawberries
Lies My Father Told Me
The Late Show
The Sunshine Boys
Death of a Salesman

The Four Seasons
The Big Chill
The Turning Point
Middle Age Crazy
Scenes from a Marriage
Who's Afraid of Virginia Woolf?
King Lear
I Never Sang for My Father
An Unmarried Woman

There are many more classics and recent releases; it is worth starting one's own collection so they can be shown at any time without having to rely on rentals.

Whatever media are used to supplement classroom teaching, they should be accompanied by discussion (before and after) to allow students to gain maximum benefit from exposure to these materials.

4. Classroom exercises based on the comments and suggestions in Table 3 can be designed and led by the professor or by groups of students. These could include simulation of age effects on mobility, sensation, perception, and memory. Role-playing exercises could also be conducted of, for instance, family members involved at different phases of the family life cycle, an older worker being supervised by a young manager, an elderly person being interviewed for admission into an institution, or other scenarios that, when acted out, could give students insights into the feelings of adults involved in difficult transitional periods of life.

5. Student groups can be formed early in the semester that meet during some of the class time (perhaps one of the three classes a week can be reserved for this purpose). These groups can be organized around the special topics described above about which students conduct research, do systematic reading, and engage in practicum work or observational field assignments at off-campus locations. These additional activities could satisfy one of the course requirements, amounting to 3 hours per week outside of class. The professor can rotate among the small groups during the class period reserved for discussion. At the end of the semester, students can turn in written projects based on their activities and present their findings or observations to the class as a whole. By sharing their experiences outside the classroom with each other, students are able to get a much broader perspective than they can from their own activity alone. In addition, in-class groups build an esprit that helps to maintain students' morale throughout the semester. The in-class groups also allow the professor (and teaching assistants, if any) to get to know each of the students and to maintain some quality con-

trol over these activities (see note in accompanying text). If the professor decides not to build any off-campus or outside class activities into the course, the small-group format can be used in a different way and accomplish some of the same goals. Random groups of students can be formed at the beginning of the year, with rotating leaders who take responsibility each week for leading a focused discussion on the topic being covered in class that week. At the end of the year, the groups can select one person to "represent" them in a panel discussion of controversial questions that other class members submit. The professor can serve as moderator of this discussion, and it can provide an enjoyable and stimulating way to finish off the semester.

Academic

1. Assign or have students select topics of interest to them within the first 4 weeks of class. If students select a topic, it should be submitted for approval by the professor. The next 4 weeks should be used for students to prepare detailed outlines (including references), which the professor then approves. The remainder of the semester is used for students to prepare their papers. The professor makes available sufficient office time to meet individually with students who need help with their papers during the latter part of the semester. Typically, the paper is due on or before the last day of class, and returned at the final exam. An alternative is to require students to submit their papers approximately 1 month before the end of the semester. If the paper is returned 2 weeks prior to the end of the semester, rather than during final exam week, students are more likely to read and digest evaluative comments and suggestions for improvement. Further, the professor can refer to a student paper in class and may, as appropriate, arrange for two or three particularly good and topically relevant papers to be presented to the class. Given the diversity of students, in terms of level and interest, who are likely to be in the class, the term paper assignment should be very flexible. Students should be able to select a topic from a wide range of areas related to adult development and aging, either dealing with special populations, conceptual issues, current controversies, or research on a new and exciting area within the field. Some appropriate term paper or research project topics, for example, could be selected or assigned to reflect strong student interest in the potential positive and negative outcomes of cognitive retraining programs or reality reorientation, the cognitive and behavioral consequences of Parkinson's disease, age differences in perceived personal autonomy, or the study of subjective levels of life satisfaction in different types of institutional settings.

2. Shorter, possibly extra-credit, projects could be assigned that consist of book reviews of either novels or monographs that deal with some particular aspect of adult development and aging. Some science fiction publications raise issues of aging in a thought-provoking manner and may serve as a superb vehicle for stimulating student thought. Papers could be five to seven pages long, and typed double-spaced. Students would be given instructions about how to prepare these, and they would have to have their choice of a book approved by the professor before they begin. The format of the report could be a brief description of the book's content, the student's evaluation of it, and a section relating ideas from the book to course content.

3. Weekly one- to two-page, typed "reaction papers" can be assigned that answer a particular question posed by the professor, or describe the student's reaction to the topic being discussed that week in class or a movie that was shown. Students would be graded on these by a simple 3-point rating system, based on how well they express themselves and how well their paper reflects mastery of course content. To make this system work, no late papers can be accepted, and the points have to add up to a significant portion of the grade by the end of the semester. Optionally, these could be assigned on an extra-credit basis.

4. Undergraduate students may be required to abstract 10 research articles at the rate of one or two per week. Abstracts must conform to a prescribed format for scientific writing and must be reviewed critically for correctness and clarity of expression as well as for content. Articles to be abstracted are selected by students from research journals that publish articles on the psychology of adult development. Students may focus on topics that would be addressed in a term paper. Such an assignment introduces students to a broader selection of the research literature than would be the case if the professor assigned 10 articles for review because a student may scan several articles before selecting one to abstract.

5. Students at any level could be required to submit a research design with the expected sophistication and tightness of the design varying with the level of the student. Students who submit particularly good and feasible designs could be encouraged to conduct the research, perhaps as an optional extra-credit component of the course, or as an independent research project earning academic credit distinct from the course that served as the stimulus for the design. Of course, the implementation of research designs mandates careful supervision and accordingly is very demanding of the professor's time. Students at a higher educational level serving as co-proctors for novice researchers may contribute substantially to the feasibility and quality of projects and at the same time gain valuable experience.

Logistic Considerations

No matter how elegant the professor's plan for a course on the psychology of adult development and aging, the course can fall flat on its face if the plan cannot be implemented. Before putting one's ideas about the course into the form of a syllabus, the professor should carefully review the practical exigencies that can intrude on the teaching and learning process.

The most important consideration is the faculty–student ratio in the class, and whether or not there will be teaching assistants available to improve this ratio. This one factor alone will permeate every aspect of the course. Written assignments, whether one or two major papers, several short assignments, or a combination thereof, must be returned promptly with careful and extensive evaluation if educational goals are to be achieved. Even more crucial, because of the potential human cost entailed, is the careful planning, monitoring, supervision, and evaluation of practicum activities. One of us will never forget the time a student's journal of practicum activities, turned in at the end of the semester, was found to contain a description of how the student had spent one afternoon a week drinking coffee with another student while doing practicum "work" at a senior center (this despite the fact that students met weekly with the professor to discuss their practicum activities). Of course, preparation of course material and examinations (which ideally would include short essay questions as well as multiple-choice items) also occupies the professor's time. Unlike some courses in psychology the content or at least the topical coverage of which remains fixed from year to year, the psychology of adult development and aging course will, as described earlier, probably vary considerably each time it is taught. This means that the professor must make allowances for course preparation time even when the course is not a new preparation.

It should be apparent from this discussion that our recommendation is for faculty to be very conservative in planning time allocations for this course. As many teaching assistants as possible should be sought from departmental resources. When graduate psychology students cannot be made available, the professor should consider other potential assistants. The most logical choice is to use a senior psychology major who has already taken the course. Creative administrative avenues can be found if the professor is determined enough and the department sufficiently flexible. Students can be reimbursed in the form of credit hours either for an undergraduate assistantship (as is the practice at the University of Massachusetts) or for an independent study or internship in which students also complete semester projects on their own. For example, a senior honors or a master's student may be conducting research for a thesis and need a group of students to help collect data in a setting where there are elderly people. The student doing the project could supervise students in the aging course who collect the data, who in turn are obtaining direct field experiences themselves. Other advanced students may be willing to volunteer to do supervision because they enjoyed their own practicum experience and want to continue it (and the accompanying recommendations the student can then ask for will provide additional incentive).

In the process of making such arrangements, the professor must be careful not to divert so much time that the project defeats its own purpose. Moreover, the professor must remember that students also do not have unlimited time to spend on the course either. They have employment, family responsibilities, other courses, and extracurricular activities that interfere with their ability to undertake excessively time-consuming class assignments, regardless of their educational value.

CURRICULUM CONSIDERATIONS

It probably strikes the reader that there is at least enough material and activities on the psychology of adult development and aging to constitute much more than a one-semester course. Apart from the content alone, the issues raised in such a course are enormously important, and will become even more so in the future.

Adult Development and Aging in Psychology Departments

Oddly enough, there apparently are many psychology departments that still do not offer a single course in the area. Whether or not any attention at all is devoted in other psychology courses to age-related issues depends primarily on the inclinations of individual faculty members and the availability of texts that include the topic. Some introductory psychology texts, for instance, include chapters on adulthood and old age (e.g., Feldman's *Understanding Psychology,* McGraw-Hill, has an excellent one). Others contain no reference at all to life-span development (e.g. Gleitman's text for Norton). Texts in upper-level courses sometimes include mention of aging (e.g. Matlin's *Perception,* Holt, Rinehart & Winston), but more often they do not. Even if the professor wanted to discuss aging relative to the topic being covered, it would be quite difficult to do so without having some text material to which to refer.

An increasing number of psychology departments do offer one course in adult development and aging. In some cases these courses are given at both the undergraduate and graduate levels, but more frequently, just at the undergraduate level. Since ordinarily only one course, if any, will be available, we have recommended broad topical coverage rather than a narrow emphasis on more specialized topics (psychopathology and aging, or aging and the environment). There are ways, though, that students can be encouraged to develop specialized knowledge on aging without taking additional courses. The faculty member in the department whose area is adult development and aging can serve as an advisor for the core of students who are interested in finding out more after having taken the survey course. Students can be helped in selecting assigned paper topics for other courses so that they give the student more knowledge about aging. For example, when taking an abnormal psychology course, the student interested in aging can be steered toward appropriate sources on psychopathology and treatment of the aged by this faculty advisor. Similarly, when taking the course on tests and measurements, the student can be advised to write a paper dealing with assessment of the elderly. Indeed, through judicious selection of assignments · and optional experiences in other psychology courses (and courses in other disciplines such as political science, sociology, economics, biology, and humanities) the student can graduate with a reasonably strong "concentration" in aging. Even without the help of a faculty advisor, students taking the initial adult development and aging course may be motivated on their own (assuming they have been well prepared with a good base of factual knowledge) to develop such a focus in their undergraduate work.

Should There Be Doctoral Programs in Adult Development and Aging?

The 1981 Boulder Conference on Training Psychologists to Work with the Elderly recommended strongly that a number of universities should develop a concentration in aging within existing programs. These could include, for instance, a concentration on aging within the clinical/counseling track, the academic/research track, or the community-social-industrial/organizational track. It was recommended that new doctoral programs *not* be developed in geropsychology. Rather, the existing doctoral programs should be expanded to allow for a subspecialty or concentration in aging. Basically, it was recommended that the concentration should include (1) a comprehensive course on adult development and aging covering developmental methods and concepts, biopsychology, cognitive psychology, personality, and social-community psychology; (2) at least one advanced seminar on a topic such as those listed above and others including psychopathology; (3) special experiences in applied psychogerontology, such as a practicum in one or more of the following: clinical/counseling, community/organizational, program evaluation and research experiences, additional internship or other supervised field experiences; and (4) dissertation research on an adult development or aging problem area. In addition to proposing that traditional doctoral programs provide the opportunity for some candidates to develop a subspecialty in aging, the Boulder Conference recommended strongly that all persons earning a doctorate in any branch of psychology have some required exposure to the study of aging.

SOME DO'S AND DON'TS

Some Don'ts

Avoid overemphasis on one segment of the population, such as the institutionalized elderly, the frail elderly, divorced adults, or battered women.

Avoid overemphasis on problems such as the shabby treatment by society of the elderly, the health problems and helplessness of the elderly, or psychopathology.

Avoid tendencies to treat as a homogeneous mass the elderly or the middle-aged or any other category of people being studied, such as the widowed, divorced, retired, or institutionalized.

Avoid a mechanistic chronological age or stage approach that neglects or submerges the life-span developmental approach.

Avoid an overemphasis on the "ivory tower" approach that focuses on abstract theory, esoteric research, and unanswerable philosophical questions. Research and theory should be well grounded in the realities of adult development and aging.

Avoid nonjudicious use of "My Aunt Tilly" anecdotes. Students at all levels, and even mature professionals, seem to be overly ready to use class or seminar time describing the life history, the peculiarities, or the problems of an elderly relative or acquaintance. Personal case histories should be used sparingly and only in relation to substantive issues. When used by the professor, they should be carefully prepared for brevity (and "Aunt Tilly's" identity disguised). The professor who does not develop procedures to limit unsolicited case history "contributions" may find that an excessive amount of class time is used nonproductively.

Avoid equating aging and death. In almost all textbooks on the psychology of adult development and aging, the final chapter is on death. It appears that in most classes the final class periods are devoted to discussions of death and dying. Whereas it is indeed recommended that bereavement, dying, and death be studied, it should be recognized that though the imminence of death is inevitable for those who have survived until very late adulthood, both death and bereavement can occur at any age. Rather than ending the class with death as the last topic, it is recommended that the final class periods be devoted to the study of successful aging. Such an approach ends the class on a more positive, upbeat, and uplifting note.

Avoid overemphasis on advocacy for some section of the population such as elderly people with incomes below the poverty level or for modification of some social or economic policy such as Medicaid. The course is on psychology, not social welfare or social change, and the focus should be on psychological approaches to understanding the individual and facilitating growth.

Avoid use of guilt as a motivator. There is a strong temptation (related to the preceding point) for professors in this area to try to impress students with the need for the members of the younger generation to work for the benefit of their elders. The negative treatment of the elderly by society (with elder abuse as an extreme example) is described in great detail, with the natural follow-up being that students should undo the wrongs fostered by the uninformed and/or unfeeling. While the idea is definitely based on well-meaning and properly motivated intentions, professors who use this approach run the risk of sending students away in droves from study or work in the area of aging. Guilt and recrimination serve as aversive conditions from which students seek relief (the old principle of negative reinforcement). Students should instead be "shaped" in a more positive manner to want to work within the field because it is so challenging, stimulating, and full of exciting potential for change.

Some Do's

Do provide a carefully prepared syllabus that is handed out the first day of class. This should describe the course objectives, required readings (text and reserve readings), and explicit goals for student performance (descriptions of assignments, extra-credit opportunities, weekly activities, examinations, and possibly the final-grade determination). List all course topics with dates and assigned readings clearly identified. Of great value is a list of references. Tell students to hold onto this syllabus (but make plenty of extra copies for when they lose theirs) because it is their "contract" for the course. You regard this as a legal document that, if they fulfill its conditions, will lead them to pass the course. You, in turn, will also fulfill your obligations to grade them according to the conditions set forth in that document.

Do attempt to coordinate classroom and experiential activities. For example, a visit by the class to a nursing home should be preceded by demographic information about the population of people in various age groups who are institutionalized, and readings and discussions on topics such as decision making regarding institutionalization, factors affecting behavioral and psychological changes following institutionalization, patterns of reinforcement within institutions, and staff–resident relationships in institutional settings.

Do attempt to allow students to tailor assignments to reflect their individual interests and career goals. When a student approaches you with an idea for a paper topic or term project, be as flexible as you can, within the limits enforced by your own time, interests, and knowledge.

Do be selective in your choice of texts. There are many new texts coming onto the market each year. Before switching from one you like to an untested new one, make sure you review the new one thoroughly to ensure it covers the topics that you want to emphasize in the course. Try to assess the appeal of the book to the students, and check the book for accuracy, clarity of organization, and readability.

Do vary depth of coverage and instructional approaches as a function of the level of students. For example, undergraduate students may be expected to study intensively one or two carefully selected texts. Postdoctoral fellows with no prior formal study of the psychology of adult development and aging would use texts for very different purposes. At the beginning of a seminar on some aspect of gerontology, they can be given the suggestion that within the next couple of weeks they review two or more basic texts simply to acquire an overview of the field, amass background information, and to identify areas for additional study, including self-study, that might otherwise go unrecognized.

CONCLUSION

The final "do" from the preceding list, recommending that depth of coverage and instructional approach should correspond to the level of the student, bears repetition. Many of the examples provided in this module pertain to the education of undergraduate students. To be sure, the majority of courses offered in adult development and aging are given at this level. There are, however, students at more advanced levels with more specialized needs, interests, and areas of expertise. Practicum experiences appropriate for undergraduate students would, obviously, not be ideal for advanced doctoral candidates or postdoctoral fellows. The opportunities and challenges for the growth of advanced students are almost endless. Doctoral candidates and postdoctoral fellows can, in addition to mastering the available literature, be involved extensively in clinical and counseling programs, community projects, program evaluation, team and individual research projects, literature reviews, preparation of review chapters, seminar participation and presentations, case presentations, preparation of research grant applications, supervision of practicum experiences for less senior students, and perhaps the teaching of liberal arts undergraduate or career preparation courses.

In conclusion, our proposed general educational approach can and should be modified as necessary to meet the needs of students at different levels. Decisions concerning emphasis on factual content, experiential involvement, scientific acumen, career skills and applications, and attitudinal sensitivity must be made for all courses. Though the details of implementing the educational goals must vary, the concerns are equally applicable to courses offered for sophomore students and doctoral candidates. Courses on the psychology of adult development and aging have the potential to be the most rewarding of a student's college or graduate school experience. It is up to the professor to use creativity, sensitivity, and attention to practical details to ensure that the course lives up to its potential.

2
Methodological Constraints— So You Want To Do Research on Aging

K. Warner Schaie

INTRODUCTION

The purpose of this module is to present material on research methodology in the psychology of aging that would not ordinarily have been presented in the traditional courses in research design and statistics encountered in psychology at both undergraduate and graduate levels. Coverage of most of the materials presented here, however, assumes that such general courses have been taken. I am thus addressing graduate students, instructors, and researchers who have good methodology grounding, who have become interested in the study of aging phenomena, or who wish to extend their instructional repertory by developing aging research methodology components or courses. We will begin by focusing on some special research problems in the developmental sciences that researchers on aging need to consider, will consider some basic designs commonly used for descriptive quasi-experimental aging studies as well as experiments involving older participants, and will address particular implications and threats to the internal and external validity of aging studies. We will then examine sampling issues and discuss some major data analysis paradigms of interest to researchers on aging, and will end with some special concerns on the ethical reporting of research results.

Special Methodological Problems in Aging Research

Age and Time

Gerontological researchers usually employ calendar age as their primary independent variable. Frequently ignored, however, is the fact that while calendar age is a time-ordered process, time of onset or duration of a given behavior is not necessarily to be correlated with age. Executive burnout, for example, could be a function of length of time on the job or of the currency of professional knowledge. Since executive burnout would usually be measured in terms of time elapsed since initial training, this phenomenon may be spuriously correlated with calendar age in those career trajectories where initial training is customary at a specific age. The same phenomenon, however, would be uncorrelated with age when observed in a population where career entry occurs over a wide age range. Executive burnout therefore is time dependent but not necessarily age related (Schaie & Hertzog, 1985).

Models of Aging

A measurement complication in the developmental sciences is that data collected over time and age are not normally distributed but, instead, represent ordered sequences whose form may vary depending upon life stage or substantive content. The most common form hypothesized to fit age-related phenomena is the well-known Gompertz curve which assumes steeply decelerating increment until a young adult asymptote followed by slowly accelerating linear decline. The implied irreversible decrement model is unduly restrictive. It does not allow for the recursive or lagged phenomena that are so characteristic of development and aging. Other models that may fit frequently observed data sets include decrement with compensation and stability throughout adulthood (cf. Salthouse, 1987; Schaie, 1973, 1977; Schaie & Hertzog, 1985). The unidirectionality of time-ordered observations, however, does present a sound basis for causal inference, in that most consequents occurring later in time cannot be said to have "caused" antecedent behaviors and events. The unidimensionality of time-ordered behaviors, therefore, provides the major rationale for applying cross-lagged correlation and linear structural analysis to developmental data or for choosing many of the fixed parameters required for model estimation.

Experiments and Quasi-Experiments

It is not possible to assign study participants randomly to different ages, birth cohorts, or measurement occasions. Age-comparative and longitudinal studies are therefore in the nature of quasi-experiments (Campbell & Stanley, 1967; Schaie, 1973, 1977). True experiments in aging research are therefore typically either within-group or age-by-treatment types of studies. Hypotheses tested by comparing nonrandom samples are subject to a variety of internal and external validity threats (to be discussed below).

Inter- and Intraindividual Differences

A major distinction among aging studies is between those that assess differences between age groups (interindividual differences) at a particular point in time and those that are concerned with changes within the same individuals across age (intraindividual differences). It should be noted that the major source of interindividual differences of interest to developmentalists are the patterns of individual differences in change within individuals. Results from studies involving comparisons of different age groups and those studying change over time within individuals are not interchangeable (cf. Labouvie, 1982; Nesselroade & Labouvie, 1985; Schaie, 1983).

Basic Design of Quasi-Experimental Aging Studies

Cross-Sectional Versus Longitudinal Methodology

Description of developmental status always involves the designation of an individual's age, the point of entry into the environment (cohort), and the point in time (period) when the dependent variable is measured. Two of these three components are ordinarily confounded, and the choice of data collection and analysis strategies should be directed by which components are of major concern (Schaie, 1965, 1977). It is widely held that the highest quality of aging data arises from longitudinal studies. However, there are many circumstances where a cross-sectional approach may indeed be the method of choice. On the other hand, if the question to be asked requires knowledge of the magnitude of intraindividual change, it cannot be answered without longitudinal data. Sometimes planned design mis-specifications may be useful when assumptions that might otherwise be unduly strong can be justified in the particular instance. For example, cohort effects are likely to be trivial when the range of ages compared is small, while period effects may be relatively trivial in many laboratory paradigms, except as expressions of reactivity or instrumentation effects (cf. Campbell & Stanley, 1967).

Data Collection Strategies

The major choice is, of course, whether one follows the same individuals over time or compares different-age individuals at the same point in time. A longitudinal sequence would follow two or more birth cohorts over a specified period of time. A cross-sectional sequence, on the other hand, would assess samples of different ages at two or more points in time. A successive accretion of data suitable for a variety of developmental analysis schemes is provided by Schaie's "most efficient design" (Schaie & Willis, 1986a, pp. 28–34).

Data Analysis Strategies

Data on different age groups collected at one point in time are *cross-sectional* in nature. We do not know whether the older group was equivalent to the younger group at an earlier age; hence, group differences may be due to either age or cohort differences or both. Single cohort *longitudinal* studies follow individuals over a specific time interval. The observed change may be a period-specific effect and thus might not be age related. Longitudinal data therefore confound effects of age and history. Another analysis method is the *time-lag* approach commonly used in the study of educational performance. Here samples of the same age are measured at different points in time. In the case of a single time-lag comparison, the difference may be due either to specific period effects, or due to cohort differences occurring prior to the observational period. If two or more appropriately selected sets of observations are available, it is possible to estimate two of three components of development, while assuming the third to be trivial or of no interest. *Cohort-sequential* studies that cross age and cohort effects and assume period to be trivial may be most useful in circumstances where an irreversible decrement model applies. *Cross-sequential* studies cross age and period and are appropriate particularly in studies of midlife or for those variables where an adult stability model appears reasonable. *Time-sequential* studies cross age and period, and may be particularly relevant in those instances where an underlying aging-with-compensation model applies. The occurrence of significant interaction effects in each instance casts some doubt on the model assumption made (Schaie, 1965, 1977).

Experimental Aging Studies

Within-Age-Group Studies

Experimental within-group designs in aging research are frequently concerned with some type of intervention paradigm designed to remediate age-related deficits in performance (cf. Krauss, 1980). In such instances a young comparison group would often be inappropriate because it may not be possible to select younger participants who have suffered such decline. Random assignment to treatment and control groups will often be successful only if the within-sample age range is reasonably limited. Otherwise, because of increasing variability with age, pretest data are needed to assure comparability of groups in small-sample studies. In any event, within-group designs should properly address the effects of intraindividual change. A powerful within-group approach involves intervention studies with groups of known developmental histories (e.g., Schaie & Willis, 1986b).

Age-Comparative Studies

The traditional paradigm in the experimental psychology of aging is to expose a young and an old group of subjects to a manipulation and then test the hypothesis that such a manipulation would be more effective for the old group and thus account for the observed age difference at base level. Main effects are of little interest in such studies since the treatment is selected because it is known to modify performance on the dependent variable, which is also known to differ by age; hence it is the interaction that is of primary interest (Baltes, Reese, & Nesselroade, 1977; Birren & Cunningham, 1985; Kausler, 1982). It is important, of course, to ascertain that the age difference in the dependent variable is not due to a failure to match on demographic or other base status variables. On the other hand, one should not inappropriately match away age differences. This could be avoided, for example, by matching relative to cohort averages. An alternative design would be to equate age groups for levels of prior practice, or to match young and old subjects on some complex behavior and then use Salthouse's (1987) molar equivalence–molecular decomposition approach to study the nature of possible underlying age effects and their compensatory mechanisms.

Many experimental aging studies suffer from inadequate cell sizes that result in inadequate power of significance tests. Minimum cell sizes should always be determined by appropriate power analyses (cf. Cohen, 1977).

Threats to Internal and External Validity

Internal Validity

Eight different threats to the internal validity of quasi-experiments have been described by Campbell and Stanley (1967) and their implications for aging research have been examined by Schaie (1977, 1988c). Of these, maturation is no threat in aging studies; it is typically the effect about which hypotheses are to be tested. However, the remaining seven threats represent rival hypotheses to the presence of maturational or age-specific effects, as follows: (1) *History* represents the impact of environmental events that could account for behavioral changes. For example, Schaie, Orshowsky, and Parham (1982) demonstrated different temporal patterns of age changes for black and white elderly. (2) *Reactivity* involves the effect of practice or testing in changing the performance of individuals at a second or subsequent assessment, independent of any maturational change (Schaie, 1988c). (3) *Instrumentation* involves the use of different equipment or test protocols across time or for the different comparison groups. This threat also includes lack of structural invariance of measures across measurement occasions (cf. Schaie, Willis, Hertzog, & Schulenberg, 1987). (4) *Statistical regression* implies that because of measurement errors, means across time will move toward the population average, leading to spurious findings of lowered performance for above-average groups or raised performance for below-average groups (Furby, 1973; Nesselroade, Stigler, & Baltes, 1980; Rogosa, 1988). Examples of a time reversal technique used to differentiate between changes due to regression effects or actual age may be found in Baltes, Nesselroade, Schaie, and Labouvie (1972) and in Schaie and Willis (1986b). (5) *Experimental mortality* becomes a problem when not all subjects originally examined are available for retest. It has been shown that dropouts typically score lower at base test than do retest survivors (Cooney, Schaie, & Willis, 1988; Riegel & Riegel, 1972; Siegler & Botwinick, 1979). Methods for assessing and adjusting for experimental mortality may be found in Schaie (1977, 1988c). (6) Differential *selection* is a problem in cross-sectional and other nonequivalent control group designs (see Baltes, Cornelius, & Nesselroade, 1979; Labouvie, 1982; Nesselroade, 1988). (7) All of the above internal validity threats can occur in *interaction*. For example, dropout effects may differ by age; for young-old individuals they are greatest due to illness, while for the old-old they are greatest due to death (Cooney, Schaie, & Willis, 1988).

External Validity

The validity of aging studies may also be threatened by the selection of samples or procedures so specific that generalizability is severely restricted (cf. Baltes, Reese, & Nesselroade, 1977; Cook & Campbell, 1979; Nesselroade, 1988; Schaie, 1978). Five different threats to the external validity of aging studies have been identified: (1) *Measurement variables* may be selected that are differentially appropriate at different age levels or different historical periods. (2) *Treatment conditions* may be differentially supportive or aversive for the young or the elderly. (3) It may not be possible to generalize across *settings* unless laboratory paradigms are indeed representative of field settings (cf. Willis, 1987). (4) Studies of *subgroups of individuals* may not be generalizable to other older groups; for example, senior center visitors or nursing home residents may not well represent the older population. (5) Generalization may be difficult across *occasions of measurement* when a study is done under unusual conditions of secular change.

Sampling Issues in Aging Studies

Frequent design criticisms are concerned with the selection of age/cohort boundaries. While it is easy to dismiss out of hand research paradigms that compare young adult college students with senior citizen center visitors, it may be much more difficult to come up with positive prescriptions. Barring a better rationale, and without knowing at what age changes are to be expected, it would make sense to place the number of selected intervals at random ages. To elucidate age-related change free of cohort confounds, it would probably be best to choose narrow age ranges at that point where such change is observed in substantial numbers of persons. Sampling requirements may differ markedly across disciplines. Certain of the secondary data analyses proposed by economists, political scientists, and sociologists involve national probability samples. By contrast, very few psychological studies are concerned with the provision of national or regional population parameters. Representative samples for the psychologist therefore may mean no more than study populations that are broad enough to cover the full range of occurrence of the behavior of interest. But even within the more limited sampling objective there are different options. One may, for example, wish to sample the occurrence of behaviors roughly proportional to their incidence within a specified parent population. Alternatively, when the primary research interest is in the mechanism of a phenomenon rather than its population distribution, it may be quite legitimate to select subjects in terms of their suitability for the study of that mechanism (cf. Keith, 1988; Nesselroade, 1988; Schaie, 1973).

Health Status and Aging Research

One major sampling issue concerns the health status of study populations. Health status may either be of direct interest as an independent variable or simply be of concern as a control variable that informs us as to the possible generalizability of the results of the findings. Under the first rubric, many studies are concerned with identifying health status consequences of demographic factors or behavioral interventions. Likewise, other studies are concerned with health status as causal influences leading to behavioral events. In these instances the question arises, however, whether the critical health status indicators should refer to the subjects' physiological state, the subjects' subjective perception of their health, or the behavioral consequences of disease (possibly unrelated to specific diagnostic entities), such as those obtained, for example, by sickness impact measures (Elinson, 1988). It would seem reasonable to expect that subjects should routinely be characterized as to their health status in at least as gross a manner as would be done for other characteristics such as age, education, and occupational status.

Measurement Development

Selection of Age-Appropriate Materials

There has been considerable discussion of the need for ecological validity of assessment instruments for the elderly (cf. Schaie, 1978). However, it is probably wise to determine whether existing instrumentation can be adapted for work with the elderly before considerable effort is invested in new methodologies. Materials specifically designed for the elderly should generally be preceded by explorative studies into the world of older people, and should involve the use of a participant-observer approach (Keith, 1988) or the participation of older persons as sources of data and judges for scaling stimuli (e.g., Scheidt & Schaie, 1978).

Equivalence of Measures Across Age and Time

Substantial methodological advances during recent years have provided formal techniques that allow us to examine the equivalence of constructs across age and time, and the efficiency with which observed variables measure the theoretical constructs in different populations and at different ages. The relevant methods are discussed by Alwin (1988) and by Schaie and Hertzog (1985). An example of a measurement equivalence study in an older population may be found in Schaie, Willis, Hertzog, and Schulenberg (1987).

Major Analysis Techniques of Particular Interest to Aging Researchers

Analysis of Variance

This technique is widely used in aging research and assumes that age groups and/or cohorts are defined as discrete intervals. Such an assumption may be valid in age-comparative studies which typically use *factorial* designs (Kausler, 1982). In descriptive and longitudinal studies direct regression approaches may be preferred, unless discrete manipulations or controls for practice or experimental mortality are involved. It should be noted that two-point *repeated measurement* ANOVAs are the exact equivalent of factorial designs employing difference scores. A variety of ANOVA schemes for various aging studies are provided by Schaie (1977), with empirical examples given in Schaie (1988c). Analysis of covariance methods are often used to adjust for inability to provide experimental controls in aging studies. In addition to grave statistical problems in this procedure, such use is problematic also because it leads to estimates under conditions not prevalent in any circumstances to which findings might be generalized.

Multivariate Analysis of Variance

Whenever multiple measures are used with the same samples that are correlated, or whenever more than two measurement occasions are to be compared, MANOVA designs would be preferred. In such analyses it is then possible to estimate effects due to nonlinear components in change over time. When significant multivariate effects are found, univariate tests are appropriate to assess the magnitude of specific contrasts (cf. Schaie & Hertzog, 1985).

Multiple Regression Analyses

In many instances multiple regression analysis will be used to determine the proportion of variance in individual differences accounted for by effects isolated in the laboratory that are represented in behaviors in real life situations (cf. Willis, 1987). Other uses involve the determination to what extent age will account for differences in the dependent variable after the effects of other competing independent variables (e.g., education, occupation, health status) have been removed. Because of high colinearity between many measures in elderly populations it is generally inappropriate to use hierarchical regression procedures. The use of simultaneous (canonical) regression analysis or newer techniques such as ridge regression is to be preferred (cf. Rogosa, 1988). Another variant of regression analysis, path analysis, has long been used by sociologists to disaggregate variance components into those associated with direct, as against mediated, effects. Current practice would prefer the use of structural equation models in these instances (see Alwin, 1988; Schaie & Hertzog, 1985; and below).

Linear Structural Analysis

If our primary interest is in studying changes or differences on theoretical constructs, then methods of linear structural analysis will become of great importance in aging research. Factor analysis can be used to reduce the large number of observable variables and to explore the structure of variable domains. More powerful than exploratory analyses, however, are the methods of confirmatory factor analysis that are used to test hypotheses about the relation between observables and theoretical constructs. Confirmatory analyses are a powerful tool used to demonstrate measurement equivalence (construct validity) over time or different subject populations (see Cunningham, 1978; Schaie & Hertzog, 1985; Schaie, Willis, Hertzog, & Schulenberg, 1987).

Structural equation models are of particular utility in aging studies because the unidirectionality of time permits sounder guides for the specification of causal paths than is possible in studies using single observation points only. Longitudinal factor analysis is a particularly useful approach to the modeling of individual differences in intraindividual change, the central focus of any individual differences approach to aging (cf. Alwin, 1988; Campbell, 1988; Joreskog, 1979; Schaie & Hertzog, 1985).

Assessment of Individual Change

While structural equation models seem to be the appropriate avenue to the assessment of measurement equivalence and the modeling of structural changes, including mean structures, there remain some very practical reasons why many investigators may wish to rely on more simplistic and direct descriptors of observed change (e.g., Schaie, 1988e). The furor over problems in interpreting change scores in developmental research started by the influential Cronbach and Furby paper (see Furby, 1973) seems to have led quantitatively unsophisticated investigators to abandon the use of change scores and for some journal editors to resist publication of change score results. This is unfortunate, since more recent work has shown that the direct assessment of change is useful in many circumstances, and that difference scores are not necessarily less reliable than other approaches (for detailed discussions see Nesselroade, Stigler, & Baltes, 1980; Rogosa, 1988.)

Event History Analysis

The study of aging involves the occurrence of discrete events that make a difference (often irreversible) to the life of individuals. It may be rather important to know how such events are timed, and what the relative importance of possible predictors might be in determining the time of occurrence of developmental transitions or disfunctions. Epidemiologists and quality control experts have long used methods of accelerated failure analysis and proportional hazard analysis to deal with similar problems in their fields. Under the name of event history analysis these methods have recently become accessible to the social and behavioral sciences (Allison, 1984).

Ethical Reporting of Research Results in Aging Studies

The Problem of Ageism in Psychological Research

Researchers interested in aging tend to examine those variables that distinguish the young and the old; differences being typically in favor of younger subjects. Only rarely are variables examined where the older person may be at advantage because of experience. Research findings may therefore provide support for stereotypes regarding the elderly or become the scientific basis for policy decisions that may disadvantage older persons (Schaie, 1988d). Researchers have an obligation, therefore, to be cautious in reporting results; specifically, they need to state the magnitude (and thus practical significance of their findings) in addition to the statistical significance (reliability) of observed differences. It should also be noted to what extent there is overlap between young and old comparison groups just as one would expect to find in studies of sex differences. Finally, it would seem appropriate to interpret the ecological relevance of small age differences (their practical significance) to make sure our findings are not misunderstood by the general public.

Collateral Data That Should Be Reported

The objectives just stated can best be achieved if research reports routinely report measures of variability (standard deviations and ranges) in addition to significance levels. In ANOVA designs it would further be appropriate to report measures of effect size, such as Omega Squared or Cohen's *d* (1977). In comparing performance levels of different age groups it would also be important to include measures of population overlap, such as the percent included in a joint distribution; and effect sizes in other relevant demographic categories (e.g., gender, education) would help to put the magnitude of age differences and changes in their proper perspective.

MODULE OUTLINE

I. Special research problems in the developmental sciences
   A. The study of age and time (Schaie & Hertzog, 1985)
      1. Time is unidirectional; antecedents and consequents must therefore be temporally distinct.
      2. Processes that have their onset and/or asymptote at a particular age are age dependent.
      3. Processes that vary in age of onset are time dependent.
   B. Models of aging (Schaie, 1973, 1988a)
      1. *Irreversible decrement* involves systematic change from a young-adult or middle-aged peak.
         (a) The Gompertz curve is a representative form of this model.
      2. *Decrement with compensation* involves age-related decline in a basic process that is compensated for by intervention or reorganization of complex behaviors.
         (a) Experienced typists maintain speed of typing even though reaction time goes up (Salthouse, 1987).
      3. *Stability* in the absence of pathology involves maintenance of optimal levels of functioning throughout adulthood.

    C. Experiments and quasi-experiments: A preview (Schaie, 1977)
      1. Experimental subjects cannot be assigned to different ages or times of measurement.
      2. Age-comparative or longitudinal studies are therefore typically quasi-experiments.
      3. Experiments in aging research are typically within-group or age-by-treatment studies (Kausler, 1982; Krauss, 1980).
    D. Inter- and intraindividual differences
       (Baltes, Reese, & Nesselroade, 1977; Schaie, 1983)
      1. Aging research differentiates between studies that assess differences between groups of individuals and those that study change within individuals.
      2. Studies of change within individuals involve both intraindividual changes and changes in interindividual differences over time.
      3. Studies of change must be longitudinal in nature.
    E. Characteristics of observations (Schaie & Hertzog, 1985)
      1. Except for demographic indicators, observed variables serve as markers of theoretically interesting constructs.
      2. Measurement equivalence of inferred constructs is usually more stable over age and time than is true for directly observed variables.
      3. A choice must be made whether developmental changes or differences are to be measured as absolute values or as relative positions.
II. Basic design of quasi-experimental aging studies
  (Campbell & Stanley, 1967; Cook & Campbell, 1979; Nesselroade & Labouvie, 1985; Schaie, 1977)
    A. Cross-sectional versus longitudinal methodology
      1. Designs of data collection must be distinguished from data analysis strategies (Schaie, 1983; Schaie & Hertzog, 1982).
      2. The age-cohort-period problem (Baltes, Cornelius, & Nesselroade, 1979; Schaie, 1965, 1986).
        (a) Definition: Development is indexed by an organism's age and cohort membership and the time-of-measurement (period) of a given response.
        (b) Similar to temperature, pressure, and volume in physics, the third factor in development is a known once the other two have been determined (two factors are always confounded).
    B. Data collection strategies (Labouvie, 1982; Schaie, 1983)
      1. Longitudinal sequences follow several cohorts over time (and age) (also cf. Campbell, 1988).
      2. Cross-sectional sequences assess samples of different ages at two or more points in time.

3. Schaie's "most efficient design" starts out with a cross-sectional sample and converts it into a series of short-term longitudinal studies (Schaie & Willis, 1986a).

C. Data analysis strategies (Schaie, 1973, 1977)

1. Single-time cross-sectional studies confound age and cohort.
2. Single-cohort longitudinal studies confound age and period.
3. Time lag studies measure samples of the same age at different times; they confound cohort and period.
4. Cohort-sequential studies assess two or more cohorts at two or more ages; period effects are assumed trivial.
5. Time-sequential studies assess two or more age groups at two or more times; cohort effects are assumed to be trivial.
6. Cross-sequential studies assess two or more cohorts at two or more times; age effects are assumed trivial.

III. Experimental aging studies
(Baltes, Reese, & Nesselroade, 1977; Kausler, 1982)

A. Within-age group studies (Krauss, 1980; Schaie & Willis, 1986b)

1. Subjects are randomly assigned to treatment and control conditions.
2. Age ranges should be reasonably small.
3. Otherwise, because of great variability, pretest data are needed to assure comparability of groups in small-sample studies.

B. Age-comparative studies (Kausler, 1982)

1. Age groups need to be matched on demographic and relevant base status variables, without matching away aging effects.
   (a) Education or occupation might be matched relative to the cohort average on these variables.
2. Groups with differential prior experience could be given practice to reach a common base criterion.
3. Main effects are of little interest, since the treatment will be selected because it is effective and older adults are likely to perform at a lower level on average than do younger subjects.
4. Age by treatment interaction is the effect of interest to determine whether treatment has differential effects by age.

IV. Threats to internal and external validity

A. Internal validity (Campbell & Stanley, 1967; Schaie, 1977, 1988b).

1. History, general environmental impact across the time period during which aging is studied.
2. Maturation, of specific interest to aging researchers, design must avoid controlling for this effect!

3. Reactivity (testing), effect of measurement operation on dependent variables being studied.
4. Instrumentation, variability of protocol or equipment across measurement occasions or comparison groups.
5. Statistical regression, effect of unreliability in spuriously raising means of low-scoring groups and lowering means of high-scoring groups over time (Baltes, Nesselroade, Schaie, & Labouvie, 1972; Furby, 1973; Nesselroade, Stigler, & Baltes, 1980; Rogosa, 1988).
6. Experimental mortality, the effect of selective sample attrition (Cooney, Schaie, & Willis, 1988; Riegel & Riegel, 1972; Siegler & Botwinick, 1980).
7. Selection, tapping particular ranges of behavior on independent variables affecting the dependent variable of interest (Nesselroade, 1988).
8. Interactions, combinations of the above threats.
   B. External validity (Cook & Campbell, 1979; Schaie, 1978)
1. Measurement variables, the same instrument may not measure same construct in different samples.
2. Treatment conditions, laboratory paradigms may have differential effects on different samples.
3. Settings, effects obtained in the laboratory may not generalize to field settings.
4. Subgroups of individuals, the same phenomenon may have different temporal patterns in different population subgroups (Schaie, Orshowsky, & Parham, 1982).
5. Occasion of measurement, developmental phenomena may be specific to particular historical periods.
   V. Sampling issues in aging studies (Schaie, 1973, 1988c)
   A. Representative samples, may represent defined populations or sets of behaviors (Nesselroade, 1988).
   B. Stratified samples, select from specific ranges of subject characteristics or phenomena.
1. Identification of demographic characteristics (e.g., age, sex, education, occupation, income).
2. Identification of health status (Elinson, 1988).
   C. Oversampling of special populations, the study of abnormal or rare behaviors of interest.
   D. Age boundaries, should be selected so as to minimize age/cohort confounds (Schaie, 1988c).
   VI. Measurement development (Schaie & Hertzog, 1985)
   A. Selection of age-appropriate materials (Schaie, 1978)
1. Participant-observer approach (Keith, 1988)
2. Ethnographic/psychometric approach (Scheidt & Schaie, 1978)

      B. Equivalence of measures across age and time (Alwin, 1988; Schaie & Hertzog, 1985; Schaie, Willis, Hertzog, & Schulenberg, 1987)

VII. Major analysis techniques of particular interest to aging researchers

      A. Analysis of variance (Schaie & Hertzog, 1985)

          1. Repeated measurement designs

          2. Factorial designs

          3. Analysis of covariance

      B. Multivariate analysis of variance

      C. Multiple regression analyses

          1. Hierarchical versus simultaneous analyses

          2. Path analysis

      D. Linear structural analysis (Alwin, 1988; Schaie & Hertzog, 1985)

          1. Factor analysis (Cunningham, 1978)

             (a) Exploratory

             (b) Hypothesis testing

          2. Causal modeling (Alwin, 1988; Campbell, 1988)

      E. Study of individual change (Rogosa, 1988; Schaie, 1988b)

      F. Event history analysis (Allison, 1984)

VIII. The ethical reporting of research results (Schaie, 1988a)

      A. The problem

          1. Effect size, magnitude of individual differences explained (Cohen, 1977).

          2. Overlap across adjacent age groups, or between young and old comparison group.

          3. Ecological relevance of age effect, does the observed age difference have a practical consequence?

      B. Collateral data that should be reported

          1. Measures of variability, standard deviations and ranges

          2. Measures of effect size, Omega Squared or Cohen's d (Cohen, 1977)

          3. Measures of population overlap, percent joint distribution.

          4. Effect sizes in other relevant demographic categories (e.g., gender, education)

ANNOTATED BIBLIOGRAPHY

Allison, P. D. (1984). *Event history analysis: Regression for longitudinal event data.* **Beverly Hills, CA: Sage.**

This monograph applies accelerated failure and proportional hazard models to the analysis of life events for which time-ordered data are available. This technique has received recent prominence in sociological and epidemiological research. It appears to be a promising method for application to longitudinal behavioral data. Heuristic examples and descriptions of relevant computer programs are included.

Kind	Recommendation	Readability	Audience
HB	** ½	3	AG

Alwin, D. F. (1988). Structural equation models in research on human development and aging. In K. W. Schaie, R. T. Campbell, W. Meredith, & S. W. Rawlings (Eds.), *Research methodology in studies of aging* (pp. 71–170). New York: Springer.

This chapter provides a tutorial describing the foundation of linear structural analysis and describing applications for the study of measurement equivalence and the testing of multivariate hypotheses for the study of developmental phenomena with several illustrations from the aging literature. Although highly technical, it is a more complete presentation than most other similar chapters, and should make the topic accessible to graduate students and researchers.

Kind	Recommendation	Readability	Audience
TC	** ½	3	AG

Baltes, P. B., Cornelius, S. W, & Nesselroade, J. R. (1979). Cohort effects in developmental psychology. In J. R. Nesselroade & P. B. Baltes (Eds.), *Longitudinal research in the study of behavior and development* (pp. 61–88). New York: Academic Press.

Provides definitions and a thorough discussion of cohort effects in behavioral research.

Kind	Recommendation	Readability	Audience
TC	* ½	2	AG

Baltes, P. B., Nesselroade, J. R., Schaie, K. W., & Labouvie, E. W. (1972). On the dilemma of regression effects in examining ability-level related differentials in ontogenetic patterns of intelligence. *Developmental Psychology, 6,* 78–84.

Discusses the Cronbach–Furby arguments about the unreliability of change scores, and describes a time-reversal technique for assessing the seriousness of regression effects in limiting the interpretation of two-point change data. Provides a fully analyzed empirical example assessing change in cognitive function from the Seattle Longitudinal Study.

Kind	Recommendation	Readability	Audience
E	**	2	AG

Baltes, P. B., Reese, H. W., & Nesselroade, J. R. (1977). *Life-span developmental psychology: Introduction to research methods.* **Monterey, CA: Brooks-Cole.**

A classic textbook (once again in print) describing methods for the study of developmental phenomena. While many technical issues are raised, the book approaches these problems so as to make them accessible for the beginner. Suitable for advanced undergraduates and service professionals as well as researchers at large. Brought up to date with some more technical supplementation [such as Schaie, Campbell, Meredith, & Rawlings (1988) (see Alwin, 1988)] it could also serve as text for a first-year graduate developmental research course.

Kind	Recommendation	Readability	Audience
TB	***	1	AU,SP

Birren, J. E., & Cunningham, W. (1985). Research on the psychology of aging: Principles, concepts and theory. In J. E. Birren & K. W. Schaie (Eds.), *Handbook of the psychology of aging* **(2nd ed., pp. 3–34). New York: Academic Press.**

Discusses the paradigms most useful in behavioral research on aging and provides an outline of questions that must be addressed by the prospective researcher.

Kind	Recommendation	Readability	Audience
RC	**	2	AG

Campbell, D. T., & Stanley, J. C. (1967). *Experimental and quasi-experimental designs for research.* **Chicago: Rand McNally.**

This classic monograph defines the difference between experiments and descriptive research and specifies appropriate paradigms for the conduct of the latter variety of quasi-experimentation, most common in research on aging.

Kind	Recommendation	Readability	Audience
HB	***	2	AG

Campbell, R. T. (1988). Integrating conceptualization, design, and analyis in panel studies of the life course. In K. W. Schaie, R. T. Campbell, W. Meredith, & S. W. Rawlings (Eds.), *Research methodology in studies of aging* (pp. 43–69). New York: Springer.

A thoughtful overview of the design of longitudinal panel studies, particularly appropriate for survey researchers, but providing many important recommendations for all researchers planning longitudinal studies.

Kind	Recommendation	Readability	Audience
TC	**	2	AG

Cohen, J. (1977). *Statistical power analysis for the behavioral sciences* (rev. ed.). New York: Academic Press.

An essential reference tool that needs to be known and kept on the shelf of every serious behavioral researcher. Contains the tables required to determine power of significance tests and to ascertain sample sizes required for valid hypothesis testing of relationships or group differences.

Kind	Recommendation	Readability	Audience
HB	*	3	AG

Cook, T. D., & Campbell, D. T. (1979). Quasi-experimentation: Designs and analysis issues for field settings. Chicago: Rand McNally.

An expansion of Campbell and Stanley (1967) with emphasis on issues of external validity. Another important reference work for those employing descriptive research paradigms in field settings.

Kind	Recommendation	Readability	Audience
HB	* 1/2	2	AG

Cooney, T. M., Schaie, K. W., & Willis, S. L. (1988). The relationship between prior functioning on cognitive and personality variables and subject attrition in longitudinal research. *Journal of Gerontology*, *43*, 12–17.

Provides an example of an empirical study of the effects of experimental mortality, segregating attrition effects into those associated with death, illness, or voluntary dropout. Data come from the Seattle Longitudinal Study.

Kind	Recommendation	Readability	Audience
E	**	3	AG

Costa, P. T., Jr., & McCrae, R. R. (1982). An approach to the attribution of aging, period, and cohort effects. *Psychological Bulletin, 92,* 238–250.

An intuitive approach to resolving the age-cohort-period problem. To understand this article, it would help to be familiar with Schaie (1965 or 1977).

Kind	Recommendation	Readability	Audience
E	* 1/2	3	AG

Cunningham, W. R. (1978). Principles for identifying structural differences: Some methodological issues related to comparative factor analysis. *Journal of Gerontology, 33,* 82–86.

A useful introduction to the design and interpretation of factor analysis studies in aging research.

Kind	Recommendation	Readability	Audience
RC	**	2	AG

Elinson, J. (1988). Defining and measuring health and illness. In K. W. Schaie, R. T. Campbell, W. Meredith, & S. W. Rawlings (Eds.). *Research methodology in studies of aging* (pp. 231–248). New York: Springer.

Definitions are given for alternate ways to measure health status in behavioral and social science studies. Emphasis is on ways to measure quality of life as impacted by disease.

Kind	Recommendation	Readability	Audience
RC	* 1/2	1	AG

Furby, L. (1973). Interpreting regression toward the mean in developmental research. *Developmental Psychology, 8*, 172–179.

A classic article that led to the premature abandonment of change scores by many researchers. Provides background for material by Nesselroade et al. (1980) and Rogosa (1988).

Kind	Recommendation	Readability	Audience
TC	*	3	AG

Garfein, A. J., Schaie, K. W., & Willis, S. L. (1988). Microcomputer proficiency in later-middle-aged and older adults: Teaching old dogs new tricks. *Social Behaviour, 3*, 131–148.

Example of an empirical within-group aging study involving the teaching of a novel skill to adults and relating effects to prior status on ability measures.

Kind	Recommendation	Readability	Audience
E	* ½	2	AG

Hertzog, C. (1987). Applications of structural equation models in gerontological research. In K. W. Schaie (Ed.), *Annual review of gerontology and geriatrics* (Vol. 7, pp. 265–294).

An up-to-date review of applications of the new linear structural equation methods to topics in aging research.

Kind	Recommendation	Readability	Audience
TC	**	3	AG

Horn, J. L., McArdle, J. J., & Mason, R. (1984). When invariance is not invariant: A practical scientist's look at the ethereal concept of factor invariance. *Southern Psychologist, 1*, 179–188.

Distinguishes between measurement invariance that involves complete equivalence of all psychometric characteristics (metric invariance) from a more relaxed criterion that requires only equivalence of structural patterns (configural invariance). Important for researchers planning comparative factor analyses studies.

Kind	Recommendation	Readability	Audience
TC	**	2	AG

Hultsch, D. F., & Hickey, T. (1978). External validity in the study of human development: Methodological considerations. *Human Development*, 21, 76–91.

A full disscussion of issues of generalizability and relevant paradigms as applied to aging research.

Kind	Recommendation	Readability	Audience
RC	* 1/2	2	AG

Jöreskog, K. G. (1979). Statistical estimation of structural models in longitudinal developmental investigations. In J. R. Nesselroade & P. B. Baltes (Eds.), *Longitudinal research in the study of behavior and development* (pp. 303–351). New York: Academic Press.

This is the basic presentation of schemes for the application of methods of linear structural analysis to longitudinal data. Should probably not be attempted before working through Alwin (1988).

Kind	Recommendation	Readability	Audience
TC	* 1/2	3	AG

Kausler, D. H. (1982). *Experimental psychology and human aging*. New York: Wiley.

An excellent graduate level presentation of designs and research findings of age-comparative manipulative studies with older persons. Needs to be supplemented by additional material on descriptive research.

Kind	Recommendation	Readability	Audience
TB	**	2	AG

Keith, J. (1988). Participant observation: A modest little method whose presumption may amuse you. In K. W. Schaie, R. T. Campbell, W. Meredith, & S. W. Rawlings (Eds.), *Research methodology in studies of aging* (pp. 211–230). New York: Springer.

A very accessible presentation of the use of ethno-methodology for nonanthropologists. Contains empirical examples of the application of participant observation techniques in a residence for older persons.

Kind	Recommendation	Readability	Audience
TC	**	1	AG

Krauss, I. (1980). Between- and within-group comparisons in aging research. In L. W. Poon (Ed.), *Aging in the 1980s* **(pp. 542–551). Washington, DC: American Psychological Association.**

Discusses under what circumstances studies of aging require young control groups and when within-age-group research is more appropriate.

Kind	Recommendation	Readability	Audience
TC	**	2	AG

Labouvie, E. W. (1982). Issues in life-span development. In B. B. Wolman (Ed.), *Handbook of developmental psychology* **(pp. 54–62). Englewood Cliffs, NJ: Prentice-Hall.**

Another view of design issues in descriptive aging research.

Kind	Recommendation	Readability	Audience
TC	**	3	AG

Nesselroade, J. R. (1988). Sampling and generalizability: Adult development and aging research issues examined within the general methodological framework of selection. In K. W. Schaie, R. T. Campbell, W. Meredith, & S. W. Rawlings (Eds.), *Research methodology in studies of aging* **(pp. 13–42). New York: Springer.**

Questions of external validity and the selection of samples in aging research are considered within a general sampling framework that (perhaps for the first time) systematically includes the temporal dimension.

Kind	Recommendation	Readability	Audience
TC	**	3	AG

Nesselroade, J. R., & Labouvie, E. W. (1985). Experimental design in research on aging. In J. E. Birren & K. W. Schaie (Eds.), *Handbook* *of the psychology of aging* (2nd ed., pp. 35–60). New York: Academic Press.

Reviews issues of designing descriptive studies in aging research and extends and updates the material first presented in Schaie (1973 and 1977).

Kind	Recommendation	Readability	Audience
TC	**	2	AG

Nesselroade, J. R., Stigler, S.M., & Baltes, P. B. (1980). Regression towards the mean and the study of change. *Psychological Bulletin, 88,* 622–637.

This article reviews the Cronbach–Furby objection to the use of change scores in developmental research, and shows under what circumstances this objection may be valid or spurious.

Kind	Recommendation	Readability	Audience
TC	* ¹/₂	3	AG

Riegel, K. F., & Riegel, R. M. (1972). Development, drop, and death. *Developmental Psychology,* 6, 306-319.

A historically important treatment of the experimental mortality problem in behavioral research on aging. Data come primarily from the authors' German longitudinal studies.

Kind	Recommendation	Readability	Audience
TC	* ¹/₂	3	AG

Rogosa, D. (1988). Myths about longitudinal research. In K. W. Schaie, R. T. Campbell, W. Meredith, & S. W. Rawlings (Eds.), *Research methodology in studies of aging* (pp. 171–209). New York: Springer.

A provocative review of traditional views of research methodology appropriate for longitudinal data. Rogosa supports the use of change scores, and emphasizes the utility of time series analyses.

Kind	Recommendation	Readability	Audience
TC	**	3	AG

Salthouse, T. A. (1987). Age, experience and compensation. In C. Schooler & K. W. Schaie (Eds.), *Cognitive functioning and social structure over the life course* (pp. 142–157). Norwood, NJ: Ablex.

A good introduction to the molar equivalence–molecular decomposition method of studying age differences. Describes the author's work on expert typists, a prime example of a data set fitting the decrement-with-compensation model.

Kind	*Recommendation*	*Readability*	*Audience*
TC	**	3	AG

Schaie, K. W. (1965). **A general model for the study of developmental change.** *Psychological Bulletin, 64,* 92–107.

This is the original exposition of the age-cohort-period problem in developmental research in psychology. More accessible (less technical) presentations are provided in Schaie (1973, 1977) and Schaie and Willis (1986a).

Kind	*Recommendation*	*Readability*	*Audience*
TC	***	3	AG

Schaie, K. W. (1973). **Methodological problems in descriptive developmental research on adulthood and aging.** In J. R. Nesselroade and H. W. Reese (Eds.), *Life-span developmental psychology: Developmental issues* (pp. 253–280). New York: Academic Press.

Provides a less technical discussion of the age-cohort-period problem than the original (1965) exposition. Also examines issues of sampling methodology in aging studies.

Kind	*Recommendation*	*Readability*	*Audience*
TC	**	2	AG

Schaie, K. W. (1977). **Quasi-experimental research designs in the psychology of aging.** In J. E. Birren and K. W. Schaie (Eds.), *Handbook of the psychology of aging* (pp. 39–58). New York: Van Nostrand Reinhold.

Applies the work of Campbell and Stanley (1967) to aging research, discusses the age-cohort-period problem, and provides paradigms for the analysis of descriptive data sets, including controls for attrition and practice.

Kind	Recommendation	Readability	Audience
TC	**	3	AG

Schaie, K. W. (1978). External validity in the assessment of intellectual development in adulthood. *Journal of Gerontology, 33,* **695–701.**

Applies the consideration of external validity (cf. Cook & Campbell, 1979) to descriptive studies of intellectual aging.

Kind	Recommendation	Readability	Audience
TC	**	1	AG

Schaie, K. W. (1983). What can we learn from the longitudinal study of adult psychological development? In K. W. Schaie (Ed.), *Longitudinal studies of adult psychological development* **(pp. 1–19). New York: Guilford Press.**

A succinct summary of the rationale for conducting longitudinal studies in aging research. Also provides a convenient schematic for the different methods of collecting and analyzing descriptive developmental data.

Kind	Recommendation	Readability	Audience
TC	**	1	AU

Schaie, K. W. (1986). Beyond calendar definitions of age, time and cohort: The general developmental model revisited. *Developmental Review, 6,* **252–277.**

Provides the conceptual framework for finessing the age-cohort-period problem by redefining one of the components of development on a noncalendar basis.

Kind	Recommendation	Readability	Audience
TC	**	3	AG

Schaie, K. W. (1987). Research methods in gerontology. In G. Maddox & R. Corsini (Eds.), *Encyclopedia of aging* **(pp. 570–573). New York: Springer.**

A nontechnical review of research issues in gerontology designed for the general reader.

Kind	Recommendation	Readability	Audience
RC	**	1	AU,GP,SP

Schaie, K. W. (1988a). **The impact of research methodology on theory-building in the developmental sciences. In J. E. Birren & V. L. Bengtson (Eds.),** *Emergent theories of aging: Psychological and social perspectives on time, self and society* **(pp. 41–58). New York: Springer.**

Reviews paradigm shifts resulting from the introduction of new schemes of data collection and data analysis. Examples cover the sequential methods and linear structural analyses applied to aging data.

Kind	Recommendation	Readability	Audience
TC	**	2	AG

Schaie, K. W. (1988b). **Internal validity threats in studies of adult cognitive development. In M. L. Howe & C. J. Brainard (Eds.),** *Cognitive development in adulthood: Progress in cognitive development research,* **pp. 241–272. New York: Springer-Verlag.**

A complete discussion of internal validity threats, their experimental control and analysis, and completely worked-out examples applying each method to data from the Seattle Longitudinal Study.

Kind	Recommendation	Readability	Audience
TC	**	3	AG

Schaie, K. W. (1988c). **Methodological issues in aging research: An introduction. In K. W. Schaie, R. T. Campbell, W. Meredith, & S. W. Rawlings (Eds.),** *Research methodology in studies of aging* **(pp. 1–11). New York: Springer.**

A nontechnical summary of major issues requiring attention by researchers on human aging.

Kind	Recommendation	Readability	Audience
RC	* ½	1	AG

Schaie, K. W. (1988d). Ageism in psychological research. *American Psychologist,* **43, 179–183.**

Discusses the manner in which inappropriate inferences from aging research can lead to policy decisions that will unfavorably affect the lives of older persons. Includes recommendations for cautions to be observed in the reporting of research results.

Kind	*Recommendation*	*Readability*	*Audience*
RC	**	1	AU,SP

Schaie, K. W. (1988e). Individual differences in rate of cognitive change in adulthood. In V. L. Bengtson & K. W. Schaie (Eds.), *The course of later life: Research and reflections.* **(pp. 65–85). New York: Springer.**

An empirical example of methods for the study of individual differences in change over time in intellectual functioning.

Kind	*Recommendation*	*Readability*	*Audience*
TC	**	3	AG

Schaie, K. W., & Hertzog, C. (1982). Longitudinal methods. In B. B. Wolman (Ed.), *Handbook of developmental psychology* **(pp. 91–115). Englewood Cliffs, NJ: Prentice-Hall.**

A formal presentaion of considerations for the application of longitudinal methods, and an exposition of research designs suitable for the analysis of longitudinal data.

Kind	*Recommendation*	*Readability*	*Audience*
TC	**	3	AG

Schaie, K. W., & Hertzog, C. (1985). Measurement in the psychology of aging. In J. E. Birren & K. W. Schaie (Eds.), *Handbook of the psychology of aging* **(2nd ed., pp. 61–92). New York: Van Nostrand Reinhold.**

Provides a technical discussion of most measurement issues addressed in this module. The discussion of multivariate approaches to the study of aging is somewhat more accessible but not as complete as Alwin (1988).

Kind	Recommendation	Readability	Audience
TC	**	3	AG

Schaie, K. W., Orshowsky, S. J., & Parham, I. A. (1982). Measuring age and socio-cultural change: The case of race and life satisfaction. In R. C. Manuel (Ed.), *Minority aging: Sociological and social psychological issues* **(pp. 223–230). Westport, CT: Greenwood Press.**

An empirical application of sequential research methodologies to the study of minority aging.

Kind	Recommendation	Readability	Audience
E	**	2	AG

Schaie, K. W., & Willis, S. L. (1986a). *Adult development and aging* **(2nd ed.). Boston: Little, Brown.**

A comprehensive account of adult development from the stage of family formation to old age and death. The introductory chapter is of particular relevance for this module as it contains an accessible account of sequential-longitudinal methodology.

Kind	Recommendation	Readability	Audience
TB	**	1	AU

Schaie, K. W., & Willis, S. L. (1986b). Can decline in adult cognitive functioning be reversed? *Developmental Psychology, 22,* **223–232.**

Empirical example of an intervention study with older persons, conducted within the context of a longitudinal study.

Kind	Recommendation	Readability	Audience
E	**	2	AG

Schaie, K. W., Willis, S. L., Hertzog, C., & Schulenberg, J. E. (1987). Effects of cognitive training upon primary mental ability structure. *Psychology and Aging, 2,* **233–242.**

Empirical example of the application of comparative factor analysis to a pretest-posttest design cognitive intervention study.

Kind	Recommendation	Readability	Audience
E	*1/2	2	AG

Scheidt, R. J., & Schaie, K. W. (1978). A taxonomy of situations for the elderly population: Generating situational criteria. *Journal of Gerontology, 33,* 872–883.

Empirical example of the application of ethno-methodology and psychological scaling methods for the development of a technique for the study of perceived competence in the elderly.

Kind	Recommendation	Readability	Audience
E	**	3	AG

Siegler, I. C., & Botwinick, J. (1979). A long-term longitudinal study of intellectual ability of older adults: The matter of selective attrition. *Journal of Gerontology, 34,* 242–245.

Kind	Recommendation	Readability	Audience
E	**	3	AG

Empirical example of the application of methods for experimental mortality analysis to data from the Duke Longitudinal Study.

Willis, S. L. (1987). Cognitive training and everyday competence. In K. W. Schaie (Ed.), *Annual review of gerontology and geriatrics* (Vol. 7, pp. 159–182). New York: Springer.

Reviews the literature on intellectual change and cognitive intervention as related to everyday behavior.

Kind	Recommendation	Readability	Audience
RC	**	2	AG

Willis S. L., & Schaie, K. W. (1988). Gender differences in spatial ability in old age: Longitudinal and intervention findings. *Sex Roles, 18,* 189–203.

Empirical example of a method to disaggregate changes over time in speed and accuracy.

Kind	Recommendation	Readability	Audience
E	**	3	AG

3
Longevity

Diana S. Woodruff-Pak and Mary Winn

INTRODUCTION

Longevity is an important, but often overlooked, issue in social and behavioral science perspectives of aging. That psychologists are beginning to recognize the relevance to their discipline of research on longevity was given evidence when the category *life expectancy* was included in *Psychological Abstracts* for the first time in 1982. Although longevity has typically been a topic considered in the realm of biology and medicine, it is becoming increasingly apparent that length of life is directly impacted by social and behavioral phenomena (Cohen & Brody, 1981). Many of the changes individuals must make in their lives to maximize their life expectancy involve psychological motivation and attitudes.

Consideration of longevity includes both the quality and the quantity of years in the lives of individuals as they age. Quality and quantity of life are closely related (Berardo, La Greca, & Hodgkins-Berardo, 1985). For example, high life satisfaction and social support are positively correlated with longevity (Berardo, 1985). Shorter life expectancy is correlated with depression (Enzell, 1984). As we improve the quality of life in later adulthood with interventions such as enhancement of social support networks and alleviation of depression, it is impossible not to also affect longevity.

A major reason making it important for psychologists to know and understand factors involved in longevity is that psychological variables significantly affect longevity. This perspective differs from the more typical point of view in the psychology of aging in which behavioral change is a dependent variable. In studying social and psychological factors affecting longevity, we are considering these factors to be independent variables. This also means that we could manipulate certain social and psychological factors and affect longevity. Naturally, the aim would be to maximize life expectancy and the quality of life by changing those social and behavioral variables that have been associated with a shortened length of life.

At present, a fair number of life-extending interventions are known (Schneider & Reed, 1985). That interventions are possible on a large scale was demonstrated in communities in Finland (Alderman, 1979). Because of the high incidence of cardiovascular disease in these communities, attitude and lifestyle interventions were undertaken on a large scale. Strategies to educate the population, to make low-fat milk and other foods low in fat more readily available, to monitor blood pressure often, and to provide optimal health care yielded dramatic results. Comparisons of a community receiving the interventions to one that did not revealed that the incidence of stroke was reduced by 40 percent over a 5-year period.

Measures of Longevity: Life Expectancy and Life Span

It is important to distinguish between *life expectancy* and *life span*. Life span is the upper limit set on human life. It is the genetic potential of the human species, and factors that appear to set this upper limit are yet to be discovered.

In their book on medical aspects in vitality and aging, Fries and Crapo (1981) make a distinction between two concepts subsumed under the term *life span*. They distinguish the maximum life potential (MLP) from life span for the general population—the idea being that only a very few of us have the genetic capacity and environmental circumstances to achieve the MLP. The age at death of the longest-lived member of the species, the MLP, is recorded to have been 120 years. No individuals with verifiable birth records have survived beyond that age. (The longest-lived human with a documented birth date was Shigechiyo Izumi, a Japanese man who died on February 21, 1986, at the age of 120 years, 7 months, and 21 days.)

Life span, according to Fries (1980, 1983), is the age at which the average individual would die if there were no disease or accidents. He asserts that this age is about 85 years and that it has been constant for centuries. Fries's position is controversial. Schneider and Brody (1983) argue that epidemiological evidence indicates that life expectancy is not maximizing at 85 but is continuing to increase beyond that upper limit.

As distinguished from MLP and life span, life expectancy is the expected age at death of the average individual, granting current mortality rates from disease and accident. It is the age at which half of a given birth cohort will be alive and half will be dead. For infants born in 1985, life expectancy was 74.7 years. This is almost 28 years longer than life expectancy for infants born in 1900. Life expectancy statistics are computed annually by life insurance companies and by governmental agencies and published as actuarial tables.

Actuarial Tables

The actuarial tables we will discuss are based on census data and predict life expectancy on the basis of age, sex, and race. An example of an actuarial table is given in the section, "Supplementary Material." It becomes clear when reading actuarial tables that the total life expectancy of an individual at birth is shorter than life expectancy at later years. The reason that life expectancy increases at older ages is because once a person survives certain critical periods, the chances for living longer are greater. For example, infancy is a time when the mortality rate is relatively high. When a baby is alive at the age of 1, he or she has a greater likelihood of surviving longer than a newborn. Between the ages of 10 and 25 life expectancy changes very little because fewer people die between these ages. The force of mortality gradually accelerates after that, and a greater percentage of the people remaining alive die with each succeeding year.

Life tables are based on recorded deaths at each age, and the life expectancy given for each age is the number of years that half the cohort born in that year will survive. For example, half of all Americans who have already reached the age of 80 years will survive to the age of 88.1 years. Some individuals who are now in their late 80s will survive to 100 years, but there are currently so few Americans in the age categories of 86 and older that the government does not even include life expectancy beyond the age of 85 on the charts.

Changes in Life Expectancy Throughout History

Studying the characteristics of human bones from the limited number of fossils of prehistoric humans that have been found, Dublin, Lotka, and Spiegelman (1949) estimated that very few prehistoric humans survived even to 40 years of age. Most met violent deaths at an early age as indicated by fractures in a large proportion of the fossilized skulls. Estimates of average age at death in Greece between 3500 B.C. and 1300 A.D. suggest a gradual improvement in life expectancy from around 18 years in the early periods to 30 years in the period around 400 B.C. Ancient Rome was an even less healthy place in which to live, with some estimates of life expectancy as low as 20 years. These mortality rates for the highest centers of civilization 2,000 years ago are worse than the mortality rate for any country in the present, but not by much. For example, United Nations data for 1982 indicated that life expectancy for males in Ethiopia was about 38 years, and for females it was 41 years.

Life expectancy in the Middle Ages was estimated to range from 30 to 35 years. Analyses for the seventeenth and eighteenth centuries indicated that life expectancy in Western Europe was between 30 and 37 years. In selected cities in the United States in this period, life expectancy estimates ranged from 25 to 36 years. In the nineteenth century, health conditions improved enough so that about 10 years was added to life expectancy. In the midnineteenth century, life expectancy estimates ranged around 40 years, and by the early twentieth century, life expectancy in the United States was between 47 and 49 years.

It is in the twentieth century that we have made the most rapid gains in human life expectancy. One consequence has been dramatic increases in the numbers of individuals reaching their 80s, 90s, and 100s (Spencer, 1987). This tremendous leap in life expectancy has resulted from medical advances, improvements in the standard of living, and improvements in our health care system (Woodruff-Pak, 1988). Consideration of future trends in longevity indicates that patterns of employment, education, and retirement must change to balance the increasing percentage of aged in the population (Vaupel & Gowan, 1986). That is, the age of the population will continue to climb if we are successful in controlling and eliminating acquired immunodeficiency disease (AIDS), which has drastically increased the rate of premature death in young adults (Kristal, 1986).

Are All Nations "Aging"?

Aging of the population is a phenomenon occurring in all developed countries, but it is not yet universal. Mortality rates are so high in underdeveloped nations that life expectancy is much lower. Additionally, the birth rates in these countries are high, so that the proportion of the aged in the population and the median ages are much lower than in developed nations. Countries in the world that have developed at a pace similar to that of the United States have shown similar advances in life expectancy. Some underdeveloped countries still have a life expectancy close to that which existed in the United States at the turn of the century. However, many Third World countries anticipate dramatic increases in the percentage of older adults in the population in the twenty-first century (Shuman, 1987).

The United States is not the oldest country in the world in terms of having the largest percentage of aged. Nineteen countries with a population of more than 1 million have a higher percentage of aged than did the United States in 1985 (Zopf, 1986). Sweden is the oldest country in terms of the percentage of old people in the population. People born in the United States also do not have the longest life expectancy. Based on data available from the United Nations in 1982, the longest life expectancy for both men and women was enjoyed by the Japanese.

Overview of Major Determinants of Life Expectancy

We will discuss the factors identified as major determinants of life expectancy with a caution about the limitations of our knowledge. Most of the data currently available on human life expectancy are correlational. It is essential to understand that correlational studies do not provide conclusive evidence about causation. For example, when high correlations were found between the incidence of lung cancer and the number of cigarettes smoked per day, many were willing to say that smoking caused cancer. Scientists were aware that such an inference was suggested by the data but not proved. Many argued that a third variable (e.g., personality) caused people to smoke and also caused lung cancer. The proof came with *experiments* showing that animals given large doses of nicotine developed cancer, while animals not given such material did not. The experimental evidence demonstrated the causal relationship.

The obvious reason why it is difficult to establish clear causal relationships in human longevity is that we cannot experiment with human lives. We simply cannot randomly assign some people to a potentially dangerous treatment while assigning another group to a nontreatment condition. Even when we carry out studies to maximize longevity and provide the experimental group with a known beneficial treatment, ethical questions are raised when we withhold the beneficial treatment from the control group. The most scandalous example of such an experiment was carried out over many decades by government researchers who treated experimental subjects who had syphilis with antibiotics and withheld treatment and even information about antibiotics from a control group who also had contracted the disease.

The only alternative to experimental research in human populations is correlational research. You examine those people who by chance happen to be exposed to beneficial or dangerous conditions, and usually you do not know if the people in the exposed group were different to begin with in terms of longevity. Studying such situations provides us with some information but does not necessarily tell us the cause.

Life-Expectancy Differences Between Males and Females

A very dramatic difference in life expectancy exists between males and females. Women of all ages and all races live longer than men of the same age and race. A female child born today has a 7-year advantage over her male counterpart. The gap in life expectancy between the sexes does narrow in later life, particularly after menopause when women become more at risk for heart disease. However, the sex difference is apparent throughout life and is especially noticeable in old age when women begin to outnumber men at a ratio of close to two-to-one. The causes of the sex difference in longevity—both biological and environmental—merit special consideration.

Potential Causes for Sex Differences in Longevity

Data to explain sex differences in longevity come from a wide variety of sources. The starting point favoring a biological explanation is that in most subhuman species females live longer. Since it is difficult to see how the environment favors female animals living in the wild, biologists interpret these data as indicating a genetic and hormonal basis for greater longevity in females.

The most widely accepted biological explanation for sex differences in human longevity involves hormones (Hazzard, 1986). Hormonal differences between males and females have a wide range of consequences, including the apparent protection of females from cardiovascular disease until after the menopause. While both men and women have heart attacks, the number one cause of death in the United States, women have them later than men.

Testosterone and estrogen affect blood-clotting mechanisms, which are an important factor in heart disease. Blood that clots more easily makes the individual more prone to a heart attack. The clotting factor in blood, called platelets, is affected by the male hormone, testosterone, so that blood is more likely to clot. Clotting is less in the presence of the female hormone, estrogen. Thus, after menopause, when estrogen levels are low and the relative amount of testosterone in women's blood is greater, they are much more likely to have heart attacks. Men are much more prone than are women to heart attacks in the third and fourth decades of their lives when testosterone output is high.

The most dramatic evidence for a hormonal effect on longevity comes from the research on castration in males. Evidence presented by Drori and Folman (1976) suggests that testosterone may be negatively related to longevity inasmuch as castrated male rats had longer-than-average life expectancies.

To evaluate the effect of castration on longevity in humans, Hamilton and Mestler (1969) compared life expectancy of twentieth century eunuchs to life expectancy of matched male and female groups. In the twentieth century only certain cancer patients, psychotics, or mentally retarded individuals were castrated. Hamilton and Mestler compared life expectancy of intact, mentally retarded men and women and mentally retarded eunuchs. Not only did the eunuchs outlive the noncastrated men by an average of 13.5 years, they also outlived the women by an average of 6.7 years. This is one of the rare instances in which men outlive women, and Hamilton and Mestler attributed the effect to testosterone. The younger the men were when they were castrated (thus, the less they were exposed to testosterone, especially if castration occurred before puberty), the longer they lived.

Castration is obviously a radical means to achieve longer life in males. Fortunately, to live a long time, neither rats nor men need to be castrated. Drori and Folman (1976) demonstrated that male rats that were exercised or that were given the opportunity to mate at least once a week lived longer than unexercised rats, rats prevented access to females, and castrated rats.

A fact suggesting a positive effect for estrogen is that women who have had children tend to live longer (once they survive childbirth.) Since estrogen production increases dramatically during pregnancy, it has been suggested that increased estrogen is responsible for the greater longevity of childbearing women. They are less susceptible to breast cancer, and they may also be less susceptible to heart disease.

While the biological arguments for sex differences in longevity are compelling, there are strong environmental (Miller, 1986; Miller & Gerstein, 1983) and biological-environmental interaction hypotheses (Stillion, 1984; Wylie, 1984). Men die at a higher rate as a result of violence and accidents, including work-related accidents. More men than women smoke, and men inhale more deeply. As more women become employed, especially as they enter into hazardous occupations that were formerly reserved for men, and as more women smoke, we might speculate that sex differences in longevity would be reduced.

Differences in Longevity Between the Races

In the United States, there is a significant difference in life expectancy between the races. Blacks have a shockingly low life expectancy when compared to the rest of the population (La Greca & Berardo, 1985). At birth, a Black male has a life expectancy over 6 years shorter than a white male. The Black–white female difference in life expectancy at birth is just over 5 years. The gap in life expectancy between Blacks and whites gradually narrows until the age of 75 when life expectancy for Black and white males is equal. For Black and white females, equal life expectancy occurs at the age of 78, and after that age, life expectancy for Black women is greater. It is likely that life expectancy becomes greater for the remaining Blacks who survive to the late 70s because the percentage of Blacks surviving to this age is so small that those left are a very select group. Undoubtedly, the lack of social advantages for Blacks as a minority group are primarily responsible for this large racial difference in life expectancy.

Asian Americans live longer than their Caucasian counterparts. This is interesting in light of the fact that old age is particularly respected and revered in Asian culture. Whether the attitudes of these individuals contribute to their longer life expectancy, or whether diet and genes are the primary causes has yet to be determined. Studies on the causes of greater longevity in American Asians may help to extend life expectancy in all races. However, relatively little research attention has been given to aging in this minority group.

Heredity and Family, Health and Lifestyle Influences on Longevity

Current evidence suggests that three major factors in human life expectancy about which we can do something are smoking, weight, and exercise. Smoking and obesity shorten life and impair health, while exercising improves health and longevity.

Hereditary and family influences on longevity include a relationship between long-lived parents and grandparents and long life (Glasser, 1981). Life expectancy is shortened if inheritable diseases run in the family. Intelligence is also inherited in part, and high intelligence is associated with long life (MacIntyre et al., 1978). Other family factors affecting longevity include mother's age at the birth of the child and birth order. Offspring live longer if they were born during a woman's prime childbearing years, and firstborns live longer than later born children (Woodruff, 1979).

Among the worst things an individual can do for health is to be overweight and to smoke. Together these two factors can take several decades off life expectancy. In addition to causing lung cancer, cigarette smoking increases the risk for cardiovascular disease (Weintraub, Klein, Seelaus, et al., 1985). Eating healthy foods such as salad and avoiding eggs and red meat add some years to life expectancy (Kahn, Phillips, Snowdon, & Choi, 1984). Light to moderate drinking is associated with greater longevity, but heavy drinking is correlated with hypertension (Arkwright, Beilin, Rouse, et al, 1982). Alcoholics often suffer from poor nutrition as well, which accelerates aging processes and death.

The role of caffeine in longevity is still unclear. Some research indicates that it is not a risk factor (Robertson et al., 1984). Other studies indicate a mild to moderate risk for heart disease, especially in men (Curatolo & Robertson, 1983; Vandenbroucke et al., 1986).

Regular exercise is exceedingly beneficial to health and longevity (Leon & Blackburn, 1977; Paffenbarger, Hyde, Wing, & Hsich, 1986; Rose & Cohen, 1977). Sexual activity is another positive correlate with living longer (Palmore, 1982). Sleeping 6 to 8 hours per night and having regular medical examinations are additional prudent health habits that correlate with long life.

People of higher socioeconomic status live longer. The more education an individual has, the higher the status of his or her occupational level, and the greater the income, the more likely he or she is to realize the genetic potential for longevity.

Lifestyle affects longevity in a number of ways. Living in a rural environment gives a slight edge in life expectancy. Social and psychological stresses influence health and longevity (La Greca, 1985). Being married is especially beneficial to the life expectancy of men, but it adds years to women's lives. Living with others as a single person is helpful, particularly for men (Ortmeyer, 1974).

The most extensive research relating personal behavior patterns to life expectancy has resulted in a description of the Type A behavior pattern involving a high-pressured, aggressive, hostile personality and a much greater risk for heart disease (Friedman & Rosenman, 1974). Other dangerous personality traits are tendencies toward risk taking and depression. Such traits lead people to die in accidents, suicide, and homicide, the fourth, eighth, and twelfth leading causes of death. Those who are adaptable and easygoing are longer lived, while rigid, dogmatic people die at an earlier than average age (Riegel, Riegel, & Meyer, 1968).

The personality quality that has been identified as characteristic of centenarians is happiness. Very long-lived people are more likely to say that their lives have been worth living and that they would do it all over again in just about the same way (Gallup & Hill, 1960). They have self-respect and self-esteem, they feel needed, and they are still happy to be alive. The special thing about centenarians seems to be the quality, not the quantity, of their lives.

COMPREHENSIVE OUTLINE

[The numbers in brackets are article numbers in the Annotated Bibliography.]

   I. Significance of longevity for social and behavioral sciences
      A. Social and behavioral phenomena impact longevity.   [5]
      B. Quality related to quantity of life.   [3, 4, 9]
      C. Psychological and social interventions affect longevity.   [1, 33]
  II. Measures of longevity
      A. Life span.   [11, 12]
      B. Maximum life potential.   [13]
      C. Life expectancy.   [32]
      D. Actuarial tables.   [40, 41]
 III. Changes in life expectancy throughout history
      A. Life expectancy in prehistoric to modern times.   [8]
      B. Life expectancy in the future.   [35]
         1. Positive trends.   [38, 41]
         2. Threat from AIDS.   [19]
         3. Trends in other nations.   [34, 43]

IV. Major determinants of life expectancy
  A. Limitations of contemporary data.   [40]
  B. Life expectancy differences between males and females
    1. Biological causes.   [7, 16, 17]
    2. Environmental causes.   [24, 25]
    3. Biological–environmental interaction hypotheses.   [36, 42]
  C. Differences in longevity between the races.   [21]
V. Heredity and family influences
  A. Longevity of parents and grandparents.   [15]
  B. Maternal age.   [40]
  C. Birth order.   [40]
  D. Intelligence.   [23]
VI. Health
  A. Cigarette smoking.   [39]
  B. Obesity.   [40]
  C. Nutrition.   [18]
  D. Exercise.   [22, 27, 31]
  E. Alcohol.   [2]
  F. Caffeine.   [6, 30, 37]
  G. Sexual activity.   [28]
  H. Sleep.   [40]
VII. Socioeconomic status.   [40]
VIII. Lifestyle
  A. Physical environment.   [40]
  B. Stress.   [20]
  C. Marital status.   [26]
  D. Type A behavior pattern.   [10]
  E. Rigidity.   [29]
  F. Life satisfaction, adjustment.   [14]

ANNOTATED BIBLIOGRAPHY

1. Alderman, M. H. (1979). Communities with unusually short life-spans: the effects of life-style modifications. *Bulletin of the New York Academy of Medicine, 55,* 357–366.

Life expectancy varies from country to country, and even from county to county. The incidence of cardiovascular disease has been shown to make a major impact on the life expectancy for any particular region. North Karelia, Finland was chosen to participate in a health and life-style intervention program because of its high incidence of cardiovascular disease, the commitment of local leadership to involvement in the project, and the stability of the population. Baseline data were obtained for North Karelia and a control community, Kuopio. Risk factors including hypertension, fat intake, and cigarette smoking were recorded. Local blood pressure monitoring stations maintained contact with individuals' referring doctors and provided treatment and education for hypertensive citizens. Diet modification was facilitated by encouraging local stores to make low-fat milk and foods available. Health care providers were trained to ensure that they were providing the best possible care to individuals who were already experiencing advanced symptoms of cardiovascular disease. The community appeared to take advantage of the intervention program. The incidence of stroke was reduced by 40% over a 5-year period. It is suggested that it is necessary to provide a link between public health and treatment of the individual that includes community education in health care.

Kind	*Recommendation*	*Readability*	*Audience*
E	**	1	GP/SP

2. **Arkwright, P. B., Beilin, L. J., Rouse, I., Armstrong, B. K., & Vandongen, R. (1982). Effects of alcohol use and other aspects of lifestyle on blood pressure levels and prevalence of hypertension in a working population.** *Circulation, 66*(1), 60–66.

The drinking habits and blood pressures of a sample of 491 males aged 20 to 45 years were examined to investigate any link between alcohol consumption and hypertension. No significant relationship was found between alcohol consumption and diastolic blood pressure. A significant positive correlation was found between systolic blood pressure and weekly alcohol consumption. The occurrence of systolic hypertension was 4 times greater for individuals who were classified as being moderate or heavy drinkers. This effect was not related to other lifestyle factors such as age, obesity, cigarette smoking, or physical activity. The similarity between blood pressures of former heavy drinkers and teetotalers suggests that the effects of alcohol consumption on blood pressure are reversible. Cigarette smoking is associated with lowered diastolic blood pressure in both drinkers and teetotalers. The authors consider possible explanations for this relationship.

Kind	*Recommendation*	*Readability*	*Audience*
E	**	2	AU

3. **Berardo, F. M. (1985). Social networks and life preservation.** *Death Studies, 9*(1), 37–50.

The author reviews the research concerning the connection between networks of social support and survivorship. There is evidence that individuals are at greater risk of deterioration in health status and also for premature mortality after the loss of a loved one. This is referred to as the "broken heart" syndrome. Differences in mortality for both married versus unmarried individuals and males versus females are considered in light of these findings. The importance of establishing and maintaining a network of social supports is stressed.

Kind	Recommendation	Readability	Audience
RC	**	1	GP

4. **Berardo, F. M., La Greca, A. J., & Hodgkins-Berardo, D. (1985). Individual lifestyles and survivorship: The role of habits, attitudes, and nutrition.** *Death Studies, 9*(1), 5–22.

Many of the determinants of survivorship cannot be directly controlled by the individual. This article presents an examination of the lifestyle characteristics and habits that impact life expectancy and may be modified by individuals. These include risk-taking behavior, nutritional practices, physical exercise, and general attitudes toward life issues. The authors note that modification of lifestyle must include a consideration of the maintenance of quality of life. The individual who monitors the characteristics of living that impact survivorship and abandons negative habits may increase both the quality and quantity of life.

Kind	Recommendation	Readability	Audience
RC	**	1	GP

5. **Cohen, J. B., & Brody, J. A. (1981). The epidemiologic importance of psychosocial factors in longevity.** *American Journal of Epidemiology, 114*(4), 451–461.

Research in longevity has increasingly examined the impact of psychosocial factors on longevity. The authors present a review of the data concerning this impact. The psychologic factors examined include intelligence, work satisfaction, and the Type A behavior pattern. Sex differences, socioeconomic status, and ethnic background are the primary sociologic factors considered. Social supports play an important interactive role in longevity and the evidence for this complex relationship is presented. Sociocultural factors—such as urbanization, lifestyle, and religion—and life change may impact longevity by potentially increasing or reducing the expected number of years of life. The authors encourage further study into the psychosocial factors in longevity. Possible sources of new evidence are cited.

Kind	Recommendation	Readability	Audience
RC	***	2	GP

6. Curatolo, P. W., & Robertson, D. (1983). The health consequences of caffeine. *Annals of Internal Medicine,* **98,** 641–653.

The authors review the evidence that links caffeine to health. The effect of caffeine is examined in relation to the following systems: the cardiovascular system, respiratory system, metabolism, gastrointestinal system, renal system, and the central nervous system. Although some data suggest that there is an increased risk of acute myocardial infarction with caffeine consumption, there are also data to suggest that no relationship exists. No direct link between caffeine and cancer or fibrocystic breast disease has been traced. The impact of caffeine on cardiac arrhythmias, gastric ulcers, and duodenal ulcers is unclear. The widespread use of caffeine-containing beverages such as coffee and tea necessitates further investigation into the health consequences of caffeine use.

Kind	Recommendation	Readability	Audience
RC	**	3	AG

7. Drori, D., & Folman, Y. (1976). Environmental effects on longevity in the male rat: Exercise, mating, castration, and restricted feeding. *Experimental Gerontology,* **11,** 25–32.

These researchers ran a number of experiments with rats to compare and contrast the effects of various measures designed to affect life expectancy. All four treatments—exercise, mating, castration, and restricted feeding—cause rats to live longer than littermates that are not exercised, are not allowed access to females to mate, are not castrated, and are fed a nonrestricted diet. The only treatment that extends the life span of rats is restricted feeding. Rats that are underfed actually exceed the life span of their species in their own longevity.

Kind	Recommendation	Readability	Audience
E	***	2	AU

8. Dublin, L. I., Lotka, A. J., & Spiegelman, M. (1949). *Length of life: A study of the life table.* **New York: Ronald Press.**

This is an old but classic book in which the authors thoroughly researched the available evidence on life expectancy at various periods during human history. Evidence is sought all the way back to prehistoric times to determine how long cave dwellers lived. Scholarship in this book is very thorough, and an extensive amount of data is presented to provide a perspective about how life expectancy for humans has changed from prehistoric to modern times.

Kind	Recommendation	Readability	Audience
HB	***	2	AU

9. Enzell, K. (1984). Mortality among persons with depressive symptoms and among responders and non-responders in a health checkup. Acta Psychiatrica Scandinavia, 69, 89–102.

Subjects for this study were obtained from a population of individuals born in 1905 who were invited to participate in a health checkup. They were evaluated by questionnaire and/or interview in order to identify those with depressive or sleep disorders. Mortality rates obtained over a 9-year period were compared for depressive and nondepressive subjects. The mortality rates for depressives were significantly higher than those for nondepressives. The author suggests that this increased mortality rate supports the theory that persons with neurotic disorders may have legitimate health concerns that can mistakenly be categorized as being symptomatic of neurosis itself. Those individuals who did not respond to the checkup invitation had higher mortality and suicide rates than those who did respond. These results could be explained by an overrepresentation of physically and mentally healthy individuals who responded to the health checkup.

Kind	Recommendation	Readability	Audience
E	**	2	AU

10. Friedman, M., & Rosenman, R. H. (1974). Type A behavior and your heart. New York: Knopf.

This book was on the best-seller list due to the authors' surprising insights about cardiovascular disease. Their data also stimulated a great deal of research on personality characteristics related to heart disease. The authors are cardiologists who observed that in addition to the typical risk factors for heart disease (smoking, obesity, high blood pressure), their patients typically shared personality characteristics including aggression, a strong drive to be upwardly mobile, a lack of sensitivity to others, and a materialistic orientation. The authors call this the Type A Personality. They devised a personality test for these characteristics. In the book they tell the story of how they came to discover the Type A Personality, and they present their research supporting their position.

Kind	Recommendation	Readability	Audience
B	***	1	GP

11. Fries, J. F. (1980). Aging, natural death, and the compression of morbidity. *The New England Journal of Medicine, 303*, 130–135.

This article presents evidence for a finite human life span and a compression of morbidity to support predictions about the future trends of life expectancy and aging. The average life expectancy has been increasing toward a theoretical optimum age of 85 years due to the suppression of infant mortality and the elimination of most acute life-threatening diseases. These developments have not led to an increase of life span (the maximum number of years a species can ideally attain) for humans. The continuation of maximization of life expectancy and stability of life span would lead to the rectangularization of survival curves. Predicted survival curves would remain at a plateau throughout the first 77 years of age and then fall sharply. As advancements in medical technology postpone the onset of chronic diseases associated with aging, individuals may enjoy more years of vigor and good health with the possibility of disability deferred until advanced old age. National health research should be directed toward delaying the onset of chronic diseases and promoting increased personal autonomy in the later years of life.

Kind	Recommendation	Readability	Audience
TC	***	2	GP

12. Fries, J. F. (1983). The compression of morbidity. *Milbank Memorial Fund Quarterly, 61*, 397–419.

The compression of morbidity would result if medical technology continues to advance in the delay of onset of chronic diseases associated with old age. Since the life span of the human race is finite, increasing life expectancy will lead to more individuals surviving to optimum age attainable by human beings without increasing the life span itself. Chronic disease is characterized by early onset that is not necessarily exposed through manifest symptomology until late in life. If medical technology can postpone the initial onset of these diseases, the symptoms may not become apparent and debilitating before the individual succumbs to natural death. The aging individual would be able to maintain productivity which would otherwise be suppressed by chronic disease. In the future, public policy should do away with mandatory retirement age, increase the selection of creative vocational opportunities, begin early health enhancement programs, and provide alternatives to institutional long-term care programs.

Kind	Recommendation	Readability	Audience
TC	***	2	SP/AU

13. Fries, J. F., & Crapo, L. M. (1981). *Vitality and aging.* San Francisco: W. H. Freeman.

The central idea presented is that patterns of aging may be altered but that the average life span is fixed. There may be an increasing period in life when the adult is healthy and vital, and that period is converging with a fixed duration of life. The form of the human survival curve is becoming ever more rectangular. The book discusses the implications of this shift in the geometry of the actuarial data. Also discussed is the concept of natural death.

Kind	Recommendation	Readability	Audience
B	**	2	AU

14. Gallup, G., & Hill, E. (1960). *The secrets of long life.* New York: Bernard Geis Associates.

Although this book is close to 30 years old, it is still a valuable resource. It presents a delightful exploration of very old age by the Gallup organization. A national survey was undertaken of individuals in their 90s or older. Over 100 individuals aged over 90 were interviewed, and the interview material is presented at length. One really gets a "feel" for some of the qualities of very old adults. An attempt is made to characterize some of the factors common to all these long-lived people. Although this is not a rigorous, scientific study, it is valuable because it presents the people as they are. The reader will feel that he or she has really experienced an interaction with some of these unique nonagenarians and centenarians.

Kind	Recommendation	Readability	Audience
B	***	1	GP

15. Glasser, M. (1981). Is longevity inherited? *Chronic Disease, 34,* 439–444.

Outcome studies on the effect of disease often control for the age of subjects and therefore assume that the age characteristics for samples are comparable. The author suggests that a further control should be introduced to guard against the possibility that different subjects may have inherited longevity endowments that might compromise the results of such research. Selected from the patients in the author's private medical practice were 457 individuals aged 40 years or older. The age of the subjects and the age of death of their parents and grandparents were collected and an analysis of the relationships between the data was performed in order to determine whether or not longevity is inherited. The results confirm the author's hypothesis that there is a positive relationship between subject's age and the parents' ages at death. The author concludes that this relationship confirms that longevity is inherited and the effect of the inheritance difference on outcome studies is strong enough to alter results significant at the $p > .05$ level. The son–father relationship had the strongest correlation value with the son–mother relationship next in strength. Evaluation of patients' inherited longevity traits appears to be necessary before studies are done to control against misleading results which can be obtained when examining the effect of disease on longevity.

Kind	*Recommendation*	*Readability*	*Audience*
E	**	2	AU

16. Hamilton, J. B., & Mestler, G. E. (1969). Mortality and survival: Comparison of eunuchs with intact men and women in a mentally retarded population. *Journal of Gerontology, 24,* 395–411.

Castration has been practiced since antiquity. In the West it was carried out to produce *castrati* singers, and in the East to provide trusted servants for the members of the imperial palace and their harems. However, in the twentieth century only certain cancer patients, psychotics, or mentally retarded individuals have been castrated. The authors compared life expectancy of 735 intact mentally retarded men, 883 intact mentally retarded women, and 297 mentally retarded eunuchs. Not only did the eunuchs outlive the noncastrated men by an average of 13.5 years, they also outlived the women by an average of 6.7 years—one of the rare instances in which men outlive women. The authors attributed the effect to testosterone. The younger the men were when they were castrated (thus, the less they were exposed to testosterone, especially if castration occurred before puberty), the longer they lived. Even men castrated between the ages of 30 and 39 lived longer than intact men. Since intact women produce some testosterone, the authors speculated that the women, like the intact men, may have died earlier as a result of having higher levels of this male hormone than did the eunuchs who had their testosterone-producing glands removed.

Kind	Recommendation	Readability	Audience
E	**	2	AU

17. **Hazzard, W. R. (1986). Biological basis of the sex differential in longevity.** *Journal of the American Geriatric Society, 34,* 455–471.

The role that hormones play in the sex differential in longevity is examined in terms of variations of the concentrations of low-density lipoprotein (LDL) cholesterol and high-density lipoprotein (HDL) cholesterol. Much of the difference in life expectancy for males and females has been attributed to the early onset and greater incidence of atherogenesis in the male population. Levels of HDL have been shown to be inversely related to atherogenic risk, while high levels of LDL appear to be related to increased risk of atherogenesis. The effects of estrogens and androgens on these lipoprotein levels are examined. Estrogen, in the absence of progesterone or any androgens, increases the concentration of HDL in the blood and decreases levels of LDL. Androgens, on the other hand, produce opposite effects. Therefore, the author concludes that the sex differential in life expectancy may be largely attributed to the presence of estrogen in the female which provides decreased risk of atherogenesis. Adoption of lifestyles that include a diet with restrictions of cholesterol and total fat, elimination of cigarette smoking, increasing aerobic exercise, and maintenance of optimal body weight may narrow the gap between life expectancies for males and females.

Kind	Recommendation	Readability	Audience
E	***	3	AG

18. **Kahn, H. A., Phillips, R. L., Snowdon, D. A., and Choi, W. (1984). Association between reported diet and all-cause mortality: twenty-one year follow-up on 27,530 adult Seventh-Day Adventists.** *American Journal of Epidemiology, 119*(5), 775–787.

The mortality rates for 27,530 adult Seventh-Day Adventists were followed to assess any relationship between all-cause mortality and diet. In 1960 the subjects responded to a questionnaire on dietary habits; follow-up on mortality continued through 1980. Mortality was determined by matching subjects to death certificate files entered during the target years. A significant negative association was found between mortality rates and green salad consumption. Mortality was found to be positively associated with the consumption of meat and eggs. Differences in strength of association were found for males and females. For males, the associations involving eggs and meat were stronger; for females, the associations involving green salad and eggs were stronger. Adjustments were made on the associations for factors such as smoking history, sex, age, health history, and year of initial exposure to the Adventist church. The authors urge caution in interpreting these results since the precise nature of the relationships is not yet fully understood.

Kind	*Recommendation*	*Readability*	*Audience*
E	**	1	AU

19. Kristal, A. R. (1986). The impact of the acquired immunodeficiency syndrome on patterns of premature death in New York City. *JAMA*, 255, 2306–2310.

Acquired immunodeficiency syndrome (AIDS) has become a leading cause of death in New York City for men aged 25 to 54 years and for women aged 25 to 39 years. Blacks and Hispanics have a significantly higher death rate from AIDS than Whites and Asians. The prevalence of drug abuse in the Black and Hispanic communities may account for the differential AIDS mortality rates. AIDS-associated deaths of individuals aged 15 to 64 years are responsible for 10% of potential life lost for males and 3.6% of potential life lost for females. The author asserts that these data illustrate the enormous increases in premature death that are attributable to AIDS, and the need for research into the psychological, medical, and biological problems associated with AIDS.

Kind	*Recommendation*	*Readability*	*Audience*
E	**	1	GP

20. La Greca, A. J. (1985). The psycho-social factors in surviving stress. *Death Studies*, 9, 23–32.

Contemporary research in the medical and psychosocial fields has explored the impact of stress on health and survivorship. The existence of a relationship between stress and cardiovascular, immunological, and central nervous system disorders has been established. The author considers factors that may intervene in this relationship. These factors include adaptation to childhood experiences, hardiness of personality, expectation of stress, social supports, and environment. Strategies that may reduce the negative impact of stress are discussed.

Kind	Recommendation	Readability	Audience
RC	**	1	GP

21. La Greca, A. J., and Berardo, F. M. (1985). The societal context of survivorship. *Death Studies*, 9, 51–71.

Patterns of survivorship are linked both to factors that are intrinsic to society and behaviors that are controlled by individuals but nevertheless are heavily influenced by societal mores. The region in which an individual resides and the race of the individual can impact his or her potential for longevity. Fifteen individual behaviors and societal policies that may influence survivorship are presented. Possible explanations for the continuation of practices that may be detrimental to life expectancy and strategies to reduce the prevalence of these practices are discussed.

Kind	Recommendation	Readability	Audience
TC	**	1	GP

22. Leon, A. S., & Blackburn, H. (1977). The relationship of physical activity to coronary heart disease and life expectancy. *Annals New York Academy of Sciences*, 301, 561–578.

This literature review examines the empirical evidence available on the relationship between physical activity, coronary heart disease (CHD), and life expectancy. The results of the studies considered are sometimes contradictory and the authors point out the design limitations that may lead to the discrepancies observed. On the whole, the evidence supports the view that there exists a negative relationship between physical activity level and incidence of CHD. Risk of myocardial infarction and mortality rate are lower for the physically active. The data, although not conclusive, suggest that exercise provides rehabilitating effects for patients recovering from myocardial infarction. The authors recommend the use of individualized exercise prescriptions as a part of a comprehensive program designed to prevent the occurrence of CHD.

Kind	Recommendation	Readability	Audience
RC	***	2	AU/SP

23. MacIntyre, N. R., Mitchell, R. E., Oberman, A., Harlan, W. R., Graybiel, A., & Johnson, E. (1978). Longevity in military pilots: 37-year followup of the Navy's "1000 Aviators." *Aviation, Space, and Environmental Medicine, 49,* 1120–1122.

The nonmilitary mortality rate for 800 military aviators who survived World War II and the Korean conflict is examined. The subjects took part in the U.S. Navy's "1000 Aviators" program which has maintained medical evaluation on these individuals over 37 years. In this population, 95 subjects died from nonmilitary causes during the 37 years. The expected mortality rate for the general population would be 208 deaths in a sample of 800 individuals. The factors that may contribute to the lower-than-expected death rate for military aviators include: preselection for service as an aviator, high intelligence level, increased on- and off-job activity, general good health, and quick learning ability. A positive correlation between parental longevity and subject's longevity was found. Cigarette smoking had the greatest negative impact on longevity of all habits investigated.

Kind	*Recommendation*	*Readability*	*Audience*
E	**	1	GP

24. Miller, G. H. (1986). Is the longevity gender gap decreasing? *New York State Journal of Medicine, 86,* 59–60.

The problem of the gender gap in longevity has inspired different explanations since it was first discussed in publication in 1953. A strictly constitutional/genetic interpretation argues that the double X chromosome in women provides protection against diseases carried as defects on one X chromosome. Since men do not have this protection, they are weaker in constitution and so have shorter life expectancy. The observation that women have a lower incidence of cardiovascular disease than men before menopause but not after menopause has led some theorists to propose that female hormones, which have a higher concentration before menopause, protect women's health and explain the gender difference in longevity. Stress has also been targeted as a causal factor in longevity, and higher stress levels for men might lead to lower life expectancy. The author suggests that it is smoking behavior that provides the answer to this puzzle and predicts that as the difference in smoking behavior between men and women becomes smaller, the gender gap in longevity will decrease and eventually disappear.

Kind	*Recommendation*	*Readability*	*Audience*
RC/TC	**	1	GP

25. Miller, G. H., & Gerstein, D. R. (1983). The life expectancy of nonsmoking men and women. *Public Health Reports, 98,* 343–349.

Research on the effect of smoking on sex differences in life expectancy has been confounded by the inclusion of traumatic death statistics in the data and by the inclusion of former smokers in the nonsmoking category. In an attempt to control for these confounds, both victims of traumatic death and former smokers were eliminated from the sample. Subjects were obtained from two samples. The first sample consisted of residents of Erie County, Pennsylvania who had died between 1972 and 1974. The names of these individuals were obtained from local death notices, and attempts were made to contact three surviving kin. Data on the age of the deceased at the time of death, cause of death, and smoking history were recorded on 4,394 decedents. The second sample consisted of 3,916 persons who lived in the area during the same years. Data on smoking habits were obtained by telephone interview. An analysis of the data showed that life expectancy for nonsmoking males and females was consistently similar. The authors concluded that the sex difference in longevity could be attributed to differences in male and female smoking patterns. It is necessary to consider this effect when preparing life expectancy tables and that data on smokers and nonsmokers not be merged. Changes in female sex-role behavior, especially the increased percentage of women smoking, should lead to a decrease in sex differences in longevity.

Kind	*Recommendation*	*Readability*	*Audience*
E	**	1	AU

26. Ortmeyer, C. E. (1974). Variations in mortality, morbidity, and health care by marital status. In C. L. Erhardt & J. B. Berlin (Eds.), *Mortality and morbidity in the United States* **(pp. 159–188). Cambridge, MA: Harvard University Press.**

This article examines the mortality rates for married individuals and compares the rates to unmarried members of the population. Life expectancy for married people is significantly longer than life expectancy for those remaining single.

Kind	*Recommendation*	*Readability*	*Audience*
E	**	3	AG

27. Paffenbarger, R. S., Jr., Hyde, R. T., Wing, A. L., & Hsieh, C. (1986). Physical activity, all-cause mortality, and longevity of col-

lege alumni. *The New England Journal of Medicine, 314,* 605–613.

The activity levels and other characteristics of lifestyle of a sample of 16,936 Harvard alumni aged 35 to 74 were examined to determine any relationships existing between these factors, all-cause mortality, and longevity. During a 12- to 16-year followup of these subjects, 1,413 alumni had died. An inverse relationship between activity level (measures of walking, sports play, and number of stairs climbed) and total mortality rate was found. The primary causes of death were determined to be cardiovascular or respiratory in nature. Energy expenditures defined as being greater than 500 kcal per week were associated with lowered death rate, although a slight increase in mortality was detected at the highest energy expenditure levels (greater than 3,500 kcal per week). When energy expenditure went above 2,000 kcal per week, the mortality rates were found to be decreased by one quarter to a third of that of less active men. The relationship between activity level and mortality rate remains significant when other factors such as hypertension, cigarette smoking, and extremes or gains in body weight are controlled. Increased activity level can reduce the mortality risks for cigarette smokers and individuals with hypertension. Maintaining an adequate activity level throughout life can lead to an increase in life expectancy of 1 to more than 2 years.

Kind	*Recommendation*	*Readability*	*Audience*
E	***	2	AU

28. Palmore, E. B. (1982). **Predictors of the longevity difference: A 25-year follow-up.** *The Gerontologist, 22,* 513–518.

A 25-year longitudinal study conducted through Duke University examined the theoretical predictors of longevity. The results of the analysis of the data collected on 252 panelists is presented. Twenty-two variables were identified as predictors of longevity and the years of impact of each were assessed. The predictors ranged over intelligence, SES, activity, sexual relations, tobacco and alcohol use, satisfaction, and health. For men, the most important indicators of longevity may be health self-rating, work satisfaction, and performance intelligence which collectively increase life expectancy by 16 years. Potentially adding 23 years collectively to a woman's life, health satisfaction, past enjoyment of sexual intercourse, and good physical functioning are strongly significant predictors of longevity.

Kind	*Recommendation*	*Readability*	*Audience*
E	***	1	GP

29. Riegel, K. F., Riegel, R. M., & Meyer, G. (1968). A study of the dropout rates in longitudinal research on aging and the prediction of death. In B. L. Neugarten (Ed.), *Middle age and aging* (pp. 563– 570). Chicago: University of Chicago Press.

The data were collected as part of a large longitudinal study of personality in older adults in Germany. The authors were interested in understanding what kind of biases were entered into the data by the dropout of subjects. Were the subjects who dropped out unique in any particular way? Among the many important insights gained by these authors was the observation that individuals who had scored high on personality test measures of rigidity and dogmatism were much more likely to have died during the course of the study. Put another way: Among the individuals who had dropped out of the longitudinal study due to death, there were significantly higher scores on the personality trait of dogmatism. Individuals who were highly dogmatic were more likely to die during the course of the study.

Kind	*Recommendation*	*Readability*	*Audience*
E	***	2	AU

30. Robertson, D., Hollister, A. S., Kincaid, D., Workman, R., Goldberg, M. R., Tung, C., & Smith, B. (1984). Caffeine and hypertension. *The American Journal of Medicine, 77*(1), 54–60.

This double-blind placebo-controlled study examines the relationship between caffeine ingestion and hypertension. The subjects were 18 individuals diagnosed as being borderline hypertensive. The control group consisted of 9 subjects who received a placebo daily over a 2-week period. The caffeine group received a placebo on the first 3 days and then received 250 mg of caffeine with meals 3 times a day for 7 days. A placebo was again given on the final 4 days of the study. The caffeine group subjects exhibited a significant increase in systolic blood pressure following the initial administration of caffeine. This effect became nonsignificant on subsequent days and no long-term effects were observed. Increases in diastolic pressure did not reach significance, and only minor increases in serum catecholamine levels and plasma renin activity were detected. It appears that chronic caffeine consumption is not associated with long-term blood pressure elevation or significant increases in plasma catecholamine levels and plasma renin activity.

Kind	*Recommendation*	*Readability*	*Audience*
E	**	2	AU

31. Rose, C. L., & Cohen, M. L. (1977). Relative importance of physical activity for longevity. *Annals New York Academy of Sciences, 301*, 671–702.

In a consideration of the relationship between longevity and physical activity, the authors collected data about on- and off-job activity levels, drinking behavior, cigarette smoking, and other lifestyle characteristics from a sample of 500 white males who had died during 1965. Physical exertion provided a more accurate prediction of longevity than two-thirds of all factors considered. Off-job activity level in particular was found to be positively associated with length of life. Differences in cigarette smoking and drinking behavior could not account for the effect of activity level on longevity. The methodological factors that can confound this type of research are extensively considered, and suggestions are made for designing studies to control for these problems.

Kind	Recommendation	Readability	Audience
E	***	2	AU

32. Schneider, E. L., & Brody, J. A. (1983). Aging, natural death, and the compression of morbidity: Another view. *The New England Journal of Medicine, 309*, 854–856.

A controversy exists about future trends of life expectancy and the health care issues that will arise as a result of these trends. The possibility exists that life expectancy may not maximize at 85 years, as Fries suggests, but will continue to increase over time. The decrease in mortality rate of individuals over 85 years of age casts doubt upon a theoretical rectangularization of survival curves. The number of individuals who live to old age will grow as life expectancy increases. There is no evidence that morbidity in the aged has decreased. The aged require more health care than any other age group and much of this need is attributed to chronic disease. Schneider and Brody caution against the assumption that the health of the elderly will improve at the rate suggested by Fries. Disability may become present in a great proportion of the population as the aged survive longer. Health care planning and policy should be directed toward management and treatment of the chronic diseases of aging.

Kind	Recommendation	Readability	Audience
TC	***	2	GP

33. Schneider, E. L., & Reed, J. D. (1985). Life extension. *The New England Journal of Medicine, 312*(18), 1159–1168.

Extending life is an attractive idea to almost all human beings. Many strategies have been promoted as anti-aging therapies. Available evidence concerning the effectiveness of some of these strategies is examined in this article. Caloric restriction, exercise, body weight, and dietary supplements are discussed. Empirical data concerning justification of anti-aging claims are reviewed. The authors suggest that future life extension research be directed toward finding specific interventions for specific problems of aging. They refer to this approach as segmental intervention.

Kind	*Recommendation*	*Readability*	*Audience*
RC	***	2–3	AU

34. Shuman, T. (1987). Third world aging. In G. Maddox (Ed.), *The encyclopedia of aging* (pp. 666–668). New York: Springer.

Aging in the Third World is a topic on which there is little or no data. Thus, this article serves as a useful resource for those seeking information on this topic. For information on longevity in the Third World, this article is useful. It discusses the increase in the older adult population of the Third World and increasing life expectancies in various of the world's underdeveloped nations.

Kind	*Recommendation*	*Readability*	*Audience*
RC	**	2	AU

35. Spencer, G. (1987). Profile of centenarians. *Statistical Bulletin of the Metropolitan Life Insurance Company, 68*(1), 2–7

Overreporting of the number of centenarians (individuals who reach the age of 100 years) has been a widespread and consistent phenomenon throughout different societies and over extended periods of time. Some of this exaggeration can be attributed to lack of proper birth documentation and some to individuals who add years to their ages to receive the attention often given to centenarians by society and especially the media. This report presents adjusted figures that more accurately reflect the number of centenarians in the U.S. population since 1940. Chances for survival to 100 years have increased from 31 per 100,000 individuals in 1900 to 1,150 per 100,000 in 1981. Some information pertaining to the likelihood of living to 100 years in different areas of the United

States is presented. Redesign of the questionnaire used in obtaining census information may alleviate some of the misrepresentation of the numbers of and characteristics of centenarians. The centenarian population is projected to continue to increase regardless of the amount of improvement in mortality.

Kind	Recommendation	Readability	Audience
TC	**	1	GP

36. Stillion J. M. (1984). Perspectives on the sex differential in death. *Death Education, 8,* 237–256.

The author provides a general overview of the current theories regarding the sex differential in death. Three different categories of theories are presented. Biogenic theories include those that suggest that chromosomal, hormonal, and metabolic differences contribute strongly to the advantage that females have in life expectancy. An alternate viewpoint looks to environmental factors to explain the differential death rates. Advances in health technology that have lowered the incidence of death associated with childbirth, hazardous working conditions for men, and concern for lower body weight among females are among the external influences believed to impact the sex differential. Theorists who favor the psychosocial approach to understanding the male disadvantage in life expectancy consider the differing behavioral and emotional expectations for boys and girls as leading to less adaptable coping behaviors for males. This may lead to increased risk of suicide and traumatic death, and also increased risk of arteriosclerotic disease. The author believes that the most useful explanation of the sex differential should incorporate all of these viewpoints. She also points out that the goal of increased longevity is only as valuable as the quality of life available to the individual.

Kind	Recommendation	Readability	Audience
RC	**	2	AU

37. Vandenbroucke, J. P., Kok, F. J., Van't Bosch, G., Van Den Dungen, P. J., Van Der Heide-Wessel, C., & Van Der Heide, R. M. (1986). Coffee drinking and mortality in a 25-year follow-up. *American Journal of Epidemiology, 123*(2), 359–361.

A 21-year followup of 2,775 Seventh-Day Adventists examined the association between coffee drinking and mortality. Data from questionnaires concerning dietary habits were analyzed. A difference was found in the effect of coffee drinking by males and females. There is no apparent connection between coffee drinking and mortality for females. For males, there is a small increase in mortality risk that is associated with consumption of coffee. This risk becomes greater as the number of cups consumed per day increases.

Kind	*Recommendation*	*Readability*	*Audience*
E	**	1	AU

38. **Vaupel, J. W., & Gowan, A. E. (1986). Passage to Methuselah: Some demographic consequences of continued progress against mortality.** *American Journal of Public Health, 76,* 430–433.

Three theories concerning future trends in life expectancy and their demographic consequences are explored. No change in mortality rates from present or a breakthrough reduction in mortality to 50% of its current rate would lead to an increase in the percentage of the population over 65 years of age by the year 2080. However, the greatest impact on population distribution would be seen under the condition of a 2% decline in mortality rates per year with a suggested increase of 27% in the over-65 age range by 2080. Using these predictions to provide insight into possibilities for the future organization of society, the authors suggest some of the challenges that may face those surviving until that time. Patterns of employment, education, and retirement will need to be precisely balanced in order to provide the aging with increased opportunity for productivity and to also allow the young to have a chance to impact society. The authors point out that societal changes that occur by the year 2080 are relevant to individuals alive today since the youth of today are the aged of tomorrow.

Kind	*Recommendation*	*Readability*	*Audience*
TC	**	1	GP

39. **Weintraub, W. S., Klein, L. W., Seelaus, P. A., Agarwal, J. B., & Helfant, R. H. (1985). Importance of total life consumption of cigarettes as a risk factor for coronary artery disease.** *The American Journal of Cardiology, 55,* 669–672.

The link that exists between cigarette smoking and increased risk for cardiovascular events has been established. This study attempts to determine if the increase in risk of cardiovascular events is influenced by recent smoking history or total life consumption of cigarettes. Current and lifetime smoking habits were determined for 1,349 patients who had previously undergone cardiac catherization to evaluate chest pain or extent of coronary artery disease (CAD). There is a significant increase in risk of CAD that is related to total life consumption of cigarettes. This risk becomes greater as the total number of cigarettes smoked over the life time increases. The effect is more extreme for the younger subjects exhibiting atypical symptoms than for more aged participants. The authors suggest that these results demonstrate that the risk associated with total life consumption of cigarettes is greater than previously believed, particularly for those individuals who would otherwise be considered to be in a low-risk category.

Kind	Recommendation	Readability	Audience
E	***	2	AU

40. Woodruff, D. S. (1979). *Can you live to be 100?* **New York: New American Library.**

This book is a positive, hopeful look at the human potential for a longer and fuller life. The elements that determine longer life are discussed, and guidelines are offered to help the reader to fulfill his or her own potential for long life. The author examines all the factors known to influence human longevity and presents them in this book. The reader is invited to consider his or her own personal potential for long life by taking a life expectancy test in Chapter 1. Subsequent chapters address the various facets affecting life expectancy from heredity and family to health, education, occupation, and lifestyle. This book is well researched and integrates all the available scholarly literature on longevity into a highly readable book.

Kind	Recommendation	Readability	Audience
B	***	1	GP

41. Woodruff-Pak, D. S. (1988). *Psychology and aging.* **Englewood Cliffs, NJ: Prentice Hall.**

A thorough grounding in the psychology of aging plus an overview of gerontology. Of particular relevance to the topic of longevity is Chapter 6 on longevity, portions of Chapter 3 on demography, Chapter 5 on physiological aging, and Chapter 18 on living, dying, and death. In Chapter 5 are presented biological theories of aging. Longevity and health are discussed in Chapter 6, which includes a description of the remarkable life of the longest-lived American, Florence Knapp, who was

114 years old on October 10, 1987. Photographs of Miss Knapp also grace the cover of the book.

Kind	Recommendation	Readability	Audience
TB	***	2	AU

42. Wylie, C. M. (1984). Contrasts in the health of elderly men and women: An analysis of recent data for whites in the United States. *Journal of the American Geriatrics Society, 32,* 670–675.

In an examination of recent research into the sex differential in longevity, several factors are presented as contributors to the higher death rate of males throughout the life span. The genetic factor in this difference is highlighted by increased male fetal and infant death rates, and the increased production of immunoglobulin associated with the presence of two X chromosomes in the female. Environmental stressors that are generally associated with "male" occupations have been advanced as a factor in the sex differential. Conclusions about this relationship must be deferred until the impact of the changing role of women in the work force on female death rate can be studied. Lifestyle differences for males and females may contribute to lower male longevity since males tend to smoke cigarettes more, take more risks when driving, and are less likely to consult health care agencies. Men also have slightly higher blood pressure levels throughout most of the life span. The author suggests that an interaction between all of these factors must be considered to explain the sex differential in death rates.

Kind	Recommendation	Readability	Audience
RC	**	1	GP

43. Zopf, P. E., Jr. (1986). *America's older population.* Houston, TX: Cap and Gown Press.

This book examines the characteristics of older people and the ways in which those characteristics are interwoven, using data for 1980 and later years. Statistics are recent and are interpreted and presented in a very large number of tables and figures. Extensive presentation of the mortality data for the United States are included along with broad coverage of mortality in other countries in the world. The author states that he wrote the book with an emphasis on social demography that brings together the data and methods of the demographer, the analyses of the sociologist, and the insights and concerns of the humanist.

Kind	Recommendation	Readability	Audience
HB	**	2	AG

SUPPLEMENTARY MATERIAL

An Exercise to Personalize Life Expectancy

A means to study longevity that makes it interesting and readily digested is to personalize it. This can be done by taking the Life Expectancy Test (Woodruff-Pak, 1988, Chapter 6) which is comprised of 32 questions identifying 32 empirically established correlates of longevity. While this test is an exercise designed to teach people about the factors relevant to life expectancy and has not been designed to actually predict when people will die, it is based on empirical data on longevity.

From the beginning of recorded history humans speculated on the causes of long life, devised myths, and invented folk remedies to extend life expectancy. More recently we have used scientific methods to determine and experiment with the causes of long life. While there is still much research to be done before we can determine accurately all of the factors affecting longevity, a large body of data has been collected that gives us some clues. This information can be used to evaluate the life expectancy of an individual. Insurance companies have been doing this for years, and the actuarial tables or life tables compiled for federal government data by insurance companies are still one of the best predictors of life expectancy available. For this reason the life tables are used as a starting point for the Life Expectancy Test. Then, in addition, the estimation of personal life expectancy personalizes the prediction by taking into account various factors in a person's background and lifestyle that make it possible to individualize the prediction.

Statisticians in insurance companies recognize the fallacy and risk in attempting to predict individual deaths on the basis of a few population parameters, and it is clear that even with the additional personal information gathered in the Life Expectancy Test, totally accurate prediction is impossible. The Life Expectancy Test must not be viewed as a scientific instrument. Rather, it should be viewed as an intellectual exercise. Nevertheless, it is an exercise that should be taken seriously. The test points out those aspects of lifestyle that may serve to lengthen or shorten life expectancy.

It is important to recognize the accuracy limitation of the Life Expectancy Test, and it is also important to understand how most of the data on longevity have been collected. These data represent the most advanced information available to scientists on longevity, but scientists still have a long way to go before they fully comprehend all the various causes of long life, especially the causes of long life in humans.

Example of an Actuarial Table

Actuarial Table*

Age	White male	White female	Black male	Black female
10	72.7	79.6	67.2	75.2
11	72.7	79.6	67.2	75.2
12	72.7	79.6	67.2	75.2
13	72.8	79.6	67.3	75.2
14	72.8	79.6	67.3	75.2
15	72.8	79.6	67.3	75.3
16	72.9	79.7	67.4	75.3
17	72.9	79.7	67.4	75.3
18	73.0	79.7	67.5	75.3
19	73.1	79.7	67.5	75.4
20	73.1	79.8	67.6	75.4
21	73.2	79.8	67.7	75.4
22	73.3	79.8	67.8	75.5
23	73.4	79.9	67.9	75.5
24	73.4	79.9	68.0	75.6
25	73.5	79.9	68.1	75.6
26	73.6	80.0	68.2	75.7
27	73.7	80.0	68.3	75.7
28	73.7	80.0	68.4	75.8
29	73.8	80.0	68.6	75.8
30	73.9	80.1	68.7	75.9
31	73.9	80.1	68.8	76.0
32	74.0	80.1	69.0	76.0
33	74.1	80.2	69.1	76.1
34	74.1	80.2	69.3	76.2
35	74.2	80.2	69.4	76.2
36	74.3	80.3	69.6	76.3
37	74.3	80.3	69.7	76.4
38	74.4	80.3	69.9	76.5
39	74.5	80.4	70.0	76.6
40	74.6	80.4	70.2	76.7
41	74.6	80.5	70.4	76.8
42	74.7	80.5	70.6	76.9
43	74.8	80.6	70.8	77.0
44	74.9	80.7	71.0	77.1
45	75.0	80.7	71.2	77.2
46	75.1	80.8	71.4	77.4
47	75.2	80.9	71.7	77.5
48	75.4	81.0	71.9	77.7
49	75.5	81.1	72.2	77.9

Actuarial Table* (Continued)

Age	White male	White female	Black male	Black female
50	75.7	81.2	72.5	78.1
51	75.8	81.3	72.8	78.3
52	76.0	81.4	73.1	78.5
53	76.2	81.5	73.4	78.7
54	76.4	81.7	73.7	78.9
55	76.6	81.8	74.1	79.1
56	76.8	81.9	74.4	79.4
57	77.1	82.1	74.8	79.7
58	77.3	82.3	75.2	79.9
59	77.6	82.4	75.6	80.2
60	77.9	82.6	76.0	80.5
61	78.2	82.8	76.5	80.9
62	78.5	83.0	76.9	81.2
63	78.8	83.3	77.4	81.6
64	79.2	83.5	77.9	81.9
65	79.5	83.7	78.4	82.3
66	79.9	84.0	78.9	82.6
67	80.3	84.2	79.4	83.0
68	80.7	84.5	79.9	83.3
69	81.1	84.8	80.4	83.7
70	81.5	85.1	80.9	84.1
71	82.0	85.4	81.5	84.6
72	82.5	85.7	82.1	85.0
73	82.9	86.1	82.7	85.5
74	83.4	86.4	83.3	86.0
75	84.0	86.8	84.0	86.5
76	84.5	87.2	84.6	87.0
77	85.1	87.6	81.2	87.4
78	85.7	88.0	81.8	87.9
79	86.2	88.4	82.4	88.5
80	86.9	88.8	87.1	89.0
81	87.5	89.3	87.8	89.6
82	88.2	89.8	88.5	90.2
83	88.8	90.3	89.3	90.9
84	89.5	90.9	90.1	91.6
85	90.2	91.5	91.0	92.4

*Life expectancies presented here are based on life tables computed for 1983 by the National Center for Health Statistics (National Center for Health Statistics, 1986).

4
The Psychology of Health: Issues in the Field with Special Focus on the Older Person

Barbara J. Felton
Tracey A. Revenson

INTRODUCTION

This module presents a current view of the psychology of health and aging. It describes, in an overview, the state of our current knowledge in the area of health psychology with special focus on older people. It presents an outline, designed for instructional use, highlighting important ideas and findings in the area. In this outline, a listing of "Unanswered Questions" is used to characterize the state of the art; it is meant to be a vehicle for promoting class discussion that bears on central questions whose resolution will constitute a real contribution to the field. Several tables, presenting basic statistics on the health status of older adults, accompany the outline.

The Bibliography that follows the outline lists all references cited earlier in the module. The Annotated Bibliography contains synopses of articles that are recommended by virtue of being (1) a classic piece in the area, (2) a major review of some relevant area, (3) an important theoretical piece directly relevant to the study of the psychology of health in late life, or (4) a recent, well-executed, empirical article important to specific topics in the field.

The module ends with a chart describing the contents of eight important review chapters we drew upon in writing this module. Health psychology covers a broad set of disciplines, and gerontological considerations of the psychology of health have concentrated on more circumscribed sets of topics. This chart offers a guide to the coverage of the diverse topics in health psychology and aging.

The psychology of health is a growing area, spurred in recent years by several major discoveries about the role of specific psychosocial factors in the etiology of illness. At present, health psychology encompasses studies of the role of social and psychological factors in the onset of illness, the psychological experience of illness, the course of recovery, the duration and intensity of chronic episodes, and the prevention of illness. Social and psychological factors are considered by health psychologists as both antecedents and moderators of people's psychological adjustment to illness or health problems. Performance on a wide variety of social and psychological tasks is also an important arena in which illness may have significant consequences.

The psychology of health in later life encompasses virtually all of the above areas. The special salience of illness to the experience of aging, due largely to the increased incidence of health problems in later life, makes health psychology a particularly important topic in the psychology of aging. The impact of health—or its absence—on the social-psychological world of the older individual has been a longstanding concern of gerontologists.

In addition to offering a context in which health issues are of paramount concern, the field of aging adds a valuable life-span developmental perspective. Gerontologists have studied age differences in psychosocial factors that influence illness (e.g., do older adults experience more stressful lives than adults under the age of 65?) as well as initiated research on possible differences in the psychological processes that govern the experience of health and illness at different points in the life span. And because gerontologists traditionally have been concerned with differences between the process of aging and the process of illness, their perspective on the relationship between psychological factors and health raises particularly important questions about the biological and psychological meanings of health and illness, as well as the overlap of disease and aging processes.

Typical of the field of health psychology, this module uses a broad definition of health, though the primary focus is on physical health rather than mental health. Variables that are presumed to reflect health include self-reported health status, functional disability, symptoms of physical distress, medical diagnosis, health behaviors (e.g., smoking, adherence to treatment regimens, reports of physician visits or of days spent in the hospital), and mortality. Functional disability, in particular, is considered a key indicator of health status among the aged; because functional disability emphasizes behavioral capabilities as well as the personal and social meaning of symptoms, it is particularly appropriate for evaluating health in an age group that typically suffers from multiple health problems.

It is tempting to organize an overview of the field by differentiating between research that evaluates the impact of social-psychological factors on the onset and course of illness from the work that evaluates the impact of health on the social psychology of the individual. These two processes, however, are seldom clearly separable, and some of the best research in the field evaluates both pathways simultaneously.

Instead, we have organized the material in this module using a "levels of analysis" approach in which we first consider individual-level processes that are involved in health and illness, then move to social-contextual processes involved in health and illness—keeping in mind that social contexts are often selected on the basis of individual-level processes and, vice versa, that many individual-level factors (e.g., coping resources) are dictated or otherwise shaped by the social context. Following this, a review of the current literature on health behaviors and the health care system illustrates more directly the interplay between environmental resources and individual behaviors in the creation of a "system" of health behaviors among older populations.

A number of psychological and social factors have been seen as critical in shaping the course of health and illness, that is, as predisposing individuals to illness, playing a role in disease etiology, influencing individual reactions to illness, and affecting recovery or rehabilitative outcomes. Psychological factors that have received the most attention in this regard are personality, stress and coping processes, and perceived control. Though some research in these areas has been extended to include consideration of older age groups, it is important to recognize that very little of the theoretical work underlying these pursuits has been generated by gerontologists and that very little empirical work addressing these linkages has included older age groups. Thus, as in much of psychology, we are still far from a clear understanding of how aging affects and is affected by the processes proposed to underlie health.

The notion that personality factors, traits, and dispositions can influence the development and course of disease has led to empirical research on a number of specific trait–disease constellations (Cohen, 1979). For example, the Type A behavior pattern has been linked to coronary heart disease in a large number of studies (Matthews & Haynes, 1986). More recent work suggests a generic disease-prone personality that predicts the onset of any of a variety of illnesses (Friedman & Booth-Kewley, 1987). Research on stress-resistance resources such as personality hardiness suggests a complementary perspective: A constellation of the personality characteristics of commitment, control, and challenge may buffer individuals under high life stress from illness (Kobasa, 1982). Yet virtually no research addresses developmental changes in these personality characteristics or possible age shifts in the linkages between personality styles and illness.

Stress and coping are factors presumably intertwined in a process through which events are cognitively appraised as challenging or threatening and thus evoke coping efforts on the part of the individual (Lazarus & Folkman, 1984). Stress has been defined most frequently as stressful life events, and empirical research has shown such events to have a consistent (though modest) deleterious impact on health (Thoits, 1983). Negative events, uncontrollable events, and events that occur "off time" in the adult life cycle are most destructive of health, and older adults, though they report fewer events than younger adults, are more likely to experience events that are negative and uncontrollable (Lazarus & DeLongis, 1983). Accordingly, empirical studies of age differences in cognitive appraisals of stress show that older people perceive stressors as more externally imposed and immutable than younger people (Folkman, Lazarus, Pimley, & Novacek, 1987). Widowhood and retirement, two prototypical stressful events of later life, take their most severe toll on health among people already in poor health or when they occur simultaneously with other stressors (Minkler, 1981; Wan, 1984). For example, the effects of forced relocation are particularly strong for those older adults already in poor health (Ferraro, 1983).

Coping behaviors differ in their effectiveness, depending on the types of stressful situations faced and the type of outcome measured (e.g., mental or physical health). In general, the individual's means of coping with a particular stressor seems to have a more clearly demonstrated impact on psychological well-being and on adjustment to illness than on illness itself (e.g., disease progression). Studies of age differences in coping styles give little reason to think that older adults' choices of coping strategies are more likely to be effective or ineffective in the situations they encounter (Felton & Revenson, 1987; Folkman, Lazarus, Pimley, & Novacek, 1987; McCrae, 1982). Some studies have found older people less likely to engage in active forms of coping (Felton, Revenson, & Hinrichsen, 1980, 1984; Irion & Blanchard-Fields, 1987); many of these are age differences in help seeking that seem to reflect older adults' cohort-specific preference for self-reliance (Veroff, Kulka, & Douvan, 1981). Many age differences in coping appear to be a function of the different types of stressors different age groups face, with older adults generally experiencing more uncontrollable stressors such as chronic health problems (McCrae, 1982).

The construct of health locus of control involves beliefs that one has control over one's future health and illness as opposed to beliefs that health is controlled by chance or by powerful others (Wallston & Wallston, 1982). The notion that real personal control leads to health, happiness, and even survival has received empirical support from Langer and Rodin's (1976) classic study, its follow-up (Rodin & Langer, 1977), and a similar study (Schulz & Hanusa, 1980) of the benefits of control-enhancing interventions in nursing homes. Research on the health locus of control variable itself has shown internal health locus of control beliefs to be linked to preventive health behaviors, recovery, and compliance with treatment (Wallston & Wallston, 1982), but studies examining these relations in older populations or exploring age-related changes in perceived control are too few from which to make generalizations.

In addition to the influence of personality factors in health and illness, it is necessary to consider the broader social context. Some features of environments may directly affect health: improving, maintaining, or deteriorating the individual's functional level by offering too much or too little in the way of environmental supports and environmental challenges (Lawton, 1981). Environments that afford some degree of personal control over decision making, as in the Langer and Rodin (1976) study cited above, seem to enhance health as well as emotional well-being. Age segregation is an environmental characteristic that plays an indirect role in health. In general, living in age-segregated buildings or neighborhoods increases social interaction, and high levels of age–peer interaction are predictors of emotional well-being of "vulnerable" community groups, including the ill elderly (Lawton, 1985). Health status has been seen as a consequence of some environmental locations and as a prompt for a variety of residential moves (Lawton, 1985; National Center for Health Statistics, 1976).

One component of the social environment critical for understanding health is social relationships. Several large-scale, longitudinal epidemiological studies have confirmed the importance of social networks in predicting morbidity and mortality among adults of all ages (Berkman & Syme, 1979). Being embedded in a network of social ties is positively related to health: Individuals who lack social ties at the time of initial measurement are more likely to die during the follow-up period, even considering the individual's prior health status and socioeconomic factors. Though these data are compelling, we know very little about the possible mechanisms through which social networks influence health status. Umberson (1987) outlines four possible mechanisms:

1. Personal characteristics (including personality, coping strategies, and psychological impairment) could affect how one deals with health concerns as well as the availability of social ties.
2. Social ties could affect compliance with medical regimens or motivation to engage in healthful behaviors.
3. Social ties could act as social supports that "buffer" the individual from the deleterious consequences of environmental stresses, life events, or chronic strains.
4. Physiological or biochemical processes such as neuroendocrine responses to the presence of others could prevent the occurrence of illness.

Studies of social support among the aged provide partial evidence for the beneficial effects of support for those under stress. Lowenthal and

Haven's (1968) classic study found that having a confidant protected older adults from the role losses of widowhood and retirement and resulted in higher levels of psychological adjustment. Other research has found evidence of a direct relationship between social support and morale among the elderly (e.g., Revicki & Mitchell, 1986). Yet some research has found social "support" to have negative consequences at times. For example, in one study, social support was related to poorer psychosocial adjustment among middle-aged and older cancer patients unless those patients were undergoing chemo- or radiotherapy or experiencing only minimal levels of functional disability (Revenson, Wollman, & Felton, 1983). It may be that the types of social support provided play a critical role in determining the value of such support: social relationships that provide a sense of reliable alliance and those that provide guidance may be particularly important in protecting older adults' mental health from the potentially deleterious effects of negative life events (Cutrona, Russell, & Rose, 1986).

Longitudinal studies are beginning to identify normal age-related changes in social networks. The Duke University studies of normal aging have shown the social networks of older adults to shift over time in composition to include a larger proportion of family members, particularly members of younger generations (Palmore, 1981). Illness imposes some changes, with older adults suffering disabilities increasing their rate of contact with family at the expense of contact with friends (Johnson & Catalano, 1983). Longitudinal data about shifts in the qualities of social relationships are badly needed to understand what types of "support" are likely to be meaningful at later life stages and available to older adults.

Health behavior is of interest since good health practices seem, especially among younger adults, to forestall the onset of illness and attenuate the disabling trajectory of most chronic illnesses (Belloc & Breslow, 1972; Breslow & Engstrom, 1980). Positive health behaviors like exercise, maintaining optimal weight, and not smoking have been found to be related to positive health outcomes, including longevity, among older adults (Palmore, 1970), but there may be a weaker association between health practices and health status in later life (Branch & Jette, 1984; Brown & McCreedy, 1986). Biological changes in late life undoubtedly complicate the relationship between a healthy lifestyle and actual health status. Life-span data on the "feedback" system between health conditions and health-promoting behavior would be enormously helpful in understanding the meaning of health behavior at different life stages. The interplay between health behaviors and social relationships is another possible source of clues about how some health behaviors shape, and are shaped by, the individual's social and psychological world (Umberson, 1987).

Older adults are major users of health care services, occupying about a third of all hospital beds and accounting for a quarter of the total health care expenditures in the country (see Shanas & Maddox, 1985). Recent trends show increased use of almost all types of services, especially outpatient services, over the past decade or so. Use of health services is better explained by need than by demographic characteristics or by the absence of financial barriers (Wolinsky & Coe, 1984; Wolinsky et al., 1983). Treatment of chronic conditions assumes a large share of the medical services used by the elderly, but most medical care settings and reimbursement policies in the United States are ill suited to these long-term care needs (Kastenbaum, 1982). Most of the long-term care of older adults is provided by family, and we have little information about the quality of such care. In professional settings, the devalued status of the elderly in our society and the chronic and/or deteriorating nature of many of their illnesses make older people particularly vulnerable to negative stereotypes and communication problems (see Haug & Ory, 1987). Better training of health care professionals as well as changes in health care policy are needed to assure older adults of high-quality medical care.

As this overview suggests, a health psychology of later life is a broad area; its purview covers a diverse set of health variables at individual, interpersonal, and social levels. While many of the research findings are tentative, they suggest promising developments in theory and future research ideas that will help clarify the transactional effects of aging and illness in late life.

OUTLINE

I. Importance of the psychology of health for later life
  A. Health is a fundamental component of "quality of life."
    1. Health status and longevity are commonly used as indicators of a society's level of development.
    2. Behavioral competence, including indices of physical health status, is considered one of the four basic components of well-being in the elderly (Lawton, 1983).
  B. Health status is an important predictor of psychological well-being in the elderly.
    1. Self-rated health status has a moderate and robust relationship with subjective well-being, as indicated by replicated secondary data analyses, statistical meta-analyses, and narrative summaries of the literature (George & Landerman, 1984; Okun, Stock, Haring, & Witter, 1984; Zautra & Hempel, 1984).
  C. The health status of the aged is a societal concern as it affects individuals' abilities to carry out social roles.

TABLE 4.1 Chronic conditions among persons 17 years of age and over, according to type of condition, age, sex, and family income, United States

17–44 YEARS									
Total	40.3	26.2	23.2	8.9	24.6	37.8	49.0	42.4	31.9
Sex									
Male	28.0	24.6	16.7	6.9	19.5	36.4	51.9	51.4	44.7
Female	51.3	27.6	29.1	10.8	29.3	39.1	46.4	34.2	20.3
Family Income*									
Less than $5,000	46.9	34.1	28.4	11.4	32.5	48.9	59.4	55.4	43.2
$5,000–$9,999	40.5	23.6	22.3	9.1	23.3	40.8	50.5	44.0	31.7
$10,000–$14,999	38.7	24.4	21.8	8.4	22.5	35.9	47.4	39.3	28.7
$15,000 or more	35.9	26.8	23.7	8.0	24.3	29.8	42.4	35.8	30.9
45–64 YEARS									
Total	204.2	33.1	35.4	42.6	88.8	126.7	68.2	114.1	63.0
Sex									
Male	148.0	29.3	28.5	40.6	97.4	101.3	68.2	140.2	73.6
Female	255.3	36.7	41.6	44.4	81.0	149.6	68.2	90.5	53.4

Family Income*

Less than $5,000	297.8	53.5	44.2	74.1	139.3	172.7	102.8	158.9	114.1
$5,000–$9,999	200.3	33.5	38.7	43.8	92.5	125.4	67.2	118.1	57.4
$10,000–$14,999	163.7	23.7	29.0	37.8	74.3	121.3	62.3	107.3	45.9
$15,000 or more	159.8	22.7	30.3	30.5	66.6	105.3	52.2	85.9	48.9
65 YEARS AND OVER									
Total	380.3	35.8	41.2	78.5	198.7	199.4	67.1	294.3	204.6
Sex									
Male	287.0	42.3	47.3	60.3	199.3	141.2	54.6	338.2	183.1
Female	450.1	31.1	36.6	91.3	198.3	240.9	76.3	262.1	220.4
Family Income*									
Less than $5,000	411.7	41.4	45.4	82.0	219.0	216.1	78.7	232.0	232.0
$5,000–$9,999	353.3	32.6	37.2	76.1	190.0	179.5	57.3	271.6	163.2
$10,000–$14,999	310.9	*	27.4	81.1	158.9	192.6	39.3	247.3	181.3
$15,000 or more	300.8	*	40.7	62.7	174.8	161.4	48.5	259.2	169.2

[a]Without heart involvement.
[b]Excludes unknown family income.
Data based on household interviews of samples of the civilian noninstitutionalized population.

Source: Division on Health Interview Statistics, National Center for Health Statistics. Selected reports from the Health Interview Survey, 1969–1973. Vital and Health Statistics, Series 10, and unpublished data from the Health Interview Survey. From Kart, Metress, & Metress (1988).

D. Illness and its concomitants are frequent experiences among older people.

1. Although acute illnesses are experienced about equally among older and younger adults, chronic illness is far more frequent among older people (See Table 1 for a listing of chronic conditions of the elderly).

   (a) Of individuals aged 65+ living outside institutions 85% report at least one chronic condition.

2. Disability is one of the most significant concomitants of illness.

   (a) About 55% of individuals living outside institutions report some limitation of activity related to chronic health conditions (National Center for Health Statistics, 1976; Shanas & Maddox, 1985) (See Tables 2 and 3).

3. Sensory impairments increase with age.

   (a) Approximately a third of individuals aged 65 to 79 have significant hearing impairments in the frequency range covering normal speech.

   (b) Decreases in good vision (20/20 without correction) are common after age 45 (Shanas & Maddox, 1985).

TABLE 4.2 Percentage of Older People Needing Help in One or More Basic Physical Activities.

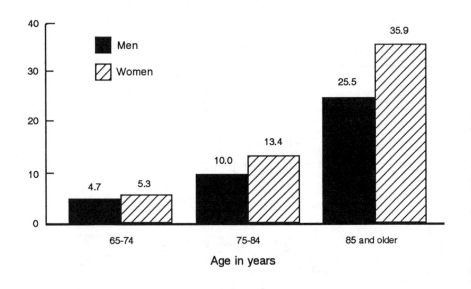

Source: National Center for Health Statistics, National Health Interview Survey, 1979–80. From Kovar (1987).

TABLE 4.3 Percentage of Older People Living in the Community Who Need Help.

	Age of men			Age of women		
	65–74	75–84	85+	65–74	75–84	85+
One or more	4.7	10.0	25.9	5.3	13.6	35.9
Walking	3.5	7.4	18.9	3.9	9.9	26.0
Going outside	2.9	5.5	18.7	3.8	10.0	28.3
Bathing	2.1	4.7	13.2	1.7	5.6	17.0
Dressing	1.5	3.2	8.6	1.3	3.4	10.2
Using the toilet	1.2	2.3	7.2	1.2	3.7	10.7
Moving from bed or chair	1.0	2.0	5.0	1.1	2.8	7.6
Eating	0.5	0.7	2.6	0.3	1.1	3.6

From Kovar (1987).

E. Psychological and social factors are needed to explain the experience of illness in old age (Siegler & Costa, 1985).
1. Psychological and social factors play at least a partial role in the etiology of most illnesses, even though we are rarely sure of the biological, psychological, and/or social processes that explain illness onset (Eisdorfer & Wilkie, 1977).
2. The course of illness is shaped by multiple social and psychological processes, including those that guide the individual's activities, residential choices, and use of health care services.
3. The experience of illness shapes the individual's social and psychological world through its influence on cognitive and psychological performance, participation in social relationships, social roles, and psychological well-being (Lawton, 1981).
4. The term *health psychology* refers to analysis and understanding of health-related behaviors at the level of the individual— a traditional province of psychology. Health psychology focuses attention on the personal, interpersonal, and contextual predictors of individual differences in behavior, and also on delineating the personal experience of health and illness (Rakowski, 1984).
F. The concept of aging as a disease is a misconception.
1. There is wide variation in health status among the elderly, with only a small percentage of elders seriously ill enough to require institutionalization.
2. Research in the psychology of health in later life can help disentangle the experience of illness from the experience of aging and thus lead to more knowledgeable interventions to improve quality of life in old age (Siegler & Costa, 1985).
II. Definitions of health and illness
A. Definitions of health vary in empirical research and gerontological theory.
1. The World Health Organization (WHO) provides the broadest definition: Health is "a state of complete physical, mental and social well-being and not merely the absence of disease and infirmity" (WHO, 1958).
2. The WHO definition of health includes its social and psychological facets as well as its physiological aspects.
(a) Distinguishing between physical and mental health is a common practice, though the "health implications" of much research often imply both facets.
(b) The correlation between health status (as measured by physicians' ratings or self-reports) and psychological well-being is consistent but not high enough to equate them (George & Landerman, 1984).

(c) The distinction between physical and mental health blurs with increasing age.

   (1) Having multiple-illness conditions and disorders that present symptoms of both physical and mental distress are more prevalent in later life (Siegler & Costa, 1985).

B. Narrower definitions of health focus on the presence or absence of illness, or on medical diagnoses for evaluations of health.

   1. The "absence of disease" model is commonly used by physicians and health care professionals, and relies upon measurement through observations, examinations, and laboratory tests.

   2. Some efforts have been made to translate medical diagnoses into psychological terms, such as a continuum of "seriousness of illness" (Wyler et al., 1971).

   3. Symptom lists provide an index of "pathology" that is not constrained by medical definitions of illness, but because symptoms are often self-reports, they are closely tied to individuals' attitudes, beliefs, and emotions about their illness experiences.

   4. Mortality is a *post facto* rudimentary index of "absence of health" that is itself clearly understandable, though there is no clear understanding of the continuum that lies between the extreme points of "health" and "death" (Kovar, 1987).

C. Most gerontologists consider the health of the elderly in terms of functional adequacy.

   1. Many agree that the "absence of disease" model is inappropriate for understanding health in later life; the multiple chronic conditions characteristic of the elderly make it important to focus on functional independence and not on cure (Kovar, 1987).

   2. A social definition of health, in which health is seen as "a state of optimum capacity for performance of the roles and tasks for which a person has been socialized" (Kovar, 1987), emphasizes behavioral capabilities and the personal and social meaning of symptoms.

   3. In evaluating health assessment measures, most gerontologists argue that health ought to be construed as a multifaceted concept that includes physical, mental, and social dimensions (Kovar, 1987).

   4. Functional health is often measured in terms of the older person's ability to perform activities of daily living, such as bathing and toilet (Katz, 1983).

D. Subjective versus objective measures of health.

   1. Subjective measures of health, usually global assessments of

overall state of health on a "poor" to "excellent" continuum, are significantly related to more "objective" measures of health, for example, physicians' ratings and disability days.

2. While often more convenient than physicians' ratings of health, self-ratings of health are not substitute measures of "objective health," as they measure other things as well as health status, for example, comparisons with age peers (Linn & Linn, 1980; Rakowski, 1984).

3. The aged frequently underestimate the extent of their health problems (Eisdorfer & Wilkie, 1977) and overestimate their overall health, leading them to be categorized as "health optimists" (Shanas et al., 1968).

4. Self-assessed health is a strong predictor of mortality among the elderly (Kaplan & Camach, 1983; Mossey & Shapiro, 1982).

Unanswered Questions

1. What factors might explain the superiority of self-rated health over physician-rated health in the prediction of mortality?

2. What processes might link mental and physical health? Which of these could be expected to differ across the life span?

3. What factors might govern the relationship between aging and disease? Are some illnesses likely to be more closely linked to "aging" than others?

III. Psychological factors in health and illness
A number of psychological and emotional factors have been found to affect the onset and course of illness. Most of the factors are themselves affected by illness as well.

A. Stress

1. Theory proposes that stress, regardless of its nature, taxes the system, so that stress weakens the organism and is thus related to illness (Selye, 1965).

2. Stress has most frequently been defined as stressful life events, or events involving major changes in one's daily life pattern (Dohrenwend & Dohrenwend, 1974).

(a) Though the *number* of life events decreases with age (Lowenthal, Thurnher, & Chiriboga, 1975), older individuals experience a higher incidence of *negative, uncontrollable* events involving loss, many of which are illness related (Aldwin & Revenson, 1985, November; Chiriboga & Cutler, 1980; Folkman, Lazarus, Pimley, & Novacek, 1987; McCrae, 1982).

(b) The meaning or stressfulness of specific events may be

different for older people than for younger people (Leventhal, 1984; Neugarten, 1979).

(c) Hassles, or short-term stresses occurring on a daily basis, may be at least as strongly predictive of health declines as negative life events (Lazarus & Folkman, 1984; Stone, Reed, & Neale, 1987).

   (1) Hassles are more prevalent among the aged than younger adults (Lazarus & DeLongis, 1983) but rated as no more stressful by older people (Kanner, Coyne, Schaefer, & Lazarus, 1981).

(d) Most life events scales include events specific to young and middle adulthood, though a few attempts have been made to develop more valid and reliable events scales for elderly populations (Amster & Krauss, 1974; Muhlenkamp, Gross, & Flood, 1975).

3. Studies of prototypical stressful events of later life have found their impact on health to be modest but significant under a variety of circumstances (Rowland, 1977; Wan, 1984).

(a) Widowhood: Some studies have found widowhood to result in a decline in older adults' reports of their health status (Thompson, Breckenridge, Gallagher, & Peterson, 1984), but others have found health changes following widowhood to be short lived (Ferraro, 1985–1986) or explainable by prior health status (Wan, 1984).

(b) Retirement: Despite commonly held notions, retirement alone often has *no* deleterious effect on health (Minkler, 1981; Rowland, 1977; Wan, 1984).

(c) Relocation: The effects of forced relocation on the health of the elderly are particularly strong for those already in ill health (Lawton, 1985), confounding the reasons for relocation with its effects (Rowland, 1977).

(d) Disasters: Studies of disasters suggest that older people suffer more physical health declines than younger adults in the short run, but that prior experience affords a probable advantage for older people (Bolin & Klenow, 1982–1983; Krause, 1987; Norris & Murrell, 1987) in long-term adjustment.

B. Coping

1. Coping refers to the thoughts and actions that people use to reduce or eliminate stressful conditions and psychological distress (Lazarus & Folkman, 1984).

(a) Coping can be directed toward solving the problem (*problem focused coping*) or toward regulating emotional distress created by the problem (*emotion-focused coping*) (Folkman & Lazarus, 1980).

(b) People use mixed patterns of coping strategies, rather than relying on a single means of coping (Fleishman, 1984; Folkman et al., 1987).

    (1) In 98% of stressful encounters, people used both problem-focused and emotion-focused modes of coping (Folkman & Lazarus, 1980).

(c) Coping efforts are shaped by the controllability of the stressor (Folkman, Lazarus, Dunkel-Schetter, DeLongis, & Gruen, 1986) and by personal resources, like mastery or personality hardiness (Fleishman, 1984; Kobasa, 1982) and education, income, and social support (Billings & Moos, 1981; Pearlin & Schooler, 1978; Thoits, 1986).

(d) Coping efforts are also shaped by cognitive appraisal processes; that is, whether the individual construes the stressful situation as posing harm, loss, threat, and/or challenge (Lazarus & Folkman, 1984; McCrae, 1982, 1984).

2. Effects of coping on health

  (a) While theoretically coping has an influence on health and health behavior, there are few empirical studies to support such a conclusion (Cassileth et al., 1984).

    (1) In one study of relocation among the aged, coping made a big difference in survival rates (Lieberman & Tobin, 1983).

  (b) Coping has a more clearly demonstrated impact on psychological well-being and on psychological adjustment to illness than on the development or progression of physical illness.

3. Age-related differences in coping

  (a) Studies of age differences in appraisal processes show older people to perceive stress as more externally imposed and less changeable than younger people (Folkman et al., 1987); they perceive themselves as less responsible for the occurrence of stress (Aldwin & Revenson, 1985, November; Blanchard-Fields & Robinson, 1987).

    (1) Older people were just as likely as younger people to make challenge appraisals even though they experience fewer challenge events (Aldwin & Revenson, 1985; McCrae, 1982).

  (b) Older people are less likely to cope by using "active" forms of coping (Felton, Revenson, & Hinrichsen, 1984; Ilfeld, 1980; Irion & Blanchard-Fields, 1987).

    (1) Most of these conclusions are based on older people's reticence to actively seek help (Aldwin & Revenson, 1987; Felton & Revenson, 1987), a phenomenon that

seems to stem from a cohort-specific emphasis on self-reliance (Veroff, Douvan, & Kulka, 1981).

(c) Many age differences in coping appear to be a function of the different types of stressors different age groups face (Felton & Revenson, 1987; McCrae, 1982), with older adults generally confronted with more uncontrollable stressors.

(d) A few studies have found older adults to be more accepting of stress and less defensive or emotionally expressive in their reactions to stress (Aldwin & Revenson, 1985, November; Felton & Revenson, 1987; Ilfeld, 1980; McCrae, 1982; Westbrook & Viney, 1983).

4. The effects of health on coping

(a) Despite wide variation within and across diagnoses, illness places universally stressful demands on its victims (Cassileth et al., 1984; Moos, 1982; Revenson & Felton, 1985, November).

(b) Although a variety of strategies are used to cope with illness, emotion-focused strategies are used more for health problems, particularly when the problems are appraised as uncontrollable (Felton et al., 1984; Folkman & Lazarus, 1980).

(1) Unfortunately, emotion-focused coping may be linked to poorer psychological adjustment to illness (Felton & Revenson, 1984).

(c) Perceptions of health problems by the aged as being natural and inevitable frequently block constructive coping efforts (Leventhal, 1984; Rodin, 1980).

(d) More than other stresses, illness prompts less active strategies (i.e., less help seeking) and greater use of intrapsychic strategies (Cicirelli, 1983, August).

(1) Older ostomy patients used less active behavioral coping (Keyes, Bisno, Richardson, & Marston, 1987).

(2) Older cancer patients desire less detailed information and less involvement in their health care (Cassileth, Zupkis, Sutton-Smith, & March, 1980).

(3) Prayer and using nonprescription drugs were common strategies for coping with illness among low-income elderly women, particularly black women (Conway, 1986).

(4) Older adults facing chronic illnesses (cancer, rheumatoid arthritis, diabetes, hypertension) were less likely to use emotional expression or information seeking than middle-aged adults (Felton & Revenson, 1987).

C. Personality
Personality factors, traits, and dispositions can influence the development and course of disease (Cohen, 1979).
1. Most research has focused on specific trait–disease constellations, such as the Type A behavior pattern.
   (a) Characterized by rapid speech, impatience, hostility, and ambition, the Type A personality has been shown to be a risk factor for coronary heart disease (CHD) independent of other risk factors, such as smoking and obesity (Matthews, 1982, 1988).
   (b) We do not know whether Type A is predictive of CHD after age 65, as most studies use age-homogeneous male samples and few have subjects over 60, and Type A may be less prevalent among older age groups (Matthews & Haynes, 1986).
2. More recent work suggests a generic disease-prone personality that predicts the onset of any of a variety of illnesses (Friedman & Booth-Kewley, 1987) or this may be a reflection of neuroticism (Costa & McCrae, 1987).
3. Personality can also act as a stress-resistance resource, such as the case of personality hardiness, which involves a constellation of the characteristics of commitment, control, and challenge (Kobasa, 1982; Magnani, 1986).
D. Control
1. Issues regarding control are particularly important to health, as restrictions on control are stress inducing and may lead to helplessness (Seligman, 1975).
2. Illness may itself impose serious restrictions on the individual's range of primary control, or the individual's exercise of direct control over the environment, e.g., the hospital (Cicirelli, 1987).
3. A sense of personal control may function as a way of reducing the negative effects of stress (Rodin, 1980), perhaps by way of increasing effective coping behaviors (Folkman, 1984).
4. Beliefs that one has control over one's future health and illness have been linked to preventive health behaviors, recovery, compliance with treatment (Wallston & Wallston, 1982).
E. Consequences of illness on psychological performance
Illness can impair psychological performance. Research has provided a beginning description of the toll taken by illness on diverse facets of performance. This research provides clues about where the process of aging diverges from the process of illness. This literature is nicely summarized in review chapters by Siegler and Costa (1985), Elias, Elias, and Elias (in press), and Siegler (1989).

1. Intellectual functioning
   (a) Health has provided a more consistently strong explanation for age-related declines in intellectual functioning than age itself.
   (b) Poorer intellectual performance seems to be a consequence of hypertension, though effects are fairly weak and studies have not always solved sampling problems or satisfactorily controlled for disease.
2. Reaction time
   (a) Declines in reaction time with age have been seen as a classic pattern, but disease processes may provide part of the explanation.
   (b) Hypertensives have been found to have slower reaction time than normotensive controls; the performance of medicated hypertensives, however, remains unclear.
3. Learning and memory
   (a) Health status seems to account for most of the age-related decline found in tasks of learning and memory such as recognition of faces, memory for names and faces, logical memory, and paired associates.
   (b) Hypertension affects Wechsler memory scale performance and neuropsychological test performance, though the effects are modest.
   (c) We are completely lacking data that would inform us about the possible role of hypertension and/or other illness conditions in early adulthood on the development of cognitive dysfunction later in life.

Unanswered Questions:

1. The definition of stress needs clarification since some types of stress are beneficial. What kinds of stress could you imagine to have positive effects on health?
2. Not all stresses are "nonspecific." What are the differences in their consequences?
3. Since health is a source of stress *and* a consequence of stress, how should we best conceptualize the link between health and stress?
4. The time lag between the onset of stress and the appearance of its consequences needs to be defined for us to correctly evaluate the impact of stressful life events on health. Design a study to evaluate the time lag between stress onset and illness.
5. If coping strategies used by adults tend to fit with the nature of the stresses typically faced at that age, is a life stage theory of coping appropriate? What would such a theory propose?
6. What is the difference between a personality-based and a coping-

based explanation of psychosocial adjustment to illness?

7. Could illness-based age differences in cognitive performance and reaction time explain any of the age differences in coping found in the literature? Could they explain age differences in the experience of stress?

IV. Social and contextual factors in health and illness
  A. Residential decision making and health
    1. Health status predicts residential location, as people move when they need more environmental support or when they can indulge in the luxury of moving to acquire more amenities (Lawton, 1985).
       (a) Cross-sectional data suggest that poor health prompts people to move to more dependent settings (National Center for Health Statistics, 1976; Newman, 1976).
       (b) Anticipated health declines, as well, play a role in decisions to move into congregate housing (Lawton, 1985).
    2. In resource-rich environments, there is some risk of incurring "excess" disability if too little challenge is provided (Lawton, 1985).
  B. Opportunities for personal control within a setting have an important impact on the health of the aged inhabitant.
    1. Degree of personal control and the positive use of opportunities for control by more functionally capable persons are important features of environments for the aged (Lawton, 1985; Lemke & Moos, 1981; Moos, 1980).
    2. Newly admitted residents of a long-term care facility participated in more activities involving physical effort and were perceived by staff as healthier if their introduction to the home provided information that increased the predictability of their new environment (Krantz & Schulz, 1980).
    3. Even among fairly disabled residents of nursing homes, providing a sense of personal responsibility or control over daily events such as visiting increased emotional well-being and activity level (Langer & Rodin, 1976; Schulz, 1976).
       (a) The longer term effects of such control-enhancing interventions are not assured (Schulz & Hanusa, 1980), though Rodin & Langer (1977) found the elevated levels of physical activity and happiness to persist among their respondents over an 18-month period.
  C. Quality of community life
     A cohesive social structure seems to contribute to lower rates of myocardial infarction; although genetic and other cultural factors cannot be definitively discounted, comparisons of death rates among adult men and women in five neighboring towns

showed the Italian community characterized by tightly knit culture composed of mutually trusting and mutually supportive members to have a strikingly low death rate from myocardial infarction (Lynn et al., 1967; Stout, Morrow, Brandt, & Wolf, 1964).

D. Social networks in health and illness
   1. Being embedded in a network of social ties is positively related to health.
      (a) Prospective studies show that individuals who lack social ties at the time of initial measurement are more likely to die during follow-up periods (Berkman & Syme, 1979; Blazer, 1982; House, Robbins, & Metzner, 1982).
      (b) Being married is the most consistently important social factor predicting delayed mortality, especially for men (Umberson, 1987).
      (c) Ongoing participation in an enduring social organization may be beneficial: Church attendance is a component of social network that postpones mortality (Berkman & Breslow, 1983).
   2. Possible mechanisms by which social networks could exert their influence on health status (Umberson, 1987):
      (a) Personal characteristics, including personality, coping strategies, and psychological impairment, could affect how one deals with health concerns *and* the availability of social ties.
      (b) Social ties could affect compliance with medical regimens or motivation to engage in healthful behaviors.
      (c) Social ties could act as social supports (see entry below) "buffering" the individual from the deleterious consequences of stress.
      (d) Physiological or biochemical processes such as neuroendocrine responses to the presence of others could prevent illness.
   3. Family relationships are related to participation in risky or health-compromising behavior; thus they may reduce mortality by performing a "social control" function (Umberson, 1987).
   4. Social support may be effective in shaping health status through its role as a stress buffer.
      (a) Individuals experiencing high stress but with good support resources should develop significantly less symptomatology than individuals experiencing high stress but with little social support (Thoits, 1982).
      (b) The beneficial effects of social support on health and well-being seem to exist regardless of the experience of

stress in many cases (Fuller & Larson, 1980; Heller & Swindle, 1983; Thoits, 1982).

(c) Having a confidant has been shown to buffer older adults from the role losses of widowhood and retirement, predicting higher levels of psychological adjustment in an elderly sample (Lowenthal & Haven, 1968).

(d) Social support acted as a stress buffer against mental but not physical health declines in studies over a 6-month period (Cutrona et al., 1986).

(e) In a sample of middle-aged and older cancer patients, social support was related to *poorer* psychosocial adjustment unless the patients were currently undergoing chemo- or radiotherapy or experiencing minimal levels of functional disability (Revenson, Wollman, & Felton, 1983).

(f) Social support may yet be best understood as elements in the older adults' "convoy" of social support; in this sense, the functions served by different network members over time may need to be considered for a full evaluation of the meaning of support (Antonucci & Akiyama, 1987).

5. While social network has an impact on health, it is also true that health status has an effect on social network.

(a) Over time, the social networks of older adults shift in composition to include a larger proportion of family members, particularly members of younger generations (Palmore, 1981).

(b) Older adults with disabilities increase their rate of contact with family at the expense of contact with friends (Johnson & Catalano, 1983).

(c) The need for social support of a particular kind may shift with illness, and thus particular types of relationships may become more central after diagnosis.

Unanswered Questions:

1. What qualities of social relationships are likely to be "supportive" for different types of stress? Are different kinds of social ties (e.g., kin vs. nonkin) likely to be particularly supportive for some types of stress? What are they?

2. Are there certain illnesses that are particularly likely to be affected by social integration? Which of the processes outlined by Umberson (1987) would be most important in explaining the link between social relationships and health?

3. What life stage differences can we expect in the link between health and social behavior? Is the nature of the relationship between

health and social relationships likely to be different among older people than younger adults?

V. Health behavior and health care systems
    A. Utilization of health care services
        1. In order to function at home, 5.2% of adults aged 65 to 74, 11.4% of adults aged 75 to 84, and 34.8% of adults aged 85 and over needed help with one or more basic physical activities such as walking, going outside, eating, bathing (U.S. Department of Health and Human Services, 1983).
        2. The elderly are disproportionately heavy utilizers of health services, occupying about a third of all hospital beds and accounting for a quarter of the total health care expenditures in the country (Kart, Metress, & Metress, 1988) (see Table 4).
           (a) Older adults' use of health care services is directly related to "need" characteristics such as functional health status and unrelated to "need-extraneous" factors like the availability of health insurance, SES, or income (Wolinsky & Coe, 1984; Wolinsky, Coe, Miller, Prendergast, Creel, & Chavez, 1983).
           (b) Having an impoverished social network, however, predicts health service use as well (Coe, Wolinsky, Miller, & Prendergast, 1985; Rundall & Evashwick, 1982).
        3. Treatment of *chronic* conditions assumes a large share of the medical services used by the elderly (Davis, 1985), but medical care settings and reimbursement policies are not well suited to these long-term care needs (Kastenbaum, 1982).
        4. Health services for older adults are offered in a variety of inpatient and outpatient settings, utilizing formal and informal caregivers (see Tables 5 and 6).
           (a) Inpatient care, offered in short-stay and long-stay hospitals and nursing homes, has been used by more and more older adults since the introduction of Medicare (Shanas & Maddox, 1985).
           (b) Outpatient services expanded during the 1970s: Although older adults' visits to doctors' offices declined, their use of hospital outpatient clinics and emergency rooms increased (U.S. Department of Health and Human Services, 1981).
           (c) Home health services, including nursing, medical care, and housekeeper services, also increased during the past decade (Shanas & Maddox, 1985).
           (d) Adult day services emerged as alternatives to nursing home care, prompted largely by cost concerns.
        5. The family provides most long-term health care to frail and disabled elderly (Brody, 1985); the bulk of care falls princi-

TABLE 4.4 Personal Health Care Expenditures ($ million) for People 65 Years of Age or Over, by Source of Funds and Type of Service: United States, 1984

| Source of funds | Total care | Type of service | | | |
		Hospital	Physician	Nursing home	Other care
Total	$119,872	$54,200	$24,770	$25,105	$15,798
Private	39,341	6,160	9,827	13,038	10,316
Consumer	38,875	5,964	9,818	12,856	10,237
Out-of-pocket	30,198	1,694	6,468	12,569	9,467
Insurance	8,677	4,270	3,350	287	770
Other private	466	196	9	182	79
Government	80,531	48,040	14,943	12,067	5,482
Medicare	58,519	40,524	14,314	539	3,142
Medicaid	15,288	2,595	467	10,418	1,808
Other government	6,724	4,920	162	1,110	532

Source: U.S. Senate Special Committee on Aging (1985). *America in transition: An aging society, 1984–85 edition* (p. 80) (an information paper). Washington, DC: U.S. Government Printing Office. From Binstock (1987).

TABLE 4.5 Utilization of Short-Stay Hospitals for Selected Age Groups, **1983**

Age group	Discharged patients				Days of care			
	Number (1000's)	Percentage distributor	Rate per 1,000		Number (1000's)	Percentage distribution	Rate per 1,000	Average length of stay (days)
All ages	38,783	100.00	167.0		268,337	100.00	1,155.2	6.9
45 to 64	8,558	22.1	192.2		65,029	24.2	1,460.6	7.6
65 to 74	5,468	14.1	334.2		50,222	18.7	3,069.5	9.2
75 to 84	4,295	11.1	504.2		42,416	15.8	4,979.6	9.9
85+	1,539	4.0	614.8		17,016	6.3	6,798.4	11.1

Source: U.S. Senate Special Committee on Aging (1985). *America in transition: An aging society, 1984–85 edition* (p. 76) (an information paper). Washington, DC: U.S. Government Printing Office. From Binstock (1987).

TABLE 4.6 Percentage Distributions of Care-givers by Relationship to 65+ Individual with Activity Limitations

	Care recipient	
	Male	Female
65 to 74		
Spouse	45	18
Offspring	21	29
Other relative	21	33
Formal	13	20
75 to 84		
Spouse	35	8
Offspring	23	35
Other relative	25	36
Formal	19	23
85+		
Spouse	20	2
Offspring	34	39
Other relative	27	36
Formal	19	23
All 65+		
Spouse	37	10
Offspring	24	34
Other relative	23	35
Formal	16	21

Source: U.S. Senate Special Committee on Aging (1985). *America in transition: An aging society, 1984–85 edition* (p. 73) (an information paper). Washington, DC: U.S. Government Printing Office. From Binstock (1987).

pally on a single caregiver: almost always a woman, and usually either a spouse or adult child (Brody, 1985; Ory et al., 1985).

D. Patient–physician relationships

Patient–provider relationships are particularly critical in old age since the health assessment of older individuals is complex and distinctions must be made between the effects of illness and the effects of aging.

1. Levels of satisfaction with medical care among the elderly are similar to other age groups and related to factors like friendliness, concern, and courteous behavior (DiMatteo & Friedman, 1982).

    (a) Lack of adequate information during a medical visit is the primary source of dissatisfaction.

2. Various survey data suggest that confidence in the medical profession is lowest among those 65 and older, particularly those of lower education and income.

    (a) This may be a cohort difference, however, as the oldest cohorts may have more communication difficulties with physicians due to language or ethnic barriers, and may have been predisposed to rely on self-care through much of their lifetime (Haug & Ory, 1987).

3. Older patients are less likely to communicate freely with their physicians, and less likely to challenge physician authority (Haug, 1979).

4. Some physicians, particularly younger ones, may be subject to ageist attitudes and behaviors that may influence the quality of the provider–patient relationship and quality of care (Kviteck et al., 1986).
   (a) Contact with elderly patients may help physicians-in-training become more sensitive and develop more realistic and optimistic attitudes (Wilson & Hafferty, 1980, 1983); however, increased contact may foster "compassionate stereotypes," which involve an overgeneralization of the neediness and helplessness of the elderly (Revenson, 1987).

E. Health behavior among the elderly
   1. Patterns of behavior may affect health and longevity more than environmental or genetic factors (Healthy People, 1979); for example, epidemiologic, clinical, and laboratory evidence links morbidity and mortality with life-style behaviors, such as smoking or alcohol use.
   2. Preventive health behavior
      (a) The consequences of good health practices for health status seem fairly clear cut when examined longitudinally among samples of adults of all ages.
          (1) In the Alameda County survey, in which 13% of respondents were 65 +, good health practices were associated with good health, independent of age (Belloc & Breslow, 1972).
              a. The number of good health practices was inversely related to mortality rates 5 1/2 and 9 1/2 years later, especially for men (Belloc, 1973; Breslow & Engstrom, 1980).
              b. When considered in old age, the association between health practices and health status is less clear (Branch & Jette, 1984; Brown & McCreedy, 1986; Palmore, 1970; Wiley & Camacho, 1980)
              c. Older adults practice more and better health habits than younger persons (Belloc & Breslow, 1972; Breslow & Engstrom, 1980; Brown & McCreedy, 1986; Harris & Guten, 1979; Wilson & Elinson, 1981), though it is possible that those with bad habits may have "died off" (Belloc & Breslow, 1972)

(i) Women practice more positive health habits than men at all stages of life (Belloc & Breslow, 1972; Brown & McCreedy, 1986; Harris & Guten, 1979)

(ii) Marital status is related to health behavior for men, with married men engaging in more health behaviors than their unmarried counterparts (Brown & McCreedy, 1986)

d. Older persons, however, are more likely to explain illness in terms of external factors, such as bad luck or the will of God and attribute their symptoms to old age and not illness; thus they may fail to seek professional help (Leventhal, 1984)

3. Compliance with medical regimens

Many of the chronic illnesses experienced by older people require continuing treatment, medication, and/or dietary and exercise regimens; the effectiveness of such treatment often depends on adherence to the prescribed regimen.

(a) The elderly are less likely to follow treatment regimens and take medication (Haug & Ory, 1987).

(1) Noncompliance is greater for complex medication regimens—those involving multiple drugs taken at different schedules—as is commonly the case for elderly patients with chronic conditions (Becker, 1985).

(2) Medication errors may be due to cognitive impairments, the patient's judgment, inadequate or miscommunication of information by physicians or pharmacists, or misunderstanding of the treatment protocol by the patient.

(b) Estimates of noncompliance are about 50% for persons with chronic conditions, and as high as 92% for short-term medication recommendations

(c) Social support is especially important in boosting compliance in long-term treatment plans (Becker, 1985), and may be especially important for elderly patients with cognitive impairments (Haug & Ory, 1987).

Unanswered Questions

1. Are health habits established in adolescence and early adulthood? If so, will improving the health habits of younger adults decrease the prevalence of chronic disease among tomorrow's elderly and thus decrease the cost and demand for health services?

2. Why do older individuals discontinue treatment regimens prematurely? What costs of adherence might outweigh the benefits?

3. What criteria do people use to identify and label themselves as healthy? Ill? At risk? How might these criteria differ for older and younger people?
4. What types of psychological and social factors may differentiate those older adults who undertake preventive health behaviors (e.g., participating in a daily exercise program, changing one's diet) from those who don't?
5. Why are certain symptoms reported to health professionals but others are not? Older women tend to report more symptoms of a minor nature than men; why is this?
6. How much illness (or how much disability) are we willing to accept as part of aging?

Bibliography

Aldwin, C. M., & Revenson, T. A. (1985, November). *Age differences in stress, coping and appraisal.* Paper presented at the annual meeting of the Gerontological Society of America, New Orleans.

Aldwin, C. M., & Revenson, T. A. (1987). Does coping help? A reexamination of the relation between coping and mental health. *Journal of Personality and Social Psychology, 53,* 337–348.

Amster, L. E., & Krauss, H. H. (1974). The relationship between life crises and mental deterioration in old age. *International Journal of Aging and Human Development, 5,* 51–55.

Antonucci, T. C., & Akiyama, H. (1987). Social networks in adult life and a preliminary examination of the convoy model. *Journal of Gerontology, 42,* 519–527. **A**

Baker, R. R. (1984). Attitudes of health care providers toward elderly patients with normal aging and disease-related symptoms. *The Gerontologist, 24,* 543–545.

Bausell, R. B. (1986). Health-seeking behavior among the elderly. *The Gerontologist, 26,* 556–559.

Becker, M. H. (1985). Patient adherence to prescribed therapies. *Medical Care, 23*(5), 539–555.

Belloc, N. B. (1973). Relationship of health practices and mortality. *Preventive Medicine, 2,* 67–81.

Belloc, N. B., & Breslow, L. (1972). Relationship of physical health status and health practices. *Preventive Medicine, 1,* 409–421.

Berkman, L. F. (1983). The assessment of social networks and social support in the elderly. *Journal of the American Geriatrics Society, 31,* 743–749. **A**

Berkman, L. F., & Breslow, L. (1983). *Health and ways of living: The Alameda County study.* New York: Oxford University Press.

Berkman, L. F., & Syme, S. L. (1979). Social networks, host resistance, and mortality: A nine-year follow-up study of Alameda County residents. *American Journal of Epidemiology, 109,* 186–204.

Billings, A. G., & Moos, R. H. (1981). The role of coping responses and social resources in attenuating the stress of life events. *Journal of Behavioral Medicine, 4*(2), 139–157.

References followed by an **A** are included in the Annotated Bibliography. References followed by an **R** are listed in the chart of review chapters at the end of this document.

Binstock, R. H. (1987). Health care: Organization, use and financing. In G. Maddox (Ed.), *The encyclopedia of aging* (pp. 307–311). New York: Springer.

Blanchard-Fields, F., & Robinson, S. L. (1987). Age differences in the relation between controllability and coping. *Journal of Gerontology, 41,* 497–501.

Blazer, D. G. (1982). Social support and mortality in an elderly community population. *American Journal of Epidemiology, 115,* 684–694.

Bolin, R., & Klenow, D. J. (1982–1983). Response of the elderly to disaster: An age-stratified analysis. *International Journal of Aging and Human Development, 16,* 283–296.

Branch, L. G. (1985). Health practices and incident disability among the elderly. *American Journal of Public Health, 75*(12), 1436–1439.

Branch, L. G., & Jette, A. M. (1984). Personal health practices and mortality among the elderly. *American Journal of Public Health, 74,* 1126–1129. **A**

Breslow, L., & Enstrom, J. E. (1980). Persistence of health habits and their relationship to mortality. *Preventive Medicine, 9,* 469–483.

Brody. E. M. (1985). Parent care as normative family stress. *The Gerontologist, 25,* 19–29.

Brown, J. S., & McCreedy, M. (1986). The hale elderly: Health behavior and its correlates. *Research in Nursing and Health, 9,* 317–329. **A**

Cassileth, B. R., Lusk, E. J., Strouse, T. B., Miller, D. S., Brown, L. L., Cross, P. A., & Tenaglia, A. N. (1984). Psychosocial status in chronic illness. *New England Journal of Medicine, 311,* 506–511.

Cassileth, B. R., Zupkis, R. V., Sutton-Smith, K., & March, V. (1980). Information and participation preferences among cancer patients. *Annals of Internal Medicine, 92,* 832–836.

Chiriboga, D. A., & Cutler, L. (1980). Stress and adaptation: Life span perspectives. In L. W. Poon (Ed.), *Aging in the 1980s* (pp. 347–362). Washington, DC: Gerontological Society of America.

Cicirelli, V. G. (1983, August). *Coping behaviors of the elderly in relation to health problems.* Paper presented at the annual meeting of the American Psychological Association, Anaheim, CA.

Cicirelli, V. G. (1987). Locus of control and patient role adjustment of the elderly in acute-care hospitals. *Psychology and Aging, 2,* 138–143. **A**

Coe, R. (1967). Professional perspectives on the aged. *The Gerontologist, 7,* 114–119.

Coe, R. M., Wolinsky, F. D., Miller, D. K., & Prendergast, J. M. (1985). Elderly persons without family support networks and use of health services: A follow-up report on social network relationships. *Research on Aging, 7,* 617–622.

Cohen, F. (1979). Personality, stress and the development of physical illness. In G. C. Stone, F. Cohen, & N. E. Adler (Eds.), *Health Psychology* (pp. 77–111). San Francisco: Jossey-Bass.

Conway, K. (1986). Coping with the stress of medical problems among Black and White elderly. *International Journal of Aging and Human Development, 21,* 39–48.

Costa, P. T., Jr., & McCrae, R. R. (1987). Neuroticism, somatic complaints and disease: Is the bark worse than the bite? *Journal of Personality, 55,* 299–316(a).

Cutrona, C., Russell, D., & Rose, J. (1986). Social support and adaptation to stress by the elderly. *Psychology and Aging, 1,* 47–54. **A**

Davis, K. (1985). Health care policies and the aged: Observations from the United States. In R. H. Binstock & E. Shanas (Eds.), *Handbook of aging and the social sciences* (2nd ed., pp. 727–744). New York: Van Nostrand Reinhold. **A R**

DiMatteo, M. R., & Friedman, H. S. (1982). *Social psychology and medicine*. Boston, MA: Olgeschlager, Gunn & Herin.

Dohrenwend, B. S., & Dohrenwend, B. P. (1974). *Stressful life events: Their nature and effects*. New York: John Wiley.

Eisdorfer, C., & Wilkie, F. (1977). Stress, disease, aging and behavior. In J. E. Birren & K. W. Schaie (Eds.), *Handbook of the psychology of aging (pp. 251–275)*. New York: Van Nostrand Reinhold. **A R**

Elias, M. F., Elias, J. W., & Elias, P. K. (in press). Biological and health influences. In J. E. Birren & K. W. Schaie (Eds.), *Handbook of the Psychology of Aging* (3rd ed.). New York: Van Nostrand Reinhold.

Felton, B. J., & Revenson, T. A. (1984). Coping with chronic illness: A study of illness controllability and the influence of coping strategies on psychological adjustment. *Journal of Consulting and Clinical Psychology, 52*, 343–353. **A**

Felton, B. J., & Revenson, T. A. (1987). Age differences in coping with chronic illness. *Psychology and Aging, 2*(2), 164–170.

Felton, B. J. Revenson, T. A., & Hinrichsen, G. A. (1984). Stress and coping in the explanation of adjustment among chronically ill adults. *Social Science and Medicine, 18*, 889–898.

Ferraro, K. F. (1983). The health consequences of relocation among aged in the community. *Journal of Gerontology, 38*, 90–96.

Fleishman, J. A. (1984). Personality characteristics and coping patterns. *Journal of Health and Social Behavior, 25*, 229–244.

Folkman, S. (1984). Personal control and stress and coping processes: A theoretical analysis. *Journal of Personality and Social Psychology, 46*, 839–852.

Folkman, S., & Lazarus, R. S. (1980). An analysis of coping in a middle-aged community sample. *Journal of Health and Social Behavior, 21*, 219–239.

Folkman S., Lazarus R. S., Dunkel-Schetter, C., DeLongis, A., & Gruen, R. J. (1986). Dynamics of a stressful encounter: Cognitive appraisal, coping and encounter outcomes. *Journal of Personality and Social Psychology, 50*, 992–1003.

Folkman, S., Lazarus, R. S., Pimley, S., & Novacek, J. (1987). Age differences in stress and coping processes. *Psychology and Aging, 2*, 171–184. **A**

Ford, C. V., & Sbordone, R. J. (1980). Attitudes of psychiatrists toward elderly people. *American Journal of Psychiatry, 137*, 571–575.

Friedman, H. S., & Booth-Kewley, S. (1987). The "disease-prone personality": A meta-analytic view of the construct. *American Psychologist, 42*, 539–555.

Fuller, S. S., & Larson, S. B. (1980). Life events, emotional support, and health of older people. *Research in Nursing and Health, 3*, 81–89.

George, L. K., & Landerman, R. (1984). Health and subjective well-being: A replicated secondary data analysis. *International Journal of Aging and Human Development, 19*, 133–156. **A**

Greene, M. G., Hoffman, S., Charon, R., & Adelman, R. (1987). Psychosocial concerns in the medical encounter: A comparison of the interactions of doctors with their old and young patients. *The Gerontologist, 27*(2), 164–168. **A**

Harris, D. M., & Guten, G. (1979). Health-protective behavior: An exploratory study. *Journal of Health and Social Behavior, 20*, 17–29.

Haug, M. R. (1979). Doctor–patient relationships and the older patient. *Journal of Gerontology, 34*(6), 852–860.

Haug, M. R. (1981). Age and medical care utilization patterns. *Journal of Gerontology, 36*, 103–111.

Haug, M. R., & Lavin, B. (1981). Practitioners or patient: Who's in charge? *Journal of Health and Social Behavior, 22*, 12–29.

Haug, M. R., & Ory, M. G. (1987). Issues in elderly patient–provider interactions. *Research on Aging, 9*(1), 3–44. **A R**

Healthy People (1979). *The Surgeon General's report on health promotion and disease prevention* (DHEW Publication No. PHS 79–550 71). Washington, DC: U.S. Government Printing Office.

Heller, K., & Swindle, R. W. (1983). Social networks, perceived social support, and coping with stress. In R. D. Felner, L. A. Jason, J. N. Moritsugu, & S. S. Farber (Eds.), *Preventive psychology: Theory, research, and practice* (pp. 87–103). New York: Pergamon Press.

Holmes, T. H., & Masuda, M. (1974). Life change and illness susceptibility. In B. S. Dohrenwend & B. P. Dohrenwend (Eds.), *Stressful life events: Their nature and effects* (pp. 45–72). New York: John Wiley. A

House, J. S., Robbins, C. A., & Metzner, H. L. (1982). The association of social relationships and activities with mortality: Prospective evidence from the Tecumseh Community Health Study. *American Journal of Epidemiology, 116*, 123–140.

Howard, J. H., Rechnitzer, P. A., Cunningham, D. A., & Donner, A. P. (1986). Change in Type A behavior a year after retirement. *The Gerontologist, 26*, 643–649.

Ilfeld, F. (1980). Coping styles of Chicago adults: Description. *Journal of Human Stress, 6*, 2–10.

Irion, J. C., & Blanchard-Fields, F. (1987). A cross-sectional comparison of adaptive coping in adulthood. *Journal of Gerontology, 41*, 502–504.

Johnson, C., & Catalano, D. (1983). A longitudinal study of family support to impaired elderly. *The Gerontologist, 23*, 612–618.

Kanner, A. D., Coyne, J. C., Schaefer, C., & Lazarus, R. (1981). Comparison of two modes of stress measurement: Daily hassles and uplifts versus major life events. *Journal of Behavioral Medicine, 4*, 1–39.

Kaplan, G. A., & Camach, T. (1983). Perceived health and mortality: A nine-year follow-up of the human population laboratory cohort. *American Journal of Epidemiology, 117*, 292–304.

Kart, C., Metress, E., & Metress, J. (1988). *Aging, health and society.* Boston, MA: Jones & Bartlett.

Kastenbaum, R. J. (1982). Healthy, wealthy, and wise? Health care provision for the elderly from a psychological perspective. In G. S. Sanders & J. Suls (Ed.s), *Social psychology of health and illness* (pp. 307–326). Hillsdale NJ: Lawrence Erlbaum.

Katz, J. L., Waines, H., Gallagher, T. F., & Hellman, L. (1977). Stress, distress and ego defenses: Psycho-endocrine response to impending breast tumor biopsy. In A. Monat & R. S. Lazarus (Eds.), *Stress and coping.* New York: Columbia University Press.

Katz, S. (1983). Assessing self-maintenance: Activities of daily living, mobility, and instrumental activities of daily living. *Journal of the American Geriatrics Society, 31*, 721–727.

Keeler, E. B., Solomon, D. H., Beck, J. C., Mendenhall, R. C., & Kane, R. L. (1982). Effect of patient age on duration of medical encounters with physicians. *Medical Care, 20*, 1101–1108.

Keyes, K., Bisno, B., Richardson, J., & Marston, A. (1987). Age differences in coping, behavioral dysfunction and depression following colostomy surgery. *The Gerontologist, 27*, 182–184.

Kobasa, S. C. (1982). The hardy personality: Toward a social psychology of stress and health. In J. Suls & G. Sanders (Eds.), *Social psychology of health and illness* (pp. 3–32). Hillsdale, NJ: Erlbaum.

Kovar, M. G. (1987). Health assessment. In G. L. Maddox (Ed.), *The Encyclopedia of Aging* (pp. 302–305). New York: Springer.

Krantz, D., & Schulz, R. (1980). Personal control and health: Some applications to crises of middle and old age. In A. Baum & J. Singer (Eds.), *Advances in environmental psychology* (Vol. 2, pp. 23–57). New York: Academic Press.

Krause, N. (1987). Satisfaction with social support and self-rated health in older adults. *The Gerontologist, 27,* 301–308.

Kvitek, S. D. B., Shaver, B. J., Blood, H., & Shepard, K. F. (1986). Age bias: Physical therapists and older patients. *Journal of Gerontology, 41,* 706–709.

Langer, E. J., & Rodin, J. (1976). The effects of choice and enhanced personal responsibility for the aged: A field experiment in an institutional setting. *Journal of Personality and Social Psychology, 34,* 191–198. **A**

Lawton, M. P. (1981). An ecological view of living arrangements. *The Gerontologist, 21,* 59–66.

Lawton, M. P. (1983). Environments and other determinants of well-being in the aged. *The Gerontologist, 23,* 349–357.

Lawton, M. P. (1985). Housing and living environments of older people. In R. H. Binstock & E. Shanas (Eds.), *Handbook of aging and the social sciences* (2nd ed., pp. 450–478). New York: Von Nostrand Reinhold. **A R**

Lazarus, R. S., & DeLongis, A. (1983). Psychological stress and coping in aging. *American Psychologist, 38,* 245–254.

Lazarus, R. S., & Folkman, S. (1984). *Stress, appraisal, and coping.* New York: Springer.

Lemke, S., & Moos, R. H. (1981). The suprapersonal environments of sheltered care settings. *Journal of Gerontology, 36,* 233–243.

Leventhal, E. A. (1984). Aging and the perception of illness. *Research on Aging, 6*(1), 119–135. **A**

Lieberman, M. A., & Tobin, S. S. (1983). *The experience of old age.* New York: Basic Books.

Linn, B. S., & Linn, M. W. (1980). Objective and self-assessed health in the old and very old. *Social Science and Medicine, 149,* 311–315.

Lowenthal, M. F., & Haven, C. (1968). Interaction and adaptation: Intimacy as a critical variable. *American Sociological Review, 33*(1), 20–30. **A**

Lowenthal, M. F., Thurnher, M., & Chiriboga, D. (1975). *Four stages of life.* San Francisco: Jossey-Bass.

Lynn, T. N., Duncan, R., Naughton, J. P., Brandt, E. N., Wulff, J., & Wolf, S. (1967). Prevalence of evidence of prior myocardial infarction, hypertension, diabetes and obesity in three neighboring communities in Pennsylvania. *The American Journal of the Medical Sciences, 88* (October), 385–391.

Maddox, G. L. (Editor-in-Chief). (1987). *The encyclopedia of aging.* New York: Springer. **A R**

Mages, N. L., & Mendelsohn, G. A. (1979), Effects of cancer on patients' lives: A personological approach. In G. C. Stone, F. Cohen, & N. E. Adler (Eds.), *Health psychology* (pp 255–284). San Francisco: Jossey-Bass.

Magnani, L. (1986). The relationship of hardiness and self-perceived health to activity in a group of independently functioning older adults. Unpublished doctoral dissertation, Adelphi University, Garden City, NY. Dissertation Abstracts International, *46*(12).

Matthews, K. A. (1982). Psychological perspectives on the Type A behavior pattern. *Psychological Bulletin, 91,* 293–323.

Matthews, K. A. (1988). Coronary heart disease and Type A behaviors: Update as an alternate to the Booth-Kewley and Friedman (1987) quantitative review. *Psychological Bulletin, 104,* 373–380(a).

Matthews, K. A, & Haynes, S. S. (1986). Type A behavior pattern and coronary disease risk. *American Journal of Epidemiology, 123,* 923–960.

McCrae, R. R. (1982). Age differences in the use of coping mechanisms. *Journal of Gerontology, 37,* 454–460. **A**

McCrae, R. R. (1984). Situational determinants of coping responses: Loss, threat, and challenge. *Journal of Personality and Social Psychology, 46,* 919–928.

Minkler, M. (1981). Research on the health effects of retirement: An uncertain legacy. *Journal of Health and Social Behavior, 22*(2), 117–129. **A**

Moos, R. H. (1980). Specialized living environments for older people: A conceptual framework. *Journal of Social Issues, 36,* 75–94.

Moos, R. H. (1982). Coping with acute health crises. In T. Millon, C. Green, & R. Meagher (Eds.), *Handbook of clinical health psychology* (pp. 129–152). New York: Plenum Press.

Mossey, J. M., & Shapiro, E. (1982). Self-rated health: A predictor of mortality among the elderly. *American Journal of Public Health, 72*(8), 800–808.

Muhlenkamp, A. F., Gross, L. D., & Flood, M. A. (1975). Perception of life change events by the elderly. *Nursing Research, 24*(2), 109–113.

National Center for Health Statistics (1976). Health characteristics of persons with chronic activity limitations, United States, 1974. *Vital and health statistics* (Series 10, No. 112). Rockville, MD: U.S. Department of Health, Education, and Welfare.

National Center for Health Statistics (1979). Current estimates from the health interview survey: U.S.—1978. *Vital and health statistics* (Series 10, No. 130). Washington, DC: U.S. Government Printing Office.

National Center for Health Statistics (1983). Americans needing help to function at home. *Advance data from vital and health statistics* (No. 92). Hyattsville, MD: Public Health Service.

National Center for Health Statistics (1986). Health promotion data for the 1990 objectives. Estimates from the National Health Interview Survey of Health Promotion and Disease Preventions, United States, 1985. *Advance data from vital and health statistics* (No. 126, (PHS) 86-1250). Hyattsville, MD: Public Health Service.

Neugarten, B. L. (1979). Time, age, and the life cycle. *The American Journal of Psychiatry, 136,* 887–894.

Newman, S. J. (1976). Housing adjustments of the disabled elderly. *The Gerontologist, 16,* 312–317.

Norris, F. H., & Murrell, S. A. (1987). Transitory impact of life-event stress on psychological symptoms in older adults. *Journal of Health and Social Behavior, 28,* 197–211.

Okun, M. A., Stock, W. A., Haring, M. J., & Witter, R. A. (1984). The social activity/subjective well-being relation: A quantitative synthesis. *Research on Aging, 6,* 45–65.

Ory, M. G., Williams, T. F., Emr, M., Lebowitz, B., Rabins, P., Salloway, J., Sluss-Radbaugh, T., Wolff, E., & Zarit, S. (1985). Families, informal supports, and Alzheimer's disease: Current research and future agendas. *Research on Aging, 7,* 623–644.

Palmore, E. (1970). Health practices and illness among the aged. *The Gerontologist, 10,* 313–316.

Palmore, E. (1981). *Social patterns in normal aging.* Durham, NC: Duke University Press.

Pearlin, L. I., & Schooler, C. (1978). The structure of coping. *Journal of Health and Social Behavior, 19,* 2–21.

Rabkin, J. G., & Struening, E. L. (1976). Life events, stress and illness. *Science, 194,* 1013–1020.

Rakowski, W. (1984). Health psychology and late life. *Research on Aging, 6*(4), 593–620. **A R**

Revenson, T. A. (1987). *Compassionate stereotypes or veridical perceptions? Rheumatologists' views of elderly patients.* Unpublished manuscript.

Revenson, T. A., & Felton, B. J. (1985, November). *Perceived stress in chronic illness: A comparative analysis of four diseases.* Paper presented at the annual meeting of the Gerontological Society of America, New Orleans:

Revenson, T. A., Wollman, C., & Felton, B. J. (1983). Social supports as stress buffers for adult cancer patients. *Psychosomatic Medicine, 45,* 321–331.

Revicki, D. A., & Mitchell, J. (1986). Social support factor structure in the elderly. *Research on Aging, 8,* 232–248.

Rodin, J., (1980). Managing the stress of aging: The role of control and coping. In S. Levine & H. Ursin (Eds.), *Coping and health* (pp. 171–202). New York: Plenum Press.

Rodin, J. (1986). Aging and health: Effects of the sense of control. *Science, 233,* 1271–1276. **A**

Rodin, J., & Langer, E. J. (1977). Long-term effects of control-relevant intervention with the institutionalized aged. *Journal of Personality and Social Psychology, 35,* 897–902. **A**

Rowland, K. F. (1977) Environmental events predicting death for the elderly. *Psychological Bulletin, 84,* 349–372.

Rundall, T. G., & Evashwick, C. (1982). Social network and help-seeking among the elderly. *Research on Aging, 4,* 205–226.

Schulz, R. (1976). Effects of control and predictability on the physical and psychological well-being of the institutionalized aged. *Journal of Personality and Social Psychology, 33,* 563–573.

Schulz, R., & Hanusa, B. H. (1980). Experimental social gerontology: A social psychological perspective. *Journal of Social Issues, 36,* 30–46.

Seligman, M. E. P. (1975). *Helplessness: On depression, development and death.* San Francisco: W.H. Freeman.

Selye, H. (1965). *The stress of life* (rev. ed.). New York: McGraw-Hill.

Shanas, E., & Maddox, G. L. (1985). Health, health resources and the utilization of care. In R. H. Binstock & E. Shanas (Eds.), *Handbook of aging and the social sciences* (2nd ed., pp. 696–726). New York: Van Nostrand Reinhold. **A R**

Shanas, E., Townsend, P., Wedderburn, D., Friis, H., Milhoj, P., & Stenouwer, J. (1968). The psychology of health. In B. Neugarten (Ed.), *Middle age and aging* (pp. 212–219). Chicago: University of Chicago Press.

Siegler, I. C. (1989). Developmental Health Psychology. In M. Storandt & G. R. VandenBos. *The Adult Years: Continuity and Change* (pp. 115–142).

Siegler, I. C., & Costa, P. T., Jr. (1985). Health behavior relationships. In J. E. Birren & K. W. Schaie (Eds.), *Handbook of the psychology of aging* (2nd ed., pp. 144–166). New York: Van Nostrand Reinhold. **A R**

Solomon, K., & Vickers, R. (1979). Attitudes of health workers toward old people. *Journal of the American Geriatric Society, 27,* 186–191.

Spence, D., Feigenbaum, E., Fitzgerald, R., & Roth, J. (1968). Medical student attitudes toward the geriatric patient. *Journal of the American Geriatric Society, 16,* 976–983.

Stenback, A., Kumpulainen, M., & Vauhkonen, M. L. (1978). Illness and health behavior in septuagenarians. *Journal of Gerontology, 33,* 57–61.

Stone, A. A., Reed, B. R., & Neale, J. M. (1987). Changes in daily event frequency precede episodes of physical symptoms. *Journal of Human Stress, 13,* 70–74.

Stout, C., Morrow, J., Brandt, E. N., Jr., & Wolf, S. (1964). Unusually low incidence of death from myocardial infarction. *Journal of the American Medical Association, 188,* 845–849.

Thoits, P. A. (1982). Conceptual, methodological, and theoretical problems in studying social support as a buffer against life stress. *Journal of Health and Social Behavior, 23,* 145–149.

Thoits, P. A. (1983). Dimensions of life events that influence psychological distress: An evaluation and synthesis of the literature. In H. B. Kaplan (Ed.), *Psychosocial stress: Trends in theory and research* (pp. 33–103). New York: Academic Press. **A**

Thoits, P. A. (1986). Social support as coping assistance. *Journal of Consulting and Clinical Psychology, 54*, 416–423.

Thompson, L. W., Breckenridge, J. N., Gallagher, D., & Peterson, J. (1984). Effects of bereavement on self-perceptions of physical health in elderly widows and widowers. *Journal of Gerontology, 39*, 309–314.

Umberson, D. (1987). Family status and health behaviors: Social control as a dimension of social integration. *Journal of Health and Social Behavior, 28*, 306–319. **A**

U.S. Department of Health and Human Services (1981). *Health United States 1981* (DHHS Publication No. (PHS) 82-1232). Washington, DC: U.S. Government Printing Office.

U.S. Department of Health and Human Services (1983). *Americans needing help to function at home.* DHHS Publication No. (PHS) 83-1250. Washington, DC: U.S. Government Printing Office.

Verbrugge, L. M. (1984). Women and men: Mortality and health of older people. In M. W. Riley, B. B. Hess, & K. Bond (Eds.), *Aging in society* (pp. 139–174). Hillsdale, NJ: Lawrence Erlbaum. **A R**

Veroff, J., Kulka, R. A., & Douvan, E. (1981). *Mental health in America.* New York: Basic Books.

Wallston, K. A., & Wallston, B. S. (1982). Who is responsible for your health? The construct of health locus of control. In A. Baum, S. E. Taylor, & J. E. Singer (Eds.), *Handbook of psychology and health* (Vol. IV, pp. 65–98). Hillsdale, NJ: Lawrence Erlbaum.

Wan, T. T. H. (1984). Health consequences of major role losses in later life: A panel study. *Research on Aging, 6*(4), 469–489. **A**

Wan, T. T. H., & Arling, G. (1983). Differential use of health services among disabled elderly. *Research on Aging, 5*, 411–431. **A**

Wentowski, G. J. (1985). Older women's perceptions of great-grandmotherhood. *The Gerontologist, 25*, 593–596.

Westbrook, M. T., & Viney, L. L. (1983). Age and sex differences in patients' reactions to illness. *Journal of Health and Social Behavior, 24*(4), 313–324.

Wiley, J. A., & Camacho, T. C. (1980). Life-style and future health: Evidence from the Alameda County study. *Preventive Medicine, 9*, 1–21.

Wilson, J. F., & Hafferty, F. W. (1980). Changes in attitudes toward the elderly one year after a seminar on aging and health. *Journal of Medical Education, 55*, 993–999.

Wilson, J. F., & Hafferty, F. W. (1983). Long-term effects of a seminar on health and aging for first-year medical students. *The Gerontologist, 23*, 319–324.

Wilson, R. W., & Elinson, J. (1981). National survey of personal health practices and consequences: Background, conceptual issues, and selected findings. *Public health reports, 96*, 218–225.

Wolinsky, F. D., & Coe, R. M. (1984). Physician and hospital utilization among noninstitutionalized elderly adults: An analysis of the Health Interview Survey. *Journal of Gerontology, 39*, 334–341.

Wolinsky, F. D., Coe, R. M., Miller, D. K., Prendergast, J. M., Creel, M. J., & Chavez, M. N. (1983). Health services utilization among the noninstitutionalized elderly. *Journal of Health and Social Behavior, 24*, 325–336.

World Health Organization (1958). Constitution of the World Health Organization, Annex J. In *The first ten years of the World Health Organization.* Geneva, Switzerland: World Health Organization.

Wyler, A. R., Masuda, M., & Holmes, T.H. (1971). Magnitude of life events and seriousness of illness. *Psychosomatic Medicine, 33*, 115–120.

Zautra, A., & Hempel, A. (1984). Subjective well-being and physical health: A narrative literature review with suggestions for future research. *International Journal of Aging and Human Development, 19*, 95–110.

Annotated Bibliography

Antonucci, T. C., & Akiyama, H. (1987). Social networks in adult life and a preliminary examination of the convoy model. *Journal of Gerontology, 42*, 519–527.

This article presents descriptive data on the social support networks of older adults using a national sample (N = 718) of adults aged 50 and older. Self-report information indicated the numbers of network members, their closeness to the respondent, the type of relation (and other structural characteristics), and the function served by each relationship for the older person. Respondents' self-reports of their social networks showed that their networks consisted of an average of 8.9 members and there were no significant differences in network size by age. Compared with the oldest age group (ages 75 through 95), the youngest age group (ages 50 through 64) was more likely to have network members who were younger, who had been known a shorter period of time, who lived closer, and who were in contact more frequently. Network members to whom the respondent felt "so close that it [was] hard to imagine life without them" were more likely to be family members than was true of other network members. Provision of support decreased with age, but there was no age difference in the amount of support received. Fewer network members provided support to the oldest group suggesting that, although there was no change in network size with age, those providing supports to older convoy members were "selectively limited."

E *U *G

Berkman, L. F. (1983). The assessment of social networks and social support in the elderly. *Journal of the American Geriatrics Society, 31*, 743–749.

This article reviews epidemiologic work on the role of social relations in the prediction of health of the elderly. Relying on data from the Alameda County study, this review evaluates the evidence for the role of social networks in mortality, and considers what facets of social relationships are most important for health. HPL data show marital ties, church and group membership, and social contacts with friends and family all have a cumulative impact on mortality. Berkman proposes that the char-

Notations following the reference citation indicate the following: **T**, a theoretical article; **E**, an empirical article; **C**, a classic in the field; **R**, a major review of the area (see chart at the end of this module). *U means that the article is recommended for undergraduate assigned reading; *G means that the article is recommended for graduate assigned reading.

acteristics of social networks that are of particular importance in predicting health are size, frequency of contact, density, intimacy, durability, geographic dispersion, and reciprocity. Berkman points to age differences in social networks (i.e., people over 70 score lower on the HPL social network index) but notes that the statistical relationship between social isolation and mortality is not different in younger and older groups of adults. Among the research needs identified are longitudinal descriptions of social networks, studies evaluating the link between social networks and specific illnesses, and research to discover the diverse types of circumstances under which older men and women derive adequate social support.

T (E) *U

Branch, L. G., & Jette, A. M. (1984). Personal health practices and mortality among the elderly. *American Journal of Public Health, 74,* 1126–1129.

The association of several health practices—physical activity, cigarette smoking, hours of sleep, alcohol consumption, and number of meals per day—with 5-year mortality rates were examined among people aged 65 and older with data from the Massachusetts Health Care Panel Study. Of 1,625 noninstitutionalized adults aged 65+, identified through a statewide probability sample in 1976, 275 (22 percent) had died by the 1980 follow-up data collection. Bivariate associations with mortality showed no relationship with health practices for females; for men, slowed-down activity was related to over twice the risk of mortality 5 years later. In multivariate analyses, age, health status, and income were all significantly associated with mortality among women but income was unrelated to mortality among men. After adjusting for these factors, only one health practice—never having smoked—was related to lower mortality, and only for women. None of the other health practices were related to mortality for men or women. These findings suggest that the relationship found between health practices and mortality for the young and middle-aged may not be generalizable to the elderly.

E *G

Brown, J. S., & McCreedy, M. (1986). The hale elderly: Health behavior and its correlates. *Research in Nursing and Health, 9,* 317–329.

This article describes the health behaviors, associated sociodemographic predictors, and health status of respondents, aged 55 years of age and older. Data were obtained through a mail survey from 386 elders (138 men, 248 women) from among 600 randomly selected members of a Northwest urban senior citizens' community. Measures included the Health Protective Behavior (HPB) score of 30 behaviors and a Health Status Index of four health indicators (Harris & Guten, 1979). The elders performed an average of 17.2 behaviors (SD = 4.9), most frequently practicing proper nutrition, adequate sleep, and not smoking. HPB scores were slightly higher for women but did not vary with age; socioeconomic status and marital status exerted small effects on health behavior. Health behaviors of males were predicted best by marital status; of females, by occupational status. HPB scores were not related to overall health status, but were weakly related to perceived health. Poorer health was related to lack of exercise and poor eating habits, but not to smoking, drinking, or weight-watching habits. In light of lack of association between health behaviors and health status, past health behavior may be more critical to current health status of elders.

R *G

Cicirelli, V. G. (1987). Locus of control and patient role adjustment of the elderly in acute-care hospitals. *Psychology and Aging*, 2(2), 138–143.

This field study used the high-constraint setting of an acute-care hospital to test the hypothesis that external locus of control is significantly related to greater adjustment among elderly patients. The sample consisted of 105 men and women, aged 60 to 93 (M = 72). Interview data provided responses to the Multidimensional Health Locus of Control scales (internality, powerful others, and chance) and constraint. Two nurses (responses averaged) provided ratings of each patient on eight items measuring patient role adjustment. Patients' self-reports of distress due to loss of independence were taken as evidence of degree of constraint. Correlations between locus of control and patient role adjustment indicated that in a high constraint environment, these elderly patients who believe powerful others have control had the best patient role adjustment.

E *G

Cutrona, C., Russell, D. & Rose, J. (1986). Social support and adaptation to stress by the elderly. *Psychology and Aging*, 1, 47–54.

This article describes a prospective study of the effects of stress and social support on the mental health and physical health of 50 elderly senior center members. Assessments at two points in time showed stability in most measures of stress, social support, physical health, and psychological well-being over 6 months. Analyses of the effects of stress and social support on physical and mental health showed physical health but not mental health to be predicted by social support. A stress-buffering interaction between stress and social support was related to mental health after 6 months, with the provisions of guidance and a sense of reliable alliance the most critical types of support provision. Individuals who were in better mental health at the initial assessment experienced fewer stressful events and higher levels of social support over the subsequent 6-month period.

E *U *G

Davis, K. (1985). Health care policies and the aged: Observations from the United States. In R. H. Binstock & E. Shanas (Eds.), *Handbook of aging and the social sciences* (2nd ed., pp. 727–744). New York: Van Nostrand Reinhold.

This chapter outlines the major health problems faced by the elderly and current health care policies to deal with them, with particular emphasis on the severely impaired elderly. The chapter provides data on health care needs among the elderly, trends in mortality, and health service utilization rates. The current U.S. health care system is described in detail, with lengthy sections on health care financing mechanisms, for example, Medicare and Medicaid. Our current health care system is described as a mix of public and privately funded services, delivered in multiple settings, financed by multiple sources, with a tendency to provide medical services in lieu of income support, housing, or social support services. The chapter concludes with guidelines for future health care policies for the aged, including a National Health plan and a more coordinated package of long-term care services.

R *G

Eisdorfer, C., & Wilkie, F. (1977). Stress, disease, aging and behavior. In J. E. Birren & K. W. Schaie (Eds.), *Handbook of the psychology of aging* (pp. 251–275). New York: Van Nostrand Reinhold.

The concepts of stress and disease play elemental roles in physiological and psychological theories of aging. This chapter focuses on the interrelations among stress, disease, and aging with two emphases: (1) the role of psychological and psychophysical stress in the development and progression of illness, and (2) the individual and joint effects of stress and disease on behavior, specifically performance tasks. Studies involving animal and human research are reviewed to support the hypothesis that patterns of behavior, specifically performance on tests of intellectual and cognitive functioning, are related to stress and disease processes independent of aging processes. Coronary heart disease, prevalent in middle and late life, is used to illustrate the complex relationships among stress, personality, psychophysiological processes, and illness.

R

Felton, B. J., & Revenson, T. A. (1984). Coping with chronic illness: A study of illness controllability and the influence of coping strategies on psychological adjustment. *Journal of Consulting and Clinical Psychology,* **52, 343–353.**

Longitudinal data on the coping strategies used by middle-aged and older adults faced with one of four different chronic illnesses ($N = 151$) were used to evaluate the role of coping in the explanation of psychological adjustment. The study distinguished between illnesses that offer few opportunities for control (rheumatoid arthritis and cancer) and those more responsive to individual and medical efforts at control (hypertension and diabetes) and evaluated the emotional consequences of two coping strategies, information seeking and wish-fulfilling fantasy. Information seeking proved to have salubrious effects on adjustment and wish-fufilling fantasy had deleterious consequences. Contrary to expectation, neither strategy's effects were modified by illness controllability: information seeking, an action-oriented strategy, was no more advantageous for patients whose illnesses afforded some controllability than for those whose illnesses were not amenable to control. Analyses of the direction of causation between coping and adjustment suggest that wish-fulfilling fantasy is linked to poor adjustment in a mutually reinforcing causal cycle. The modesty of the effects of coping, however, demand replication of results to confirm the conclusions drawn here.

E *G

Folkman, S., Lazarus, R.S., Pimley, S., & Novacek, J. (1987). Age differences in stress and coping processes. *Psychology and Aging,* **2, 171–184.**

This cross-sectional study compared younger and older community-dwelling adults in their experience of daily hassles and of coping with them. The younger group was composed of 75 couples (*M* age women

39.6; *M* age men 41.4). The older group (*n* = 141) had a mean age of 68.9 years for women and 68.3 years for men. In a home interview, each individual indicated the coping strategies he or she had used with respect to one of the hassles the individual reported on the Hassles Scale. The younger group experienced more hassles in the areas of finances, work, home maintenance, personal life, and family and friends than did their older counterparts; they also appraised their hassles as more changeable than the older group. Age differences in coping strategies were striking and consistent. Younger people used proportionately more confrontive coping, planful problem solving, and social support and were less likely to employ distancing, acceptance of responsibility, and positive reappraisal than older people. Overall, the findings tend to support a developmental interpretation: Given that older adults face more unchangeable situations, the coping patterns that emerge are age appropriate.

E *U *G

George, L. K., & Landerman, R. (1984). Health and subjective well-being: A replicated secondary data analysis. *International Journal of Aging and Human Development, 19*, 133–156.

This article uses secondary data analysis to look at the relationship between health and subjective well-being; it presents, as well, a discussion of the strengths and weaknesses of replicated secondary data analysis and points out strategies to follow in order to encompass both empirical and conceptual replications in a secondary data analysis effort. Seven data sets were selected to examine the relation between self-rated health and subjective well-being. The zero-order correlations found ranged from .03 to .48; the 95% confidence interval for the relationship was between .29 and .35. Variations in the sizes of the correlations were due, in part, to differences in the measures used. Using 10 variables (sociodemographic, social support, and social activity variables) as controls in analyses across the data sets, results showed the relationship between health and well-being to be robust net of multiple controls. Physician-assessed health showed weaker relationships with subjective well-being and these correlations did not remain significant net of theoretically relevant covariates. The relation between health and subjective well-being was found to be conditoned by age and stronger for measures of negative rather than positive affect.

E *G

Greene, M. G., Hoffman, S., Charon, R., & Adelman, R. (1987). Psychosocial concerns in the medical encounter: A comparison of the interactions of doctors with their old and young patients. *The Gerontologist, 27*(2), 164–168.

Doctor-patient interviews were analyzed for differences between younger and older patients. It was hypothesized that older patients would raise more psychosocial concerns with their physicians, but that doctors would raise those issues less frequently with older patients and be less responsive to older patients about these issues. Five physicians (all less than 40 years old) interviewed four "older" (65 +) and four "younger" (45 or younger) patients each during follow-up visits. Age groups were matched for sociodemographic characteristics, and patients' conditions were rated as "severe" or "not severe." Audiotapes of the interviews, rated for content and process (questioning, support, informing), showed that psychosocial issues were raised more, by *both* patient and doctor, in the younger patient interactions. As hypothesized, physicians raised fewer psychosocial concerns with older patients, and were less responsive to them when older patients raised them than when younger patients did so.

E *U

Haug, M. R., & Ory, M. G. (1987). Issues in elderly patient-provider interactions. *Research on Aging, 9* (1), 3–44.

This article reviews major issues relevant to understanding the implications of provider–patient interactions for elderly patients. The study of provider–patient interactions is central to a health psychology of aging not only because older people are heavy users of health services but also because the elderly individual has a special need for respect and dignity in these encounters. Given the paucity of studies on patient–provider interaction with elderly samples, the authors draw on existing findings with varied age groups to speculate on those effects of patient–provider relationships that would be particularly critical for elderly populations. Two major areas are addressed: (1) the process of provider–patient interactions, which includes communication issues and congruence between patient expectations and the reality of the medical visit, and (2) the outcome of those interactions, which includes discussion of compliance with treatment regimens, patient satisfaction, and continued utilization of health care services. The authors suggest that one look at three components of patient–provider interactions: the provider (in terms of gender, stereotyping, communication style), the patient (cohort influences, health attitudes and beliefs, symptoms), and the context of care (i.e., the type of health care setting). The majority of research has focused on the physician as the health care provider and on interactions in outpatient settings. The authors suggest that important research questions lie in the effects of patients' gender, race, and extreme old age on their interactions with care providers, as well as the influence new forms of care (e.g., HMOs) will have.

R *U *G

**Holmes, T. H., & Masuda, M. (1974). Life change and illness suscepti-
bility. In B. S. Dohrenwend & B. P. Dohrenwend (Eds.), *Stressful life
events: Their nature and effects* (pp. 45–72). New York: Wiley.**

This report describes the development of one of the first, but still widely used, measures of stressful life events, the Social Readjustment Rating Scale (SRSS) and its use in early (1967–1972) studies of stress and illness. Interviews and questionnaires—with an unspecified sample—generated 43 life events that would require adaptive or coping behavior. These events were then rated by a heterogeneous sample of convenience of 394 subjects, according to the relative degree of readjustment necessitated by their occurrence. The ratings, with high consensus within the sample (correlations averaging .94 between discrete groups), resulted in a rank ordering and rating of the events which became the Schedule of Recent Experience (SRE). Two successful replications of the ratings are described, as well as cross-cultural studies indicating a high degree of similarity (correlations of .72 -.89). Finally, retrospective and prospective studies using the SRE and describing its relationship to health are presented. Overall, greater stress scores are related to a higher incidence of symptoms and illnesses, and greater illness severity.

E C *G

**Langer, E. J., & Rodin, J. (1976). The effects of choice and enhanced
personal responsibility for the aged: A field experiment in an institutional setting. *Journal of Personality and Social Psychology, 34*, 191–
198.**

This article describes a landmark study of the effects of enhanced personal responsibility and choice on a group of nursing home residents. A field experiment was undertaken on the notion that the debilitated condition of many of the aged residing in institutions was, at least in part, a result of living in a relatively decision-free environment and thus a potentially reversible condition. An experimental group ($N = 47$) of residents was given a communication emphasizing their responsibility for themselves; a comparison group ($N = 44$) was given a communication stressing staff's responsibility for them. To bolster the communication, residents in the experimental group were given the freedom to make choices and the responsibility of caring for a plant rather than having decisions made and the plant taken care of for them by the staff, as was true of the comparison group. Questionnaire ratings by residents and nurses and behavioral measures showed a significant improvement for the experimental group over the comparison group on alertness, active participation, and a general sense of well-being 3 weeks after the intervention.

E C *U *G

Lawton, M. P. (1985). Housing and living environments of older people. In R. H. Binstock & E. Shanas (Eds.), *Handbook of aging and the social sciences* (2nd ed., pp. 450–478). New York: Van Nostrand Reinhold.

This chapter reviews the literature on residential arrangements of the elderly and relates current knowledge in this area to policy issues. The chapter is organized around the central theme of the older adult's stance toward the environment—primarily, whether that stance is a proactive or a passive stance. Thus Lawton presents a model of residential decision making that organizes the literature on moving versus staying, the occurrence of amenity moves and assistance moves, environmental push, involuntary relocation, the search for housing, the effects of residential relocation and remaining in place. The chapter discusses environmental gerontology and public policy, outlining housing policy needs, constraints on fulfillment of those needs, feasible policy directions for housing services in place, relocation assistance, and housing choices. Though health is not a central focus of any section of this chapter, health is seen as playing a key role in determining what types of residential decisions are made by older adults, and is an important criterion for evaluating housing adequacy and the quality of residential decisions made.

R *G

Leventhal, E. A. (1984). Aging and the perception of illness. *Research on Aging*, 6(1), 119–135.

This article describes two studies assessing age differences in illness perceptions based on a model of cognitive and emotional representations of illness. In Study 1, 174 subjects (77 male, 97 female) ranging in age from 20 to 75+ rated 20 illnesses on a number of adjective scales. Few age differences were found in cognitive representations of illness, that is, causes, consequences, identity, and time line. A decrease with age was found on the emotional dimensions of anger, fear, and shame, although fear of cancer remained constant across age groups. Willingness to alter diet declined with age except in relation to ulcer and diabetes. Study 2 utilized open-ended pilot interviews with 32 members of a coalition for the aging aged 50 to 80. While ascribing generally positive meanings to aging, respondents cited fatigue and changes in appearance, cognitive abilities, and health as signs of aging in themselves and others. The positive perceptions of these older people may be due to their continued good health, making future illness seem less likely. It is also suggested that their decreased fear of illness may be due to increased experience in coping with illness as a function of aging.

E *G

Lowenthal, M. F., & Haven, C. (1968). Interaction and adaptation: Intimacy as a critical variable. *American Sociological Review, 33*(1), 20–30.

This study examined whether level of social interaction, specifically presence or absence of a confidant, affected morale and mental health status among a community sample of elderly (60+). A strong and clear relationship was found between presence of a confidant and positive adjustment. Respondents experiencing increases in social interaction yet lacking a confidant were more likely to be depressed than those who had a confidant but whose level of general social interaction decreased. Those who had retired or become widowed within 7 years but who had a confidant expressed more satisfaction than those still married or working but lacking a confidant. This effect was not true for those suffering from serious illness, due perhaps to the increased strain of illness on closer relationships. Women were more likely to have a confidant than men; married people were most likely to have a confidant and single people least. Those of higher socioeconomic status were more likely to have a confidant, especially among men. Men were more likely than women to name their spouse as confidant. Having a confidant indeed serves as a buffer against social and role losses. Having at least one stable and intimate relationship appears to be a better predictor of positive morale and mental health than sheer level of social interaction.

E C *U *G

Maddox, G. L. (Ed.-in-Chief). (1987). *The encyclopedia of aging.* New York: Springer.

The following sections included in *The Encyclopedia of Aging* are relevant to the study of psychology and health in later life. These sections are brief, to-the-point treatments of the issues. "Geriatric Medicine" describes social and psychological aspects of patient care, diagnosis, medical assessment (including functional ability, recognition of symptoms of mental impairment, and consideration of the patient's social network), rehabilitation, and medical effects. In the section titled "Health Assessment" the WHO definition of health is presented, followed by standard measures of health status in the elderly and other instruments developed for health research. The relationship between disease status, functional health, and self-reported health is addressed. The value of "Health Beliefs" as predictors of health behavior is considered. "Health Care: Organization, Use and Finance" presents useful charts of statistical data in many areas, for example, health care expenditures, utilization in short-stay hospitals. The section on "Health Care Policy" discusses health care financing in the United States since the American Revolution in the context of the types of illnesses faced by elderly individuals. It concludes with a discussion of how current health care trends will affect the health care needs of the elderly in the future and suggests avenues for policy reform.

R Selected entries: *U *G

McCrae, R. R. (1982). Age differences in the use of coping mechanisms. *Journal of Gerontology, 37,* 454–460.

Two cross-sectional studies assessed the influence of age on the use of 28 coping mechanisms. In the first study, 255 community-dwelling healthy volunteers completed a questionnaire describing their coping efforts. Three age groups were formed: 24–49 ($n = 88$), 50–64 ($n = 81$), and 65–91 ($n = 86$). Life events that occurred during the previous year were classified as challenge, loss, or threat events. One such event was selected for each subject and respondents indicated which of 118 coping behaviors they employed for this event. Ten of 20 coping behaviors showed age differences: When type of stressor was statistically controlled for, no evidence emerged for the hypothesis that mature and effective coping responses were more often found among the middle-aged than among younger and older adults. In Study 2, respondents identified a threat, challenge, and loss event, and described how they coped with each event. Findings showed that controlling for the type of stressor eradicated most age differences in coping: Middle-aged and older adults were less likely to engage in only 2 types of coping behaviors, hostile reaction and escapist fantasy, than younger adults. The author concludes that the older people in the sample coped in much the same way as younger people and where they employed different coping mechanisms, it was largely because of the different types of stress they face.

E *G

Minkler, M. (1981). **Research on the health effects of retirement: An uncertain legacy.** *Journal of Health and Social Behavior, 22*(2), 117–129.

This review article examines the existing research on the health and retirement relationship, including recent refinements in the study of life events. The paper first explores the theoretical perspectives and definitional bases of retirement as a stressful life event and as a process model as proposed by Robert Atchley. The second section reviews the few research studies that have attempted an empirical examination of the health effects of retirement and produced conflicting results. The author concludes that these studies were hampered by sampling and methodological problems that also precluded generalizations from the findings. The fact that the research to date has neither strongly supported nor refuted the hypothesis that retirement has a significant influence on health status underscores the need for further rigorous research of retirement, within a broad sociopolitical context. Additionally, it is suggested that life events stress scales be refined and tailored to an older age group in order to foster the integration of the study of retirement with the life events perspective.

T *G

Rakowski, W. (1984). **Health psychology and late life.** *Research on Aging, 6*(4), 593–620.

Psychological literature pertinent to understanding the health psychology and health behaviors of older adults is reviewed. Health psychology refers to analysis and understanding of health-related behaviors at the level of the individual; health psychology focuses attention on the personal, interpersonal, and contextual predictors of individual differences in behavior. In covering many topic areas of health psychology—health attitudes and beliefs, symptom recognition, predictors of health service utilization—the author notes the lack of research with older populations or research examining age differences in these phenomena. To a great extent, the health psychology of late life is grounded in circumstances associated with chronic illness, which is characterized by periods of relative health interspersed with periods of acute exacerbations. Thus, the author proposes that health and illness are not separate endpoints of a single continuum and should be differentiated as elements of a late-life health psychology. A conceptual model is presented of the factors leading to elders' decisions to take health actions.

R *G

Rodin, J. (1986). **Aging and health: Effects of the sense of control.** *Science, 233*, 1271–1276.

This article reviews the evidence for the relation between health, aging, and a psychological sense of control. The author maintains the thesis that the relation between health and control may grow stronger in old age, as a result of three processes: (1) control-relevant experiences may increase markedly with age; (2) age may moderate the relationship between control and health, for example, through immune system functioning, stress, or symptom labeling; and (3) age may moderate the relationship between control and health behaviors, for example, seeking medical care. Studies are reviewed that demonstrate the detrimental health effects of restricting control in older populations and the beneficial health effects of control-enhancing interventions.

T *U *G

Shanas, E., & Maddox, G. L. (1985). **Health, health resources and the utilization of care. In R. H. Binstock & E. Shanas (Eds.),** *Handbook of aging and the social sciences* **(2nd ed., pp. 696–726). New York: Van Nostrand Reinhold.**

This chapter considers the social and behavioral aspects of illness as they affect the health and health care of the elderly. In addition to discussing the use of various health care services by the elderly and the mechanisms by which they are financed, the authors discuss issues in the definition of health and illness in old age that would affect health service utilization. These include the definition of health itself (including individuals' self-reports), psychological and social predictors of health, and use of medical care, and the relation between illness and functional capacity. This chapter also includes discussions of psychological impairment among the elderly and the role of the family in health care.

Drawing on the material in the chapter, the authors raise key research issues about the relation of aging, illness, and health care that are essential to the formation of health care policy.

R *G

Siegler, I. C., & Costa, P. T., Jr. (1985). Health behavior relationships. In J. E. Birren & K. W. Schaie (Eds.), *Handbook of the psychology of aging* (2nd ed., pp. 144–166). New York: Van Nostrand Reinhold.

This chapter takes a psychological approach to the questions (1) How does health affect behavior with advancing age? and (2) How does behavior affect health with advancing age? Using data on human populations from a variety of disciplines, the authors examine health–behavior relationships among older people without illness that severely restricts their functioning. To address the effects of health on behavior, the authors summarize a number of studies within the major areas in the psychology of aging: personality, cognitive and intellectual functioning, adjustment, performance, and learning and memory. The complementary topic of the effects of behavior on health and health-related behaviors reviews research on health habits among the elderly, stress and personality as antecedents of disease, health perceptions (e.g., self-rated health), patient–physician relationships, and compliance. Throughout the chapter, the authors point out methodological concerns in the research that may affect the findings, and stress the fact that there are many gaps in our knowledge about health–behavior relationships among the elderly.

R *G

Thoits, P. A. (1983). Dimensions of life events that influence psychological distress: An evaluation and synthesis of the literature. In H. B. Kaplan (Ed.), *Psychosocial stress: Trends in theory and research* (pp. 33–103). New York: Academic Press.

This chapter evaluates the research on the psychological effects of major life events. It asks, more specifically, What types of life events influence psychological disturbance, and how do life events actually affect mental health—directly, indirectly, and/or interactively. Thoits identifies three types of research designs used in research in this area and examines a number of methodological features of this research that may account for the modest size of the correlation between life events and psychological distress typically found; for example, problems with dependent variables, including timing of measurement, problems of content and contamination in life events measures, and dubious assumptions about causal ordering. Thoits finds promise in the possibility that specific kinds of events are associated with particular outcomes and identifies characteristics of events that are particularly strongly associated with psychological outcomes: undesirability, uncontrollability, unexpectedness, and major magnitude of events. She proposes that models need to specify the form of the relationship between life events and psychological disorder, consider the time clustering of events, and more fully explore the dimensions of events associated with specific disorders. Her consideration of the theoretical processes that could account for findings in this area focuses on "self processes" that damage self-esteem or otherwise decrease people's sense of mastery.

T R *G

Umberson, D. (1987). Family status and health behaviors: Social control as a dimension of social integration. *Journal of Health and Social Behavior, 28,* 306–319.

This empirical study sought to explain the link between marital status and mortality by examining evidence for the idea that family operates as a social control mechanism, reducing people's participation in risky health behavior. Data from a national sample of 2,246 adults, in which widowed and divorced adults were oversampled, were used to examine the relationship between family structure and health risk. Health behavior variables used in analyses consisted of two lifestyle variables (an orderly lifestyle scale and a risk-taking behavior scale) and four substance use/abuse measures. Marital status and parenting status were the primary independent variables and, in fact, proved to be related to health risk behavior. Parenthood had a deterrent effect, particularly strong for licit and illicit substance abuse. Marital status showed even more consistently constructive effects: Except for marijuana use, divorced and widowed adults were more likely than the married to engage in negative health behaviors and less likely to experience an orderly lifestyle. The author concludes that, within the theoretical framework of social integration, family roles promote social control of health behaviors that affect subsequent mortality.

E *G

Verbrugge, L. M. (1984). Women and men: Mortality and health of older people. In M. W. Riley, B. Hess, & K. Bond (Eds.), *Aging in society* (pp. 139–174). Hillsdale, NJ: Lawrence Erlbaum

This chapter provides a broad overview of the differences among older men and women in health behavior and mortality, drawing on multiple sources, including Census Bureau data and the Health Interview Survey. The author raises research questions based on these differences with implications for the funding and planning of health services for older people. Older women tend to have more chronic health problems while older men have a higher incidence of more serious conditions leading to decreased life expectancy. Older women are more likely to curtail their usual activities due to an illness, visit physicians more frequently, and take more medications. The majority of nursing home residents are women; that older men are more likely to have a living spouse may account for this. Five explanatory factors are provided for these gender differences: (1) inherited risk (women may be biologically protected from disease prior to menopause); (2) acquired risk (greater risk for men through work roles, choice of leisure activities, smoking and alcohol consumption); (3) illness attitudes and enabling factors (e.g., women may be more sensitive to physical discomfort, more accustomed to dealing with physicians due to child bearing and rearing; more frequent medical care may contribute to greater longevity through early detection while men seem more likely to neglect health problems); (4) illness behavior (women's willingness to curtail activities for illness may be beneficial); and (5) reporting behavior. Changing gender roles, increased awareness of positive health behaviors, and improved medical care should decrease these gender differences for future cohorts of older people. This piece contains a number of excellent statistical tables from the Census Bureau and Health Interview surveys.

R *G

Wan, T. T. H. (1984). Health consequences of major role losses in later life: A panel study. *Research on Aging, 6*(4), 469–489.

This study focused on the health impacts of major role losses such as retirement and widowhood and their interaction in later life. Using the Longitudinal Retirement History Survey, the study sample included 1,804 males and 672 females who had worked before 1969 and who remained alive in 1977. Five exogenous váriables including age, recency of retirement, recency of widowhood, total annual income, and number of physician contacts were analyzed using a LISREL model to determine the impact of each on physical health. Physical health was measured at 2 time points 2 years apart. The significance of the impact of the exogenous variables was measured both with and without controls for prior physical health. Among the major findings, it was shown that recency of role losses, through either retirement or widowhood, had a relatively negligible influence on the physical health of older adults in later life, and that elderly persons who have a favorable level of physical health in later life are those who experienced better health at the early stage of the aging process, irrespective of major role losses, economic status, and age.

E *G

Wolinsky, F. D., & Coe, R. M. (1984). Physician and hospital utilization among noninstitutionalized elderly adults: An analysis of the Health Interview Survey. *Journal of Gerontology, 39,* 334–341.

This study evaluated the ability of predisposing, enabling, and need characteristics to explain physician utilization and hospital utilization by older adults. Using data on 15,899 noninstitutionalized adults (ages 60+ years) from the Health Interview Survey, this study was the first to evaluate Anderson's model in a national sample of older adults. Actual number of visits to physicians during the preceding 12-month period and number of nights spent in a hospital during the preceding 12-month period were the dependent variables. Predisposing, enabling, and need characteristics explained 3% and 5% of the variance in physician and hospital utilization, respectively. When the utilization variables were recoded to truncate the upper ranges of these variables (13+ physician visits per year and 15+ nights in the hospital were each given a single code), the predictor set explained 20% and 9% of the variance in physician and hospital utilization. The unique contribution of the need characteristics accounted for 56.8% to 66.7% of the variance explained in physician utilization and 74.5% and 77.7% of the variance explained in hospital utilization, suggesting that an apparently equitable system is operative in elderly adults' use of health services.

E *G

Review Chapters and Articles in Health Psychology and Aging

	Davis	Eisdorfer & Wilkie	*Encyclopedia*	Haug & Ory	Rakowski	Shanas & Maddox	Siegler & Costa	Verbrugge
Health Statistics								
Morbidity								
Prevalence of Specific Conditions								
Mortality								
Life Expectancy								
Disability								
Mental Disorder								
Impact of health/illness on behavior								
Mental Health/Well-being								
Personality								
Coping								
Cognitive Functioning								
Other Performance								
Functional Ability								
Physiological/Biological Processes								
Impact of behavior on health/illness								
Stress								
Personality								
Attitudes and Beliefs								
Symptoms								
Health Habits/Lifestyle								
Self-Reported Health								
Health behavior								
Preventive Health Behavior								
Compliance								
Medication Use								
Seeking Health Care								
Predictors of Health Behavior								
The health care setting								
Physician-Patient Relationships								
Stereotyping by Professionals								
Patient Satisfaction								
Role of the Family in Health Care								
Health care policy								
Health Care Needs of the Elderly								
Utilization of Health Services								
Health Care Costs/Financing								
Hospitalization								
Long-term Care								
Outpatient/Community Service								
Research issues								
Definition of Health/Illness								
Health Assessment								
Cohort Differences								
Sex Differences								
Social Class Differences								
Cross-Cultural Comparisons								
Research Design Issues								

5
Mental Health and Aging

Steven H. Zarit and Diana Spore

I. Introduction: Developmental Perspectives on Mental Health and Aging
   A. Normative versus pathological change
   B. Plasticity and compensation
   C. Negative stereotypes of aging and their effects on behavior
   D. The importance of cohort
   E. Age of onset versus age of patient
   F. Developmental patterns in psychiatric syndromes
II. Disorders of Aging
   A. Prevalence of disorders in late life
   B. Disorders with onset typically before late life
      1. Schizophrenia
         a. Incidence and prevalence in the whole population
         b. Patterns of change during adulthood
         c. Is there a late-life form of schizophrenia?
      2. Bipolar disorders (Manic Depression)
         a. Incidence and prevalence
         b. Patterns of change during adulthood
      3. Anxiety disorders
         a. Incidence and prevalence
         b. Are there anxiety disorders in old age?
      4. Personality disorders
         a. Clinical examples of change
         b. Is there late-life onset?
   C. Disorders with Onset Throughout Adulthood
      1. Unipolar Depression
         a. Incidence and prevalence
         b. Theories of depression
         c. Is late onset different from early onset?
      2. Alcoholism
         a. Rates of onset in early and late life
         b. Are there different etiological factors in late life?

3. Suicide
D. Disorders primarily of aging
  1. Paraphrenia
    a. Prevalence
    b. Etiological factors
  2. Dementia
    a. Definition and types of dementia
    b. Prevalence of dementia
    c. Alzheimer's disease (AD)
      i. Description of disease
      ii. Incidence and prevalence
      iii. Theories of AD
        — cholinergic
        — genetic
        — aluminum
        — head trauma
        — other
    d. Multi-infarct dementia
      i. Description
      ii. Incidence and prevalence
      iii. Etiology
    e. Other dementias
  3. Delirium and reversible dementia
    a. Description
    b. Estimates of prevalence
    c. Causes
  4. Somatic disorders
III. Assessment
  A. Differential diagnosis: Are cognitive problems due to dementia, delirium, depression, normal aging?
    1. Distinguishing features and overlap
    2. Can AD be differentiated reliably from other dementias?
  B. Functional assessment
    1. Purposes of functional assessment
      a. Identify assets and deficits in current situation
      b. Identify goals for treatment and/or indicators to evaluate treatment
      c. Develop a treatment plan
    2. Approaches to functional assessment
      a. Omnibus batteries—OARS, CARE
      b. Measures, tests, ratings
      c. Self-monitoring
IV. Treatment of Mental Health Problems
  A. Principles of treatment with older persons
  B. Individual psychotherapy

Despite increased attention to problems of aging, mental health problems of elders are often ignored, receiving either inadequate or no treatment. Much of the problem is due to the fact that the elder with a mental disorder has two stigmas, being older and mentally ill. Avoidance and neglect of problems of older persons with mental disorders lead to a self-fulfilling prophesy: Little is done to help patients out of the belief that they cannot improve, and as a result, they do not obtain help that might alleviate their problems.

Accumulating evidence from several disciplines suggests a more optimistic picture. Many mental health problems of the elderly are partly or completely reversible. There are also often treatable components of irreversible problems. The foundation for this positive view comes from a life-span developmental perspective on late-life mental disorders. First and foremost, this perspective suggests the potential for healthy and successful aging. There are many paths to successful aging, which suggests that aging and pathology are not necessarily synonymous (Butler & Lewis, 1983; Rowe & Kahn, 1987). Studies of the aging process suggest a complex pattern that includes not only decline but also growth and compensation (Baltes, 1987). While some abilities decline with age, others depend on experience. Some people may show increments in these abilities at least into their 80s (Schaie & Hertzog, 1983). A primary barrier to continued growth in late life is the negative stereotypes and labels that affect self-esteem of older people, as well as the way they are treated by others (Atchley, 1988; Rodin & Langer, 1980). Contributing to these stereotypes are generational or cohort differences. Older people are different in many ways from the young, and while these differences are often taken as signs of aging, evidence from studies that follow several generational groups over time (cohort-sequential studies) suggests that cohort is a primary determinant of many of these differences (Schaie & Hertzog, 1983). An implication of these investigations is that we can understand elders by learning about the generational influences that affected their development.

Two specific life-span considerations pertaining to mental health problems of late life are distinguishing between the age of the patient and the age of the problem and identifying the longitudinal course of mental health problems. To some extent, the negative expectations about older patients arise from confusing the age of the patient and age of the problem (Zarit, 1980). People with a chronic mental health problem that did not respond to treatment when they were younger may also not improve when older. This type of treatment failure, however, may be ascribed to the person's age, not the chronicity of the problem. There has also been surprisingly little attention to the long-term course and outcome of common mental health problems. The identification of different outcomes for persons with similar disorders may lead to development of more effective programs of treatment (Miller, 1986).

In following these observations, mental health problems of older persons can be differentiated according to whether age of first onset is primarily earlier in the life span or primarily in late life or whether they occur throughout adulthood. Issues of aging are likely to be relevant for any older person with a mental disorder, whatever the age at first onset. But treatment of a recurrent disorder should also focus on issues related to previous episodes, including types of intervention that were effective. In contrast, issues of aging are more likely to be relevant in the etiology and treatment of problems with first onset in late life.

The mental disorders with onset typically earlier in life include schizophrenia, bipolar disorders (manic depression), anxiety disorders, and personality disorders. There is controversy in each case concerning whether new cases of these problems develop in old age or if there is a late-life variant. Nonetheless, it is clear that the vast majority of cases have their first onset earlier in life, and the course is often chronic. Schizophrenia can be used to illustrate this pattern.

Schizophrenic disorders are perhaps the major mental health problem across the life span, with a lifetime prevalence as high as 1% of the population. Felix Post (1980), a pioneer in research on schizophrenic symptoms in the elderly, concludes from a review of the clinical literature that onset of schizophrenia is typically in early and middle life, though paranoid disorders, including paranoid schizophrenia, are more likely to originate during middle and late life. (The paranoid disorders are discussed below.) The outcome of schizophrenia is still somewhat controversial. Post (1980) suggests schizophrenics have a higher mortality rate than the general population but that significant numbers also experience some lessening of symptoms as they age, although they often remain impaired in social functioning. Long-term follow-up of younger people with schizophrenic episodes has found that some individuals are markedly improved, and that others experience sufficient lessening of symptoms to function effectively in social and occupational roles. For many, however, the disorder is chronic and unrelenting (Clausen, 1986; Tsuang, 1986).

Other syndromes with onset primarily during early and middle adulthood include bipolar disorders (manic depression), anxiety disorders, and personality disorders. Lithium carbonate is an effective treatment for bipolar disorders, including with older people. Anxiety among the elderly has received surprisingly little attention, except from some clinicians (see Verwoerdt, 1980, 1981). Significantly, current epidemiological studies identify phobic reactions as having a high prevalence among older people (Kramer, German, Anthony, Von Korff, & Skinner, 1985; Weissman, Myers, Tischler, Holzer, Leaf, Orvaschel, & Brody, 1985). Many older people suffering from anxiety show a continuation of symptoms from earlier life, although new cases have also been noted. That many tranquilizing drugs can produce paradoxical reactions that increase symptoms of anxiety contributes to this problem. Similarly, little is known about the course of personality disorders. Cross-sectional studies indicate that a diagnosis of personality disorder is made most often during the years 25 to 44, and that the prevalence of identified cases among the elderly is quite low (Verwoerdt, 1981). Whether this decline occurs because many people improve or because clinicians do not look for this problem in late life cannot be determined. While the prevalence is not known, older persons with lifelong personality disorders are not uncommon in clinical settings serving the elderly. Older persons with these inflexible, maladaptive personality styles are more difficult to treat, and may have a more chronic course of other symptoms, such as depression (Thompson, Gallagher, & Czirr, 1988).

Depressive disorders may occur anytime during the life span. Estimates of the prevalence of depression across the life span vary, depending on the criteria used to identify cases or problems. Studies that use DSM-III criteria for Major Depressive Disorder (the most severe type of unipolar depression) have generally reported highest rates to be among the middle aged, and somewhat lower prevalence in late life. As an example, Weissman and Myers (1978) found the prevalence of major depression to be 1.9% among persons aged 26 to 45, 6.3% among those 46 to 64, and 5.4% after age 65. Other studies have reported even lower rates of major depression among the elderly (for reviews, see Blazer, 1982; Blazer, Hughes, & George, 1987). Significant numbers of older people, however, have prominent symptoms of depression, without reaching DSM-III cutoffs for diagnosis of Major or Minor Depression. Blazer and associates (1987), for example, found that 8% of a community-living older population met diagnostic criteria for an affective disorder (including major depression and other diagnoses), while another

19% had significant depressive symptoms, though failing to fall within established diagnostic categories. Gurland and his associates (1980) have reported similar rates of depressive symptoms. Longitudinal study of these subjects has found that symptoms are often chronic and many persons may meet criteria for diagnosis of clinical depression at follow up (Gurland et al., 1987). These findings raise the question of whether the criteria for clinical depression should be broadened in later life.

Current theories of depression stress genetic, biochemical, behavioral, cognitive, and social factors (for reviews, see Gaylord & Zung, 1987; Zarit & Zarit, 1984). Biological investigations have emphasized the possibility of a genetic predisposition and the role of neurotransmitters. Behavioral approaches have identified low rates of positive reinforcement and poor social skills as important. Cognitive approaches highlight the tendency for depressed persons to make overly negative evaluations of themselves and others. With the exception of genetic theories, each of these approaches suggests an increasing vulnerability to depression with age.

There is, as yet, little clarification of another important issue: the significance of age at first onset of depression. Age of onset has been found to be unrelated to the duration of current episodes of depression (Lewinsohn, Fenn, Stanton, & Franklin, 1986). Delusional symptoms, however, may be more prominent among late-onset cases (Meyers & Greenberg, 1986).

Alcoholism is another significant mental health problem that can occur anytime during the adult years. Peak prevalence is in middle age, although significant numbers of persons with alcohol problems have been identified in later life (Zimberg, 1987). It is generally believed that about two-thirds of elderly alcoholics became alcoholics earlier in life, while one-third either developed the problem in late life or had a worsening of a pattern of occasional problem drinking. Losses and other stresses, including death of a spouse, retirement, health problems, and marital problems, often contribute to development of a drinking problem in old age. Clinicians may underestimate the occurrence of alcohol problems in older persons, because they do not expect to find it and so fail to inquire, or because cognitive symptoms are ascribed to dementia rather than the effects of alcohol. Smaller amounts of alcohol may be harmful to older persons because the body metabolizes alcohol more slowly, and because of the possibility of interactions with prescription medications (Zimberg, 1987). Alcohol can also increase cognitive symptoms of dementia patients.

While suicide is often thought to be a problem of the young, rates among older people are high. In fact, the group at greatest risk of suicide is older white males (Miller, 1979). Risk factors include depression, physical illness, and social isolation.

Disorders with onset primarily in middle or late life include paranoid disorders, dementia, delirium, and somatic problems. For paranoid disorders, symptoms can range from a single, encapsulated delusion to an extensive delusional system accompanied by first-rank symptoms of schizophrenia. Cases that meet diagnostic criteria for paranoid schizophrenia tend to have onset earlier in life (20s or 30s), while those problems that occur for the first time in the 40s or later usually have a more circumscribed symptomatology. Several etiologies have been suggested for these late-life disorders, including bilateral hearing loss, exacerbation of a personality pattern characterized by difficulties with interpersonal relationships, and an underlying dementia or delirium (Post, 1980).

Dementia is perhaps the most devastating of late-life problems. It is characterized by a progressive deterioration of memory and other cognitive abilities, and of the person's ability to manage daily activities. Once thought to be a universal condition of aging, dementia is now known to be the result of specific disease processes that affect some, but not all, older persons. Common types of irreversible dementias (i.e., dementias for which there is no current treatment) are Alzheimer's disease, multi-infarct dementia, and Pick's disease. Many patients with Parkinson's disease will also develop dementia. Dementia symptoms, including memory loss and disorientation, may also be caused by a variety of potentially treatable problems (National Institute on Aging Task Force, 1980). Prevalence of moderate and severe cases of dementia is estimated between 4 to 7% of the population over 65 (Mortimer, 1980, 1986). While data are incomplete, it is estimated that prevalence among 80-year-olds may be as high as 20% of the population.

Alzheimer's disease (or Senile Dementia of the Alzheimer Type) is the most frequent cause of dementia, accounting for 50 to 70% of cases. Alzheimer's disease is characterized by a particular type of brain pathology that involves formation of senile (or neuritic) plaques, neurofibrillary tangles, and selected loss of certain types of brain neurons (Cummings & Benson, 1983). There may be both a familial (or inherited) form and a nonfamilial form, and the possibility of other subtypes cannot be ruled out (Mayeux, Stern, & Spanton, 1985). Theories of the cause of Alzheimer's disease have focused variously on genetic, neurochemical, aluminum toxicity, viral, and immunological factors. Recent discoveries highlight the possibility that an abnormality or malfunction at a site on chromosome 21 may be important in the etiology of Alzheimer's disease. Despite an intensive search for treatment, there is nothing that can currently be done to reverse or retard the progression of this disease.

Multi-infarct dementia, which involves accumulation of brain damage as a result of multiple small strokes or infarcts, accounts for approximately 10 to 20% of cases of dementia. (Another group of cases has evidence both of Alzheimer and multi-infarct pathology.) Risk factors involved in multi-infarct dementia are similar to those for heart disease and other types of stroke.

Reversible dementia and delirium are syndromes in which prominent cognitive disturbances are potentially treatable. Reversible dementia (sometimes called "pseudodementia") is characterized by symptoms that are similar to (and in some instances virtually indistinguishable from) the irreversible dementias such as Alzheimer's disease. Delirium is marked by more dramatic symptoms that may include impairment in patients' awareness of self or surroundings, hallucinations, disturbances of the wake–sleep cycle, and altered psychomotor behavior that can range from hyperactivity to catatonic stupor (Lipowski, 1983). Similar causes can give rise to delirium or reversible dementia, including drug toxicity or interaction, metabolic disorders, malnutrition, and infections (National Institute on Aging Task Force, 1980). Many older people experience mild symptoms of delirium in late afternoon or early evening, especially in strange surroundings (Cameron, 1941; Evans, 1987). This phenomenon is sometimes called "sundowner's syndrome." Some depressed older persons also have a degree of cognitive impairment typical of dementia, though these symptoms generally improve with treatment of the depression. It is noteworthy that dementia patients are especially susceptible to delirium, and some improvement in their cognitive status can be achieved by identifying and treating causes of delirium.

Finally, another type of problem with onset typically in middle or late life is preoccupation with somatic symptoms, including exaggeration of physical symptoms, expression of affect through somatic symptoms, and excessive preoccupation with illness (hypochondriasis) (Verwoerdt, 1981). Prevalence of somatic disorders is not known, though their sufferers often present a considerable challenge for treatment.

Psychological assessment of older persons with mental health problems contributes to diagnosis and treatment planning. The most common diagnostic issue is to identify if cognitive symptoms are due to dementia, delirium, depression, or normal aging. There are no definitive medical or psychological tests that identify dementia or specific types of dementia such as Alzheimer's disease. Diagnosis is made by establishing that symptoms and history are typical of dementia and by ruling out treatable conditions, including depression and the conditions that can cause reversible dementia symptoms (McKhann et al., 1984; National Institute on Aging Task Force, 1980; Zarit, Orr, & Zarit, 1985). Dementia is characterized by impairment in memory and at least two other cognitive abilities, decreased ability to manage one's personal affairs and personal care, and by a history of gradual progression. That dementia can coexist with both delirium and depression (Reifler, Larson, & Hanley, 1982; NIA Task Force, 1980) complicates the diagnostic process. Mental status tests, which assess recall of simple information and orientation, are an effective way of identifying obvious cognitive deficits, but there is considerable overlap between dementia and normal populations, especially among people with less education (Anthony, LeResche, Nias, Von Korff, & Folstein, 1982). Because of this overlap and the implications of a diagnosis of dementia, Kahn and Miller (1978) have proposed that dementia be diagnosed only when all other possible causes of cognitive symptoms have been ruled out. Diagnostic criteria specific to Alzheimer's disease have been proposed, though examination of brain tissue at autopsy remains necessary for definitive diagnosis (McKhann et al., 1984).

In addition to contributing to diagnosis, another function of assessment is to identify patients' functional abilities. A functional assessment can identify assets and problems in the current situation and goals for treatment, as well as contribute to the development of a treatment plan. A variety of structured interviews, psychological tests, and other measures have been used with older populations to evaluate functioning (Lawton, 1986; Zarit, Eiler, & Hassinger, 1985).

In psychological interventions with older adults, there are both continuities and discontinuities with treatment of younger persons (Gatz, Popkin, Pino, & VandenBos, 1985). Among the continuities is the recognition that many of the approaches to individual and group psychotherapy with younger adults are effective with older adults. There are, however, some unique barriers to treatment of older persons, including attitudes of professionals and of older persons themselves and the lack of third party payment through Medicare for most mental health services. Kahn (1975) stresses the importance of maximizing the older person's remaining independence by planning treatment according to what he calls the "principle of minimum intervention." In this approach, interventions that are least disruptive of an older person's usual functioning and living arrangements are preferred, whenever possible. Emphasis is placed on brief, rather than long-term, care and community interventions over institutionalization as ways of maximizing the older person's control over his or her life and for supporting independence (see also Zarit, 1980).

Psychotherapeutic approaches that have been used with the elderly include psychoanalytic, behavioral, cognitive, Rogerian, and eclectic approaches (see Gatz et al., 1985; Storandt, 1983). Knight (1986) provides a conceptual model of psychotherapy with older adults in which he identifies five topics and three themes that typically characterize treatment. The topics of therapy are (1) chronic illness and disability, (2) death and dying, including grieving, (3) love, marriage, and sexuality, (4) the meaning of aging and growing older, and (5) ethnicity and aging. Major themes that emerge from therapy are (1) empowerment, (2) enjoyment, and (3) life review. Knight (1986) also stresses the importance of examining patients' feelings about their therapists (transference) and therapists' feelings about their older clients (countertransference). He suggests one must look at the interactions in a particular therapist–patient relationship to understand these processes, rather than relying on some formula or theory.

A specific focus of research has been the outcome of psychotherapy of depression. Studies have suggested good immediate and long-term outcome (Thompson, Gallagher, & Breckenridge, 1987). Approaches to treatment of depression in the elderly have in common an emphasis on the therapist taking an active role, educating the patient about depression and how to use treatment, and using homework and other tasks (Zarit & Zarit, 1984).

Group work has been used extensively with older persons over the years, although reports have often been characterized by an oversimplification about how groups work or about uses with disparate populations. Groups have the potential for certain therapeutic effects that make them especially attractive as a treatment approach with the elderly, such as creating opportunities for social interactions and exchanges, and identifying with and learning from people in similar situations. The application of group techniques varies, however, depending on the type of clients and the setting. Groups have been used for treatment of mental disorders, such as depression (Thompson, Gallagher, Nies, & Epstein, 1983), for examination of stressful life events such as widowhood (DeBor, Gallagher, & Lesher, 1982), and for enhancing the transition to late life through life review (Lewis & Butler, 1974) and similar approaches.

Despite the attention given to family problems and conflict, little has been written about family therapy. A major exception is the work of Herr and Weakland (1979) who apply a communication framework for assessing and treating family disorders. Knight (1986) identifies some practical considerations, such as whether the presenting problem is new and how to use alliances between therapist and various family members to further treatment goals.

Two areas of considerable importance that cut across these various types of treatment are interventions with dementia patients and their families and interventions in institutional settings. Although dementia patients themselves have limited ability to initiate change, they may be responsive to environmental contingencies (Hussian, 1986), as well as to the mood and tone of people around them (Zarit et al., 1985). Families of dementia victims, as well as caregivers of elders with other impairments, are often under considerable stress. Interventions with family members can be helpful by providing more information about patients' disease and behavior, teaching caregivers how to manage the patient more effectively, and identifying people or agencies who can provide assistance (Zarit et al., 1985). Support groups have been an important source of assistance for caregivers, typically providing them with information and the kind of emotional support that comes from people who have been through similar experiences. Other interventions may be useful as well, including individual counseling for the primary caregiver and family meetings that address issues of conflict and support.

Institutional settings are quite varied, ranging from retirement communities in which older residents are largely independent to skilled nursing facilities. Interventions depend on the type of population and problem. In retirement communities, interventions are more likely to focus on life enhancement or prevention of problems. In nursing homes, a variety of interventions are possible to treat specific mental health problems of residents or to enhance the functioning of all residents (Butler & Lewis, 1983; Smyer, Cohn, & Brannon, 1988). The institution, however, functions as a community, with its own rules and assumptions that will affect how interventions are carried out. Perhaps the most obvious example is that the staff who have the greatest impact on residents are the nurses' aides (Smyer et al., 1988). Interventions that change how they interact with residents may have the most enduring effects, while brief treatment provided by a professional will have more limited benefits.

I. Introduction: Developmental Perspectives on Mental Health and Aging
   A. Normative versus pathological change: The prospects for successful aging

Butler, R. N., & Lewis, M. I. (1983). Healthy, successful old age. Chapter 2 from *Aging and mental health* (3rd ed.). St. Louis, MO: Mosby.

Rowe, J. W., & Kahn, R. L. (1987). Human aging: Usual and successful. *Science, 237*, 143–149.

   B. Plasticity and compensation

Baltes, P. B. (1987). Theoretical propositions of life-span developmental psychology: On the dynamics between growth and decline. *Developmental Psychology, 23*, 611–626.

Hussian, R. A., (1981). The compensatory model: Explaining age-related differences. In *Geriatric psychology: A behavioral perspective.* New York: Van Nostrand Reinhold.

   C. Negative stereotypes of aging and their effects on behavior

Rodin, J., & Langer, E. (1980). Aging labels: The decline of control and the fall of self-esteem. *Journal of Social Issues, 36*, 12–29.

Supplemental Readings:

Pruchno, R., & Smyer, M. A. (1983). Mental health problems and aging: A short quiz. *International Journal of Aging and Human Development, 17*(2), 123–140.

Atchley, R. C. (1988). *Social forces and aging: An introduction to social gerontology* (5th ed.). Belmont, CA.: Wadsworth.

D. The importance of cohort

Supplemental Readings:

Schaie, K. W., & Hertzog, C. (1983). Fourteen-year cohort-sequential analyses of adult intellectual development. *Developmental Psychology, 19*, 531–543.

E. Age of onset versus age of patient

Zarit, S.H. (1980). Mental health and aging: An overview. Chapter 1, from *Aging and mental disorders.* New York: Free Press.

F. Developmental patterns in psychiatric syndromes

Miller, N. E. (1986). Introduction: The prediction of psychopathology across the life-span. In L. Erlenmeyer-Kimling & N. E. Miller (Eds.), *Life-span research on the prediction of psychopathology* (pp. 1–17). Hillsdale, NJ: Lawrence Erlbaum.

II. Disorders of Aging
   A. Prevalence of disorders in late life

Robins, L. N., Helzer, J. E., Weissman, M. M., Orvaschel, H., Gruenberg, E., Burke, J. D., Jr., & Regier, D. A. (1984). Lifetime prevalence of specific psychiatric disorders in three sites. *Archives of General Psychiatry, 41,* 949–958.

Kramer, M., German, P. S., Anthony, J. C., Von Korff, M., & Skinner, E. A. (1985). Patterns of mental disorders among the elderly residents of Eastern Baltimore. *Journal of the American Geriatrics Society, 33*(4), 236–245.

Weissman, M. M., Myers, J. K., Tischler, G. L., Holzer, C. E., III, Leaf, P. J., Orvaschel, H., & Brody, J. A. (1985). Psychiatric disorders (DSM-III) and cognitive impairment among the elderly in a U.S. urban community. *Acta Psychiatrica Scandinavica, 71,* 366–379.

Supplemental Readings:

American Psychiatric Association (1987). *Diagnostic and statistical manual of mental disorders* [DSM-III-R] (3rd ed., rev.). Washington, DC: Author.

   B. Disorders with onset typically before late-life
      1. Schizophrenia
         a. Incidence and prevalence in the whole population
         b. Patterns of change during adulthood
         c. Is there a late-life form of schizophrenia?

Post, F. (1980). Paranoid, schizophrenia-like, and schizophrenic states in the aged. In J. E. Birren & R. B. Sloane (Eds.), *Handbook of mental health and aging.* Englewood Cliffs, NJ: Prentice-Hall.

Clausen, J. A. (1986). A 15- to 20-year follow-up of married adult psychiatric patients. In L. Erlenmeyer-Kimling & N. E. Miller (Eds.),

Life-span research on the prediction of psychopathology (pp. 175–194). Hillsdale, NJ: Lawrence Erlbaum.

Tsuang, M. T. (1986). Predictors of poor and good outcome in schizophrenia. In L. Erlenmeyer-Kimling & N. E. Miller (Eds.), *Life-span research on the prediction of psychopathology* (pp. 195–203). Hillsdale, NJ: Lawrence Erlbaum.

    2. Bipolar disorders (Manic Depression)
       a. Incidence and prevalence
       b. Patterns of change during adulthood

Gaylord, S. A., & Zung, W. W. K. (1987). Affective disorders among the aging. In L. L. Carstensen & B. A. Edelstein (Eds.), *Handbook of clinical gerontology* (pp. 76–95). New York: Pergamon Press.

    3. Anxiety disorders
       a. Incidence and prevalence
       b. Are there anxiety disorders in old age?

Verwoerdt, A. (1980). Anxiety, dissociative and personality disorders in the elderly. In E. W. Busse & D. G. Blazer (Eds.), *Handbook of geriatric psychiatry* (pp. 368–380). New York: Van Nostrand Reinhold.

    4. Personality disorders
       a. Clinical examples of change
       b. Is there late-life onset?

Bergmann, K. (1978). Neurosis and personality disorder in old age. In A. D. Isaacs & F. Post (Eds.), *Studies in geriatric psychiatry* (pp. 41–76). New York: Wiley.

Verwoerdt, A. (1981). Personality disorders. Chapter 7 in *Clinical geropsychiatry* (2nd ed.). Baltimore: Williams and Wilkins.

Supplemental Readings:

Thompson, L. W., Gallagher, D., & Czirr, R. (1988). Personality disorder and outcome in the treatment of late-life depression. *Journal of Geriatric Psychiatry, 21*(2), 133–146.

    C. Disorders with Onset Throughout Adulthood
       1. Unipolar Depression
         a. Incidence and prevalence

Blazer, D., Hughes, D. C., & George, L. K. (1987). The epidemiology of depression in an elderly community population. *The Gerontologist, 27*, 281–297.

Weissman, M. M., & Myers, J. K. (1978). Affective disorders in a US urban community. *Archives of General Psychiatry, 35*, 1304–1311.

Gurland, B. J., Dean, L., Cross, P., & Golden, R. (1980). The epidemiology of depression and dementia in the elderly. In J. O. Cole & J. E. Barrett (Eds.), *Psychopathology of the aged*. New York: Raven Press.

         b. Theories of depression

Gaylord, S. A. & Zung, W. W. K. (1987). Affective disorders among the aging. In L. L. Carstensen & B. A. Edelstein (Eds.), *Handbook of clinical gerontology* (pp. 76–95). New York: Pergamon Press.

Blazer, D. G., II. (1982). *Depression in late life.* St. Louis, MO: Mosby.

Zarit, S. H., & Zarit, J. M. (1984). Depression in later life: Theory and assessment. In J. P. Abrahams & V. Crooks (Eds.), *Geriatric mental health: A clinician's guide.* (pp. 21–39). New York: Grune & Stratton.

Supplemental Readings:

Breslau, L. D., & Haug, M. R. (Eds.). (1983). *Depression and aging: Causes, care, and consequences.* New York: Springer.

Fry, P. S. (1986). *Depression, stress, and adaptations in the elderly: Psychological assessment and intervention.* Rockville, MD.: Aspen.

Akiskal, H. S., & McKinney, W. T., Jr. (1973). Depressive disorders: Toward a unified hypothesis. *Science, 182,* 20–29.

Beck, A. T., Rush, D., Shaw, D., & Emery G. (1979). *Cognitive therapy of depression.* New York: Guilford.

Lewinsohn, P. M., Muñoz, R. F., Youngren, M. A., & Zeiss, A. M. (1978). *Control your depression.* Englewood Cliffs, NJ: Prentice-Hall.

Seligman, M. A. P. (1975). *Helplessness.* San Francisco: Freeman.

Klerman, G. L., Weissman, M. M., Rounsaville, B. J., & Chevron, E. S. (1984). *Interpersonal psychotherapy of depression.* New York: Basic Books.

  c. Is late onset different from early onset?

Lewinsohn, P. M., Fenn, D. S., Stanton, A. K., & Franklin, J. (1986). Relation of age at onset to duration of episode in unipolar depression. *Psychology and Aging, 1,* 63–68.

Meyers, B., & Greenberg, R. (1986). Late-life delusional depression. *Journal of Affective Disorders, 11*(2), 133–.

  2. Alcoholism
    a. Rates of onset in early and late life
    b. Are there different etiological factors in late life?

Mishara, B. L., & Kastenbaum, R. (1980). *Alcohol and old age.* New York: Grune & Stratton.

Zimberg, S. (1987). Alcohol abuse among the elderly. In L. L. Carstensen & B. A. Edelstein (Eds.), *Handbook of clinical gerontology* (pp. 57–65). New York: Pergamon Press.

  3. Suicide

Osgood, N. J. (1985). *Suicide in the elderly: A practitioner's guide to diagnosis and mental health intervention.* Rockville, MD.: Aspen.

Osgood, N. J., & McIntosh, J. L. (Eds.) (1986). *Suicide and the elderly: An annotated bibliography and review.* Westport, CT: Greenwood Press.

Miller, M. (1979). *Suicide after sixty: The final alternative.* New York: Springer.

D. Disorders primarily of aging
   1. Paraphrenia
     a. Prevalence
     b. Etiological factors

Post, F. (1980). Paranoid, schizophrenia-like, and schizophrenic states in the aged. In J. E. Birren & R. B. Sloane (Eds.), *Handbook of mental health and aging* (pp. 591–615). Englewood Cliffs, NJ: Prentice-Hall.

   2. Dementia
     a. Definition and types of dementia

Butler, R. N., & Lewis, M. I. (1983). Organic brain disorders. Chapter 5 in *Aging and mental health* (3rd ed.). St. Louis, MO: C.V. Mosby.

Cummings, J. L. (1987). Dementia syndromes: Neurobehavioral and neuropsychiatric features. *Journal of Clinical Psychiatry, 48*(5, Suppl.), 3–8.

Cummings, J. L, & Benson, D. F. (1983). *Dementia: A clinical approach.* Boston: Butterworth.

National Institute on Aging Task Force (1980). Senility reconsidered. *Journal of the American Medical Association, 244*(3), 259–263.

Zarit, S. H., Orr, N. K., & Zarit, J. M. (1985). Causes of memory loss: Alzheimer's disease, other dementias, and conditions with similar symptoms. Chapter 2 in *The hidden victims of Alzheimer's disease: Families under stress.* New York: New York University Press.

Supplemental Readings:

Melnick, V. L., & Dubler, N. M. (Eds.) (1985). *Alzheimer's disease: Dilemmas in clinical research.* Clifton, NJ: Humana Press.

Roach, M. (1985). *Another name for madness.* Boston: Houghton-Mifflin.

     b. Prevalence of dementia

Mortimer, J. A. (1986). Epidemiology of dementia: International comparisons. In G. Maddox & J. Brody (Eds.), *Epidemiology and aging.* New York: Springer.

Mortimer, J. A., & Schuman, L. M. (Eds.). (1981). *The epidemiology of dementia.* New York: Oxford University Press.

Weissman, M. M., Myers, J. K., Tischler, G. L., Holzer, C. E., III, Leaf, P. J., Orvaschel, H., & Brody, J. A. (1985). Psychiatric disorders (DSM-III) and cognitive impairment among the elderly in a U.S. urban community. *Acta Psychiatrica Scandinavica, 71*, 366–379.

     c. Alzheimer's disease
       i. Description of disease

Butler, R. N., & Lewis, M. I. (1983). Organic brain disorders. Chapter 5 in *Aging and mental health* (3rd ed.). St. Louis, MO: C. V. Mosby.

Cummings, J. L. (1987). Dementia syndromes: Neurobehavioral and neuropsychiatric features. *Journal of Clinical Psychiatry*, *48*(5, Suppl.), 3–8.
Cummings, J. L, & Benson, D. F. (1983). *Dementia: A clinical approach.* Boston: Butterworth.

Supplemental Readings:

Cummings, J. L., & Zarit, J. M. (1987). Probable Alzheimer's disease in an artist. *Journal of the American Medical Association*, *258*, 2731–2734.

ii. Incidence and prevalence

Mortimer, J. A. (1986). Epidemiology of dementia: International comparisons. In G. Maddox & J. Brody (Eds.), *Epidemiology and aging.* New York: Springer.
Mortimer, J. A., & Schuman, L. M. (Eds.). (1981). *The epidemiology of dementia.* New York: Oxford University Press.

iii. Theories of AD
— cholinergic
— genetic
— aluminum
— head trauma
— other

Reisberg, B. (Ed.). (1983). *Alzheimer's disease: The standard reference.* New York: The Free Press.
Davies, P., & Wolozin, B. L. (1987). Recent advances in the neurochemistry of Alzheimer's disease. *Journal of Clinical Psychiatry*, *48* (5, Suppl.), 23–30.
Mayeux, R., Stern, Y., & Spanton, S. (1985). Heterogeneity in dementia of the Alzheimer type: Evidence of subgroups. *Neurology*, *35*, 453–461.
St. George-Hyslop, P. H., Tanzi, R. E., Polinsky, R. J., Haines, J. L., Nee, L., Watkins, P. C., Myers, R. H., Feldman, R. G., Pollen, D., Drachman, D., Growdon, J., Bruni, A., Foncin, J.-F., Salmon, D., Frommelt, P., Amaducci, L., Sorba, S., Piancentini, S., Stewart, G. D., Hobbs, W. J., Conneally, M., & Gusella, J. F. (1987). The genetic defect causing familial Alzheimer's disease maps on chromosome 21. *Science*, *235*, 885–890.

d. Multi-infarct dementia
i. Description
ii. Incidence and prevalence
iii. Etiology

Cummings, J. L., & Benson, D. F. (1983). *Dementia: A clinical approach.* Boston: Butterworth.
Reisberg, B. (Ed.). (1983). *Alzheimer's disease: The standard reference.* New York: The Free Press.

e. Other dementias

Cummings, J. L., & Benson, D. F. (1983). *Dementia: A clinical approach.* Boston: Butterworth.

Cummings, J. L. (1987). Dementia syndromes: Neurobehavioral and neuropsychiatric features. *Journal of Clinical Psychiatry, 48* (5, Suppl.), 3–8.

3. Delirium and reversible dementia
   a. Description
   b. Estimates of prevalence
   c. Causes

Butler, R. N., & Lewis, M. I. (1983). Organic braln disorders. Chapter 5 in *Aging and mental health* (3rd ed.). St. Louis, MO: C. V. Mosby.

Evans, L. K. (1987). Sundown syndrome in institutionalized elderly. *Journal of the American Geriatrics Society, 35,* 101–108.

Cameron, D. E. (1941). Studies in senile nocturnal delirium. *Psychiatric Quarterly, 15,* 47–53.

Lipowski, Z. J. (1983). Transient cognitive disorders (delirium, acute confusional states) in the elderly. *American Journal of Psychiatry, 140,* 1426–1436.

National Institute on Aging Task Force (1980). Senility reconsidered. *Journal of the American Medical Association, 244*(3), 259–263.

Wells, C. E. (1979). Peudodementia. *American Journal of Psychiatry, 136,* 895–900.

Zarit, S. H., Orr, N. K., & Zarit, J. M. (1985). Causes of memory loss: Alzheimer's disease, other dementias, and conditions with similar symptoms. Chapter 2 in *The hidden victims of Alzheimer's disease: Families under stress.* New York: New York University Press.

4. Somatic disorders

Verwoerdt, A. (1981). Somatic expression of psychiatric illness. Chapter 9 in *Clinical geropsychiatry* (2nd ed.). Baltimore: Williams & Wilkins.

III. Assessment
   A. Differential diagnosis: Are cognitive problems due to dementia, delirium, depression, normal aging?
      1. Distinguishing features and overlap

Anthony, J. C., LeResche, L., Nias, U., Von Korff, M. R., & Folstein, M. F. (1982). Limits of the 'Mini-mental state' as a screening test for dementia and delirium among hospital patients. *Psychological Medicine, 12,* 397–408.

Butler, R. N., & Lewis, M. I. (1983). Diagnostic evaluation. Chapter 9 in *Aging and mental health* (3rd ed.). St. Louis, MO: C. V. Mosby.

Kahn, R. L., & Miller, N. E. (1978). Assessment of altered brain function in the aged. In M. Storandt, I. C. Siegler, & M. F. Elias (Eds.), *The clinical psychology of aging* (pp. 43–69). New York: Plenum Press.

Lezak, M. D. (1986). Neuropsychological assessment. In L. Teri & P. M. Lewinsohn (Eds.), *Geropsychological assessment and treatment* (pp. 3–38). New York: Springer.

Poon, L. W. (Ed.). (1986). *Handbook for clinical memory assessment of older adults*. Washington, DC: American Psychological Association.

Reifler, B. V., Larson, E., & Hanley, R. (1982). Coexistence of cognitive impairment and depression in geriatric outpatients. *American Journal of Psychiatry, 139*, 623–624.

Thompson, L. W., Gong, V., Haskins, E., & Gallagher, D. (1987). Assessment of depression and dementia during the late years. In K. W. Schaie (Ed.), *Annual Review of Gerontology and Geriatrics, Volume 7*, (pp. 295–324). New York: Springer.

Zarit, S. H., Orr, N. K., & Zarit, J. M. (1985). How to assess for dementia. Chapter 3 in *The hidden victims of Alzheimer's disease: Families under stress*. New York: New York University Press.

2. Can AD be differentiated reliably from other dementias?

McKhann, G., Drachman, D., Folstein, M., Katzman, R., Price, D., & Stadlan, E. M. (1984). Clinical diagnosis of Alzheimer's disease. *Neurology, 34*, 939–944.

Storandt, M., Botwinick, J., Danziger, W. L., Berg, L., & Hughes, C. P. (1984). Psychometric differentiation of mild senile dementia of the Alzheimer type. *Archives of Neurology, 41*, 497–499.

B. Functional Assessment
    1. Purposes of functional assessment
        a. Identify assets and deficits in current situation
        b. Identify goals for treatment and/or indicators to evaluate treatment
        c. Develop a treatment plan
    2. Approaches to functional assessment
        a. Omnibus batteries—OARS, CARE
        b. Measures, tests, ratings
        c. Self-monitoring

Hussian, R. A., & Davis, R. L. (1985). *Responsive care: Behavioral interventions with elderly persons*. Champaign, IL: Research Press.

Lawton, M. P. (1986). Functional assessment. In L. Teri & P. M. Lewinsohn (Eds.), *Geropsychological assessment and treatment* (pp. 39–88). New York: Springer.

Zarit, S. H., Eiler, J., & Hassinger, M. J. (1985). Clinical assessment. In J. E. Birren & K. W. Schaie (Eds.), *Handbook of the psychology of aging* (2nd ed., pp. 725–754). New York: Van Nostrand Reinhold.

IV. Treatment of Mental Health Problems
    A. Principles of treatment with older persons

Butler, R. N., & Lewis, M. I. (1983). General treatment principles. Chapter 8 in *Aging and mental health* (3rd ed., pp. 171–195). St. Louis, MO: C. V. Mosby.

Gatz, M., Popkin, S. J., Pino, C. D., & VandenBos, G. R. (1985). Psychological interventions with older adults. In J. E. Birren & K. W. Schaie (Eds.), *Handbook of the psychology of aging* (2nd ed., pp. 755–785). New York: Van Nostrand Reinhold.

Kahn, R. L. (1975). The mental health system and the future aged. *The Gerontologist, 15*(No. 1, Pt. 2), 24–31.

Knight, B. (1985–1986). Therapists' attitudes as explanation of underservice of elderly in mental health: Testing an old hypothesis. *International Journal of Aging and Human Development, 22,* 261–269.

Smyer, M. A., & Pruchno, R. A. (1984). Service use and mental impairment among the elderly. Arguments for consultation and education. *Professional Psychology: Research and Practice, 15,* 528–537.

Zarit, S. H. (1980). Principles of treatment: A model of community care. Chapter 10 in *Aging and mental disorders* (pp. 255–281). New York: The Free Press.

B. Individual psychotherapy
   1. General considerations

Hussian, R. A., & Davis, R. L. (1985). *Responsive care: Behavioral interventions with elderly persons.* Champaign, IL: Research Press.

Knight, B. (1986). *Psychotherapy with older adults.* Beverly Hills, CA: Sage.

Storandt, M. (1983). *Counseling and therapy with older adults.* New York: Springer.

   2. Psychotherapy of depression

Thompson, L. W., Gallagher, D., & Breckenridge, J. S. (1987). Comparative effectiveness of psychotherapies for depressed elders. *Journal of Consulting and Clinical Psychology, 55,* 385–390.

Thompson, L. W., Davies, R., Gallagher, D., & Krantz, S. (1986). Cognitive therapy with older adults. In T. Brink (Ed.), *Clinical gerontology: A guide to assessment and intervention* (pp. 245–279). New York: Haworth Press.

Zarit, J. M., & Zarit, S. H. (1984). Depression in later life: Treatment. In J. P. Abrahams & V. Crooks (Eds.), *Geriatric mental health: A clinician's guide* (pp. 41–54). New York: Grune & Stratton.

C. Group psychotherapy
   1. General considerations

Toseland, R. (in press). Group work with older adults. New York: New York University Press.

   2. Uses with specific populations
      a. Depression

Thompson, L. W., Gallagher, D., Nies, G., & Epstein, D. (1983). Evaluation of the effectiveness of professionals and nonprofessionals as instructors of "Coping with Depression" classes for elders. *The Gerontologist, 23,* 390–396.

b. Life review

Lewis, M. I., & Butler, R. N. (1974). Life review therapy: Putting memories to work in individual and group psychotherapy. *Geriatrics, 29,* 165–169.

c. Widows' groups

DeBor, L., Gallagher, D., & Lesher, E. (1982). Group counseling with bereaving elders. *Clinical Gerontologist, 1.*

D. Family psychotherapy

Herr, J. J., & Weakland, J. H. (1979). *Counseling elders and their families.* New York: Springer.

E. The case of dementia: Interventions with patients and families

1. Interventions with patients

Hussian, R. A. (1986). Severe behavioral problems. In L. Teri & P. M. Lewinsohn (Eds.), *Geropsychological assessment and treatment* (pp. 121–144). New York: Springer.

2. Interventions with caregivers

a. Goals
b. Approaches
c. Outcome

Zarit, S. H., Orr, N. K., & Zarit, J. M. (1985). *The hidden victims of Alzheimer's disease: Families under stress.* New York: New York University Press.

Pinkston, E. M., & Linsk, N. L. (1984). *Care of the elderly: A family approach.* New York: Pergamon Press.

Supplemental Readings:

Mace, N. L., & Rabins, P. V. (1981). *The thirty-six hour day.* Baltimore, MD: Johns Hopkins University Press.

F. Interventions in institutions

Butler, R. N., & Lewis, M. I. (1983). Proper institutional care. Chapter 11 in *Aging and mental health* (3rd ed., pp. 283–329). St. Louis, MO: C. V. Mosby.

Hussian, R. A., & Davis, R. L. (1985). *Responsive care: Behavioral interventions with elderly persons.* Champaign, IL: Research Press.

Smyer, M. A., Cohn, M. D., & Brannon, D. (1988). *Mental health consultation in nursing homes.* New York: New York University Press.

Smyer, M. A., & Frysinger, M. (1985). Mental health interventions in the nursing home community. In M. P. Lawton and G. Maddox (Eds.), *Annual Review of Gerontology and Geriatrics, Volume 5* (pp. 283–320). New York: Springer.

Akiskal, H. S., & McKinney, W. T., Jr. (1973). **Depressive disorders: Toward a unified hypothesis.** *Science, 182,* 20–29.

This paper evaluates various theories of depression, and proposes a comprehensive model in which depression is the common outcome of several different pathways. Etiological factors such as genetic, biochemical, or early experience may work singly or in combination. Experimental and clinical literature supporting different theories are reviewed, including research on object loss in primates, pharmacologically induced depression, and learned helplessness. The common outcome proposed is that etiological factors affect the biology of reward and punishment, resulting in biochemical changes and associated behaviors.

Kind	*Recommendation*	*Readability*	*Audience*
TC	***	2	AU,AG

Anthony, J. C., LeResche, L., Nias, U., Von Korff, M. R., & Folstein, M. F. (1982). Limits of the "mini-mental state" as a screening test for dementia and delirium among hospital patients. *Psychological Medicine, 12,* **397–408.**

This study examined the use of a commonly used cognitive screening test, the Mini–Mental State Examination (MMSE) with a sample of patients admitted to a general medical ward. Focus of the study was to provide data on the MMSE with a sample not seeking psychiatric treatment and with a broader range of sociodemographic characteristics than previous samples. Subjects were administered the MMSE, and then rated independently by a psychiatrist for the presence of dementia, delirium, and other mental disorders. The use of the standard cutoff for the MMSE (23 or less indicates impairment) was associated with a false positive rate of 39% and a false negative rate of 4.7%. All subjects with false positive diagnoses had less than a high school education. This paper highlights the limitations of relying on a mental status test alone for determining diagnosis. The MMSE is reprinted in an appendix to the article.

Kind	*Recommendation*	*Readability*	*Audience*
E	**	3	SP,AG

Atchley, R. C. (1988). *Social forces and aging: An introduction to social gerontology* **(5th ed.). Belmont, CA: Wadsworth.**

This most recent edition of a landmark and leading text on social gerontology is up to date, comprehensive, integrated, and well referenced.

Atchley's authoritative creation on aging is especially noteworthy for its multidisciplinary approach, setting it apart from other texts in this area. Carefully and clearly written chapters present an in-depth and timely overview of aging-related topics and issues (e.g., employment and retirement; physical, psychological, and social aging; health and social services for older adults; social policy; the economy; successful adaptation to aging).

Kind	Recommendation	Readability	Audience
TB	***	1	AU,AG,SP,GP

Beck, A. T., Rush, D., Shaw, D., & Emery, G. (1979). *Cognitive therapy of depression.* **New York: Guilford.**

This book presents the cognitive theory of depression and a psychotherapy approach derived from it that uses cognitive and behavioral techniques. The cognitive theory emphasizes that depression is the result of exaggerated ways of perceiving events. Depression is characterized by the cognitive triad, in which patients hold negative views of themselves, their experiences, and the future. While there may be some life events that contribute to these negative perceptions, cognitive theory holds that depression results not from the events themselves but from exaggerated evaluations of them or their implications. The treatment approach involves making patients aware of cognitions that evaluate themselves and their experiences, identifying cognitions that involve exaggerations, and then modifying these thought patterns. The therapist–client relationship and behavioral techniques are also seen as important to treatment outcome. This book has had a major influence on clinicians and researchers alike, and represents a major landmark in the literature on depression.

Kind	Recommendation	Readability	Audience
TB	***	2	SP,AG

Blazer, D. G., II. (1982). *Depression in late life.* **St. Louis, MO: Mosby.**

This book provides a comprehensive and in-depth discussion of depression and aging. Theories of depression, diagnosis, and treatment issues are discussed thoroughly. Particular attention is given to epidemiology of depression, especially the prevalence of symptoms of depression in community-living elderly who are not necessarily seeking treatment. Chapters focus on unipolar and bipolar disorders, bereavement, depressive neurosis, and depressive disorders associated with illness and alcohol use. Attention is devoted to major treatment approaches, including psychotherapy, family therapy, medication, other biological approaches, and treatment of depression in institutions.

Kind	Recommendation	Readability	Audience
TB	***	1	SP,AU,AG

Blazer, D., Hughes, D. C., & George, L. K. (1987). The epidemiology of depression in an elderly community population. *The Gerontologist,* **27, 281–297.**

This study reports on findings from a community survey of 1,300 community-living adults aged 60 years or older. Subjects were selected from urban and rural areas of five counties in North Carolina as part of the National Institute of Mental Health Epidemiologic Catchment Area studies. Each respondent completed the Diagnostic Interview Schedule (DIS), a structured interview designed to assess the severity and frequency of psychiatric symptoms and to yield a DSM-III diagnosis. The results indicated that approximately 1% of the sample had a DSM-III diagnosis of Major Depression while another 7% had various other diagnoses of affective disorder. Another 19% of the sample had significant depressive symptoms, though not meeting diagnostic criteria. The results indicate that diagnostic categories omit significant numbers of older people experiencing depressive symptoms.

Kind	Recommendation	Readability	Audience
E	**	2	SP,AG

Breslau, L. D., & Haug, M. R. (Eds.). (1983). *Depression and aging: Causes, care, and consequences.* **New York: Springer.**

This book notably provides an eclectic collection of perspectives, held by a variety of experts in the field, on multiple issues of depression and aging: definitions of depression in old age, nosology, epidemiology and diagnostic considerations; etiology; treatment and care; and the consequences for an individual as well as social/societal level. In the final chapter of this volume, Breslau and Haug attempt to create an integrated conceptual model of depression in older people, taking into account developmental changes and aging-associated vulnerabilities (or insufficient capacities) to developmental/aging processes and to depression, as well as the consequences of depressive disorders.

Kind	Recommendation	Readability	Audience
HB	**	2	AG,SP

Butler, R. N., & Lewis, M. I. (1983). *Aging and mental health* (3rd ed.). St. Louis, MO: C. V. Mosby.

This book provides an introduction to the problems of mental health and aging. Chapters cover normal adaptation as well as psychopathology. A positive psychosocial approach is taken that stresses that aging is not synonymous with decline. Rather, it is a period with potential for growth and development. Chapters on psychopathology are oriented around DSM-III categories and provide reviews of major problems of aging. Treatment approaches are reviewed, including individual and group psychotherapy, prevention of institutionalization, and care within institutions.

Kind	*Recommendation*	*Readability*	*Audience*
TB	***	1	AU,AG

Cameron, D. E. (1941). Studies in senile nocturnal delirium. *Psychiatric Quarterly, 15,* 47–53.

Patients with nocturnal delirium (or sundown syndrome) were evaluated by being placed in a darkened room much earlier in the day than when symptoms usually develop. This procedure resulted in appearance of symptoms of delirium and agitation within an hour. Another procedure involved blindfolding patients and asking them to identify the location of five objects in the room. With longer duration of blindfolding, subjects began misidentifying the location of objects. The results suggest that immediate visualization is important in maintaining cognitive functioning in many older persons. Decreased visualization caused by darkness may contribute to the development of nocturnal delirium.

Kind	*Recommendation*	*Readability*	*Audience*
E	***	2	AG

Clausen, J. A. (1986). A 15- to 20-year follow-up of married adult psychiatric patients. In L. Erlenmeyer-Kimling & N. E. Miller (Eds.), *Life-span research on the prediction of psychopathology* (pp. 175–194). Hillsdale, NJ: Lawrence Erlbaum.

Clausen reports findings from a follow-up study of a cohort of *married* psychiatric patients initially admitted to a mental hospital in the 1950s. Diagnoses on admission included schizophrenia, severe psychoneurosis, character disorder, or affective psychosis. Through use of clinical summaries, rediagnosis was attempted with the Research Diagnostic Criteria.

This chapter provides data on patients' current functioning, treatment history during the 15-to-20-year time span since initial hospitalization, and life histories. In general, favorable outcomes are correlated with acuteness of onset, the existence of a definite precipitant, later age at initial onset of psychiatric symptomatology, and good "premorbid status." Although the majority of patients have been treated for psychiatric symptoms since initial hospitalization, most were functioning adequately a great deal of the time. Outcome data tended to be more favorable for males than for females. Case studies are provided.

Kind	Recommendation	Readability	Audience
E	**	2–3	SP,AG

Cummings, J. L. (1987). Dementia syndromes: Neurobehavioral and neuropsychiatric features. *Journal of Clinical Psychiatry,* **48**(5, Suppl.), 3–8

The diseases causing dementia are described, including their symptoms and brain pathology. Common disorders, such as Alzheimer's-type dementia and vascular dementias, and rarer diseases, are both reviewed. Diagnostic considerations such as EEG and CT scan findings are discussed. An emphasis is placed on differentiating symptoms such as aphasia, amnesia, apraxia, and agnosia, which occur when the cerebral cortex is damaged, from symptoms that suggest subcortical involvement, for example, bradyphrenia, memory impairment, cognitive disturbance, personality and mood changes. Alzheimer type and Pick's disease are associated with cortical symptoms. Vascular or multi-infarct dementia, tumors, and brain infections can present with both cortical and subcortical symptoms. Depression and hydrocephalus are associated with subcortical symptoms.

Kind	Recommendation	Readability	Audience
RC	**	3	SP,AG

Cummings, J. L, & Benson, D. F. (1983). *Dementia: A clinical approach.* **Boston: Butterworth.**

This book provides a comprehensive review of causes of dementia. Chapters cover the most common dementing disorders, including Alzheimer's disease and multi-infarct dementia, as well as rarer types. Reversible causes of dementia are also reviewed. Chapters emphasize prevalence, etiology, brain pathology, presenting symptoms, and diagnostic indicators of each disorder. Disorders are classified according to whether they involve primarily cortical or subcortical areas of the brain. Neuropsychological and medical approaches to diagnosis are discussed. While stressing the importance of ruling out treatable causes of dementia, the authors also indicate signs and symptoms that point toward specific types of dementia. This book is probably the most complete reference on dementia.

Kind	Recommendation	Readability	Audience
TB	***	2,3	SP,AG

Cummings, J. L., & Zarit, J. M. (1987). Probable Alzheimer's disease in an artist. *Journal of the American Medical Association, 258,* 2731– 2734.

This article describes the deterioration in artistic ability in a painter afflicted with Alzheimer's disease. While most investigations of dementia emphasize verbal abilities, nonverbal artistic functions may also be altered significantly. The patient in this case study was a 75-year-old man who was an amateur painter. Changes in his artistic abilities are illustrated by a series of paintings he made around the time of the onset of the disease and as it progressed. Motivation and organizational ability, rather than visual spatial performance, were affected first. As the disease progressed, there was a gradual simplification of themes and color. Shading and perspective were gradually lost. These changes corresponded to deterioration in performance on neuropsychological tests. This study suggests possible neuropsychological and neuropathological bases of artistic ability as well as the specific effects of Alzheimer's disease.

Kind	Recommendation	Readability	Audience
E	***	2	SP,AU,AG

Davies, P., & Wolozin, B. L. (1987). Recent advances in the neurochemistry of Alzheimer's disease. *Journal of Clinical Psychiatry, 48*(5, Suppl.), 23–30.

This chapter reviews the neuropathology associated with Alzheimer's disease (neuritic plaques, neurofibrillary tangles, granulovacuolar degeneration) and summarizes research on the neurochemistry of these changes. Studies of amyloid, the protein at the core of neuritic plaques, focus on the question of its origins, whether it is carried by serum or is derived from material in brain neurons. Recent work has identified a precursor of this protein to be located on chromosome 21, in the region where possible abnormalities in familial cases of Alzheimer's disease have also been identified. The accumulation of aluminum in plaques and neurofibrillary tangles may also be significant, although aluminum levels are similar to normal aging. Deficits in neurotransmitters, particularly the cholinergic system that synthesizes acetylcholine, are pronounced in Alzheimer's disease. Neurons that synthesize acetylcholine have their origins in the nucleus basalis of Meynert, a region of the basal forebrain. These cells are differentially affected in Alzheimer's disease, with more than 75% lost. GABA and norepinephrine may also be affected, at least in subgroups of patients. Neuropeptides, especially somatostatin, are also affected in Alzheimer's.

Kind	Recommendation	Readability	Audience
RC	**	3	AG

Evans, L. K. (1987). Sundown syndrome in institutionalized elderly. *Journal of the American Geriatrics Society,* **35**, 101–108.

Patients in a nursing home were screened for the presence of "sundown syndrome" which involves increased agitation, restlessness, and cognitive impairment around the hour of sunset. Sundown syndrome is commonly reported for older patients in nursing homes and hopsitals, and represents a significant management problem. Eighty-nine nursing home residents over age 60 were evaluated with an inventory to identify sundown behaviors. Eleven subjects were found to have evidence of sundown syndrome. Factors associated with sundown syndrome were the presence of dementia, dehydration, being awakened at night, and recent admission to the facility.

Kind	Recommendation	Readability	Audience
E	**	2	SP,AG

Fry, P. S. (1986). *Depression, stress, and adaptations in the elderly: Psychological assessment and intervention.* **Rockville, MD: Aspen.**

This well-referenced, comprehensive text is identified as being targeted primarily at clinical practitioners. Additionally, it will be an extremely useful resource for clinical faculty as well as students interested in an *in-depth* introduction to clinical issues with the elderly segment of the population, especially those elders dwelling in the community rather than in institutions. Informative chapters focus on age- and aging-related issues, clinical assessment of various conditions and disorders (e.g., clinical depression, cognitive impairments and disorders, stress reactions, and coping strategies), management, and treatment dimensions (support, interpersonal, cognitive–behavioral, group, family, psychopharmacological, and integrated therapies). Attention is given to issues revolving around grief, death, and dying. In the book's final chapter, Fry explores future directions in caring for older people—with a timely emphasis on a community-based and community-oriented system of care.

Kind	*Recommendation*	*Readability*	*Audience*
Clinical text	**	2–3	SP,AG

Gatz, M., Popkin, S. J., Pino, C. D., & VandenBos, G. R. (1985). Psychological interventions with older adults. In J. E. Birren & K. W. Schaie (Eds.), *Handbook of the psychology of aging* (2nd ed., pp. 755–785). New York: Van Nostrand Reinhold.

This review of the treatment literature emphasizes four themes: (1) that there are both continuities and discontinuities between interventions made with older and younger age groups, (2) the different ways clinical knowledge is generated ranging from case studies to controlled evaluations of outcome, (3) how the types of problems of older people require choosing certain treatment approaches, and (4) some common factors that emerge from reviewing diverse treatment approaches used with the elderly. The chapter begins by reviewing barriers to psychological intervention, including: (1) client variables, such as not being psychologically minded and the age of therapists, (2) therapist variables such as lower expectations for outcome and countertransference, and (3) features of the mental health system such as reimbursement procedures. The chapter then reviews approaches to individual and group treatment, as well as other community and institutional interventions. Support is presented for continuity in treatment of older people compared to younger persons. Common factors associated with positive outcomes were increasing feelings of control and hope, establishing a positive relationship with the therapist, facilitating clients to find meaning in the events of their lives, and creating opportunities for learning.

Kind	*Recommendation*	*Readability*	*Audience*
HB	***	2	SP,AG

Gaylord, S. A., & Zung, W. W. K. (1987). Affective disorders among

the aging. In L. L. Carstensen & B. A. Edelstein (Eds.), *Handbook of clinical gerontology*. New York: Pergamon Press.

This chapter reviews affective disorders in the elderly, including symptoms, types of disorders, diagnostic issues, assessment, prevalence, etiology, and treatment. Current genetic, biochemical, and psychological theories of depression are discussed. Treatment approaches reviewed are medications, electroconvulsive therapy, and individual and group psychotherapy. The chapter is useful for providing an overview of the literature on affective disorders.

Kind	Recommendation	Readability	Audience
HB	**	2	SP,AU,AG

Herr, J. J., & Weakland, J. H. (1979) *Counseling elders and their families*. **New York: Springer.**

This landmark book provides an overview of a family therapy approach to treatment of problems of older people. The authors apply a systems approach to family therapy drawn from the Palo Alto School, as well as other theorists. Practical suggestions for conducting therapy are made, including how to develop a therapeutic relationship and how to formulate helpful communication. Procedures for assessing families, determining goals, and making interventions are described, with several case examples that illustrate application of these approaches.

Kind	Recommendation	Readability	Audience
TB	***	2	SP,AG

Hussian, R. A. (1981). *Geriatric psychology: A behavioral perspective.* **New York: Van Nostrand Reinhold.**

This practical clinical manual is noteworthy for its clarity, level of detail, appeal to practitioners, and optimal use of good clinical examples. In addition to providing a detailed, very understandable overview of effective behavioral strategies and techniques, Hussian proposes a "compensatory model of aging" for explaining age-related differences and for understanding inappropriate behavior to be a result of inadequate adaptation to aging/changes. Problem behaviors discussed include paranoid behavior, wandering, self-stimulatory behavior, depression, anxiety, and urinary incontinence.

Kind	Recommendation	Readability	Audience
TB	**	2	SP,AU,AG

Hussian, R. A., & Davis, R. L. (1985). *Responsive care: Behavioral interventions with elderly persons.* **Champaign, IL: Research Press.**

This very practical and useful manual, targeted at clinicians and care-givers, provides an excellent and detailed overview of age-associated problems as well as behavioral techniques and strategies. Behavioral interventions are aimed at altering or modifying the duration, intensity, frequency, or location of specific target behaviors. Notably, attention is given to the influence of values or attitudes in labeling specific behaviors as problematic. In addition to assessing behaviors objectively, the general goal is to increase adaptive and/or appropriate behaviors (e.g., behavioral deficits), to decrease maladaptive and/or inappropriate behaviors (e.g., behavioral excesses), or to change the particular location or context of a problematic response (e.g., although masturbation is a normal behavior, it is deemed inappropriate to participate in self-stimulation in the lobby area of a nursing home). Problematic behaviors discussed include minimal social interaction, low involvement with group activities, low self-care skills (i.e., behavioral deficits), physical aggression, unwarranted chronic demandingness, excessive shouting (i.e., behavioral excesses).

Kind	Recommendation	Readability	Audience
Clinical	***	1	SP,GP,AU,AG

Kahn, R. L. (1975). The mental health system and the future aged. *The Gerontologist, 15*(No.1, Pt. 2), 24–31.

Although this intriguing article was written well over a decade ago, it remains of tremendous value and significance. Kahn discussed the changing mental health ideologies from the early 1900s, focusing analytically on custodialism. Predicted future changes in the characteristics of mental health professionals and older adults are discussed. This well-written paper is especially noteworthy for its still timely "guiding principles" for service delivery and suggestions for beneficial mental health system-level changes.

Kind	Recommendation	Readability	Audience
RC	***	2	SP,AU,AG

Kahn, R. L., & Miller, N. E. (1978). Assessment of altered brain function in the aged. In M. Storandt, I. C. Siegler, & M. F. Elias (Eds.), *The clinical psychology of aging* **(pp. 43–69). New York: Plenum Press.**

This chapter reviews approaches to the assessment of dementia and delirium in older patients. Models of the relation of brain impairment to cognitive functioning are reviewed, with an emphasis on individual differences. Psychometric and clinical approaches to assessment are presented, including a review of commonly used tests. It is stressed that in the absence of definitive diagnostic criteria, false positive diagnoses of dementia have more harmful consequences than false negative diagnoses. As a result, the diagnosis of dementia should not be made unless evidence is strong and treatable disorders have been clearly ruled out. This paper also describes the different patterns of response of dementia and delirium patients to standard mental status examinations.

Kind	Recommendation	Readability	Audience
RC	***	2	SP,AG

Klerman, G. L., Weissman, M. M., Rounsaville, B. J., & Chevron, E. S. (1984). *Interpersonal psychotherapy of depression*. New York: Basic Books.

This approach to understanding and treating depression places an emphasis on interpersonal behavior. Antecedents of depression are seen in disruptions of interpersonal relationships in childhood, as well as more recent events that affect social behavior. In turn, depression has an impact on social behavior and communication. Treatment involves identifying and modifying social and interpersonal problems, including interpersonal role disputes, role transitions, interpersonal deficits, and depression associated with grief reactions. Features of the therapy are an emphasis on the here and now, encouragement of expression of affect to teach its management, analysis of communication problems, behavior change techniques such as role playing and decision analysis, and use of the therapeutic relationship to support change.

Kind	Recommendation	Readability	Audience
TB	**	2	SP,AG

Knight, B. (1985–1986). Therapists' attitudes as explanation of underservice of elderly in mental health: Testing an old hypothesis. *International Journal of Aging and Human Development, 22*, 261–269.

This study tests the assumption that therapists have negative attitudes about the elderly. Therapists' attitudes are commonly cited as a principal reason older people are underserved in the mental health system. A semantic differential and the Silverman revision of Kogan's Older Person Scale were used to measure attitudes. Subjects were a sample of therapists recruited from community mental health centers and a group of college students. Results indicated that therapists' attitudes were more positive than college students. Work site was more important than attitudes, however, in determining if a therapist worked with elderly clients. The results suggest system level variables may be a more important barrier to service delivery for older adults than attitudes of mental health workers.

Kind	Recommendation	Readability	Audience
E	**	2	AU,AG

Knight, B. (1986). *Psychotherapy with older adults*. Beverly Hills, CA: Sage.

The author, a clinician and researcher at a community mental health center, provides a conceptual overview to psychotherapy with older adults, and illustrates his approach with numerous case examples. Knight's model of psychotherapy with older adults identifies five topics and three themes that characterize treatment. The topics of therapy are (1) chronic illness and disability, (2) death and dying, including grieving, (3) love, marriage, and sexuality, (4) the meaning of aging and growing older, and (5) ethnicity and aging. Major themes of psychotherapy are (1) empowerment of the older person, (2) enjoyment of one's life, and (3) life review. Knight also stresses the importance of examining patients' feelings about their therapist (transference) and therapists' feelings about their older clients (countertransference). He discusses the various ways that assumptions made by clients and therapists based on differences in age between them can interfere with treatment process. He suggests looking at the particular interactions between client and therapist to understand these processes, rather than relying on a formula.

Kind	Recommendation	Readability	Audience
TB	***	1	SP,AU,AG

Kramer, M., German, P. S., Anthony, J. C., Von Korff, M., & Skinner, E. A. (1985). Patterns of mental disorders among the elderly residents of Eastern Baltimore. *Journal of the American Geriatrics Society*, *33*(4), 236–245.

This paper presented prevalence rates of specific mental disorders and *severe* cognitive impairment for 3,481 participants, aged 18 and above, in the Eastern Baltimore Mental Health Survey, which is part of the National Institute of Mental Health Epidemiologic Catchment Area studies. This particular survey is especially notable for its oversampling of individuals aged 65 and over. The interview schedule included a modified Diagnostic Interview Schedule (DIS) and Mini-Mental State Examination. Substantial age differences were found for 6-month prevalence rates of the 11 DIS/DSM-III mental disorders as well as for point prevalence rates for severe cognitive impairment. Excluding major depressive disorder and severe cognitive impairment, prevalence rates for all disorders tended to be highest for individuals in the 18 to 64 age group and lowest for people aged 75 and over. Conditions with prevalence rates above 1% in the 65 to 74 age group were phobic disorder (12.1%), severe cognitive impairment (3.0%), alcohol use disorder (2.1%), obsessive compulsive disorder (2.2%), and dysthymia (1.0%). Conditions with prevalence rates above 1% among respondents in the 75+ age group were phobic disorders (10.1%), severe cognitive impairment (9.3%), major depression (1.3%), and dysthymia (1.1%). For those aged 75 and over, no cases of schizophrenia were identified. Rates of major depression were highest for those respondents in the 18 to 64 age group (2.5%), lower for the 65 to 74 age group (0.7%), and then higher for the 75+ age group (1.3%). In contrast, cognitive impairment rates showed a consistent and *marked* increase associated with advanced age (3.0% for the 65 to 74 age group, 9.3% for the 75+ age group). Relationships of sex, race, educational level, size of household, and marital status with prevalence rates were examined.

Kind	Recommendation	Readability	Audience
E	***	2–3	SP,AU,AG

Lewinsohn, P. M., Fenn, D. S., Stanton, A. K., & Franklin, J. (1986). Relation of age at onset to duration of episode in unipolar depression. *Psychology and Aging, 1,* 63–68.

This study considers longitudinal and developmental issues in depression. There is extensive variability in the duration of episodes of unipolar depression, but there has been little investigation of determinants of duration. The hypothesis that duration of episodes is longer with late onset is based on evidence that risk factors for depression, such as biological factors and social losses, increase with age. A total of 2,020 subjects from four different samples were evaluated, and included significant numbers of persons over age 65. Unipolar depression was determined using the Schedule for Affective Disorders and Schizophrenia (SADS) Interview Schedule. Diagnosis was determined using the Research Diagnostic Criteria. Age of onset was not found to be related to duration of the most recent episode. Gender, however, was associated with duration, with women reporting being depressed for a longer period of time. Episodes of depression were generally relatively brief, with only 27% lasting more than 1 year.

Kind	Recommendation	Readability	Audience
E	***	2	AG

Lewinsohn, P. M., Muñoz, R. F., Youngren, M. A., & Zeiss, A. M. (1978). *Control your depression.* Englewood Cliffs, NJ: Prentice-Hall.

This book is designed as a self-help manual for treatment of depression. Based on successful classes for treating depression, the book reviews theories of depression, with an emphasis on the behavioral theory. The behavioral theory stresses the relation between depressed mood and the events in a person's life, particularly, engaging in pleasant and unpleasant events. A series of structured exercises are presented that help persons to assess if they are depressed and to plan and then implement treatment. In addition to the focus on pleasant and unpleasant events, chapters deal with social skills and cognitive aspects of depression.

Kind	Recommendation	Readability	Audience
TB	***	1	GP,SP,AU

Lewis, M. I., & Butler, R. N. (1974). Life review therapy: Putting memories to work in individual and group psychotherapy. *Geriatrics, 29,* 165–169.

This article posits that a spontaneous process of life review often occurs in late life, and may be specifically stimulated as part of psychotherapy in order to facilitate change. Some clients may be aware of the process, but for others it may be manifested in a variety of indirect ways from a mild nostalgia to garrulousness or depression. Life review can be enhanced through several means, including having clients make a written or taped autobiography, construct a genealogy, make pilgrimages to significant places in one's life, and construct summations of one's life work. Life review can also be facilitated in an age-integrated psychotherapy group. Although many obstacles must be overcome to develop a successful group, the outcome can involve development of meaningful relationships and the creative use of life experiences by older adults.

Kind	Recommendation	Readability	Audience
case study	***	1	SP,AU,AG

Lezak, M. D. (1986). Neuropsychological assessment. In L. Teri & P. M. Lewinsohn (Eds.), *Geropsychological assessment and treatment* (pp. 3–38). New York: Springer.

Neuropsychological assessment can contribute to differential diagnosis, document the course of a condition, identify features of the patient's mental condition that relate to the capacity for self-care and response to treatment, and contribute to research on brain–behavior relations. Two distinct approaches to assessment have been taken: (1) the clinical approach, which identifies individual differences in patients' symptoms and how they solve test problems, and (2) the psychometric approach, which is based on performance on normative tests. The clinical approach has more flexibility for an in-depth examination of performance, while the psychometric approach has greater objectivity and more systematically examines different functions. A combination of these approaches with elderly patients is recommended, in which standardized tests are interpreted in the light of age-related decrements that may affect performance (e.g., sensory loss) and more flexible testing approaches can be instituted. This chapter also reviews tests of different neuropsychological functions and comprehensive test batteries. Two cases are presented for illustration of the author's approach to assessment.

Kind	*Recommendation*	*Readability*	*Audience*
RC	**	2	SP,AG

Mace, N. L., & Rabins, P. V. (1981). *The thirty-six hour day.* **Baltimore: Johns Hopkins University Press.**

Mace and Rabins have sensitively written an easily understood guide for families providing care to members with dementia. It is characterized by accurate and helpful information, sure-to-be-familiar case examples, and very practical, detailed suggestions on how to adjust to difficult changes, address problematic issues, and manage inappropriate behaviors that may be encountered every day. Chapters focus on diagnostic concerns, treatment, and care of the family member's loved one (e.g., problems encountered in daily care, behavioral and medical problems, mood disturbances, difficulties arising when the impaired family member is still living independently, legal and financial issues, alternative living arrangements). Attention is given to the needs of the family members—as caregivers and as human beings (e.g., the need for taking time out for themselves, avoiding isolation, taking part in support groups, recognizing and understanding their own emotions).

Kind	*Recommendation*	*Readability*	*Audience*
E	***	1	GP

Mayeux, R., Stern, Y., & Spanton, S. (1985). Heterogeneity in dementia of the Alzheimer type: Evidence of subgroups. *Neurology,* **35, 453– 461.**

A series of 121 patients with Alzheimer's disease were evaluated for current symptoms, and a smaller group of 50 were followed longitudinally at 3-month intervals for a period of 6 months to 4 years. Based on the initial and longitudinal evaluations, four subgroups are proposed: (1) benign, with little or no progression of symptoms, (2) myoclonic, characterized by the presence of myoclonis or other dyskinesias and a rapid deterioration, (3) extrapyramidal, in which patients have Parkinsonlike symptoms such as bradykinesia, rigidity, problems with gait, tremor, and a masklike expression, and where intellectual and functional decline is severe, including more frequent occurence of psychotic symptoms, and (4) typical, with gradual progression of symptoms. It is suggested that the extrapyramidal subtype may be experiencing deficiencies in two major neurotransmitter systems, cholinergic and dominergic. The myoclonus group was younger when the disease developed. This study suggests the need for careful characterization of Alzheimer patients to identify significant subgroups.

Kind	*Recommendation*	*Readability*	*Audience*
E	**	3	SP,AG

McKhann, G., Drachman, D., Folstein, M., Katzman, R., Price, D., & Stadlan, E. M. (1984). Clinical diagnosis of Alzheimer's disease. *Neurology,* **34, 939–944.**

This paper presents criteria for diagnosis of Alzheimer's disease. No definitive diagnostic test exists as yet for Alzheimer's disease, except for confirmation at autopsy of the presence of characteristic brain pathologies, such as neuritic plaques and neurofibrillary tangles. The clinical criteria proposed permit classification of cases as probable or possible Alzheimer's disease, based on history and clinical characteristics. Probable Alzheimer's disease is established through identification of progressive impairment of memory and other cognitive functions, no disturbance of consciousness, absence of other systemic or brain diseases that might cause the cognitive impairment, the absence of plateaus in the disease. A history of sudden onset, focal neurological symptoms, and seizures or gait problems early in the disease make the diagnosis of Alzheimer's uncertain. A definite diagnosis of Alzheimer's is based on these clinical criteria and confirming evidence obtained at autopsy.

Kind	*Recommendation*	*Readability*	*Audience*
RC	***	2	SP,AG

Melnick, V. L., & Dubler, N. M. (Eds.). (1985). *Alzheimer's disease: Dilemmas in clinical research.* **Clifton, NJ: Humana Press.**

This very timely and intellectually provocative volume raises ethical, moral, practical, and theoretical issues regarding much-needed research on patients afflicted with Alzheimer's disease. Notably, informed consent issues are dealt with in a thorough and thoughtful manner (e.g., proxy consent, veritable competency of cognitively impaired patients to refuse or assent consent, critical concerns revolving around usage of institutionalized demented people in research protocols). In the final chapter, suggested guidelines for future research endeavors—primarily of interest to clinical researchers as well as reviewers of research proposals—are provided.

Kind	Recommendation	Readability	Audience
E	**1/2	2–3	AG

Miller, M. (1979). *Suicide after sixty: The final alternative.* **New York: Springer.**

Although generally considered to be a problem of the young, suicide rates are high among the elderly, with older white males having the highest rates of any group in the population. This book reviews data on the prevalence and causes of suicide and discusses prevention approaches. Risk of suicide in late life is increased by the presence of depression, chronic illness, and social isolation, such as might follow widowhood or other losses. Alcohol and drug abuse and retirement may also be precipitants.

Kind	Recommendation	Readability	Audience
TB	**	1	GP,SP,AU,AG

Miller, N. E. (1986). Introduction: The prediction of psychopathology across the life-span. In L. Erlenmeyer-Kimling & N. E. Miller (Eds.), *Life-span research on the prediction of psychopathology* **(pp. 1–17). Hillsdale, NJ: Lawrence Erlbaum.**

This eloquently written introduction to a volume provides an overview of several clinical longitudinal studies of psychopathology. Notably, it incorporates a series of intellectually provocative methodological, practical, conceptual, substantive, and developmental issues regarding the understanding of and life-span prediction of psychopathologic disorders.

Kind	Recommendation	Readability	Audience
RC	**	2–3	AG

Mishara, B. L., & Kastenbaum, R. (1980). *Alcohol and old age.* **New York: Grune & Stratton.**

This book attempts to address two opposing branches of literature (use vs. abuse) on alcohol and aging issues: (1) the positive aspects of alcohol use, and (2) the detrimental aspects of alcohol use. Attention is given to two general types of problem drinkers or alcoholics in later life: those who had drinking problems when young and throughout adulthood and those who have started to abuse alcohol in old age. Addressed topics include an overview of alcohol use issues in old age; criteria for determining if an older person has a drinking problem; physiological effects of alcohol use; epidemiological information; the effect of alcohol use on an elder individual's health status; benefits associated with use of alcoholic beverages among institutionalized elderly people.

Kind	Recommendation	Readability	Audience
TB	**	2	AU,AG

Mortimer, J. A. (1986). Epidemiology of dementia: International comparisons. In G. Maddox & J. Brody (Eds.), *Epidemiology and aging.* New York: Springer.

This paper reviews prevalence of dementia, using available epidemiological surveys from around the world. Rates of moderate and severe dementia in developed countries range from approximately 3.0% to 7.7% of the population over age 65. Prevalence in less developed countries is much lower, averaging around 2.2 cases per 1,000 persons. This lower rate is the result of higher birth rates and lower life expectancies in these countries. Projections for the next 25 years show the prevalence of cases will increase in both developed and less developed countries, though the relative differences between them can be expected to remain the same, given current birth rates. Although rates of overall prevalence are similar in developed countries, differences in rates of various types of dementia may provide information about possible etiology. As an example, Alzheimer's disease is the most common cause of dementia in Western Europe and the United States, while Japanese studies indicate a higher rate of multi-infarct dementia.

Kind	Recommendation	Readability	Audience
RC	**	2	AG

Mortimer, J. A., & Schuman, L. M. (Eds.). (1981). *The epidemiology of dementia.* New York: Oxford University Press.

This book reviews available epidemiological data on the incidence and prevalence of dementia. Evidence from Western Europe and the United States suggests some variation in rates, although this may be the result of differences in how cases are identified, rather than actual prevalence.

Chapters discuss diagnostic issues, etiology including genetic models, and methodological problems in the study of dementia.

Kind	Recommendation	Readability	Audience
TB	**	2	SP,AU,AG

National Institute on Aging Task Force (1980). Senility reconsidered. *Journal of the American Medical Association, 244*(3), 259–263.

This article emphasizes the various disorders in the elderly that are associated with symptoms of dementia and delirium. It is stressed that virtually any disturbance of the "internal environment" of an older person can result in cognitive disturbances. Among the treatable causes of cognitive impairment are drug toxicities, depression, and stress such as from relocation. It is proposed that irreversible dementia be a diagnosis of exclusion, arrived at only after treatable conditions have been ruled out. This article sets a standard for medical evaluation for possible dementia.

Kind	Recommendation	Readability	Audience
RC	***	2	SP,AG

Osgood, N. J. (1985). *Suicide in the elderly: A practitioner's guide to diagnosis and mental health intervention.* **Rockville, MD: Aspen.**

Suicide occurs more frequently among older than among younger people. In fact, suicide rates are higher among older male adults (over age 70) than any other sex-age grouping in the national population. In comparison to younger people, when elders attempt to take their own lives, they are usually successful, more frequently use lethal means, and are not simply expressing a cry for help. This book provides an excellent overview of issues revolving around suicide and aged individuals; it includes age- and aging-related issues; prevalence rates; causal factors; diagnostic criteria (e.g., characteristics associated with older people who are at suicidal risk) and assessment considerations; intervention or prevention strategies (including pharmacological interventions, support groups, a variety of creative therapies, life review therapy, techniques for coping with stresses and changes in later life).

Kind	Recommendation	Readability	Audience
Clinical text	**	2–3	SP,AG

Pinkston, E. M., & Linsk, N. L. (1984). *Care of the elderly: A family approach.* **New York: Pergamon Press.**

This book describes application of a behavioral treatment approach to problems of aging. Utilizing home interviews and all members of the patient's family who are available, treatment plans are developed that emphasize reinforcement of positive behavior and control of problems. Treatment examples provide outcome data that document the effectiveness of this approach.

Kind	Recommendation	Readability	Audience
TB	***	2	SP,AG

Poon, L. W. (Ed.) (1986). *Handbook for clinical memory assessment of older adults.* **Washington, DC: American Psychological Association.**

This collection of articles provides in-depth reviews on major issues of memory assessment of the elderly. Sections cover different models of memory assessment, instruments for evaluation of symptoms and complaints about memory, assessment of the effects of depression, and the use of external validators. Articles review normal memory in aging and clinical problems such as changes due to Alzheimer's disease and other dementias.

Kind	Recommendation	Readability	Audience
HB	***	2,3	SP,AG

Post, F. (1980). Paranoid, schizophrenia-like, and schizophrenic states in the aged. In J. E. Birren & R. B. Sloane (Eds.), *Handbook of mental health and aging* **(pp. 591–615). Englewood Cliffs, NJ: Prentice Hall.**

This excellent scholarly work provides a comprehensive, well-referenced review of paranoid, schizophrenialike, and schizophrenic states in older people. The distinction between age of onset versus aging of the patient was noted, reflecting the fact that these disorders are life-span problems. Post integrates findings of studies done on two types of elders: those who experienced these disorders for the first time in later life and those who experienced "breakdowns" earlier in life and were followed up and studied in later life. The following issues were discussed: terminology, nosology, clinical descriptions of various disorders (e.g., simple paranoid psychosis, schizophrenialike illnesses, paranoid schizophrenia states, persistent organic paranoid psychoses, schizoaffective illnesses), epidemiology, etiological concerns (revolving around hereditary, personal and interpersonal, and physical factors), prognosis, and treatment.

Kind	Recommendation	Readability	Audience
RC	***	2–3	AG
(in HB)			

Pruchno, R., & Smyer, M. A. (1983). Mental health problems and aging: A short quiz. *International Journal of Aging and Human Development, 17*(2), 123–140.

A 16-item quiz, created to assess factual knowledge about a variety of mental health and aging issues (e.g., psychotherapeutic efficacy with older adults, suicide prevalence rates, drug abuse, psychiatric disorder prevalence rates among nursing home residents) was administered to two groups of undergraduate students: 301 undergraduates enrolled in an introductory science course and 91 undergraduates enrolled in a course on aging. At pretest, the science group attained a mean score of 7.581 and the aging group attained a mean score of 7.143. Increases in mean scores were not found for either group at the 2-month retest. Item-to-item correlations were positive but low. Quiz items were documented with supporting research for the purposes of promoting discussion, stimulating further research, and presenting a succinct overview of important theoretical and empirical issues in the area of mental health and aging.

Kind	Recommendation	Readability	Audience
E	**	1	SP,AU,AG

Robins, L. N., Helzer, J. E., Weissman, M. M., Orvaschel, H., Gruenberg, E., Burke, J. D., Jr., & Regier, D. A. (1984). Lifetime prevalence of specific psychiatric disorders in three sites. *Archives of General Psychiatry, 41*, 949–958.

This paper presents lifetime prevalence rates for specific DSM-III psychiatric disorders for participants aged 18 and above from three sites (New Haven, Connecticut; Baltimore, Maryland; and St. Louis, Missouri) of the National Institute of Mental Health Epidemiologic Catchment Area studies. Estimates were derived through the use of a Diagnostic Interview Schedule (DIS). Leading diagnoses were alcohol abuse or dependence, major depressive disorder, phobia, antisocial personality, and drug abuse and dependence. Antisocial personality and alcohol abuse and dependence ("acting-out disorders") predominated in males. Depressive and anxiety disorders (specifically, phobias) predominated in females. Intersite comparisons were made for all psychiatric disorders, with consideration given to the demographic correlates of sex, age, race, and educational level. Notably, compared to males, females were not found to have higher total rates of all disorders examined. This is in striking contrast to findings from prior studies showing that females are more psychiatrically impaired than are males. Significant differences were not found between rates among blacks versus whites. Low levels of psychiatric disorders were generally correlated with rural residence and higher levels of education. Unexpectedly, the 25 to 44 age group was found to have the highest rates for most psychiatric disorders. Only rates for severe cognitive impairment (based on point prevalence rates determined from the Mini-Mental State Examination) were found, as was expected, to increase consistently with advancing age. Generally, the lowest lifetime prevalence rates for studied psychiatric disorders were found for those aged 65 and above.

Kind	Recommendation	Readability	Audience
E	**	2–3	AG

Rodin, J., & Langer, E. (1980). Aging labels: The decline of control and the fall of self-esteem. *Journal of Social Issues, 36*, 12–29.

This article provides a good review of several empirical studies on how negative labeling of and stereotypes about older people may contribute to and influence behavior. Resultant behavior might then serve to "confirm" common stereotypes about the elderly and ultimately lead to diminished sense of control over one's own life and lowered self-esteem. The authors succinctly describe the (mis)labeling process (including reasons for why it may be occurring) and discuss past research on held stereotypes playing a role in interactions involving older adults. It should be noted that the focus is on how stereotypes about aging affect the behavior of other people, not of the elder. This paper's value is enhanced by its discussion of how and what environmental interventions may serve to beneficially alter the consequences of negative labeling processes and "overattribution" to deficits associated with aging.

Kind	Recommendation	Readability	Audience
RC	**	2	AG

Rowe, J. W., & Kahn, R. L. (1987). Human aging: Usual and successful. *Science, 237*, 143–149.

This paper reemphasizes the need to view the normal segment of the older population as a heterogeneous group, rather than merely to focus on differences between diseased and nondiseased elderly individuals. The authors discuss the need to recognize and utilize in future research a conceptual distinction between "usual" and "successful" aging, two subcategories of the conventional "normal" category. With respect to successful aging, the focus is on extrinsic factors playing a positive or neutral role in the adaptation to aging process. Empirical findings regarding the physiological (carbohydrate metabolism, cognitive functioning, osteoporosis) and psychosocial (control or autonomy, social support) domains are provided to support the proposed distinction between usual and successful aging. Thereafter, the authors delineate an agenda for future research: to incorporate the proposed conceptual distinction in gerontological research, to increase our knowledge base about transitions in later life (most notably, those in the positive or "successful" direction), to study the influence of physiological and psychosocial components singly and interdependently with respect to successful aging. The article is of great value through its overall emphasis on the promotion of holistic health and its presentation of aging as a time of potential growth.

Kind	*Recommendation*	*Readability*	*Audience*
RC	**	2–3	AU,AG

Schaie, K .W., & Hertzog, C. (1983). **Fourteen-year cohort-sequential analyses of adult intellectual development.** *Developmental Psychology*, *19*, 531–543.

This paper reports findings from a landmark study on adult intellectual development, based on data from two 14-year longitudinal sequences of seven birth cohorts (1956 to 1970; 1963 to 1977) as well as four cross-sectional sequences (1956, 1963, 1970, and 1977). Performance ratings on five of Thurstone's 1948 Primary Mental Abilities (PMA) Test subtests—Verbal Meaning, Space, Inductive Reasoning, Number, and Word Fluency—are reported. Results showed that there are clearly age-correlated decrements in PMA performance on all subtests for subjects aged 60 and over. These performance decrements in later life are believed to be of practical importance as well as statistical significance. In addition, some statistically significant declines were shown in some PMA subtests prior to age 60. In short, although age-related declines are clearly evident after the age of 60, some small decrements are occurring earlier. Schaie and Hertzog discuss potential explanations (e.g., effects covarying with time of measurement) for these early declines, recommending caution in interpreting these findings. Reliable cohort differences were found for Space, Reasoning, and Verbal Meaning subtests. Consistent gender differences were found across the life span: females tended to perform better on Word Fluency; males performed better on

Number and Space subtests. This paper emphasizes considerable interindividual differences in performance.

Kind	*Recommendation*	*Readability*	*Audience*
E	***	3	AG

Smyer, M. A., Cohn, M. D., & Brannon, D. (1988). *Mental health consultation in nursing homes.* **New York: New York University Press.**

This book presents a comprehensive overview of mental health problems in nursing homes. Emphasizing the nursing home as a community, the authors examine interventions aimed at the different members of the community (e.g., staff, patients, families). Interventions need to be planned with an understanding of how staff and patients function within the nursing home environment. Different models of consultation are also discussed, including providing direct service or working with staff or families to increase their effectiveness. Specific assessment and intervention skills relevant to nursing homes are reviewed. Additional chapters emphasize systems-level interventions that alter job patterns and service delivery within the nursing home.

Kind	*Recommendation*	*Readability*	*Audience*
TB	***	2	SP,AG

St. George–Hyslop, P. H., et al. (1987). The genetic defect causing familial Alzheimer's disease maps on chromosome 21. *Science, 235,* **885–890.**

This paper describes recent research looking at possible genetic defects as a cause of Alzheimer's disease. It has been recognized for some time that some large families have multiple cases of Alzheimer's disease. While this does not imply inheritance of all cases, the possibility of autosomal dominant transmission in these familial cases is raised. The finding that older patients with Down's syndromes develop Alzheimer-type brain pathology suggests the possibility for a genetic abnormality on the 21st chromosome. Research was conducted with four large families in which there were multiple cases of Alzheimer's disease. Pedigree and clinical data were collected from these families to document numbers of affected persons and to confirm diagnosis. A genetic marker in affected individuals was identified on chromosome 21. The localization is near the region in which a gene that synthesizes amyloid has been identified. This discovery may assist in understanding the biochemical changes that occur in Alzheimer's disease.

Kind	Recommendation	Readability	Audience
E	***	3	AG

Storandt, M. (1983). *Counseling and therapy with older adults.* **New York: Springer.**

This easily understood text will be of interest mostly to students interested in an *introduction* to psychotherapy and counseling with older people. It presents a very general overview of the area, including brief chapters on different theoretical perspectives and therapies (psychodynamic, behavioral, and cognitive–behavioral) with limited discussion of their associated effectiveness with elderly individuals. Applications to groups, families, and the institutionalized setting are also dealt with in a succinct and clear manner.

Kind	Recommendation	Readability	Audience
TB	**	1	AU,AG,SP

Thompson, L. W., Davies, R., Gallagher, D., & Krantz, S. (1986). Cognitive therapy with older adults. In T. Brink (Ed.), *Clinical gerontology: A guide to assessment and intervention* **(pp. 245–279). New York: Haworth Press.**

This chapter reviews the use of cognitive therapy with older adults. An important aspect of a cognitive approach is the therapeutic relationship in which warmth and acceptance plays a facilitating role. As treatment progresses, the therapist is relatively active in keeping the focus on depressive symptoms and the faulty assumptions that cause them. Specific issues in treating older adults are highlighted. Older depressed patients may learn at a slower rate, so the repetitions involved in cognitive therapy actually work well with this group. Clients may also hold beliefs about not being able to change, or that they cannot be happy unless they return to a previous situation in their lives. These issues must be addressed directly in the therapy by testing the global nature of their expectations. While results of cognitive therapy are generally positive, some factors associated with poorer outcome are a more severe initial level of depression, features of an endogenous depression, evidence of a preexisting personality disorder, and a weaker social network. Case examples are presented.

Kind	Recommendation	Readability	Audience
RC	***	2	SP,AG

Thompson, L. W., Gallagher, D., & Breckenridge, J. S. (1987). Comparative effectiveness of psychotherapies for depressed elders. *Journal of Consulting and Clinical Psychology, 55,* 385–390.

Older persons with a diagnosis of a major depressive disorder were randomly assigned into three treatment conditions: behavioral, cognitive, or brief psychodynamic therapy. Additionally, one third of subjects were held out of treatment for a 6-week waiting period. After the 6-week period, subjects in all three treatments showed improvement, compared to wait list controls. At the end of therapy, 52% of subjects reached criteria indicating remission of symptoms, while another 18% were significantly improved. There were no differences among treatment groups in outcome. Results suggest that improvement rates of older patients are comparable to those of younger people receiving psychotherapy for depression.

Kind	*Recommendation*	*Readability*	*Audience*
E	***	2	SP,AG

Thompson, L. W., Gallagher, D., & Czirr, R. (1988). Personality disorder and outcome in the treatment of late-life depression. *Journal of Geriatric Psychiatry, 21*(2), 133–146.

This clinical paper reports findings of a study examining two general issues: (1) whether Axis II formulations increased during an episode of major depressive disorder, and (2) whether there is a relationship between the presence/absence of an Axis II diagnosis and psychotherapeutic outcome. The 79 subjects were randomly placed in one of three therapy groups (brief psychodynamic, cognitive, or behavior therapy) or in a delayed control condition group, and were administered the Structured Interview for DSM-III Personality Disorders (SIDP) under two separate conditions. When rating usual self 33% were diagnosed as having a personality disorder, and over 66% provided retrospective evidence of having had a personality disorder when in a major depressive episode. Findings suggested that there is an increase in symptoms, particularly avoidant and dependent-type features, sufficient for the diagnosis of personality disorder when older adults experienced a major depressive disorder. Also, data suggested that those individuals who presented evidence of a personality disorder when describing their usual selves, in comparison to those who did not, were less likely to have positive therapeutic outcomes or be labeled as "successes" (based on Axis I diagnosis at conclusion of therapy).

Kind	*Recommendation*	*Readability*	*Audience*
E	*	2–3	SP,AG

Thompson, L. W., Gallagher, D., Nies, G., & Epstein, D. (1983). Evaluation of the effectiveness of professionals and nonprofessionals as instructors of "Coping with Depression" classes for elders. *The Gerontologist, 23,* 390–396.

This article describes adaptation of coping with depression classes for a community setting, and compares the results of classes led by a professional and a trained older person. Results were that depression was lowered in both types of classes, with gains maintained at the 2-month follow-up. There were few differences due to type of group leader.

Kind	Recommendation	Readability	Audience
E	**	3	AU,AG

Thompson, L. W., Gong, V., Haskins, E., & Gallagher, D. (1987). Assessment of depression and dementia during the late years. In K. W. Schaie (Ed.), *Annual Review of Gerontology and Geriatrics, 7,* 295–324.

This chapter reviews current issues in the assessment of dementia and depression. Commonly used interviews and self-rating scales for depression are evaluated in light of available data. Both approaches are limited by reluctance of many elders to admit to negative symptoms and because of the overlap of somatic symptoms and depression. Mental status tests and neuropsychological approaches to dementia are described, including factors that make assessment of older people more problematic, such as decreased energy, speed of processing, and sensory impairment. Procedures for identifying different types of dementia are reviewed. A useful section reviews the evidence of cognitive impairment in older depressed patients, and the problem of differentiating depression and dementia.

Kind	Recommendation	Readability	Audience
RC	**	2	SP,AG

Tsuang, M. T. (1986). Predictors of poor and good outcome in schizophrenia. In L. Erlenmeyer-Kimling & N. E. Miller (Eds.), *Life-span research on the prediction of psychopathology* (pp. 195–203). Hillsdale, NJ: Lawrence Erlbaum.

This chapter reports findings on clinical variables—at admission and at follow-up 30 to 40 years later—of 200 schizophrenic patients in the Iowa 500 project. Schizophrenia was operationally defined by stringent research criteria. Subjects were interviewed with the Iowa Structured Psychiatric Interview form. Tsuang provides an outcome analysis according to admission variables derived from original medical records. Ratings on four outcome variables—psychiatric, residential, occupational, and marital—were used to assess which variables were predictive of good or fair and poor outcome. Generally, a poor overall outcome was described for schizophrenic subjects in this sample. Indeed, over half of the patients evidenced substantial and serious psychiatric symptomatology 30 to 40 years after admission. Predictors of poor outcome included thought blocking, memory deficit, social withdrawal, younger age of onset, and hallucinations. In contrast, predictors of good outcome were persecutory delusions, hyperactivity, flight of ideas, and euphoria.

Kind	*Recommendation*	*Readability*	*Audience*
E	**	2–3	SP,AG

Verwoerdt, A. (1981). *Clinical geropsychiatry* **(2nd ed.). Baltimore: Williams & Wilkins.**

Utilizing a psychodynamic theoretical orientation and DSM-III nomenclature, Verwoerdt provides an overview of various psychiatric conditions, including organic mental disorders, paranoid and thought disorders, affective disorders, personality disorders, and somatoform disorders. Attention is given to the psychological, social, and biological domains of aging. The relationship of age and aging to diagnosis is a strong theme throughout this text. For instance, the interactional relationship of aging processes and personality disorders is addressed. In addition to discussing various relatively lifelong patterns of maladaptive interactions with the environment, Verwoerdt describes behavior disorder that may arise for the first time in later life ("age-specific behavior disorders"), including disorders that are associated with alterations in the older person's time perspective and those that are a result of psychopathology developing in old age (e.g., organic brain syndrome).

Kind	*Recommendation*	*Readability*	*Audience*
TB	**	2–3	SP,AG

Weissman, M. M., Myers, J. K., Tischler, G. L., Holzer, C. E., III, Leaf, P. J., Orvaschel, H., & Brody, J. A. (1985). Psychiatric disorders (DSM-III) and cognitive impairment among the elderly in a U. S. urban community. *Acta Psychiatrica Scandinavica, 71,* **366–379.**

This paper presents prevalence rates of specific mental disorders and *severe* cognitive impairment for 2,588 surveyed community-dwelling participants aged 65 and above from the Yale University site of the National Institute of Mental Health Epidemiologic Catchment Area studies. The interview schedule included a modified Diagnostic Interview Schedule (DIS) and Mini-Mental State Examination. The paper reports findings on demographic and social functioning characteristics of the respondents, including age, gender, race, education level, marital status, living arrangements, employment and economic status, health, functional ability, and social support. Data revealed a 6.7% 6-month prevalence rate of psychiatric disorders and a 3.4% point prevalence rate of severe cognitive impairments. Psychiatric disorder prevalence rates were slightly higher for females than males. Affective and anxiety disorders (particularly phobia) were most commonly found among sampled older adults. Uncommon psychiatric conditions included alcohol abuse/dependence (0.7%), somatization disorder (only one case), schizophrenia (0.3%), panic disorder (0.1%), obsessive compulsive disorder (0.7%). There were no cases found for anorexia nervosa or drug abuse. The authors emphasize the relative psychiatric well-being of *noninstitutionalized* older adults. However, the paper notes that the relative risk for cognitive disorders and for physical conditions/diseases increases substantially with advancing age. Due to increased longevity and increasing numbers of elders, it should be expected that the absolute numbers of individuals with severe cognitive impairments will increase in the future, even if rates per se do not increase and most older people are not affected.

Kind	*Recommendation*	*Readability*	*Audience*
E	**	2–3	SP,AU,AG

Zarit, J. M., & Zarit, S. H. (1984). Depression in later life: Treatment. In J. P. Abrahams & V. Crooks (Eds.), *Geriatric mental health: A clinician's guide* (pp. 41–54). New York: Grune & Stratton.

This chapter reviews brief psychotherapy approaches to the treatment of depression that have been used with older persons. The behavioral approach of Lewinsohn and Beck's cognitive behavioral treatments is described in detail. The behavioral approach emphasizes the relation of pleasant events and mood. In cognitive–behavioral treatment, depression is viewed as the result of making overly negative interpretations of events. Several common features are found in both treatments including use of a structured and collaborative approach, focusing on the events and feelings that the client experiences in everyday situations, teaching clients how to use the therapy approach, and having clients monitor their own mood, thoughts, and behavior. Specific problems implementing these approaches with older adults include the fact that a client's maladaptive behavior or thoughts may have a longer history, and the interplay of illness and depression. Sometimes, too, therapists must be advocates for older clients, helping them obtain benefits or services that will materially affect their situation.

Kind	Recommendation	Readability	Audience
RC	**	2	SP,AG

Zarit, S. H., Eiler, J., & Hassinger, M. J. (1985). Clinical assessment. In J. E. Birren & K. W. Schaie (Eds.), *Handbook of the psychology of aging* (2nd ed., pp. 725–754). New York: Van Nostrand Reinhold.

This chapter reviews assessment approaches for older persons. In the area of cognitive assessment, a neuropsychological model is proposed, which relates cognitive constructs to brain function. Literature on intelligence and aging are reinterpreted in the light of this model. Deficits on performance-type subtests appear related to their being more demanding, and thus requiring more neural resources than verbal tests. Problems of cognitive assessment include that norms may be cohort specific and that various impairments may have an effect on cognitive performance. Assessment of behavior and personality emphasizes the use of direct observation and reports from older clients, including self-monitoring. Issues in differential diagnosis and assessment of dementia are also reviewed.

Kind	Recommendation	Readability	Audience
RC	**	2	AG

Zarit, S. H., Orr, N. K., & Zarit, J. M. (1985). *The hidden victims of Alzheimer's disease: Families under stress*. New York: New York University Press.

This book presents an approach that stresses identification of potentially treatable aspects of the caregiver's situation. The starting point is assessment of the patient, including ruling out the presence of treatable disorders or treatable aspects of the dementia. A model for interventions with caregivers is proposed, including providing them with information about their relative's disease and its effects on behavior, teaching a problem-solving approach to management of behavioral problems, and increasing the social support they receive. Procedures for individual counseling, groups, and family meetings are discussed.

Kind	Recommendation	Readability	Audience
TB	**	2–3	GP,SP,AU,AG

Zarit, S. H., & Zarit, J. M. (1984). Depression in later life: Theory and assessment. In J. P. Abrahams & V. Crooks (Eds.), *Geriatric mental health* (pp. 21–39). New York: Grune & Stratton.

This chapter provides an overview of current theories of depression and their relevance to depression in later life. Diagnostic issues are stressed, including whether depression in late life is similar to or different from depression with earlier onset. Specific diagnostic approaches are evaluated and suggestions made for psychosocial assessment.

Kind	*Recommendation*	*Readability*	*Audience*
RC	**	2	SP,AU,AG

Zimberg, S. (1987). Alcohol abuse among the elderly. In L. L. Carstensen & B. A. Edelstein (Eds.), *Handbook of clinical gerontology* (pp. 57–65). New York: Pergamon Press.

Alcoholism is often a hidden problem among the elderly. While rates of alcoholism peak between ages 35 and 50, it remains a significant problem in later life. A distinction is proposed between early-onset and late-onset alcoholism for the elderly. Older patients with early onset are likely to experience more medical complications, while age at onset provides information about etiological factors that may be useful for planning treatment. Assessment and treatment approaches are reviewed, and suggestions are made for prevention of alcohol abuse among the elderly.

Kind	*Recommendation*	*Readability*	*Audience*
RC	**	1	SP,AU,AG

6

Sexuality and Aging

Jodi L. Teitelman

INTRODUCTION

Literature Review

Researchers, clinicians, and advocates in gerontology have worked hard in the past two decades to dispel the concept of total asexuality in old age. These efforts, occurring within a context of more societal openness and candor about sexual matters in general, have resulted in considerable progress. Many people now recognize that older people not only have sex but "like sex, want sex, feel they need sex for their physical and psychological well-being and are frustrated when they do not have sex" (Starr, 1985, p. 106).

Sadly though, equal numbers of individuals do not acknowledge this. If societal consciousness is examined as a whole, it is clear that many erroneous myths, conceptions, and notions regarding sex and aging cling tenaciously (Kaas, 1981). Some of the most pervasive stereotypes are that sexual drive and activity do and should decline with old age and that older people who speak of having sex lives are either sinful, deranged, or exaggerating (Butler, 1978; Corby & Solnick, 1980). Similarly, sex may be viewed as deviant in old age, for example, "the dirty old man or woman syndrome." Some individuals may accept active sexuality for aging men but, adhering to a sexist double standard, find sex for aging women abhorrent (Kuhn, 1976). Even people who do accept on a cognitive level the actuality of sex in old age may have difficulty believing that, subjectively, older individuals find sex to be as exciting, provocative, and stimulating as younger people do.

These stereotypes, and general emotional resistance to the idea of gerontological sexuality, may be an extension of the "incest taboo" and the anxiety people experience when witnessing or imagining their parents or other elders engaged in sexual activities. The discomfort may reflect an anachronistic extension of Victorian morality which viewed sex only as intercourse and intercourse as appropriate only for conception. Sex for communication, recreation, or pleasure was therefore considered to be unnecessary and, in fact, immoral. Also, in contemporary society, sexuality is most frequently equated with youthful standards of attractiveness, particularly for women. This idea, continually reinforced by the popular media, may effectively inhibit the thought of sex among individuals of less than youthful and athletic appearance and who perhaps are chronically ill or have physical disabilities. Finally, sex can be empowering, and for those individuals who prefer to view the elderly as dependent and powerless, acknowledging the validity of sexuality in old age can be threatening (Falk & Falk, 1980).

A major consequence of this stereotyping is that the elderly either actually come to believe the erroneous myths or avoid desired expression of sexual needs, for fear of societal ridicule or censure (Kaas, 1981). By accepting society's false beliefs, however, some elderly individuals may be barring themselves from sexual and intimate experiences that could be of benefit to their physical health (Runciman, 1980) and their emotional well-being (Butler & Lewis, 1976; Leviton, 1973; Stimson, Wase, & Stimson, 1981). Although it must be recognized that some older adults genuinely have no desire to engage in sexual activities, as is true for some younger adults, for those who do—and they are many—an active, vibrant sex life may prove to be therapeutic and health promoting in a variety of ways.

Research on age changes in hormonal and reproductive functioning reveal little that would be prohibitive of continued sexual enjoyment and activity (see Comfort, 1980; Corby & Solnick, 1980; Weg, 1980, 1983). Women typically experience their last menstruation in midlife, resulting in both a rapid loss of the female sex hormone, estrogen, and a loss of fertility (National Institute on Aging, 1987; Schiff & Wilson, 1978). The estrogen loss of menopause, combined with normal biological age changes, leads to a reduction in the elasticity and lubricating abilities of the vagina. In most cases, however, women readily adapt to these changes, sometimes with the judicious use of hormone replacement therapy, and the potential for orgasm and subjective enjoyment of sex remains unimpaired in postmenopausal women.

Aging men experience some decline in production of the male sex hormone, testosterone, but there is little convincing evidence at this point that men experience a magnitude of change sufficient to constitute a "male menopause" (Futterwheit, Molitch, Morley, & Cherlin, 1984). While older men experience some testicular atrophy, and may have problems with prostate gland enlargement, the penis does not change in size or weight, fertility remains intact, and the potential for sexual enjoyment continues (Harman, 1978, 1981).

The noted sexologists William Masters and Virginia Johnson have examined sexual responsivity across the life span and have concluded that while physiological changes do take place with age, the capacity for both functioning and fulfillment does not disappear (Masters, 1986; Masters & Johnson, 1981). The excitement stage of sex, during which the body becomes physically aroused, increases in length with age; it takes longer for women's vaginas to lubricate and for men to have an erection. The pre-orgasmic plateau phase, during which sexual tension is at its height, is also extended in duration. Orgasm is experienced more rapidly, somewhat less intensely, and more spasmodically by both genders. Also, the two-stage orgasm of sense of ejaculatory inevitability followed by actual semen expulsion experienced by younger males blurs into a one-stage ejaculation for older men. Resolution, during which the body returns to its baseline pre-arousal state, occurs more rapidly, but it typically takes an older man longer to be able to sustain another erection; in other words, there is a longer refractory period.

Early researchers were interested in examining the effects of these age changes on frequency of sexual activities. More recent research, in contrast, has begun to explore the implication of these changes for the subjective experience or more qualitative aspects of sex in old age. Early cross-sectional data taken from the Duke Longitudinal Study (Newman & Nichols, 1960; Pfeiffer, 1974; Pfeiffer & Davis, 1972) and other early cross-sectional studies (for review see White, 1982) indicated generally low frequencies of sexual activity for older adults compared to their young and middle-aged counterparts, particularly for females and unmarried individuals. It bears noting, however, that the definition of sexual activity in these studies was typically limited to heterosexual intercourse, and that the subjects sampled at the time constituted a cohort of individuals raised during a period of strict sexual conservatism. It may be that low levels of activity reported at that time reflected the attitudes and behaviors of that specific older generation, rather than any physical changes in sexual functioning caused by age per se (Starr, 1985; Traupmann, 1984). Later analysis of Duke Longitudinal Study data to control for a possible cohort effect did, indeed, reveal stability of sexual activity patterns from mid- to late life (George & Weiler, 1981). Those who, possibly because of social upbringing, were sexually conservative and inactive in midlife carried that pattern through their later years; those who were more sexually active in middle age continued to be so in old age.

Brecher's more recent (1984) national survey indicated declining frequencies of reported sexual activity for each successive decade, but also clearly demonstrated that there are many older people who continue to have ongoing active sexual experiences. Of even more importance is that these older individuals are experiencing their sex lives as exciting, enjoyable, and pleasurable, and as an important part of their lives (Adams & Turner, 1985; Brecher, 1984; Martin, 1981; Persson, 1980; Starr, 1985; Starr & Weiner, 1981).

While age per se then does not preclude sexual functioning and enjoyment, it must be acknowledged that there are potential barriers to sexual expression to which the elderly may be particularly vulnerable. Physical health problems of self and/or partner(s), for instance, are one of the most frequently cited reasons for refraining from sexual activity in old age (Pfeiffer & Davis, 1972). The chronic illnesses endemic in the older population may lead to pain, discomfort, fatigue, and/or disability, resulting in curtailment of sexual drive and/or function (see Corby & Solnick, 1980; Friedeman, 1978; Walz & Blum, 1987; Woods & Herbert, 1979). Hospitalization and surgery (Kentsmith & Eaton, 1979) or the diagnosis of terminal illness (Rezendes, 1981) can further exacerbate the situation, as can the prescription of medications that impair sexual desire and/or ability (Long, 1980).

In the current cohort of elderly, the availability of a marital partner has been found to be a crucial determinant of ongoing, active sexual expression (Brecher, 1984; Pfeiffer & Davis, 1972; Persson, 1980; Newman & Nichols, 1960; Starr & Weiner, 1981). This is particularly true for women who, in the current generation of elderly, have been strongly socialized against seeking sexual intimacy outside the bonds of marriage. Because women tend to outlive their husbands, many more women than men are single in late life, thus sexually inactive (Corby & Zarit, 1983; Turner & Adams, 1983). Not surprisingly, then, research shows consistently lower rates of reported frequency of sexual activity for older females than males. Although multiple male partners and lesbian relationships have been suggested as viable alternatives for older women (Cavan, 1973), there is little evidence to suggest that this is a readily acceptable solution for women after a lifetime of monogamy and heterosexuality (Ludeman, 1981).

A strong predictor of sexual activity in late life, as noted earlier, is one's earlier pattern of activity. Those who are most sexually active in midlife tend to be so in old age (George & Weiler, 1981; Martin, 1981). Sexuality, then, appears to be a stable and continuous function across the life span.

One's attitude toward and comfort with sexuality have an obvious impact on one's sex life at any age, and this is particularly true for older individuals exposed to societal notions of their asexuality. Those who do not ascribe to societal sanctions against sex in old age and those who are relatively well balanced emotionally and psychosexually will, of course, be likely to have more active and healthy sex lives (Brecher, 1984; Corby & Solnick, 1980; Friedman, 1978; Hays, 1984; Persson, 1980; Starr & Weiner, 1981; Walz & Blum, 1987). Personality factors, such as locus of control, may also have an influence on certain types of sexual behavior (Catania & White, 1982). Finally, within the context of a discussion of psychosocial influences on late-life sexuality, it should be noted that most sexual activity for the current generation of elders does occur within the context of a marital relationship. Thus, clearly, the emotional health of the marriage (Campden-Main & Sara, 1983; Corby & Solnick, 1980; Persson,1980) and the effect of age-related changes such as retirement on the marriage (Appleton, 1981) will influence sexuality. The onset of marital problems, such as boredom of partners with one another, can clearly be a barrier to ongoing, enjoyable sexual expression (Masters & Johnson, 1981).

Equally, however, it cannot be assumed that all sexual activity occurring among older individuals is strictly marital or heterosexual. Data on the sexual patterns and adaptation to aging of older gays have begun to emerge in the gerontological literature of the past decade (Bennett & Thompson, 1980; Berger, 1980; Gray & Dressel, 1985; Harry & DeVall, 1978; Kelly, 1977; Kimmel, 1978; Laner, 1978), although researchers are beginning only now to look at the lives of older lesbians (Genevay, 1980; Kehoe, 1986; Laner, 1979). The majority of studies, though revealing as much heterogeneity for homosexual elders as for heterosexuals, do show consistent patterns of relatively good adjustment to old age and ongoing sexual interest and activity for both older lesbians and gays (Raphael & Robinson, 1981).

Also, while the majority of late-life sexual activity occurs among the independent, community-dwelling elderly, the sexual intimacy needs of those older adults residing in long-term care facilities cannot be ignored. While studies indicate generally low levels of sexual activity among nursing home residents, at least some are active and many others indicate they would be active if opportunity allowed (Kaas, 1978; Wasow & Loeb, 1979). Lack of privacy (Kaas, 1978; White, 1982), negative staff attitudes (Blackwell & Hunt, 1980; Kassel, 1983), administrative difficulties (Miller, 1980; Szasz, 1983), and the nonromantic atmosphere of the institutional environment, all reduce the incentive of residents to be sexually interested or involved. Gerontologists recommend a number of possible interventions to facilitate residents' opportunity for sexual expression, including new privacy policies, the availability of conjugal rooms, more romantic social programming, and sex education and sensitization for both staff and residents (Burnside, 1981; Walz & Blum, 1987).

For both the institutionalized and noninstitutionalized elderly, psychologists, psychiatrists, and other mental health professionals can be helpful in facilitating sexual expression and growth. Older couples and individuals presenting with marital problems and/or nonorganic sexual dysfunction are equally responsive to psychotherapeutic and sex therapy techniques as younger individuals (Comfort, 1980; Corby & Solnick, 1980; Felstein, 1983; Masters & Johnson, 1981; Meyers, 1985; Renshaw, 1984). Unique transference and countertransference issues may need to be dealt with in interactions between young therapists and elderly clients (Apfel, Fox, Isberg, & Levine, 1984); nevertheless, with adequate therapist awareness and knowledge, these issues can usually be resolved and used therapeutically. Therapists involved in more general areas of counseling and therapy as well need to be aware of sexuality as an issue for older adults, as it may emerge as an area of focus in a variety of disorders, for example, depression, or paranoia (Liptzin, 1984).

Education of the elderly in matters of sexuality appears also to be facilitative of understanding and growth (Schmall & Staton, 1981). A wealth of reports appear in the literature indicating the success of sex education programs in increasing the sexual awareness, knowledge, enjoyment, and activities of older participants (Guarino & Knowlton, 1980; Salamon & Charytan, 1984; Sviland, 1980; West, 1983; White & Catania, 1982). While most of these programs were not evaluated empirically, the anecdotal findings are suggestive of education as a powerful tool in enhancing elders' sexuality.

Whether working with or teaching about the older adult in the community or in the nursing home, males or females, homosexuals or heterosexuals, the issue of human sexuality is a significant one. As more professionals become knowledgeable in this area and as research becomes increasingly sophisticated in order to advance that knowledge, the older population will benefit. It is hoped that, through the refutation of inhibiting, defeating stereotypes of late-life sexuality, older adults will experience more freedom to explore and express their natural sexual desires and needs.

Implementing the Curriculum

Most people today will readily give lip service to the notion that sexuality is normal and natural, regardless of age. In actually expressing such a concept to students in the classroom, however, the issue may become one that is surprisingly volatile and emotional. While the majority of students find study of gerontological sexuality provocative and interesting (not to mention a welcome break from more tedious areas of their curriculum!), it is not uncommon to find students who are resistant to such teaching efforts.

Perhaps because of religious views, personal experiences, or unresolved conflicts, some students may refuse to participate in discussion of sexual matters or may openly express disgust. Discussion of late-life masturbation and homosexuality, in particular, may elicit strong emotional reactions from a minority of students. Thus, it is important for the instructor, while continuing to respect the diversity of sexual opinions inherent in the classroom, to encourage openness and recognition of the realities of sex in old age. It may be helpful for the instructor to convey that, while the student may not *like* the fact that masturbatory and homoerotic activities occur in old age, such activities do indeed occur. To be an effective gerontologist interacting with older patients and clients, this reality must be addressed and resolved with one's own personal feelings, however incongruent they may seem to be.

Conversely, open exploration of certain topics may elicit a sense of relief for some students. For example, frank and nonjudgmental discussion of homosexuality seems to "give permission" for gay and lesbian students to (usually privately) express to the instructor their sexual orientation and/or interest in the area. Many a term paper title has been changed once students realized it was "OK" to pursue an interest in older gays and lesbians!

It may also be helpful to remind students that what is really known about sexuality in old age is actually quite limited. The number of well-controlled empirical studies in the area is less than overwhelming, and cohort analyses of sexual thoughts and behaviors across the life span are only now emerging in the literature. Students should be encouraged to cast a critical eye on the extant gerontological sexuality research and to begin to think of better ways in which the complexities of sexuality across the life span might be explored.

As with the teaching of any human sexuality curriculum, it is, of course, imperative that the instructor be aware of his or her own sexual values and how this impacts upon teaching efforts. Based on rigorous examination of one's own experiences and taboos, the instructor must bring to the classroom a sense of ease and comfort with the subject. Acceptance of one's own sexuality can help the instructor create an atmosphere that facilitates open discussion, and can make instruction in this area a dynamic (and fun) experience.

COMPREHENSIVE OUTLINE

Content Outline	References (#1–104)	Supplemental Materials (#105–114)
I. Attitudes and Beliefs About Sex in the Elderly		
A. Impact of social stereotypes	19. Corby & Solnick (1980) 40. Kaas (1981) 102. Winn & Newton (1982) 74. Robinson (1983)	111. Walz & Blum (1987) 112. White (1982)
B. Negative stereotypes	9. Butler (1978) 47. Kuhn (1976) 11. Cameron (1970)	108. Genevay (1981)
C. Reasons for stereotyping	25. Falk & Falk (1980)	
D. Some evidence of positive attitudes	50. LaTorre & Kear (1977) 75. Roff & Klemmack (1979)	

E.   Sexual thoughts of
     elderly

7.   Brecher (1984)
12. Cameron & Biber
     (1973)
15. Cavan (1973)
43. Keller, Eakes,
     Hinkle, & Hughsten
     (1978)
56. Ludeman (1981)
62. Newman & Nichols
     (1960)
68. Portonova, Young,
     & Newman (1984)
80. Smith & Schmall
     (1983)
81. Snyder & Speitzer
     (1975)
85. Starr & Weiner
     (1981)

II. Benefits of Late-Life
     Sexuality
     A.   Physical
     B.   Psychological

76. Runciman (1980)
10. Butler & Lewis
     (1976)
52. Leviton (1973)
87. Stimson, Wase, &
     Stimson (1981)

III. Physical Aspects of
     Sexuality and Aging
     A.   Hormonal/
          reproductive
          changes (general)

          1. Females

     2. Males

     B.   Changes in sexual
          responsiveness

17. Comfort (1980)
19. Corby & Solnick
     (1980)
95. Weg (1980)
97. Weg (1983b)
21. Coulam (1981)
61. National Institute
     on Aging (1987)
78. Schiff & Wilson
     (1978)
29. Futterwheit, Molitch,
     Morley, & Cherlin
     (1984)
35. Harman (1981)
34. Harman (1978)
13. Campden-Main &
     Sara (1983)
18. Corbett (1981)
19. Corby & Solnick
     (1980)
56. Ludeman (1981)
58. Masters (1986)
59. Masters & Johnson
     (1981)
63. O'Connor & Flax
     (1977)

114. Carroll
     (1978)
113. Freideman
     (1979)

66. Pfeiffer & Davis (1972)
73. Rezendes (1981)
92. Walz & Blum (1987)
103. Woods (1979)
104. Woods & Herbert (1979)

B. Availability of partner
7. Brecher (1984)
18. Corbett (1981)
20. Corby & Zarit (1983)
37. Hays (1984)
62. Newman & Nichols (1960)
64. Persson (1980)
66. Pfeiffer & Davis (1972)
85. Starr & Weiner (1981)

C. Previous patterns
19. Corby & Solnick (1980)
28. Friedeman (1978)
31. George & Weiler (1981)
57. Martin (1981)
62. Newman & Nichols (1960)
66. Pfeiffer & Davis (1972)

D. Psychosocial factors
1. Locus of control
14. Catania & White (1982)

2. Attitudes toward sex
7. Brecher (1984)
19. Corby & Solnick (1980)
28. Friedeman (1978)
37. Hays (1984)
64. Persson (1980)
85. Starr & Weiner (1981)
92. Walz & Blum (1987)

3. Health of relationship
3. Appleton (1981)
7. Brecher (1984)
13. Campden-Main & Sara (1983)
19. Corby & Solnick (1980)
59. Masters & Johnson (1981)
64. Persson (1980)

VI. Homosexuality in Old Age
24. Dressel & Avant (1983)
69. Raphael & Robinson (1981)

A. Older gays
4. Bennett & Thompson (1980)
5. Berger (1980)
32. Gray & Dressel (1985)
36. Harry & DeVall (1978)
44. Kelly (1977)
46. Kimmel (1978)
48. Laner (1978)

B. Older lesbians
30. Genevay (1980)
42. Kehoe (1986)
49. Laner (1979)

VII. Sex in the Long-Term Care Facility
A. Extent of activity and interest
39. Kaas (1978)
89. Szasz (1983)
93. Wasow & Loeb (1979)
100. White (1982)

B. Barriers to sexual expression
6. Blackwell & Hunt (1980)
38. Hussian & Davis (1985)
39. Kaas (1978)
41. Kassel (1983)
89. Szasz (1983)
100. White (1982)

107. Film: *Rose by Any Other Name*
110. Miller (1975)

VIII. Facilitating Older Adults' Sexual Function
A. Therapy and counseling
2. Apfel, Fox, Isberg, & Levine (1984)
17. Comfort (1980)
19. Corby & Solnick (1980)
26. Felstein (1983)
53. Liptzin (1984)
59. Masters & Johnson (1981)
60. Myers (1985)
71. Renshaw (1983)

109. Campden-Main (1980)

B. Education
33. Guarino & Knowlton (1980)
77. Salamon & Charytan (1984)
79. Schmall & Staton (1981)
88. Sviland (1980)
99. West (1983)
101. White & Catania (1982)

IX. Late-Life Affection, Love, and Intimacy
7. Brecher (1984)
10. Butler & Lewis (1976)

105. Film: *Minnie Remembers*

22. Datan & Rode-   106. Film: *A*
    heaver (1983)   *Ripple of*
27. Fitzgerald, McKellar,   *Time*
    Lener, & Copans
    (1985)
51. Laury (1980,
    January)
54. Livson (1983)
67. Porcino (1981)
70. Reedy, Birren, &
    Schaie (1981)
85. Starr & Weiner
    (1981)
86. Steffl (1981)
94. Wax (1982)
98. Weiss (1983)

ANNOTATED BIBLIOGRAPHY

1. **Adams, C. G., & Turner, B. F. (1985). Reported change in sexuality from young adulthood to old age.** *The Journal of Sex Research, 21*(2), **126–141.**

This is one of the very few studies that have attempted to examine qualitative and subjective aspects of late-life sexuality. Using Laws's (1980) life-span developmental model of sexuality as a framework, the authors administered questionnaires to 102 individuals (aged 60 to 85 years). Subjects provided information on current sexual activities and feelings, and as they recalled these when they were younger (age 20 to 30 years). All types of sexual activity were reported as tending to decline over the years, but few of these were of statistical significance. Thirty-eight percent of the women and 14 percent of the men reported increases with age for at least one of the variables measured, suggesting that women were more likely to have benefitted from recent changes in social norms for sexual behavior.

Kind	*Recommendation*	*Readability*	*Audience*
E	***	2	AU and above

2. **Apfel, R. J., Fox, M., Isberg, R. S., & Levine, A. F. (1984). Counter-transference and transference in couple therapy: Treating sexual dysfunction in older couples.** *Journal of Geriatric Psychiatry, 17*(2), **203–214.**

The authors describe some of the countertransference and personal, emotional responses of a seminar class of five young female psychiatric residents conductiong sex/marital therapy with middle-aged couples. Two cases emerging from this course are presented. The authors conclude that, despite problems of transference and countertransference, therapy potentially can provide both young therapists and older clients opportunities for increased sexual understanding and growth.

Kind	Recommendation	Readability	Audience
Clinical	**	2	SP

3. Appleton, W. S. (1981). Effect of retirement on marriage. *Medical Aspects of Human Sexuality, 15*(10), 78–87.

This nonempirical discussion highlights the fact that retirement (of husband, wife, or both) requires a period of adjustment in marriage. Increased privacy and leisure time may mean more shared activities and sexual intimacy. If not dealt with appropriately, however, retirement may lead to too much unproductive time with one another and eventual disillusionment and unhappiness. A commentary by M. A. Bartusis, M.D. on the future impact of today's rise in dual career marriages is included.

Kind	Recommendation	Readability	Audience
Review article	*1/2	1	GP, SP, or AU and above

4. Bennett, K.C., & Thompson, N. L. (1980). Social and psychological functioning of the ageing male homosexual. *British Journal of Psychiatry, 137,* 361–370.

This study aimed to test the accuracy of negative stereotypes about homosexuality in a sample of 478 Australian gay men of various ages. No confirmation of destructive stereotypes was found. Old and young homosexuals were equally involved and satisfied with their involvement in the gay community, and showed no differences in terms of psychological well-being. Older gays were, however, more inclined to conceal their sexual orientation and to describe their orientation as being beyond their control.

Kind	Recommendation	Readability	Audience
E	**	2	SP or AU and above

5. Berger, R. M. (1980). Psychological adaptation of the older male homosexual. *Journal of Homosexuality,* 5(3), 161–175.

In this study, using societal reaction theory as its framework, 112 homosexuals (aged 41 to 77) generally reported themselves as well-adjusted, self-accepting, and satisfied with life. Most respondents were sexually active, and over half were in a monogamous relationship. Older age was correlated with less depression and fewer psychosomatic symptoms, and regression analyses showed advancing age to be a significant predictor of greater self-acceptance and life satisfaction, and fewer psychosomatic symptoms.

Kind	Recommendation	Readability	Audience
E	**	2	SP or AU and above

6. Blackwell, D. L., & Hunt, S. S. (1980). Sexuality and aging: Staff attitudes toward sexual expression among aged nursing home residents. *Journal of Minority Aging,* 5(3), 273–277.

A questionnaire with items on attitudes and policy toward residents' sexuality was completed by 585 nursing home staff (all levels; professional and paraprofessional). Those respondents who had higher income and more education were more approving of residents' sexual expression. Most (62.6%) indicated that if they actually "saw older people have intercourse," they would "ignore it," 32.3% would "report it," and 5.1% would "intervene directly and attempt to stop it." Interestingly, the highest percentages of those staff who would ignore residents' sexual expression were clerical staff (81.5%) and nursing staff (65.0%); those most likely to report it or intervene were activity directors (58.3%) and administrative staff (47.3%).

Kind	Recommendation	Readability	Audience
E	**½	2	SP or AU and above

7. Brecher, E. M. (1984). *Love, sex and aging: A Consumer's Union report.* **Boston: Little, Brown.**

This book encompasses a nationwide survey conducted by Consumer's Union in 1978–1979. Results from 4,246 respondents over the age of 50 are presented and discussed. Not only does the book present a wealth of self-report data on older adults' patterns of sexual behavior, but issues of intimacy, affection, marriage, and other heterosexual and homosexual relationships are addressed as well. The frequencies of various responses to each item are reported and supported by selected passages from individual responses; these responses can provide rich illustrative material for lecture preparation, as many of them are revealing and candid, and some are quite humorous.

Kind	*Recommendation*	*Readability*	*Audience*
TB	***	1	GP and above

8. Burnside, I. M. (1981). Sexuality in nursing homes: A need for sensitivity and compassion. *Generations,* *6*(1), 22–23, 41.

The author, a leader in the field of gerontological nursing, notes that nursing home staff often have difficulty handling sexual situations, particularly if they involve cognitively impaired residents or homosexual behaviors. Burnside recommends several strategies to enhance residents' sexuality, including the use of a sexual health history inventory, in-service education, implementation of social activities, and sex education programs for residents.

Kind	*Recommendation*	*Readability*	*Audience*
Clinical	**	2	SP

9. Butler, R. N. (1978). Psychosocial aspects of reproductive aging. In E. L. Schneider (Ed.), *Aging*: **Vol. 4.** *The aging reproductive system.* **New York: Raven Press.**

This chapter focuses on cultural attitudes toward sexuality in old age and how these affect the actual sexual behavior of the elderly, usually in a negative way. Some health problems that may adversely affect sexual functioning of the elderly are presented, and possible medical interventions for some of these conditions are suggested.

Kind	*Recommendation*	*Readability*	*Audience*
RC	**	2	SP or AU and above

10. Butler, R. N., & Lewis, M. I. (1976). The second language of sex. *Sex after sixty.* **New York: Harper & Row. Also reprinted in R. L.**

Solnick (Ed.). (1980). *Sexuality and aging* (rev. ed.). Los Angeles: University of Southern California.

The emotional benefits of continued sexuality in late life are discussed. A good sex life can contribute to self-esteem and interpersonal closeness, serve as reaffirmation of one's own body, be a mechanism for defying ageist stereotypes, and serve as a source of feelings of personal control. Butler and Lewis emphasize that sex is more than a physical act, and involves communication and motivation.

Kind	Recommendation	Readability	Audience
RC	**	1	GP and above

11. Cameron, P. (1970). **The generation gap: Beliefs about sexuality and self-reported sexuality.** *Developmental Psychology, 3*(2), 272.

This very brief report presents data from a study conducted with 317 males and females aged 18 to 79 years. Although by now dated, this study was one of the first to begin to explore this area. Respondents of all ages, including the elderly themselves, rated older people as significantly less knowledgeable about sex, interested in sex, sexually active, and sexually skilled.

Kind	Recommendation	Readability	Audience
E	*½	2	AU and above

12. Cameron, P., & Biber, H. (1973). **Sexual thought throughout the life-span.** *The Gerontologist, 13*, 144–147.

Subjects ($N=4,420$) between the ages of 8 and 99 were asked about their thoughts within the preceding 5 minutes. Frequency of both passing and focal thoughts about sex had a curvilinear relationship for both genders, typically peaking in the teenaged and young adult years.

Kind	Recommendation	Readability	Audience
E	*½	2	AU and above

13. Campden-Main, B. C., & Sara, M. L. (1983). **Sex in the later years.** *Medical Aspects of Human Sexuality, 17*(3), 81–91.

Written by two sex therapists, this article focuses on guidelines for therapy primarily with elderly married couples. Recommendations for approaches to sex/marital therapy appropriate for older couples are discussed, including provision of information about normal age changes, recommending the setting aside of "relationship-building time," and having husband and wife vary the initiation of sexual activities.

Kind	Recommendation	Readability	Audience
Clinical	**	2	SP

14. Catania, J. A., & White, C. B. (1982). Sexuality in an aged sample: Cognitive determinants of masturbation. *Archives of Sexual Behavior*, *11*(3), 237–245.

In this study, 30 community-dwelling elderly were interviewed with regard to their masturbatory behavior. Regression analysis showed that an internal locus of control was the strongest predictor of high frequency of masturbation. Masturbation, it was concluded, may be a healthy mechanism through which the elderly can avoid helplessness and depression, asserting control over their sexuality.

Kind	Recommendation	Readability	Audience
E	**	3 (statistics)	AG

15. Cavan, R. S. (1973). Speculations on innovations to conventional marriage in old age. *The Gerontologist*, *13*, 408–411.

This paper explores the possibility of the elderly accepting alternatives to traditional monogamous marriage as methods of fulfilling their intimacy and sexual needs (e.g., nonmarital cohabitation, homosexual/ lesbian relationships, group marriage and communal arrangements, and co-marital contacts). There is little evidence to suggest that the author's provocative ideas have been embraced by the elderly with any degree of significance. Also, her contention that the elderly desire "dependence on younger kin" is questionable.

Kind	Recommendation	Readability	Audience
Theoretical Article	*½	2	AU and above

16. Christenson, C. V., & Johnson, A. B. (1973). Sexual patterns in a group of older never-married women. *Journal of Geriatric Psychiatry*, *6*(1), 80–98.

This early paper presents data collected by Kinsey and associates in the 1940s and 1950s on 71 never-married women between 50 and 69 years of age. Constituting a somewhat elite group in terms of education and professional status, the sexual patterns of the various respondents were mixed. For the subjects as a group, all sexual activities declined in frequency with advancing age, but a small group of women continued to actively seek sexual outlets, primarily through masturbation and coitus.

Kind	*Recommendation*	*Readability*	*Audience*
E	*½	2	AU and above

17. Comfort, A. (1980). Sexuality in later life. In J. E. Birren & R. B. Sloane (Eds.), *Handbook of mental health and aging*. Englewood Cliffs, NJ: Prentice-Hall.

Although the title implies a comprehensive approach, this brief chapter focuses primarily on sexual physiology and hormonal functioning, and some of the older studies on frequency of sexual activity in old age. The chapter concludes with a good summary of basic counseling strategies and clinical issues in dealing with sexual dysfunctions.

Kind	*Recommendation*	*Readability*	*Audience*
Clinical	**	2	AU and above

18. Corbett, L. (1981). The last sexual taboo: Sex in old age. *Medical Aspects of Human Sexuality*, *15*(4), 117–131.

This article provides brief introductory overviews of basic issues in geriatric sexuality, including normal physiological age changes in sexual response for men and women; psychosocial factors contributing to possible cessation of sexual activity in old age; the advantages of sexual relationships between older women and younger men (and vice versa); the effects of prostate surgery on sexual functioning; homosexuality in old age; and sex in nursing homes. This is a good introduction for the reader without an advanced background in the area.

Kind	*Recommendation*	*Readability*	*Audience*
Review Article	**	2	SP

19. Corby, N., & Solnick, R. L. (1980). Psychosocial and physiological influences on sexuality in the older adult. In J. E. Birren & R. B. Sloane (Eds.), *Handbook of mental health and aging*. Englewood Cliffs, NJ: Prentice-Hall.

This chapter offers an excellent, comprehensive overview of the major psychosocial and physiological issues in gerontological sexuality, and is of interest to both researchers and clinical practitioners. Physiological aspects covered include hormonal changes with age, differences in sexual responsivity, and diseases and surgical procedures that affect sexual expression. The section on psychosocial factors summarizes studies indicating frequency and extent of sexual activity and interest in old age, and explores the following psychosocial influences in depth: marital status, past sexual patterns, attitudes and social conventions, and midlife changes (physical and psychological effects). The section concludes with separate discussions of the married elderly, older people alone, and elderly homosexuals. Sexual dysfunctions are described, and various treatment modalities overviewed. Therapeutic measures discussed include individual and couple-oriented sexual counseling, group therapies, hormonal replacement therapies, and penile prosthetic devices.

Kind	Recommendation	Readability	Audience
RC	***	2	AG or SP

20. **Corby, N., & Zarit, J. M. (1983). Old and alone: The ummarried in later life. In R. B. Weg (Ed.),** *Sexuality in the later years: Roles and behavior.* **New York: Academic Press.**

The two noted authors briefly overview the social and sexual patterns of older widowers and widows, and never-married individuals (primarily focusing on women). Implications for future policy research and education are presented. This is a good, solid, but noncomprehensive introduction to this particular area.

Kind	Recommendation	Readability	Audience
RC	*$^1/_2$	2	AU and above or SP

21. **Coulam, C. B. (1981). Age, estrogens, and the psyche.** *Clinical Obstetrics and Gynecology, 24,* **219–229.**

This technically oriented article examines possible causes of psychological problems seen in some perimenopausal women. The author concludes that, although estrogen changes do exert some impact on brain catecholamines, causing psychological problems, normal age changes in neurotransmitters and stressful environmental and social occurrences around the time of menopause are more influential factors.

Kind	Recommendation	Readability	Audience
Review	**	3	AG or SP
Article			(some knowl-
			edge in neu-
			roendocrinology
			required)

22. **Datan, N., & Rodeheaver, D. (1983). Beyond generativity: Toward a sensuality of later life. In R. B. Weg (Ed.), *Sexuality in the later years: Roles and behavior*. New York: Academic Press.**

The authors propose that there are two types of love: procreative, which affirms the future through generativity, and existential, which affirms the present by seizing onto current moments of intimacy. The authors strongly recommend early socialization into awareness of both types of love, so that sexual and sensual activities may continue into the post-childbearing years, and so that the elderly will not be seen, by themselves and others, as "desexualized."

Kind	Recommendation	Readability	Audience
RC	**	2	AU and above

23. **deNicola, P., & Peruzza, M. (1974). Sex in the aged. *Journal of the American Geriatrics Society*, 22(8), 380–382.**

The results of research with 85 subjects, aged 62 to 81 years, are briefly reported. It was concluded that continued sexual activity in the aged is normal and therapeutic. The roles of health, environment, and social and psychological factors in sexuality of the elderly are discussed.

Kind	Recommendation	Readability	Audience
E	*1/2	2	SP or AU and above

24. **Dressel, P. D., & Avant, W. R. (1983). Range of alternatives. In R. B. Weg (Ed.), *Sexuality in the later years: Roles and behavior*. New York: Academic Press.**

The chapter begins with an overview of the concept of sexual orientation, noting some of the inherent problems in its operationalization and conceptualization. The authors provide an interesting and thoughtful analysis of research existing at that time on homosexual elders. Various social constraints that restrict the sexual freedom of older people of all

sexual orientations are also discussed. The chapter concludes with recommendations for new areas and improvements in research concerning
sexual orientation in the elderly.

Kind	Recommendation	Readability	Audience
RC	**1/2	2	AG

25. **Falk, G., & Falk, U. S. (1980). Sexuality and the aged.** *Nursing Outlook, 28*(1), 51–55.

The authors set forth the thesis that sexual behavior in the elderly is
ridiculed, when not actually forbidden by society, and use case studies
and research examples to illustrate their point. The article makes interesting reading; the case studies are thought provoking and occasionally
elicit anger.

Kind	Recommendation	Readability	Audience
Review Article	**	2	SP or AU and above

26. **Felstein, I. (1983). Dysfunction: Origins and therapeutic approaches. In R. B. Weg (Ed.),** *Sexuality in the later years: Roles and behavior.* **New York: Academic Press.**

Both the psychogenic and organic causes of sexual dysfunction in older
men and women are overviewed. According to Felstein's very thorough
discussion, impotence may occur due to a variety of physically based
causes or may be psychologically induced. Dysfunction in women is
covered somewhat more generally in this chapter with a discussion of
causes and treatment of dyspareunia, vaginismus, and anorgasmia. The
chapter concludes with a brief review of late-life sexual dysfunction
research and therapy being conducted in the United Kingdom.

Kind	Recommendation	Readability	Audience
Clinical	**	2	SP

27. **Fitzgerald, R. V., McKellar, A., Lener, W., & Copans, S. A. (1985). What are the essential ingredients for a long, happy marriage?** *Medical Aspects of Human Sexuality, 19*(3), 237–257.

Three psychiatrists and a biologist present their thoughts on predictors
and characteristics of durable marriages. Although a few empirical stud-

ies are cited, most of the factors discussed appear to be based on the authors' clinical observations, and on common sense. Sexual compatibility is an important part of long-standing marriages, but may not necessarily be the most important component. Good health and economic stability are also mentioned as crucial to the satisfaction of older married couples.

Kind	Recommendation	Readability	Audience
Theoretical	*½	1	SP or AU
Article			and above

28. Friedeman, J. S. (1978). Factors influencing sexual expression in aging persons: A review of the literature. *Journal of Psychiatric Nursing and Mental Health Services, 16*(7), 34–37.

This article presents a comprehensive review of variables believed to influence the expression of sexuality in the elderly. These include demographic factors, the individual's belief system and knowledge about sex, prior patterns of sexuality, social-economic resources, and physical and emotional health. Areas in which research is lacking are noted, and the article concludes with suggestions for further inquiry.

Kind	Recommendation	Readability	Audience
Review	**	3	SP and AG
Article			

29. Futterwheit, W., Molitch, M. E., Morley, J. E., & Cherlin, R. S. (1984). Is there a male climacteric? *Medical Aspects of Human Sexuality, 18*(4), 147–171.

This technically written article presents the views of four endocrinologists on the validity of the concept of a male climacteric. A range of opinions is presented; however, the majority contend that, while the male sex hormone testosterone declines with age, accompanied by some loss in sexual ability, it is not as dramatic or abrupt as the estrogen depletion seen in menopausal women.

Kind	Recommendation	Readability	Audience
Review	**	3	SP and AG
Article			

30. Genevay, B. (1980). Age kills us softly when we deny our sexual

identity. In R. L. Solnick (Ed.), *Sexuality and aging* (rev. ed.). Los Angeles: University of Southern California.

Taking a feminist perspective, the author describes the twofold barrier of ageism and sexism which prohibits the fulfillment of intimacy and sexual needs in older women. Although examples of both compliance with and defiance of restrictive stereotyping in older heterosexuals is discussed briefly, more emphasis is placed on the problems, coping skills, and positive experiences of lesbian women as they age. The author exhorts readers to explore their personal values about sexuality and to allow freedom of choice in sexual expression.

Kind	Recommendation	Readability	Audience
Review Article	**	2	AU and above

31. George, L. K., & Weiler, S. J. (1981). Sexuality in middle and late life: The effects of age, cohort and gender. *Archives of General Psychiatry*, *38*(8), 919–923.

The data presented here are derived from the second longitudinal study at Duke University, where subjects were tested four times over a 6-year period. Most subjects reported consistent and stable levels of sexual activity across all four testing times. Younger cohorts, however, reported higher levels of sexual activity than older age-cohort groups. These results suggest that patterns of sexual activity and interest remain fairly stable across the life span, and that the lower rates of sexual activity. reported by today's elderly reflect a cohort effect.

Kind	Recommendation	Readability	Audience
E	***	2	AG

32. Gray, H., & Dressel, P. (1985). Alternative interpretations of aging among gay males. *Gerontologist*, *25*(1), 83–87.

Data from Jay and Young's (1979) self-report questionnaire completed by 4,212 gay males (age range = 16 to 78) were analyzed. Older gays were more likely to wish to keep their sexual orientation a secret. More important, length of time actively involved in homosexual activity and subculture emerged as a better predictor of certain behaviors and attitudes than age per se. The authors predict (in this pre–AIDS crisis article) that increasingly accepting or at least tolerant attitudes toward homosexuality will improve the circumstances of future cohorts of aging gays.

Kind	*Recommendation*	*Readability*	*Audience*
E	**	2	AU and above

33. Guarino, S. C., & Knowlton, C. N. (1980, October). Planning and implementing a group health program on sexuality for the elderly. *Journal of Gerontological Nursing*, **pp. 600–603.**

The authors relate their experiences as faculty supervising nursing students conducting a workshop on "Building Relationships" for older adults in a residential hotel. Information on didactic content and outcomes is presented in only very general terms; in contrast, descriptions of group processes and recommendations for future similar groups are quite clear and helpful.

Kind	*Recommendation*	*Readability*	*Audience*
Clinical	**	2	SP or AU and above

34. Harman, S. M. (1978). Clinical aspects of aging of the male reproductive system. In E. L. Schneider (Ed.), *Aging:* **Vol. 4.** *The aging reproductive system.* **New York: Raven Press.**

Much of the information in this good foundation chapter is highly technical, focusing on hormonal and metabolic age-related changes that affect the sexual functioning of older males. Of particular interest to generalists are the sections on age changes in sexual behavior, physiology, and fertility.

Kind	*Recommendation*	*Readability*	*Audience*
RC	**	3	AG and SP

35. Harman, S. M. (1981). Aging, sexual activity and sex hormones in healthy men. *Generations*, *6*(1), **10–13.**

Data from 76 healthy male volunteers in the Baltimore Longitudinal Study of Aging are presented. Although no significant decrease in testosterone or increase in estrogen was found, the frequency of self-reported sexual activity decreased with age. Higher frequency of sexual activity in older men was correlated with higher serum testosterone levels. This article includes a glossary of terms and an overview of male reproductive endocrine physiology; however, portions of the article are worded quite technically.

Kind	Recommendation	Readability	Audience
E	**	3	AG or SP

36. Harry, J., & DeVall, W. (1978). Age and sexual culture among homosexually oriented males. *Archives of Sexual Behavior*, 7, 199–209.

Data on 243 homosexuals, ranging in age from the 20s to 40s, are reported in this interesting, but not specifically gerontological, study. Although evidence of a "youth orientation" in the gay subculture was found, considerable variability existed between individuals. Older men, middle-class men, and/or frequenters of gay bars were more likely to evidence preference for someone younger than themselves as sexual partners.

Kind	Recommendation	Readability	Audience
E	**	2	AU and above

37. Hays, A. M. (1984). Intimacy and sexuality in the elderly: Discussion. *Journal of Geriatric Psychiatry*, 17(2), 161–165.

Writing from a nursing perspective, the author provides an introductory overview of factors that may have a negative impact on sex in the elderly, maintaining that age per se is not a primary contributor to sexual decline. Negative factors include absence of a partner, poor education and attitudes, and health problems.

Kind	Recommendation	Readability	Audience
Review Article	*1/2	2	SP

38. Hussian, R. A., & Davis, R. L. (1985). Discharge program: Inappropriate sexual behavior. In *Responsive care: Behavioral interventions with elderly persons*. Champaign, IL: Research Press.

Several reasons for inappropriate sexual behavior in institutions (i.e., reactions to medication, stroke, dementia, and ongoing history of such behavior) are listed. Specific behavioral strategies for assessment and management of inappropriate sexual behavior are then discussed.

Kind	Recommendation	Readability	Audience
Clinical	**	2	SP

39. Kaas, J. (1978). Sexual expression of the elderly in nursing homes. *The Gerontologist*, *18*, 372–378.

In this study of 85 elderly nursing home residents and 207 staff members, both staff and residents considered lack of privacy to be the major deterrent to sexual expression. Most residents reported that they did not feel sexually attractive or interested in sex, indicating the strong repressive effect of the environment on sexual behavior.

Kind	Recommendation	Readability	Audience
E	**	2	AU and above or SP

40. Kaas, M. J. (1981). Geriatric sexuality breakdown syndrome. *International Journal of Aging and Human Development*, *13*(1), 71–77.

In an analogy to Kuypers and Bengtson's Social Breakdown Theory, the author posits that the normal physiological slowing of sexual response places aging individuals in a position of increased susceptibility to negative cues provided by the social environment. Typically, such cues are that sex is inappropriate or sinful for the elderly. In response, older adults may repress their sexual feelings. Sexual skills and abilities may then indeed atrophy, threatening self-esteem, and making the individual susceptible to a repetition of the breakdown process. Kaas recommends community sex education and education of the elderly as interventions for reversing the vicious breakdown process.

Kind	Recommendation	Readability	Audience
Theoretical Article	**	2	AU or SP

41. Kassel, V. (1983). Long-term care institutions. In R. B. Weg (Ed.), *Sexuality in the later years: Roles and behavior*. New York: Academic Press.

The cognitive and physical impairments of nursing home residents, combined with lack of education and awareness of staff, often lead to restrictive attitudes toward residents' sexuality and an assumption that residents are, in fact, asexual. While many ill and disabled residents are frankly not interested in sexual activity, for others the drives toward sex and intimacy are strong. Those working with the aged are admonished to be sensitive to these remaining needs in both heterosexual and homosexual residents.

Kind	Recommendation	Readability	Audience
RC	**	2	SP or AU and above

42. Kehoe, M. (1986). Lesbians over 65: A triply invisible minority. *Journal of Homosexuality*, *12*(6), 157–161; and, A portrait of the older lesbian. *Journal of Homosexuality*, *12*(6), 157–161.

The first article describes results of a survey polling 50 lesbians aged 65 to 85 residing in all areas of the United States. The data illustrate the over-65 lesbian to be in relatively good physical health and in excellent, stable mental health. Many are currently not involved in a sexual/affectional relationship, but this is involuntary, and most consider sexuality important. The second article is a more personal essay on the survivorship and strengths of "gynophiles" (i. e., older lesbians), particularly those retiring from the academic community.

Kind	Recommendation	Readability	Audience
E	**	1	AU and above

43. Keller, J. E., Eakes, E., Hinkle, D., & Hughston, G. A. (1978). Sexual behavior and guilt among women: A cross-generational comparison. *Journal of Sex and Marital Therapy*, *4*(4), 259–265.

Forty-five white married women aged 20 to 81 completed the Bentler Heterosexual Behavior Scale and the Mosher Forced-Choice Guilt Inventory. Analyses revealed lower levels of sexual experience and greater levels of guilt with increasing age. The authors interpret their findings as confirming the prediction that older women, acculturated into more sexually restrictive values during their upbringing, would express greater guilt about their sexual feelings, even with the sanction of marriage.

Kind	Recommendation	Readability	Audience
E	**	2	AG

44. Kelly, J. (1977). The aging male homosexual: Myth and reality. *The Gerontologist*, *17*(4), 328–332.

Data from a study of 241 gay men of all ages (including a subset of interviews with 36 individuals over the age of 65) are presented. The researcher found little evidence for the negative stereotypes associated with aging homosexuals; however, social and legal discrimination against gays, combined with the stigma associated with aging, were problematic for some. Kelly concludes that there is nothing intrinsically problematic about being an aging homosexual per se, but that societal discrimination can cause considerable problems.

Kind	Recommendation	Readability	Audience
E	**½	2	AU and above

45. Kentsmith, D. K., & Eaton, M. T. (1979). Sex during sickness. *Treating sexual problems in medical practice.* **New York: Arco.**

The direct and indirect effects of a broad array of illnesses and surgical procedures on sexual functioning are overviewed. Sexuality in long-term hospitalization and techniques for sexual counseling of the disabled are discussed very briefly.

Kind	Recommendation	Readability	Audience
TB (chapter)	**	2	SP

46. Kimmel, D. C. (1978). Adult development and aging: A gay perspective. *Journal of Social Issues, 34*(3), 113–130.

This primarily theoretical paper is based on pilot research conducted by the author with 14 older gay men. Using Levinson's developmental framework, Kimmel illustrates the diversity of developmental processes across the life span for gays, with some common patterns. One commonality evidenced was the relatively good adjustment of older gays and the lack of adherence to negative, homophobic social stereotypes. Developmentally, homosexuality was found to create both unique advantages and problems with aging. Kimmel notes that it is crucial to consider cohort effects when discussing such developmental patterns. The author calls for more research in this area and for more advocacy to support community and health services for older gays and lesbians.

Kind	Recommendation	Readability	Audience
T/E	**½	2	AU and above

47. Kuhn, M. E. (1976). Sexual myths surrounding the aging. In W. W. Oaks, G. A. Melchiode, & I. Ficher (Eds.), *Sex and the life cycle* **(35th Hahnemann Symposium). New York: Grune & Stratton.**

The author of this chapter, a vocal advocate for the elderly and national convener of the Gray Panthers, asserts that societal ageism is responsible for negative sexual myths about older adults. A call is made for changes in attitude and behavior, in order to permit the elderly to meet their needs for intimacy and affection.

Kind	Recommendation	Readability	Audience
RC	**	2	AU and above

48. Laner, M. R. (1978). Growing older male: Heterosexual and homosexual. *The Gerontologist*, *18*(5), 496–501.

The results of a nonreactive study comparing content of personals advertisements by homosexual and heterosexual males is presented. Counter to the stereotype of accelerated self-perceptions of aging in homosexual men, a higher proportion of early middle-aged homosexuals placing advertisements was not found. Similarly, seekers of young or younger-than-self partners were not overrepresented in the homosexual group. Interestingly, though, fewer homosexuals reported their own age.

Kind	Recommendation	Readability	Audience
E	**	2	AU and above

49. Laner, M. R. (1979). Growing older female: Heterosexual and homosexual. *Journal of Homosexuality*, *4*(3), 267–275.

The content of nationally distributed personals advertisements for lesbians ($N=273$) and nonlesbians ($N=229$) was analyzed. In contrast to the researchers' predictions, the vast majority of personals were placed by young and early middle-aged adults. More lesbians stated their own age and, while more lesbians did not indicate any age preference for the partner sought, many more heterosexual women clearly expressed desire for a partner older than themselves. Contrary to stereotypes, lesbians appeared generally to be seeking long-range, committed relationships and were not looking for partners dramatically younger than themselves. In this otherwise interesting article, the author's conclusion about heterosexual women's alleged "accelerated aging" is confusing and appears unfounded.

Kind	Recommendation	Readability	Audience
E	**	2	AU and above

50. LaTorre, R. A., & Kear, K. (1977). Attitudes toward sex in the aged. *Archives of Sexual Behavior,* **6,** 203–213.

In this study, 80 college students and 40 nurses and nurses aides in an institution for the elderly responded to three stories: one each on decision making, coitus, and masturbation, with variations in age and gender of the main character. Although neither subject group expressed more negative attitudes toward sex in the aged, sex was viewed as less credible for older story characters. Coitus was rated more favorably for the male characters in the study, and masturbation for the female characters. Nursing home staff members had more negative attitudes toward the sexual stories than did students, regardless of age of main character.

Kind	Recommendation	Readability	Audience
E	**	2	AU and above

51. Laury, G. V. (1980, January). Sensual activities of the aging couple. *Medical Aspects of Human Sexuality,* **pp. 32–37.**

Despite its misleading title, this article is basically an exhortation to physicians to disregard societal stereotypes of geriatric asexuality and to recognize the lifelong need for intimacy, coital or noncoital. The general discussion includes two illustrative case examples. A commentary on sexual dysfunction is provided by Dr. Alex Comfort; additional comments are presented by Drs. Stanley Cath and Susan Krinsky.

Kind	Recommendation	Readability	Audience
Clinical	*1/2	2	SP

52. Leviton, D. (1973). The significance of sexuality as a deterrent to suicide among the aged. *Omega,* **4,** 163–174.

Using a multidisciplinary approach, the author contends that the self-esteem and relationship values attached to a good sex life are deterrents to depression, isolation, and suicide in the elderly. Sexual therapy and interventions can be useful in countering dysfunction or loss leading to despair. The ideas presented are broad and speculative and, as the author states, require empirical testing.

Kind	Recommendation	Readability	Audience
Theoretical Article	*1/2	2	AU and above

53. Liptzin, B. (1984). Clinical perspectives on sexuality in older patients. *Journal of Geriatric Psychiatry, 17*(2), 167–181.

This article is comprised of a series of interesting vignettes illustrating the variety of ways in which sexuality may be an issue in psychiatric practice with geriatric patients. Issues covered include the effects of various psychopathologies on sexual function, the effects of life events and changing relationships on sexuality, and perceived threats to one's masculinity or femininity in old age.

Kind	*Recommendation*	*Readability*	*Audience*
Clinical	**½	2	AU and above

54. Livson, F. B. (1983). Gender identity: A life-span view of sex role development. In R. B. Weg (Ed.), *Sexuality in the later years: Roles and behavior.* **New York: Academic Press.**

The author proposes a life-span model of sex roles and gender identity. Beginning in midlife, men and women take on roles and characteristics considered appropriate to the opposite sex (i.e., move toward androgyny), without relinquishing their own previously developed masculine and feminine traits. Women become more assertive and instrumental, while men become more nurturant and expressive. Because traditional masculine roles and traits are typically more highly valued, many older women begin to experience better mental health and self-image than in their younger years. This chapter provides a nice theoretical overview of a very important and integral aspect of human sexuality.

Kind	*Recommendation*	*Readability*	*Audience*
TC	**½	2	AU and above

55. Long, J. W. (1980). Many common medications can affect sexual expression. *Generations, 6*(1), 32–33.

The major drug categories that potentially may impair sexual functioning are presented. Excellent summaries of specific drugs' effects in males and females are inserted in the article. Of particular interest to psychologists might be the various psychotropics mentioned.

Kind	*Recommendation*	*Readability*	*Audience*
Clinical	***	2	SP

56. Ludeman, K. (1981). The sexuality of the older person: Review of the literature. *The Gerontologist*, *21*(2), 203–208.

The author summarizes the major literature in the areas of physiological age changes in sexual responsivity, attitudes toward sex in the elderly, and sexual activity/interest rates in old age. Tests to assess sexual attitudes and interests are described, followed by a critique of the literature and suggestions for future exploration. This evaluative review, while not exhaustive, offers a good integrative introduction to the central foci of this area of research. (Unfortunately, several of the sources cited in the text are omitted in the list of references.)

Kind	Recommendation	Readability	Audience
Review	**½	2	SP or AU and above

57. Martin, C. E. (1981). Factors affecting sexual functioning in 60–79-year old married males. *Archives of Sexual Behavior*, *10*(5), 399–420.

Data from 188 married male participants in the Baltimore Longitudinal Study of Aging are presented. Frequency of sexual expression was found to be unrelated to most demographic indices, and to self-reported marital adjustment and attractiveness of wives, but prior and present rates of sexual activity were closely related. Most respondents reported a reasonable contentedness with their current sexual funtioning. Premature ejaculation was experienced by 21% of the least active and 8% of the most active; potency problems by 75% of the least active, 19% of the most active.

Kind	Recommendation	Readability	Audience
E	**½	2	AU and above or SP

58. Masters, W. H. (1986). Sex and aging—expectations and reality. *Hospital Practice*, *21*(8), 175–198.

Dr. Masters provides an in-depth summary of the major aging changes in physiological sexual response, identified through research at the Masters and Johnson Institute. Written in fairly technical language for a medical professional audience, the article also discusses major chronic disorders, medications, and psychological/relationship problems that may impair sexuality. The author strongly advocates continued, regular sexual activity across the life span and educational efforts to help aging persons recognize certain changes as normal.

Kind	Recommendation	Readability	Audience
E	**	3	SP or AG

59. Masters, W. H., & Johnson, V. E. (1981). Sex and the aging process. *Journal of the American Geriatrics Society, 29*(9), 385–390. Also reprinted in *Medical Aspects of Human Sexuality,* 1982, *16*(6), 40–57.

Masters and Johnson present a summary of the normal changes in sexual responsivity seen with advancing age in males and females. The Widow(er) Syndrome (i.e., sexual dysfunction following a long period of abstinence because of a spouse's illness and death) is described. The authors explore the deleterious effects of marital boredom on sexual expression and exhort older couples to be spontaneous and experimental.

Kind	Recommendation	Readability	Audience
Review Article	**	2	SP or AU and above

60. Myers, W. A. (1985). Sexuality in the older individual. *Journal of the American Academy of Psychoanalysis, 13*(4), 511–520.

The author reviews existing psychoanalytic literature on sexuality and the elderly, lamenting the paucity of such materials. Examples from the author's case load, illustrating some of the transference and countertransference dynamics that may emerge when sexual issues are involved in psychoanalysis, are presented.

Kind	Recommendation	Readability	Audience
Clinical Article	**	2	SP or AU and above (with some background in psychoanalytic issues and terminology)

61. National Institute on Aging (D-HHS). (1987). *The menopause time of life.* **Silver Spring, MD: National Institute on Aging.**

This pamphlet, written for a general audience, provides an excellent overview of menopause, including its effects and self-care strategies for optimizing the menopause experience. The more controversial aspects of this topic (e.g., use of estrogen replacement therapy) are treated both rationally and sensitively. Single copies of this brochure are available free of charge from: National Institute on Aging Information Center, 2209 Distribution Circle, Silver Spring, MD 20910.

Kind	Recommendation	Readability	Audience
Review	***	1	GP

62. Newman, G., & Nichols, C. R. (1960). Sexual activities and attitudes in older persons. *Journal of the American Medical Association,* **173, 33–35.**

Data from one of the pioneer descriptive studies on sex in old age (i.e., the Duke University Longitudinal Study) are presented here. Results of the study indicated that sexual interest and activity decline in old age, but cessation of sexual activity is related more to health problems in one or both of the partners involved than to age per se. In addition, over one-half of the married persons surveyed remained sexually active.

Kind	Recommendation	Readability	Audience
E	*1/2	2	AU and above

63. O'Connor, J., & Flax, C. (1977). The effects of aging in human sexuality. *Nursing Care, 10*(7), 24–27.

Normal age changes in sexual response, problems of impotence, and problems that may arise with menopause are discussed. Some of the material is, by now, outdated. Additionally, the authors explain that young males typically don't select older female partners "not simply because women age more rapidly than men, but because of strong unrecognized cultural undercurrents" (p. 24). While the latter assertion is most probably true, there is no evidence to support the former. These minor flaws mar an otherwise good introduction to the issue.

Kind	Recommendation	Readability	Audience
Review Article	**	2	SP or AU and above

64. Persson, G. M. (1980). Sexuality in a 70-year old urban population. *Journal of Psychosomatic Research, 24*(6), 335–342.

In this empirical study, 46 percent of 166 elderly males and 16 percent of 266 elderly females reported they were still sexually active (i.e., had intercourse at least once in the past 2 to 3 months). The vast majority of those reporting continued sexual activity were married. In both men and women, continued sexual intercourse was associated with good mental health and a positive attitude toward sex in old age. Sexually active women also tended to have younger husbands, self-reported better marriages, and more positive attitudes toward sex in general.

Kind	Recommendation	Readability	Audience
E	**	2	AU and above or SP

65. Pfeiffer, E. (1974). Sexuality in the aging individual. *Journal of the American Geriatrics Society, 22*, 481–484.

Statistics from the Duke University Longitudinal Study are presented as evidence that sexual activity continues to be important for many older individuals. Implications of these findings for clinical practice are discussed, most notably the need to create private environments for the elderly.

Kind	Recommendation	Readability	Audience
E	**	2	AG or SP

66. Pfeiffer, E., & Davis, G. C. (1972). Determinants of sexual behavior in middle and old age. *Journal of the American Geriatrics Society, 20*, 151–158.

Using data from the Duke University Longitudinal Study, the researchers found level of sexual functioning in younger years, age and sex of subject, and subjective and objective health ratings to be important determinants of sexual behavior in later life. For women specifically, past sexual enjoyment, marital status, and age were the most critical factors.

Kind	Recommendation	Readability	Audience
E	**	2	AG or SP

67. Porcino, J. (1981). Growing older female: With love, sex and intimacy. *Generations*, *6*(1), 8–9, 40.

Postmenopausal physical changes and the effects of certain disease processes that may necessitate sexual adaptation are briefly overviewed. Alternatives to traditional heterosexual intercourse are also discussed.

Kind	Recommendation	Readability	Audience
Review Article	**	1	GP or SP

68. Portonova, M., Young, E., & Newman, M. A. (1984). Elderly women's attitudes toward sexual activity among their peers. *Health Care for Women International*, *5*, 289–298.

In this study, 120 older ($\bar{X}$ age = 71) community-dwelling women read one each of six brief vignettes of a sexually active older individual: Vignettes varied in terms of gender, marital status (married or widowed), and place of residence (apartment or nursing home). Results indicated generally positive attitudes toward active sexuality for both older males and females. Analysis of variance did reveal, however, that attitudes were more positive toward individuals described as married and dwelling independently.

Kind	Recommendation	Readability	Audience
E	**	2	AU and above

69. Raphael, S., & Robinson, M. (1981). Lesbians and gay men in later life. *Generations*, *6*(1), 16–18.

This article provides a brief overview of family, friend, and long-term love relationships among older lesbians/gays, pointing out that while sex drive diminishes somewhat with age for both males and females, most remain sexually active and interested in intimacy and relationships. The authors describe research showing that the diverse patterns of adjustment to aging by older gays and lesbians are similar to those of heterosexuals. Finally, the need for sensitivity to gay/lesbian issues among service providers to older adults is underscored.

Kind	Recommendation	Readability	Audience
Review Article	**	2	AU and above or SP

70. Reedy, M. N., Birren, J. E., & Schaie, K. W. (1981). Age and sex differences in satisfying love relationships across the adult life span. *Human Development*, *24*, 52–66.

Young, middle-aged, and older couples nominated by others as having happy marriages (*N* = 102) completed a Q-sort task describing dimensions of love. Emotional security was rated as the most important component of love for all ages, and love was considered to be more than just genital sexuality across the life span. Older couples, however, had significantly higher ratings on the emotional security and loyalty dimensions, and lower rankings on sexual intimacy and communication than younger and middle-aged couples. These differences may be attributable to developmental changes (e.g., physiological changes in sexual responsivity) or generational effects (e.g., attitudes of different cohorts).

Kind	Recommendation	Readability	Audience
E	**	2	AG

71. Renshaw, D. C. (1983). Sex, intimacy and the older woman. *Women and Health*, *8*(4), 43–54.

This somewhat rambling article defines and discusses several forms of intimacy that remain important for older women (and men as well). Intimacy may be physical, social, intellectual, emotional, spriritual, or sexual. The author notes that many older adults have benefitted from participation in a brief sex therapy program offered at the Loyola College Sex Clinic. Particular attention is paid in this article to the importance of emotional intimacy for late-life women; barriers to, bridges to, and benefits of such intimacy are outlined.

Kind	Recommendation	Readability	Audience
Theoretical	**	1	GP, SP, or AU and above

72. Renshaw, D. C. (1984). Geriatric sex problems. *Journal of Geriatric Psychiatry*, *17*(2), 123–138.

Normal and pathological needs for late-life intimacy, as well as normal age-related changes in physical sexual response, are discussed. Some suggestions whereby professionals can assist older clients and patients in maximizing sexual function are given. The article also provides brief coverage of chronic disease and drug/alcohol abuse as barriers to late-life sexual functioning.

Kind	Recommendation	Readability	Audience
Clinical	**	2	SP

73. Rezendes, J. B. B. (1981). The triple whammy: Aging, sexuality and terminal illness. *Generations*, 6(1), 19–21, 43.

The dying elderly are almost always assumed to be asexual. Clinical observations indicate, however, that while sex drive and performance may be reduced in such patients, sexual and intimacy needs remain intact. Some common fears and reactions of terminally ill elderly with regard to their sexuality are clearly and succinctly addressed, and guidelines for professionals are offered.

Kind	Recommendation	Readability	Audience
Clinical	**	1	SP or AU and above

74. Robinson, P. K. (1983). The sociological perspective. In R. B. Weg (Ed.), *Sexuality in the later years: Roles and behavior*. New York: Academic Press.

As the author aptly notes, research efforts have overlooked the concept of the *potential* for sexuality and sensuality in the later years. Social barriers to active sexual expression (delineated clearly in this chapter) include health problems, stigmatization, institutionalization, objections of children, and for many women, lack of access to male partners. The author contends that if social barriers could be eradicated, sexual potential in late life would be quite high. She notes that old age can bring welcomed improvement in relationships, more freedom in choosing sex roles, increased emphasis on intimacy and affection, and greater opportunity to explore new alternatives.

Kind	Recommendation	Readability	Audience
RC	**	2	AU and above or SP

75. Roff, L. L., & Klemmack, D. L. (1979). Sexual activity among older persons: A comparative analysis of appropriateness. *Research on Aging*, 1(3), 390–398.

In this study, 210 adults rated the perceived appropriateness of various sexual behaviors for older persons. The researchers found no stereotyping of the elderly as asexual in subjects' responses. Most respondents believed older persons to be interested in and capable of sexual activity, and considerd this appropriate (at least among married individuals).

Kind	Recommendation	Readability	Audience
E	**	2	AU and above

76. Runciman, A. P. (1980). Sexual problems in the senior world. In R. L. Solnick (Ed.), *Sexuality and aging* (rev. ed.). Los Angeles: University of Southern California.

This chapter summarizes some of the determinants of sexual behavior in old age, including psychological factors. Masters and Johnson's findings on changes in sexual responsivity with age are integrated into the material. This informal chapter provides thorough, if somewhat disjointed, coverage of the topic.

Kind	Recommendation	Readability	Audience
RC	*1/2	2	SP or AU and above

77. Salamon, M. J., & Charytan, P. (1984). A sexuality workshop program for the elderly. *Clinical Gerontologist*, 2(4), 25–35.

A series of sexuality workshops offered through a multidisciplinary, holistic preventive health center with an elderly clientele is described. Pre- and postworkshop measures revealed significantly enhanced self-reported knowledge about sexuality and more positive attitudes, and a nonsignificant trend toward improved life satisfaction.

Kind	Recommendation	Readability	Audience
E	**	2	SP

78. Schiff, I., & Wilson, E. (1978). Clinical aspects of aging of the female reproductive system. In E. L. Schneider (Ed.), *Aging*: Vol. 4. *The aging reproductive system*. New York: Raven Press.

In the first part of this relatively technical article, the authors describe thoroughly the development of the female reproductive organs and aging-related changes in these organs. The second section briefly covers cancer, sexual responsivity, pregnancy, contraception, clinical evaluation, and therapy for pre- and postmenopausal women, with emphasis on diagnostic and treatment issues.

Kind	Recommendation	Readability	Audience
RC	**	3	AG or SP

79. Schmall, V. L., & Staton, M. (1981). Sex education for older adults. *Generations*, 6(1), 24–26.

Older adults, their family members, and their care providers need to be educated about late-life sexuality if such sexual functioning is to be optimized. General guidelines for teaching the elderly about sex, particularly in group settings, and an overview of sexual information older adults need to know are given.

Kind	Recommendation	Readability	Audience
Clinical	*½	1	SP or AU

80. Smith, M. M., & Schmall, V. L. (1983). Knowledge and attitudes toward sexuality and sex education of a select group of older people. *Gerontology and Geriatrics Education*, 3(4), 259–269.

In this study, interviews were conducted with 32 community-dwelling men and women ranging in age from 65 to 74 years. Although many respondents expressed discomfort in talking about sex, the vast majority (90%) felt that sex education would be beneficial for older adults. The authors suggest that such education should be multifaceted, offering classes and group discussions, as well as self-study materials. Although subjects reported preference for peers to lead such groups, they also indicated great enjoyment interacting with young interviewers. Thus the authors conclude that interpersonal qualities, not age of the leader(s), would be most influential in determining the success of such a group.

Kind	Recommendation	Readability	Audience
E	**	2	SP or AU and above

81. Snyder, E. E., & Speitzer, E. (1975). Attitudes of the aged toward non-traditional sexual behavior. *Archives of Sexual Behavior*, 5, 249–254.

Using data drawn from the National Opinion Research Center, a 65+ group and an under-64-years group were examined. The researchers noted a correlation between increased age and conservatism in attitudes toward premarital sex, extramarital sex, and homosexuality. Although age proved to be a correlate of conservative sexual attitudes, so did gender, church attendance, social and economic status, and parenthood, for both older and younger cohorts. The authors conclude that there may be a considerable range of variability in sexual attitudes among older adults.

Kind	Recommendation	Readability	Audience
E	*1/2	2	AU and above

82. Solnick, R. L. (1980). Sexual responsiveness, age and change: Facts and potential. In R. L. Solnick (Ed.), *Sexuality and aging* (rev. ed.). Los Angeles: University of Southern California.

The chapter begins with a summary of the author's research where erectile responsivity of older males was improved using such interventions as biofeedback and sexual fantasy. This is followed by a survey of studies observing changes in sexual activity with age and a discussion of emotional, societal, and physical determinants of sexuality. The author accomplishes an interesting integration of empirical and humanistic concerns.

Kind	Recommendation	Readability	Audience
E/R	**	2	AU and above or SP

83. Solnick, R. L., & Birren, J. (1977). Age and male erectile response and sexual behavior. *Archives of Sexual Behavior, 6*(1), 1-9.

In this laboratory study, the erection rate of younger subjects while viewing an erotic film was 5.8 times faster than that of older subjects, and their average increase in penile circumference was significantly larger. Both age groups found the film to be erotic, and little anxiety was expressed by either old or young subjects. While the results confirmed a slowing down of erectile response with age, the authors note that this should in no way preclude enjoyment of sex. They recommend that aging males be made aware of this normal change in order to avoid anxiety and depression.

Kind	Recommendation	Readability	Audience
E	**	2	AU and above

84. Starr, B. D. (1985). Sexuality and aging. In C. Eisdorfer (Series Ed.), *Annual review of geriatrics and gerontology* (Vol. 5, M. P. Lawton & G. C. Maddox, Eds.). New York: Springer.

This chapter critiques early research indicating a sharp decline in sex with age on the basis of methodological flaws and, more important, for failing to explore the meaning and experience of sexuality for older adults. The author exhorts researchers to continue recent efforts begun to determine such phenomenological aspects. Relying heavily on the Starr–Weiner (1981) report, but citing other research as well, the author illustrates that the elderly as a whole clearly "like sex, want sex, feel they need sex for their physical and psychological well-being and are frustrated when they do not have sex" (p. 106). In summary, this review provides a thoughtful, comprehensive summary of gerontological research in sexuality.

Kind	Recommendation	Readability	Audience
RC	***	2	AG

85. Starr, B. D., & Weiner, M. B. (1981). *The Starr-Weiner report on sex and sexuality in the mature years.* **New York: McGraw-Hill.**

This book reports verbatim how elderly persons themselves view their sexuality. Presented in a straightforward, clear manner and with nontechnical language, the book was developed through the efforts of two researchers who obtained 800 responses from individuals aged 60 to 91 to a questionnaire about sexual beliefs and practices. These responses are reported throughout the book under various chapter headings: For each chapter, the results and implications of responses to pertinent survey questions are discussed, and actual illustrative responses are presented. Most responses indicated not only a global acceptance of sexuality in the elderly, but continued interest in personal sexual expression. (The general trend toward overwhelming acceptance of most aspects of sexuality may, of course, be partially attributable to subject selection factors.) With this qualification in mind, however, the book is strongly recommended for its candid, thoughtful, and sometimes humorous insights into late-life sexuality.

Kind	Recommendation	Readability	Audience
E	***	2	AG, SP, or AU and above

86. Steffl, B. M. (1981). Touch and human sexuality in later life. *Generations,* **6(1), 27–28.**

The needs for warmth and touch, as well as the difficulty older persons often have in meeting these needs, is discussed. Steffl warns that ethnic and cultural differences in touch behavior need to be respected, and calls for more research on the meaning of touch to the elderly. The article concludes with some very helpful and specific guidelines to the appropriate use of loving touch.

Kind	Recommendation	Readability	Audience
Clinical	**	1	SP

87. Stimson, A., Wase, J. F., & Stimson, J. (1981). Sexuality and self-esteem among the aged. *Research on Aging, 3*(2), 228–239.

Factor analysis was used to examine constructs of self-esteem in older ($\overline{X}$ age = 68 years) men and women. For older males, confidence in sexual performance was a crucial part of overall self-esteem. This was not found to be true for older females; however, women who judged themselves as "not sexually attractive," according to societally proscribed youthful standards, expressed low feelings of self-worth.

Kind	Recommendation	Readability	Audience
E	**	2	AU and above

88. Sviland, M. A. P. (1980). A program of sexual liberation and growth in the elderly. In R. L. Solnick (Ed.), *Sexuality and aging* (rev. ed.). **Los Angeles: University of Southern California.**

The chapter is prefaced with several pages discussing the myth of asexuality in old age, rates and potential of sexual expression, and barriers to sexuality imposed by societal values. The core of the chapter describes techniques used in a program designed to enhance the sexuality of elderly couples. The author briefly reports several cases where couples derived benefit from participation in this therapy program, but more rigorous evaluative data is not presented.

Kind	Recommendation	Readability	Audience
Clinical	**	2	SP or AU and above

89. Szasz, G. (1983). Sexual incidents in an extended care unit for aged men. *Journal of the American Geriatrics Society, 31*(7), 407–411.

Nursing home staff's responses to an anonymous questionnaire indicated that residents' sexual behaviors considered most problematic were sex talk, sexual acts (e.g., public masturbation, touching or grabbing staff), and implied sexual behavior (e.g., reading pornography, requesting unnecessary genital care). A later in-service discussion session revealed that such incidents occurred daily, but were primarily caused by 20% to 25% of the residents. Sexual behaviors considered appropriate were private masturbation and brief, limited hugging and kissing between staff and residents.

Kind	Recommendation	Readability	Audience
E	**	2	SP or AU and above

90. Traupmann, J. (1984). Does sexuality fade over time? A look at the question and the answer. *Journal of Geriatric Psychiatry, 17*(2), 149–159.

As the author notes, the idea that sexuality declines with age is very common in popular culture. Factors contributing to this notion are discomfort with parental sexuality, the emphasis on youth seen in the popular media, and ageism in general. The author contends that, while some cross-sectional research suggests a decline in frequency of sexual activity with age, many older couples and individuals continue to engage in active and vibrant sex lives. Rejection of ageist misconceptions about late-life sexuality and previous active patterns appear to be the best predictors of ongoing active sexual expression. The article concludes with a reminder that the quality of intimacy in relationships is an important factor in sexuality at any age and cannot be ignored.

Kind	Recommendation	Readability	Audience
Review Article	***	2	SP or AU and above

91. Turner, B. F., & Adams, C. A. (1983). The sexuality of older women. In E. W. Markson (Ed.), *Older women: Issues and prospects.* Lexington, MA: Lexington Books.

This chapter, although focusing primarily on older women, also describes age-related changes in aging men, because (as the authors note) for most women, sexual activity is heterosexual. The effects of chronic disease on sexuality are discussed, with particular emphasis on cancer and heart disease. Developmental sexual changes are covered for both men and women, as are the effects of changing sexual attitudes across cohorts and alternatives to heterosexual intercourse for older women. Other changes that may be of benefit to older women include advances that enhance the longevity of males, reeducation and counseling of older men, and early training of future generations of older men.

Kind	Recommendation	Readability	Audience
R	**	2	AU and above

92. Walz, T. H., & Blum, N. S. (1987). *Sexual health in later life.* **Lexington, MA: Lexington Books.**

This straightforward, lay-oriented book provides a good general overview of the topic. The authors begin with a general discussion of physical age-related changes in sexuality, effects of various chronic illnesses and medical regimens on adult sexuality and specific recommendations for overcoming the barriers to sexuality imposed by illness. Concrete guidelines for maintaining healthy sexuality are offered, as well as more general prescriptions for maintaining physical and mental health. The authors conclude with two commendable chapters on dealing with disapproval of sexual activity by others and on homosexual relationships in late life.

Kind	*Recommendation*	*Readability*	*Audience*
TB	**1/2	1	GP

93. Wasow, M., & Loeb, M. B. (1979). Sexuality in nursing homes. *Journal of the American Geriatrics Society,* **27(2), 73–79. Also reprinted in R. L. Solnick (Ed.),** *Sexuality and aging* **(rev. ed.). Los Angeles: University of Southern California, 1980.**

In this survey of 63 older nursing home residents and staff members, results indicated that some residents retained at least moderate levels of sexual interest. They were typically not sexually active, however, due to perceived lack of opportunity and inhibiting attitudes of staff. This article effectively demonstrates the repressive effect of lack of knowledge on sexual expression and underscores the need for continuing sexual education of both nursing home staff and residents.

Kind	*Recommendation*	*Readability*	*Audience*
E	**	2	AU and above or SP

94. Wax, J. (1982). Sex and the single grandparent. In S. H. Zarit (Ed.), *Readings in aging and death: Contemporary perspectives* **(2nd ed.). New York: Harper & Row.**

This warm, personal, and nontechnical article, originally published in 1975, offers excerpts from interviews with older unmarried couples living together for purposes of companionship and/or overt sexual activity. Although the supportive statistics presented are outdated and the author occasionally appears condescending, this humorous and humane article provides a clear illustration of the lifelong needs of men and women for intimacy and affection.

Kind	Recommendation	Readability	Audience
Review Article	**	1	GP

95. Weg, R. B. (1980). The physiology of sexuality in aging. In R. L. Solnick (Ed.), *Sexuality and aging* (rev. ed.). Los Angeles: University of Southern California.

Good coverage of aging-related changes in the sexual anatomy and responsivity of males and females is provided. Other topics covered include the effects of illness and disease on sexuality, and treatment interventions for health care workers to provide to older patients experiencing sexual problems. This is recommended as a nice overview of major issues in sexuality and aging.

Kind	Recommendation	Readability	Audience
RC	**1/2	2	AU and above or SP

96. Weg, R. B. (1983a). Introduction: Beyond intercourse and orgasm. In R. B. Weg (Ed.), *Sexuality in the later years: Roles and behavior.* New York: Academic Press.

Dr. Weg traces the historical development of research in human sexuality. She notes that few researchers have considered sexuality beyond its genital aspects and encourages the furtherance of research on relationships and feelings across the life span.

Kind	Recommendation	Readability	Audience
RC	*1/2	2	AU and above

97. Weg, R. B. (1983b). The physiological perspective. In R. B. Weg (Ed.), *Sexuality in the later years: Roles and behavior.* New York: Academic Press.

Despite its limiting title, the author begins her holistically oriented chapter with overviews of the historical, social/attitudinal, and personal aspects of sexuality in old age. The content on the physical aspects of aging includes an overview of research on age-related changes in sexual response in men and women. The hormonal changes associated with the female premenopausal climacteric and with males of the same age are presented thoroughly and in detail. Brief overviews of homosexuality and masturbation are provided, followed by a discussion of the negative impact of medication misuse/substance abuse, chronic illnessess, and surgical procedures on older adults' sexuality. Also covered are the potential benefits of hormonal replacement therapies, sex and marital counseling, and lifelong sexual education. This is a useful overview of a multitude of factors related to the physiology of aging, with a humanistic touch.

Kind	*Recommendation*	*Readability*	*Audience*
RC	***	2	AU and above or SP

98. Weiss, L. J. (1983). Intimacy and adaptation. In R. B. Weg (Ed.), *Sexuality in the later years: Roles and behavior*. New York: Academic Press.

The chapter presents a National Institute on Aging–sponsored study on age changes in intimacy and the role of intimacy in adaptation to stress and loss in old age. The Weiss Intimacy Rankings (WIR) measure and measures of stressful life events, morale, and psychosomatic symptoms were administered to 171 men and women aged 21 to 72. For both men and women, marital intimacy declined precipitously with age, although rising again for postretirement women. Spousal intimacy, though, was generally found to be a mediator of late-life stress. The author notes that the "empty nest" for women and retirement for men appeared to initiate lower degrees of intimacy; thus, it is unlikely that aging and its accompanying stresses result in increased potential for intimacy.

Kind	*Recommendation*	*Readability*	*Audience*
E	**	2	AG

99. West, H. L. (1983). Sexuality and aging: An innovative educational approach. *Gerontology and Geriatrics Education, 4*(1), 61–66.

A decision-making simulation game used in workshops on sexuality for older adults, family members of older relatives, and service providers to the elderly is described. The author reports that, in pre- and postworkshop measures, participants' knowledge and attitudes toward late-life sexuality changed in a positive direction. The simulation, however, occurred within the context of more global workshops (see White & Cantania, 1982). Therefore, it is not possible to determine whether the game was itself responsible for the positive impact, or if it was other aspects of the intervention that initiated the desired change.

Kind	Recommendation	Readability	Audience
E	*1/2	2	SP

100. White, C. B. (1982). Sexual interest, attitudes, knowledge, and history in relation to sexual behavior in the institutionalized aged. *Archives of Sexual Behavior, 11*(1), 11–21.

Interviews with 269 nursing home residents (mean age for males = 81, mean age for females = 83) revealed that, while 91% reported themselves as sexually inactive, 17% said they were interested in sex but lack of privacy and/or partners were deterrents to activity. Regression analyses revealed that sexual attitudes, knowledge, and prior history were all significantly predictive of current activity. Thus, while the nursing home environment poses clear obstacles to sexual fulfillment, institutionalization does not necessarily have to mean the end of sexual functioning. A nice feature of this article is a table providing an excellent, concise summary of 24 early (1925 to 1975) research studies on frequency of sexual activity in the elderly

Kind	Recommendation	Readability	Audience
E	**1/2	2	AU and above

101. White, C. B., & Catania, J. A. (1982). Psychoeducational intervention for sexuality with the aged, family members of the aged and people who work with the aged. *International Journal of Aging and Human Development, 15*(2), 121–138.

This article describes the outcome of a three-session educational program about geriatric sexuality. Three separate groups were tested: community-residing elderly, relatives of older adults (unrelated to test group), and nursing home staff, and each experimental group ($N = 30$) had a control group. Regression analyses revealed significant pre-to-posttest positive changes in knowledge and attitudes in all three groups, and posttest scores were significantly more positive than those of the control group participants. Older participants reported increased frequencies of sexual intercourse and masturbation, and greater sexual satisfaction. Although the long-term impact of the intervention is not known, this straightforward information-providing intervention seems promising as a mechanism for enhancing older adults' sexuality.

Kind	Recommendation	Readability	Audience
E	**	3(Statistics)	AG

102. Winn, R. L., & Newton, N. (1982). Sexuality in aging: A study of 106 cultures. *Archives of Sexual Behavior, 11*(4), 283–298.

A cross-cultural analysis of 106 of the 293 datasets on traditional societies contained in the Human Relations Area Files is presented. In most of these cultures, some form of sexual activity was reported as present by observers in older men (70%) and women (84%), and sexual interest remained high for both genders. In 23% of the cultures, the onset of old age was associated with lessened sexual inhibition, particularly for women. Very few instances of societal censure or ridicule of sexual behavior in old age were noted. In those cases where it occurred, however, it did have an inhibiting effect on elders' sexuality, suggesting the importance of cultural/societal attitudes in late-life sexual behavior.

Kind	*Recommendation*	*Readability*	*Audience*
E	**	2	AU and above

103. Woods, N. (1979). Adaptation to hospitalization and illness. In N. Woods (Ed.), *Human sexuality in health and illness* (2nd ed.). St. Louis: C. V. Mosby.

Topics covered in this interesting chapter are the effects of hospitalization on sexual feelings and behavior; sexuality and the sick role; cultural/ethnic differences in sex roles; dynamics of sexual acting out of patients; interventions for eliminating embarrassing situations; encouraging privacy and facilitating sexual needs; confronting staff sexism; and dealing with one's own feelings when sexually aroused by a patient. Several excellent brief case examples are offered to stimulate thought and discussion.

Kind	*Recommendation*	*Readability*	*Audience*
RC	**½	2	SP or AU and above

104. Woods, N., & Herbert, J. M. (1979). Sexuality and chronic illness. In N. Woods (Ed.), *Human sexuality in health and illness* (2nd ed.). St. Louis: C. V. Mosby.

Sexuality is discussed within the framework of four chronic illnesses: diabetes mellitus, heart disease, hypertension, and chronic renal failure. Each condition's effects on male and female sexual responsivity and fertility are presented. Guidelines for clinical assessment of biological and psychosocial factors affecting sexuality and suggestions for health care interventions to optimize sexual functioning are provided. An excellent set of review questions concludes the chapter.

Kind	Recommendation	Readability	Audience
RC	**	2	SP or AU and above

SUPPLEMENTARY MATERIALS

I. Reviewed and Recommended Audiovisuals

105. *Minnie Remembers*   1976   5 min   Color   16 mm

This dramatic film, illustrating a poem written by Donna Swanson, depicts an older woman (Minnie) reliving memories from the past. She recalls the affection and closeness she used to experience with family members, lamenting her present loneliness and the fact that nobody touches her anymore. The film is poignant in its portrayal of the life-long need for intimate touch and love. Purchase $125.00; Rental $25.00.

Available from: Mass Media Ministries
                2116 North Charles Street
                Baltimore, MD 21218
                (301) 727-3270

106. *A Ripple of Time*   1974   24 min   Color   16 mm and video

A 54-year-old woman and a 68-year-old man are filmed relating to each other sexually in a variety of ways. The film is tasteful and aesthetically pleasing; the participants are attractive and often playful. This is a very explicit film, including scenes depicting full nudity, male and female genitals, sexual intercourse, and oral sex. The film is generally an excellent and provocative resource for demonstrating the potential for sexual expression, affection, and intimacy throughout the life span. (Produced by Laird Sutton, National Sex Forum.) Purchase $400.00 (16mm), $340.00 (video); Rental $60.00 (16mm).

Available from: Multi-Focus, Inc.
                1525 Franklin Street
                San Francisco, CA 94109
                (800) 821-0514
                (In CA call collect at (415) 673-5103.)

107. *Rose by Any Other Name* 1979 15 min Color 16mm and video

In this film by Judith Keller, a 79-year-old nursing home resident, Rose Gordon, is seen cuddling and laughing in bed with Mr. Morris, another elderly resident. When this relationship comes to the attention of the home's administrator, Rose is told she must leave the home if she continues to spend the night with Mr. Morris. In fear of being "expelled" from the home and despite her daughter's attempt to help, Rose agrees to stop seeing Mr. Morris. Mr. Morris becomes despondent, and in another conversation with the administrator, Rose relates how angry she is at the way his policy intrudes on her private life and how lonely she now feels. The administrator remains unmoved and repeats his ultimatum. In the film's final scene, Rose is caught in Mr. Morris's room by the administrator and the head nurse. The administrator says, "I'm sorry, Rose, but you leave me no other choice." The film purposely ends with Rose's fate remaining unresolved and ambiguous. This entertaining, nonexplicit film is an excellent stimulus for triggering thoughts and feelings about continuing needs for privacy, affection, and sex in the institutional environment. Purchase $350.00 (16mm), $250.00 (video); Rental $40.00 (16mm).

Available from: Multi-Focus, Inc.   or   Focus International, Inc.
1525 Franklin St.
San Francisco, CA 94109
(800) 821-0514
(In CA call collect at
(415) 673-5103.)

14 Oregon Drive
Huntington Station
New York, NY 11746
(516) 549-5320

II. Structured Discussion Tool

108. Genevay, B. (1981). It's time we sat down and talked about sex— again. *Generations,* 6(1), 14–15, 41.

Subtitled "A playscript for older people, their families and those in the helping professions," a scenario of a 72-year-old widow having a sexual relationship with a 62-year-old man, and her various family members, is presented. Although some may find the dialogue and situation unrealistic, the two-page script can be used as an excellent tool for focusing on issues of sexuality and aging for discussion. The author, in fact, suggests a number of potential areas for discussion that may be stimulated by reading this playscript.

109. Campden-Main, B. C. (1980, August). Quiz: Sexual counseling of older patients. *Medical Aspects of Human Sexuality,* pp. 80–85.

The quiz presents a series of sex-oriented scenarios that the health or mental health professional is likely to encounter in clinical practice with older patients. Some of the material in this quiz will probably not be known to individuals without some specific training in sex counseling and in geriatrics; however, the quiz provides an interesting and educational introduction to therapeutic issues in sexuality of the elderly, and could easily be used to construct a discussion.

110. Miller, D. B. (1975). Sexual practices and administrative policies in long-term care institutions. *Journal of Long-Term Care Administration, 3*(3). Also in R. L. Solnick (Ed.) (1980). *Sexuality and Aging.* (rev. ed.). Los Angeles: University of Southern California.

Although written for administrators, information is provided that could be potentially enlightening and sensitizing to a broader-based audience. On page 170 (in the 1980 reprinting) there is a list of the "possible range of institutional sexual partners," both heterosexual and homosexual, that nursing home staff may encounter in their residents. These scenarios can be used to structure a discussion regarding how the individual, if he or she were an administrator, would respond personally and professionally, and how this would impact upon the formulation of policy for his or her facility.

III. Pre- and Posttest Questionnaires

111. Walz, T. H., & Blum, N. S. (1987). Adult sexuality knowledge and attitude test (ASKAT). In *Sexual health in later life.* Lexington, MA: Lexington Books.

This series of 49 true-false items on various aspects of sexuality in older adults is readily useable as a pre- and posttest measure of knowledge. Also included are 17 questions to assess individual feelings, attitudes, and values regarding late-life sexuality. The ASKAT inventory can be found on pages 9-14, and a key with correct answers to the knowledge items is included in an appendix.

112. White, C. B. (1982). A scale for the assessment of attitudes and knowledge regarding sexuality in the aged. *Archives of Sexual Behavior, 11*(6), 491–502.

The Aging Sexual Knowledge and Attitudes Scale (ASKAS) was designed to assess cognitions about sex in old age among older respondents, family members of older adults, care providers, and volunteers, and is highly appropriate for use as an educational tool and/or a pre- and posttest measure. The ASKAS comprises 61 items (35 knowledge-oriented true-false questions and 26 attitudinal items). The scale has been demonstrated as acceptable on all indices of reliability (range of reliability coefficients presented = .72–.91). Use of the ASKAS in experimental research has shown it to be a valid research measure, and as the author notes, this scale also has potential utility in both educational and clinical settings.

113. **Friedeman, J. S. (1979). Development of a sexual knowledge inventory for elderly persons.** *Nursing Research, 28,* 372–374.

A 30-item Sexual Knowledge Inventory for Elderly Persons (SKE) was administered to 100 older women. as well as to 40 nursing faculty and 86 nursing students. The instrument was revised to contain 25 items (included, with appropriate responses, in the article). The SKE can be used not only to assess sexual knowledge of the elderly, but as a teaching tool for audiences of all ages.

114. **Carroll, K. (Ed.) (1978).** *Sexuality and aging.* Inservice Guide, Human Development Series. Available from Ebenezer Center for Aging and Human Development, 2626 Park Avenue, Minneapolis, MN 55407. $4.00 plus postage and handling.

This 35-item true-false questionnaire on physical and psychological aspects of late-life sexuality may also be useful as a pre- and postknowledge measure. Brief supportive information and references are provided with the correct answers for each item.

IV. Additional Resources

115. **Schmall, V. L. (1981). Resources: Aging and sexuality.** *Generations, 6*(1), 46–48.

A helpful compilation of resources, current as of 1981, is provided. The descriptive and access information given for 10 publications, 17 media presentations, and 9 organizations could potentially be of great assistance in lecture preparation and class presentation.

116. Davis, R. H. (1980). Sex on the screen. *The Gerontologist, 20*(6), 631–635.

Several films on sex and aging are reviewed: *Sex and Aging . . . Elders Speak Out, Love After Sixty, Sexuality and Aging,* and *Rose by Any Other Name.* Additional films are mentioned but not reviewed. While much of the acquisition information is no longer current, this article is of potential use to those beginning to think about which audiovisual resources might be appropriate to their instructional needs.

117. Smith, M. M., & Schmall, V. L. (1983). Resources on sexuality and aging. *Gerontology and Geriatrics Education, 3*(4), 266–269.

Presented as an afterword to an empirical article by the author, descriptive and access information is provided for 12 publications (books, training manuals, etc.) and 17 media presentations (games, films, slides/tapes).

SUMMARY

Paramount in the understanding of late-life sexuality is the realization that sex for older people, as for people of any other age, cannot be limited in conceptualization to an act or acts involving the meeting of a pair of genitals. In addition to such overt activities, human sexuality in the elderly includes one's sense of gender identity, one's need for intimacy and affection, and one's desire for warmth and contact through hugging, kissing, fondling, and cuddling (Butler & Lewis, 1980; Laury, 1980; Porcino, 1981; Steffl, 1981). Although early research did not attempt to look at these aspects of sex, more recent surveys of the sex lives of the elderly recognize these as integral components (Brecher, 1984; Starr & Weiner, 1981; Wax, 1982). The results of these studies send a strong message concerning the importance of each of these in the sexual expression and experiences of older adults. In fact, particularly in many long-standing relationships, it is these more intimate, emotional aspects of sexuality, rather than the more genital aspects, to which couples attribute their success in togetherness (Brecher, 1984; Fitzgerald, McKellar, Lener, & Copans, 1985; Reedy, Birren, & Schaie, 1981; Starr & Weiner, 1981).

In striving for scientific credibility in this area of inquiry, the quantitative aspects of sex in old age are often examined in isolation from its emotional, subjective and qualitative aspects. Effective mental health researchers, teachers, and practitioners need to achieve a balance between the generation of accurate, easily quantifiable data and the simultaneous recognition of aspects of real-life human sexuality that do not easily fit within the parameters of empirical research. An awareness of the true facts of late-life sexuality plus sensitivity to the whole gamut of emotions and experiences involved in sex is one of the most helpful combinations the mental health professional can bring to his or her work with older adults.

Starr (1985), in an excellent review of the literature, notes that the phenomenological approach only recently taking hold in this area of research is an appropriate one. Early studies provided the numbers, in terms of frequency of late-life sexual activity compared to patterns of sexual frequency in young and middle-aged adults. The most potentially fruitful area of focus for the present and future becomes the thoughts, feelings, and subjective experiences of older adults who are sexually active and engaged. The qualitative approach allows an understanding, not only of when and how often older adults "have sex," in whatever form that might take, but how they experience it as well. Recent research has indeed begun to explore these areas (Adams & Turner, 1985; Brecher, 1984; Starr & Weiner, 1981), and future researchers are encouraged to continue in that direction, as a means for advancing knowledge of true applicability in this important and provocative area of gerontology (Weg, 1983a).

7
Ageism

Dean Rodeheaver

"I am not mad, only old."
May Sarton, *As We Are Now*

Introduction

Imagine that you are driving down a busy street. Suddenly, a car moves out of an intersection ahead and slowly enters the lane in front of you. If you are like many people, even as you swerve to avoid a collision, you are forming an impression of the driver of that car. As you pass, you check to confirm your impression. And, if you are like many people, you nod approvingly at your prescience when you see that the driver is short and white haired.

There is, of course, some basis in fact for the impression you formed. However, the ease with which such incidents confirm people's expectations of older drivers and the equal ease with which they ignore counterinstances—older people who drive well or bad drivers who are not old—reflect that set of attitudes, beliefs, and stereotypes known as ageism.

The term *ageism* was coined by Robert Butler, the first director of the National Institute on Aging (NIA). Since 1969, Butler has written extensively on the existence in America of a deep-seated prejudice against the aged. This prejudice is expressed in socially accepted negative attitudes, erroneous beliefs, stereotypes, and discriminatory behaviors and practices. Lack of knowledge about the process of aging and old people has produced a set of false *beliefs* arising primarily from the notion that aging causes inevitable and irreversible changes. These beliefs, now known not to be characteristic of the aged population, include the following (Butler, 1975a, 1975b; see also Comfort, 1976a; 1976b):

1. Aging brings an end to productivity.
2. The aged naturally desire to disengage from society.
3. Older people are inflexible, set in their ways.

Module prepared for Division 20 of the American Psychological Association.

4. Senility is a normal part of aging.

5. The aged are (or should be) serene and accepting of these changes.

Ageism also comprises a deep and profound set of prejudicial, negative *attitudes* about aging and the elderly. Butler (1969) has written: "Age-ism reflects a deep-seated uneasiness on the part of the young and middle-aged—a personal revulsion to and distaste for growing old, disease, disability; and fear of powerlessness, 'uselessness,' and death" (p. 243). These negative attitudes toward aging can affect *behavior* toward the aged. Anxiety and fear can prevent dealing effectively with the elderly, an ineffectiveness Butler calls "benign ageism" (1980). Ageism can also be expressed more directly in the form of disdain, dislike, avoidance, epithets, or other, more "malignant" forms of ageism. Ageism also permits and encourages *discriminatory practices* against the elderly in health care, employment, social services, and public policy.

As a consequence of ageism, the plight of the aged is more easily ignored and the old may be denied opportunities to remain healthy, independent, and receive services. Furthermore, they are denied opportunities for social interaction and to influence younger generations. The consequence: "Ageism allows the younger generations to see older people as different from themselves; thus they subtly cease to identify with their elders as human beings" (Butler & Lewis, 1982, p. xvii). Finally, the pervasiveness of ageism inhibits the personal growth of the aged themselves, who may internalize ageist attitudes and beliefs and act the way they conclude an older person is supposed to act.

This module examines beliefs about and attitudes and behaviors toward aging and the aged in America, including historical and cross-cultural perspectives on ageism, reflections of ageism in contemporary society, the consequences of ageism, and strategies for change.

THE EMERGENCE OF CONTEMPORARY AGEISM

It is sometimes comforting to believe that ageism is a recent phenomenon—this reinforces a nostagia for "the good old days" when everything was simpler and life was better for everyone. Historians have found, however, that American society has always been characterized by ambivalence—a combination of positive and negative feelings—toward the aged (Achenbaum, 1978). More important, throughout our history, there are rarely any periods when popular beliefs about aging reflected the reality of aging in America—myths and stereotypes about aging have always existed. Moreover, most other societies demonstrate attitudes, beliefs, and behaviors that could be considered ageist to some degree (Nydegger, 1983). Contemporary ageism in America, then, differs primarily in the degree to which it is expressed and in its forms of expression.

The current popular image of aging appears to have been shaped by three forces: economic change, evolving cultural ideals, and increasing scientific understanding of the life course (Achenbaum, 1978; Fischer, 1978; Jensen & Oakley, 1982–1983; Tibbitts, 1979). The transformation of America from a rural, agricultural economy to an urban, industrial economy in the late 1800s created a demand for an efficient, a productive, and an educated work force. Suspicions that older workers were outdated were confirmed at the turn of the century by scientific studies demonstrating that biological, intellectual, and social decrements were part of the aging process. The emerging highly competitive economy also helped give rise to the notion that the death and displacement of the aged were a natural part of social evolution—progress toward a better society; the youthful hero, productive, efficient, and technologically educated, replaced the experienced elder as the ideal of maturity (Gruman, 1978; Phillipson, 1982). Thus, the aged lost valued social roles and no new ones arose to replace them. The aged still lack a well-defined place in American society, a situation that lies at the heart of contemporary ageism. Lacking a clearly defined, visible, and valued role, the aged may be segregated from other age groups and are subject to erroneous and potentially destructive social perceptions.

THE AMERICAN WAY OF AGING

Images of the aged in America—in the media, on greeting cards, in literature, and in popular language and humor—reflect their low status (Cheren, 1984, August–September; Spicker, Woodward, & Van Tassel, 1978). One common image portrays old age as second childhood (Arluke & Levin, 1984, August–September). Impulsive, cranky, stubborn, or silly, absent-minded older characters in advertisements and movies or on television, for example, are like children in mood and manner. Their dress, when not clearly out of fashion, is often childish. They suffer the physical problems of children, most notable in their extreme concern over regularity and incontinence. And they are often assumed to enjoy the activities and playthings of children; compare, for example, the crafts, games, and recreational programs for seniors listed in local newspapers to the activities of kindergarten children.

Many aspects of the image of aging are more straightforwardly negative, as is illustrated by the language used to refer to aging or the aged. Such common terms as "crone," "biddy," "coot," "codger," or "gomer" far outnumber positive terms in daily use and in the dictionary; there are, indeed, few positive words to choose from when referring to the elderly (Nuessel, 1982; 1984, August–September). These words imply that the aged possess personality quirks, outdated manners, bad habits, and other displeasing traits and relegate the aged to a subordinate status. The language Americans use also demonstrates some avoidance of aging: Both young and old dislike words that denote age—"old man," "old woman," the "aged," the "aging"—and prefer, instead, age-neutral terms like "senior citizen," "retired American," or "mature American" (Barbato & Feezel, 1987). Negative images of the elderly are also reflected to some extent in the stereotypic desexed, senile oldsters who are the butt of greeting cards and popular jokes (Davies, 1977; Richman, 1977), in advice books for the elderly (Arluke, Levin, & Suchwalko, 1984), in the tendency of college textbooks to include the elderly only in sections describing social problems (Kalab, 1985), and in the preoccupation with the sorrows and losses of aging in poetry (Sohngen & Smith, 1978).

The most pervasive image problem the elderly face, however, is that they simply have no image at all: They are absent from popular culture. Nowhere is this more evident than on television. From news programs to commercials to television series, older characters are scarce (Davis, 1984, August–September; Davis & Davis, 1985). When they do appear, older characters are often stereotyped, unrealistically portraying old age as either exclusively joyous or exclusively sorrowful. For example, Davis and Davis (1985) noted that older television characters either experience no health problems at all or are physically incapacitated. Furthermore, the lack of development of these characters within programs suggests that, when they are present, the old are unimportant.

How are these images reflected in the attitudes and beliefs of individuals? Ambivalent or negative images of aging have been noted within subgroups of society, many of whom are directly responsible for the care and well-being of the elderly. Concern has been expressed about ageist attitudes and beliefs among social workers (Greene, 1983), audiologists and speech pathologists (Boone, 1985), nursing home administrators (Keith, 1977), and students in the health care professions (Levenson, 1981).

Of greater concern has been evidence of ageism among children, especially in elementary schools (Hickey, Hickey, & Kalish, 1968; Kogan & Shelton, 1962): Children commonly state that they would not like to be like the elderly and support their preference with a number of stereotypic beliefs about growing old. How many of these beliefs and attitudes children acquire from their parents is hard to determine, but images of the elderly in the media and in literature have been examined. One source of ageism among children may be television: Old people are relatively absent from commercial television; they are nonexistent in children's television (Davis, 1984, August–September). Likewise, in children's literature, there are few aged characters and those who do appear are typically uninteresting, unimportant, and unimaginative (Ansello, 1977). They are rarely the principal characters, they often have no occupation, they are less healthy and less self-reliant than other characters, and they are passive (Ansello, 1977, 1978; Barnum, 1977; Seefeldt, Galper, Serock, & Jantz, 1978). The foundations of ageism, then, may be laid very early.

THE CONSEQUENCES OF AGEISM

Scholars in the field of adult development and aging have suggested that the negative image of aging in America contributes to the personal, social, physical, and economic problems of the aged. Culturally accepted stereotypes about aging may become for the aged a set of expectations that governs their behavior and their image of themselves (Zinberg, 1976): They act "old" not because they *are* old but because they have learned how someone who is old is *supposed* to act. Moreover, they may internalize negative attitudes and begin to hate or be ashamed of themselves. In order to avoid such negative self-images, some may dissociate themselves from their age peers, claiming, as research has shown, to be middle aged even into their seventies. As Comfort has written, "We have a lifetime of indoctrination with the idea of the difference and inferiority of the old, and on reaching old age we may be prejudiced against ourselves" (1976b, p. 4).

The absence of elderly characters in literature and the media exacerbates the problem by denying young and old alike realistic models of the aging process (Davis & Davis, 1985; Rodin & Langer, 1980; Rosow, 1974): With no clearly defined roles and no realistic role models, how does one know how to grow old? Furthermore, research has also shown that, while age may be less important in forming initial impressions of people than their sex or their appearance, it may be critical in developing expectations about their abilities, needs, and actions (Lawrence, 1975). Thus, a self-fulfilling prophecy is formed in which socially accepted stereotypes abound, few alternatives are available, and the aged and younger generations adopt the stereotypes. The aged may begin to act according to the stereotypes, thereby confirming and sustaining them.

Other scholars have pointed out more tangible consequences of ageism, including discrimination in health care, employment, and the development of public policies and services. There is great concern, for example, that physicians and psychiatrists may overlook or misdiagnose the health problems of the aged because older patients are members of a devalued group and because their problems are erroneously assumed to be the result of growing old and, therefore, are incurable (Butler, 1975a, 1975b; Goodstein, 1985; Ray, Raciti, & Ford, 1985). The aged themselves can become unwitting accomplices in poor health care (Hesse, Campion, & Karamouz, 1984)—health care professionals are not the only people who believe that to be old is to be sick, tired, and incurable, myths and stereotypes that are reinforced by the media (Davis & Davis, 1985).

Ageism may also be related to wage and employment discrimination and, thereby, to the ability of the aged to remain productive and to live independently. Ageist attitudes and stereotypes have been found in studies of decision making among managers and personnel officers (Rosen & Jerdee, 1976; Schwab & Heneman, 1978) and may consequently prevent the elderly from being given jobs or promotions. Furthermore, stereotypic assumptions about productivity and financial need may contribute to wage discrimination: Older workers are assumed to be less productive and to need less money, so they are offered low-paying jobs or are denied promotions (Wanner & McDonald, 1983).

Finally, ageism may hinder attempts to solve the problems of the aged—solutions to problems that are produced in part by ageism are, paradoxically, impeded by ageism. Some research (e.g., see Roscoe, 1985) finds the problems of aging and the aged to be minimized, suggesting that many of their problems would never be addressed were it not for the power of the "gray lobby." Moreover, one component of ageism may involve blaming the victim: The problems of aging are not addressed because of the ageist belief that the aged themselves are responsible for their dilemma due to their unproductivity, lack of thrift, or senility (Estes, 1979). A more serious problem may be that policies and programs intended to solve the problems of the aged reinforce their marginal status and the socially accepted stigmatization of the aged: If they need this much help, some may believe, they must be very badly off indeed (Estes, 1979).

DOUBLE AND TRIPLE JEOPARDY: AGEISM, SEXISM, AND RACISM

Prejudice against the aged is compounded by the fact that the majority of elders are female and by the fact that the poorest social and economic conditions among the aged are found among the minority aged. Ageism is intertwined with sexism and racism.

Research findings on ageism and sexism are clear and consistent: When negative attitudes are held about the elderly, they are especially negative about elderly women. The typical stereotype of the older woman characterizes her as sick, sexless, uninvolved except in her family and at church, and alone (Payne & Whittington, 1976). Indeed, she is often used as a standard for what *not* to be: A widely acknowledged insult is the suggestion that an old man has become a woman (Silverman, 1977). A significant bias against older women is found on television (Davis & Davis, 1985), in humor (Davies, 1977), and in literature (Peterson & Karnes, 1976). Older women suffer the consequences of ageism and sexism in economics (Minkler & Stone, 1985; Palmore & Manton, 1973; Porcino, 1983) and in health care (Butler & Lewis, 1982; Keith, 1977; Lillard, 1982; Porcino, 1983; Ray et al., 1985; Steuer, 1982): They are poorer and are considered undesirable as patients. Their problem is confounded by a lack of concern among women's groups for older women (Bell & Schwede, 1985; Datan, 1981; Lewis & Butler, 1972) and in public policy (Datan, 1989; Porcino, 1983; Rodeheaver, 1987b).

The minority aged face a peculiar bias: They are virtually invisible in research on adulthood and aging. Studies of ageism and racism are relatively rare. It is clear, however, that following a lifetime facing prejudice, Blacks, Chicanos, Native Americans, and other minority group members reach old age facing the double jeopardy of ageism and racism (Kasschau, 1977). This is especially true with regard to income and education (Palmore & Manton, 1973). The combined effects of ageism and racism are apparent in health care, also: The minority aged face discrimination in diagnoses and quality of care, for example (Butler & Lewis, 1982). Finally, elderly minority women face triple jeopardy. For example, while the economic condition of the aged has improved dramatically in recent decades, the majority of elderly black women still can anticipate living in or near poverty (Pinkney, 1984).

Ageism, sexism, and racism should not be considered expressions of the same problem, though: They differ in history and intensity (Hopkins, 1980). Ageism presents a peculiar set of problems. First, all subgroups of American society will experience ageism to some extent (Kasschau, 1977). Second, the economic and educational problems of the aged have not responded to civil and equal rights measures (Palmore & Manton, 1973). Third, an awareness that ageism is wrong has not made its way into social consciousness to the extent that an awareness of sexism and racism has (see Sigelman & Sigelman, 1982, on this point). Thus, special efforts to undermine ageism are called for.

STRATEGIES FOR CHANGE

If ageism represents a pervasive and systematic prejudice, then corresponding systematic efforts at change are also required, including changing the social system that supports ageism; the ageist images of our culture; and the attitudes, beliefs, and behaviors of individuals (Hess, 1974). A variety of consciousness raising and social change strategies have been suggested (see Feldman, 1977), most of which are based on four assumptions:

1. Knowledge about the aging process is necessary to change beliefs.
2. Greater exposure to the elderly can improve attitudes and falsify stereotypes.
3. The elderly themselves must become more visible and more powerful in fighting discrimination.
4. Scholars in the field of adult development and aging must change the focus of their inquiry.

The presence among schoolchildren of negative attitudes and errone-ous beliefs underscores the need for more information about aging. Integrating information on aging and ageism into the school curriculum has been suggested as one way of accomplishing this goal (Seefeldt, Jantz, Galper, & Serock, 1977; Sorgman & Sorensen, 1984). This would require, though, some examination of the attitudes and beliefs of educa-tors since the learning environment may be more influential in forming students' attitudes than the material they are presented (Seltzer, 1977; Wilhite & Johnson, 1976).

Children's contact with the elderly has been diminished by age segre-gation in housing and activities and is accentuated by the absence of elderly characters from the media and literature. Presenting more old characters, with diverse attributes, in a variety of roles, lifestyles, and settings is a necessary step toward breaking down stereotypes and pre-venting their being acquired (Davis & Davis, 1985; Seefeldt et al., 1977, 1978). And some school systems are increasing opportunities for contact between children and the elderly through counseling or intergenera-tional school programs (Peacock & Talley, 1984; Seefeldt et al., 1978).

The need for information and contact is not limited to elementary schools: Studies show that students in professional schools may develop more negative attitudes toward the aged over the course of their educa-tion (Levenson, 1981). Using naturalistic observation, collecting personal life histories, and learning to examine social and cultural backgrounds have been suggested as strategies for increasing sensitivity to the diverse needs and problems and the strengths in coping and adapting of the elderly (Allen & Burwell, 1980; Hesse et al., 1984; Levenson, 1981; Patterson, 1981). In addition, some counseling in death anxiety may be helpful among those who intend to work with the ill elderly. Studies of social workers find that those who are most receptive to working with the elderly have the *highest* levels of death anxiety, suggesting that they are also more receptive to the self-examination that such casework may require (Greene, 1983; Salter & Salter, 1976).

Discriminatory practices in housing and employment that limit the visibility and opportunities of the elderly should also be examined. In-creasing the variety of roles available to the elderly—through work or family responsibilities, for example—may diminish stereotypes about their abilities (Peacock & Talley, 1984; Tibbitts, 1979). Another common, though subtle, form of discrimination involves treating the aged like dependent children. Greater personal control and responsibility among the elderly in a variety of settings is associated with more positive self-images (Rodin & Langer, 1980). In the long run, such empowerment of the elderly themselves helps them fight their own victimization (Com-fort, 1976a, 1976b).

Finally, experts in the field of aging are shifting their attention to strategies for reducing functional limitations that may appear among the elderly: Rather than examining the nature and extent of decline, there is a focus on prevention, recovery, and compensation of problems that are no longer assumed to be caused by age itself (Butler, 1982; Riley & Bond, 1983). Educating the public about the aging process is also becoming an integral part of the study of aging (Peterson, 1985).

SUMMARY AND CONCLUSIONS

Ageism comprises a set of negative attitudes toward and erroneous beliefs, often generalized as stereotypes, about the aged. These attitudes and beliefs are accompanied by discriminatory practices and behaviors. Ageism is evidenced in America by a tendency to treat the elderly like children, by commonly used negative labels, and by stereotypical images in literature and the media. As a result of this socially accepted prejudice, the elderly themselves may restrict their activities and hold negative self-images; society in general and particularly children are denied models of how to grow old; health, income, and independence may be jeopardized; and the problems of the elderly may be minimized or overlooked. Furthermore, cultural patterns of sexism and racism mean that the problems of aging in America are worse among women and minority group members. Ageist attitudes and beliefs can be changed, however. Increasing knowledge about aging, greater exposure to and experience with the aged, seeking an end to age discrimination, and studying ways to prevent and compensate problems experienced by some elderly are all promising strategies for adapting our society to the needs of elders.

COMPREHENSIVE OUTLINE

References

I. Introduction and Definition
   A. Ageism as a set of negative attitudes,   Butler, 1969, 1975a,
       beliefs, stereotypes, and behaviors   1975b; Comfort,
                                             1976a, 1976b
     1. Beliefs   Butler, 1975a,
        (a) End of productivity   1975b
        (b) Disengagement
        (c) Inflexibility
        (d) Senility
        (e) Serenity
     2. Attitudes and behaviors   Butler, 1969, 1980

    (a) Uneasiness, distaste, ineffective-
        ness (benign ageism)
    (b) Dislike, avoidance (malignant
        ageism)
  3. Consequences   Butler, 1975a,
    (a) Problems ignored   1975b; Butler &
    (b) Opportunities denied   Lewis, 1982
    (c) Age segregation
    (d) Inhibited personal growth
II. The Emergence of Contemporary Ageism
  A. Historical and cross-cultural viewpoints
    1. Continued presence of ambivalence   Achenbaum, 1978
       toward aged
    2. Ageism in other cultures   Nydegger, 1983
  B. Historical changes shaping contempo-
    rary ageism
    1. Change to urban, technological   Achenbaum, 1978,
       economy   Fischer, 1978;
    2. Emerging cultural ideal of efficiency,   Gruman, 1978;
       productivity, education   Jensen & Oakley,
    3. Scientific studies showing age-related   1982–1983;
       decline   Phillipson, 1982;
  C. Absence of roles, emergence of segre-   Tibbits, 1979
    gation and erroneous beliefs
III. The American Way of Aging   Cheren, 1984,
                                 August–
                                 September;
                                 Spicker et al.,
                                 1978

  A. Images of old age
    1. As second childhood   Arluke & Levin,
                                 1984, August–
                                 September
    2. Negative images in language   Nuessel,1982, 1984,
                                 August–
                                 September;
                                 Barbato & Feezel,
                                 1987
    3. Other negative images   Arluke et al., 1984;
     (a) Humor   Davies, 1977;
     (b) Advice books   Kalab, 1985;
     (c) Textbooks   Richman, 1977;
     (d) Poetry   Sohngen &
                                   Smith, 1978
    4. Absence from the media   Davis, 1984,

B. Images, attitudes, and beliefs
 1. Among special groups
  (a) Social workers
  (b) Audiologists/speech pathologists
  (c) Nursing home administrators
  (d) Students in health care
 2. Among schoolchildren

  (a) Children's television

  (b) Children's literature

IV. The Consequences of Ageism
 A. Inhibited personal growth
  1. Expectations
  2. Negative self-image
  3. Self-prejudice
 B. Problems in socialization
  1. No role models

  2. Age used in assigning roles
  3. Self-fulfilling prophecy created
 C. Tangible consequences
  1. Assumption of incurable illnesses leading to poor quality health care

  2. Wage and employment discrimination

  3. Social problems minimized or overlooked

August–September; Davis & Davis, 1985

Greene, 1983
Boone, 1985
Keith, 1977
Levenson, 1981
Hickey et al., 1968; Kogan & Shelton, 1962
Davis, 1984, August–September
Ansello, 1977, 1978; Barnum, 1977; Seefeldt et al., 1978

Zinberg, 1976

Comfort, 1976a

Davis & Davis, 1985; Rodin & Langer, 1980; Rosow, 1974
Lawrence, 1975

Butler, 1975; Goodstein, 1985; Hesse et al., 1984; Ray et al., 1985
Rosen & Jerdee, 1976; Schwab & Heneman, 1978; Wanner & McDonald, 1983
Estes, 1979; Roscoe, 1985

V. Double and Triple Jeopardy: Ageism,
   Sexism, and Racism
   A. Ageism and sexism
      1. Negative stereotypes of older women   Payne & Whit-
      2. Bias against older women   tington, 1976;
                                                   Silverman, 1977

         (a) On television   Davis & Davis, 1985
         (b) In humor   Davies, 1977
         (c) In literature   Peterson & Karnes,
                                                   1976
         (d) In economics   Minkler & Stone,
                                                   1985; Palmore &
                                                   Manton, 1973;
                                                   Porcino, 1983

         (e) In health care   Butler & Lewis,
                                                   1982; Keith,
                                                   1977; Lillard,
                                                   1982; Porcino,
                                                   1983; Ray et al.,
                                                   1985; Steuer, 1982

         (f) In the women's movement   Bell & Schwede,
                                                   1985; Datan,
                                                   1981; Lewis &
                                                   Butler, 1972
         (g) In public policy   Datan, 1989;
                                                   Rodeheaver,
                                                   1987b

   B. Ageism and racism
      1. Double jeopardy among minority
         aged
         (a) In education and income   Kasschau, 1977;
                                                   Palmore & Man-
                                                   ton, 1973
         (b) In health care   Butler & Lewis,
                                                   1982
      2. Triple jeopardy and minority-aged   Pinkney, 1984
         women
   C. Ageism as distinct from sexism and   Hopkins, 1980
      racism
      1. Experienced by all subgroups   Kasschau, 1977
      2. Little impact of civil and equal rights Palmore & Manton,
                                                   1973
      3. Lack of social awareness   Sigelman & Si-
                                                   gelman, 1982

VI. Strategies for Change

    Feldman, 1977;
Hess, 1974

  A. Education and intergenerational contact
    1. Increased knowledge
      (a) In schools   Seefeldt et al., 1977; Sorgman & Sorensen, 1984

      (b) Among educators   Seltzer, 1977; Wilhite & Johnson, 1976

    2. Increased intergenerational contact
      (a) On television   Davis & Davis, 1985
      (b) In literature   Seefeldt et al., 1978
      (c) In schools   Peacock & Talley, 1984; Seefeldt et al., 1978

    3. Among students in professional schools   Allen & Burwell, 1980; Greene, 1983; Hesse et al., 1984; Levenson, 1981; Patterson, 1981; Salter & Salter, 1976

  B. Diminished discrimination
    1. Increasing roles   Peacock & Talley, 1984; Tibbits, 1979

    2. Increasing control and responsibility   Rodin & Langer, 1980

    3. Empowering the old to fight victimization   Comfort, 1976a, 1976b
  C. New research focus
    1. Prevention, recovery, compensation   Butler, 1982; Riley & Bond, 1983

    2. Educating the public   Peterson, 1985
VII. Summary and Conclusions
  A. Ageism defined
  B. Evidence of ageism
  C. Consequences of ageism
  D. Worst problems among women and minorities
  E. Possibilities for social change

Annotated Bibliography

Achenbaum, W. A. (1978). *Old age in the new land.* Baltimore, MD: Johns Hopkins University Press.

Historical examination of the social status of the aged in America. Achenbaum considers the recurrent ambivalence toward the aged and the separation between popular, political, and scientific rhetoric about aging and the reality of aging which have characterized aging in America.

Kind	*Recommendation*	*Readability*	*Audience*
Book	***	1–2	AU,AG

Allen, J. A., & Burwell, N. Y. (1980). Ageism and racism: Two issues in social work education and practice. *Journal of Education for Social Work, 16(2),* 71–77.

Discusses strategies for dealing with the effects of ageism and racism through the social work curriculum, including the need to appreciate and integrate the strengths and needs of age and racial groups.

Kind	*Recommendation*	*Readability*	*Audience*
TA	*	1	SP

Ansello, E. F. (1977). Age and ageism in children's first literature. *Educational Gerontology, 2,* 255–274.

Examined 656 juvenile picture books and first readers and found a generally boring portrayal of the elderly. Rather than in overtly negative images, the aged were presented as engaged in routine and mundane activities and as unimportant, unexciting, and unimaginative.

Kind	*Recommendation*	*Readability*	*Audience*
EA	**	1–2	GP,AU,AG

Ansello, E. F. (1978). Ageism—The subtle stereotype. *Childhood Education, 54,* 118–122.

Suggests that educators have played a role in perpetuating ageism, that children's books are also at fault. Describes research finding few old characters in children's literature—particularly women and minority aged—and portrayals of old people as passive.

Kind	Recommendation	Readability	Audience
RA	**	1	SP

Arluke, A., & Levin, J. (1984, August–September). Another stereotype: Old age as second childhood. *Aging*, pp. 7–11.

Compares images of the aged in the media to images of children in terms of dress, appearance, activities, playthings, and physical problems. Suggests that such infantilization encourages otherwise impermissible actions toward the elderly, diminishes their status, and distracts those who might otherwise work for improvement and empowerment.

Kind	Recommendation	Readability	Audience
RA	**	1	GP

Arluke, A., Levin, J., & Suchwalko, J. (1984). Sexuality and romance in advice books for the elderly. *The Gerontologist, 24*, 415–419.

Finds that while sexuality is advocated, remarriage and dating are denied or discouraged, thwarting sexual activity among those who are not already married.

Kind	Recommendation	Readability	Audience
EA	**	1–2	GP,SP,AU,AG

Barbato, C. A., & Feezel, J. D. (1987). The language of aging in different age groups. *The Gerontologist, 27*, 527–531.

Examined preferences among several age groups for terms referring to the elderly. The lay public preferred terms that did not connote age and old age *per se*—senior citizen, retired person, mature American—over those that did—e.g., elderly or the aged.

Kind	Recommendation	Readability	Audience
EA	**	1–2	AU,AG

Barnum, P. W. (1977). Discrimination against the aged in young children's literature. *Elementary School Journal, 77*, 301–306.

Examined literature for preschool to third-grade children from 1950 to 1974. The aged appeared infrequently, engaged in fewer social interactions, were more passive, less healthy, and less self-reliant than other characters.

Kind	Recommendation	Readability	Audience
EA	**	1–2	SP

Bell, M. J., & Schwede, K. M. (1985). Roles, feminist attitudes, and older women. *Women & Politics, 5*(1), 5–22.

Discusses perceptions of age differences in public and private spheres of feminism.

Kind	Recommendation	Readability	Audience
RA	**	2	AG

Blue, G. F. (1978). The aging as portrayed in realistic fiction for children. 1945–1975. *The Gerontologist, 18,* 187–192.

Examined books known to have elderly characters and found they did not contain negative stereotypes. The aged were portrayed in a variety of life-styles and health statuses, engaging in diverse behaviors, and the books included multidimensional character development.

Kind	Recommendation	Readability	Audience
EA	*	2	AU,AG

Boone, D. R. (1985). Ageism: A negative view of the aged. *ASHA, 27,*51–53.

Discusses the impact of ageism on speech and learning and communication disorders.

Kind	Recommendation	Readability	Audience
RA	*	1	SP

Borges, M. A., & Dutton, L. J. (1976). Attitudes toward aging: Increasing optimism found with age. *The Gerontologist, 16,* 220–224.

Older respondents rated old age more positively and were more likely to see possibilities for happiness and adaptation.

Kind	Recommendation	Readability	Audience
EA	*	2	AU,AG

Brubaker, T. H., & Powers, E. A. (1976). The stereotype of "old"—a review and alternative approach. *Journal of Gerontology, 31,* 441–447.

Attempts to reconcile studies finding both positive and negative stereotypes about aging among the old themselves. Hypothesizes that, as objective indicators of old age increase, one's self-definition as old will increase; if previous self-concept is positive, positive stereotypes are adopted.

Kind	Recommendation	Readability	Audience
TA	**	2–3	AU,AG

Butler, R. N. (1969). Age-ism: Another form of bigotry. *The Gerontologist, 9,* 243–246.

First-published description of ageism and its relation to policy and the problems of the aged.

Kind	Recommendation	Readability	Audience
TA	***	1	GP,SP,AU,AG

Butler, R. N. (1975a). Psychiatry and the elderly: An overview. *American Journal of Psychiatry, 132,* 893–900.

Notes the failure of psychiatrists to provide services, treatment, and research commensurate with the needs of the aged and that many conditions medical or socioeconomic in nature are labeled senility and remain untreated.

Kind	Recommendation	Readability	Audience
RA	**	2	SP,AG

Butler, R. N. (1975b). Why survive? Being old in America. New York: Harper & Row.

Pulitzer Prize–winning examination of aging in America, including descriptions of health, housing, transportation, crime, and other problems faced by the aged, and the role of ageism in creating and maintaining those problems.

Kind	Recommendation	Readability	Audience
Book	***	1	GP,SP,AU,AG

Butler, R. N. (1980). Ageism: A foreword. *Journal of Social Issues, 36,* 8–11.

Compares benign ageism—anxiety and fear that prevent dealing effectively with the elderly—and malignant ageism—characterizing the aged as worthless.

Kind	Recommendation	Readability	Audience
TA	*	1	GP,SP,AU,AG

Butler, R. N. (1982). The triumph of age: Science, gerontology, and ageism. *Bulletin of the New York Academy of Medicine, 58,* 347–361.

Examines the growth of the study of aging and the emergence of a "new gerontology" which searches for functional compensation or total recovery of losses, but is also accompanied by new fears that increasing longevity will be associated with greater incidence of debility and senility in extreme old age.

Kind	Recommendation	Readability	Audience
RC	**	2	SP,AU,AG

Butler, R. N., & Lewis, M. I. (1982). *Aging and mental health* **(3rd ed.). St. Louis, MO: C. V. Mosby.**

Discusses issues in mental health policies and services for the aged, including problems related to ageism, racism, and sexism.

Kind	Recommendation	Readability	Audience
Text	***	1–2	GP,SP,AU,AG

Cheren, C. E. (Ed.) (1984, August–September). Ageism in America. *Aging* **(346).**

Collection of articles on ageism in America, including discussions of language, television, and programs designed to redefine children's understanding of old age.

Kind	Recommendation	Readability	Audience
Journal	**	1	GP

Comfort, A. (1976a). *A good age*. New York: Crown.

The ABCs of growing old, including a brief description of ageism and the need for its victims to fight it.

Kind	Recommendation	Readability	Audience
Book	**	1	GP

Comfort, A. (1976b). Age prejudice in America. *Social Policy*, 7(3), 3–8.

Examines the importance of "sociogenic aging"—the impact of folklore, prejudice, and misconceptions—to the experiences of the elderly. Suggests that ageism takes two new forms: thoughtless ageism; and overstating the injustices faced by the aged in order to correct them, thereby creating further stigmatization.

Kind	Recommendation	Readability	Audience
TC	**	1	GP

Datan, N. (1981). The lost cause: The aging woman in American feminism. In B. Justice & R. Pore (Eds.), *Towards the second decade: The impact of the women's movement on American institutions* (pp. 119–125). Westport, CT: Greenwood.

Suggests aging women are at a historical and political crossroad, experiencing the narrow confines of ageism and historical discrimination against women. Notes political, educational, and demographic changes that are likely to increase the power of older women.

Kind	Recommendation	Readability	Audience
RC	***	1–2	GP,SP,AU,AG

Datan, N. (1989). Aging women: The silent majority. *Women's Studies Quarterly*, 17, 12–19.

Discusses the disregard for older women in psychological research, training, practice, and mental health policy.

Kind	Recommendation	Readability	Audience
RA	***	1–2	GP,SP,AU,AG

Davies, L. J. (1977). Attitudes toward old age and aging as shown by humor. *The Gerontologist, 17,* 220–226.

Discusses the generally negative attitudes toward the aged expressed in humor, especially with regard to physical, sexual, social, and mental abilities. Notes that attitudes toward old women are particularly negative.

Kind	Recommendation	Readability	Audience
EA	**	2	AU,AG

Davis, R. H. (1984, August–September). TV's boycott of old age. *Aging,* pp. 12–17.

Notes that there are few elderly characters on television, that older women are notably absent, and that the old are generally either extremely healthy or extremely unhealthy. Discusses the youth orientation on television, for example, in commercials and television newscasters, and describes the invisibility of the aged on children's programs.

Kind	Recommendation	Readability	Audience
RA	**	1	GP

Davis, R. H., & Davis, J. A. (1985). *TV's image of the elderly.* **Lexington, MA: D. C. Heath.**

Discusses television as communicator, socializer, and conveyor of social values and notes that increasing age is associated with increasing invisibility on television. Notes the particularly negative portrayals of women, unrealistic portrayals of health problems, and the conspicuous absence of the aged on children's shows and in commercials.

Kind	Recommendation	Readability	Audience
Book	***	1	GP,SP,AU,AG

Estes, C. L. (1979). *The aging enterprise.* **San Francisco: Jossey-Bass.**

Examines the social conditions and social policies that maintain the marginality and the stigmatization of the aged. Emphasis on the importance of class, race, and sex.

Kind	Recommendation	Readability	Audience
Book	***	1–2	GP,SP,AU,AG

Feldman, H. (1977). Penelope, Molly, Narcissus, and Susan. In L. E. Troll, J. Israel, & K. Israel (Eds.), *Looking ahead: A woman's guide to the problems and joys of growing older* (pp. 73–80). Englewood Cliffs, NJ: Prentice-Hall.

Discusses the variety of individual approaches to old age among women and suggests strategies for implementing social change.

Kind	Recommendation	Readability	Audience
RC	**	1	GP

Fischer, D. H. (1978). *Growing old in America*. New York: Oxford University Press.

Examines political, economic, and social changes that led to the diminished status of the aged in America.

Kind	Recommendation	Readability	Audience
Book	***	2	AU,AG

Golden, H. M. (1976). Black ageism. *Social Policy, 7*(3), 40–42.

Examines the multiple jeopardy faced by aging blacks: ageism, racism, and sexism among black women.

Kind	Recommendation	Readability	Audience
TA	**	1	GP,SP

Goodstein, R. K. (1985). Common clinical problems in the elderly: Camouflaged by ageism and atypical presentation. *Psychiatric Annals, 15,* 299–311.

Notes that clinical problems in the elderly are characterized by idiosyncratic presentation, requiring the clinician to examine the roles of experience, heredity, coping style, and physical and emotional status. Further suggests that ageism and the atypical presentation of disease among the aged often lead to assumptions of incurability.

Kind	Recommendation	Readability	Audience
RC	**	2	SP

Greene, R. (1983). Ageism, death anxiety, and the case worker. *Journal of Social Service Research,* **7(1),55–69.**

Found that death anxiety was higher among social workers with a geriatric case load than among those without. Death anxiety also increased with number of years practicing up to 6 or 7 years.

Kind	Recommendation	Readability	Audience
EA	**	2	SP,AU,AG

Gruman, G. J. (1978). Cultural origins of present-day "ageism": The modernization of the life cycle. In S. F. Spicker, K. M. Woodward, & D. D. Van Tassel (Eds.), *Aging and the elderly: Humanistic perspectives in gerontology* **(pp. 359–387). Atlantic Highlands, NJ: Humanities Press.**

Examines the historical and ideological context in which ageism emerged, especially in relation to social Darwinism, positivism, and neo-positivism and changes in notions of maturity and vigor in adulthood.

Kind	Recommendation	Readability	Audience
TC	**	2–3	AG

Herrick, J. W. (1983). Interbehavioral perspectives on aging. *International Journal of Aging and Human Development, 16,* **95–124.**

Notes the emphasis in geropsychology on physiologically based changes and the tendency to overlook learned behaviors, thereby contributing to ageism.

Kind	Recommendation	Readability	Audience
TA	**	2–3	AU,AG

Hess, B. B. (1974). Stereotypes of the aged. *Journal of Communication, 24,* **76–85.**

Examines the nature of communication about the aged in terms of the social system, the message itself, the message receiver, and the media.

Kind	Recommendation	Readability	Audience
RA	**	1–2	GP,SP,AU,AG

Hesse, K. A., Campion, E. W., & Karamouz, N. (1984). Attitudinal stumbling blocks to geriatric rehabilitation. *Journal of the American Geriatric Society, 32,* **747–775.**

Discusses three stumbling blocks among the aged themselves to successful rehabilitation: the assumption that rehabilitation is useless because to be old is to be sick; the assertion that dependency is a right earned by long life; feeling too tired to work hard on rehabilitation.

Kind	Recommendation	Readability	Audience
TA	*	1–2	SP

Hickey, T., Hickey, L., & Kalish, R. A. (1968). Children's perceptions of the elderly. *Journal of Genetic Psychology, 112,* **227–235.**

Examines the nature of children's attitudes and beliefs about the elderly.

Kind	Recommendation	Readability	Audience
EA	**	2	AU,AG

Hopkins, T. J. (1980). A conceptual framework for understanding the three "Isms"—Racism, ageism, sexism. *Journal of Education for Social Work, 16(2).* **63–70.**

Analyzes the difference between ageism, sexism, and racism and notes that different histories, dynamics, and intensities suggest they should not be considered the same problem.

Kind	Recommendation	Readability	Audience
TA	**	2	AU,AG

Ivester, C., & King, K. (1977). Attitudes of adolescents toward the aged. *The Gerontologist, 17,* **85–89.**

Found that most adolescents had positive attitudes toward the elderly, especially among the white middle class.

Kind	Recommendation	Readability	Audience
EA	**	2	AU,AG

Jensen, G. D., & Oakley, F. B. (1982–1983). Ageism across cultures and in perspective of sociobiologic and psychodynamic theories. *International Journal of Aging and Human Development, 15,* 17–26.

Considers sociobiologic and psychodynamic explanations for ageism in industrial societies, including the emergence of larger populations of the aged without sociocultural strategies to incorporate them, their contribution versus their cost to families, the psychological threat posed by aging and death, and failures in identification.

Kind	Recommendation	Readability	Audience
TA	**	2–3	AG

Kahana, E., Liang, J., Felton, B., Fairchild, T., & Harel, Z. (1977). Perspectives of aged on victimization, "ageism," and their problems in urban society. *The Gerontologist, 17,* 121–129.

Found a small proportion of older people reported experiencing discrimination or personal rejection and that most did not consider ageism to be a major issue in their lives. Suggest reluctance to admit membership in a stigmatized group and lack of age group consciousness.

Kind	Recommendation	Readability	Audience
EA	**	2–3	SP,AU,AG

Kalab, K. A. (1985). Textbook reference to the older population. *Educational Gerontology, 11,* 225–235.

Investigated references to the aged population in introductory sociology and introductory gerontology texts. Sociology texts referred to the aged most often in sections on stratification and inequality, using the term "old people." Gerontology texts used more terms for the aged, especially "the elderly."

Kind	Recommendation	Readability	Audience
EA	*	2	AU,AG

Kalish, R. A. (1979). The new ageism and the failure models: A polemic. *The Gerontologist, 19,* 398–402.

Describes the "new ageism" which contributes to the stigmatization of the aged by asserting their need for help and asserting the need for expert solutions to their problems.

Kind	Recommendation	Readability	Audience
TA	***	2	AU,AG

Kasschau, P. L. (1977). Age and race discrimination reported by middle-aged and older persons. *Social Forces, 55,* 728–742.

Examines experience of race and age discrimination among blacks, Mexican-Americans, and whites, reported for themselves, their friends or acquaintances, or in society generally. Blacks had experienced the most race discrimination, but there were no dramatic differences between the groups in age discrimination.

Kind	Recommendation	Readability	Audience
EA	**	2	AG

Kearl, M. C. (1981–1982). An inquiry into the positive personal and social effects of old age stereotyping among the elderly. *International Journal of Aging and Human Development, 14,* 277–290.

Suggests that ageism provides a relative advantage for the old by providing an example of unsuccessful aging with which they can favorably compare themselves and by enhancing participation in and support of coalitions and programs for the old.

Kind	Recommendation	Readability	Audience
TA	***	2	AU,AG

Kearl, M. C., Moore, K., & Osberg, J. S. (1982). Political implications of the "New Ageism." *International Journal of Aging and Human Development, 15,* 167–184.

Finds the existence of a social problem ideology about aging and an associated belief in the need for federal intervention, particularly among the young and the elderly. Suggests that this exemplifies a new ageism characterized by the assertion that the aged as a group require help from others.

Kind	Recommendation	Readability	Audience
EA	**	3	AG

Keith, P. M. (1977). An exploratory study of sources of stereotypes of old age among administrators. *Journal of Gerontology*, 32, 463–469.

Examined age stereotypes held by nursing home administrators. Found that those with the most negative attitudes were those with the greatest proportion of female patients; positive labeling of the aged depended on their possessing socially desirable characteristics (male, mobile, and financially independent).

Kind	Recommendation	Readability	Audience
EA	**	2	SP,AU,AG

Kogan, N. (1979). Beliefs, attitudes, and stereotypes about old people: A new look at some old issues. *Research on Aging*, 1, 11–36.

Notes that the connection between beliefs, attitudes, and behaviors toward the old has not been clearly established because of methodological and conceptual problems in research on ageism.

Kind	Recommendation	Readability	Audience
RA	***	2–3	AU,AG

Kogan, N., & Shelton, F. (1962). Beliefs about "old people:" A comparative study of older and younger samples. *Journal of Genetic Psychology*, 100, 93–111.

One of the earliest studies of beliefs and attitudes about the aged. Found elementary school children and adolescents and the elderly themselves held negative attitudes toward aging.

Kind	Recommendation	Readability	Audience
EA	**	1–2	AU,AG

Lawrence, J. H. (1975). The effect of perceived age on initial impres-

sions and normative role expectations. *International Journal of Aging and Human Development, 5,* 369–391.

Found that age cues were not used as often as other cues in forming initial impressions and typically were used in conjunction with other cues. However, age cues seemed to become important in assigning social roles.

Kind	Recommendation	Readability	Audience
EA	**	2–3	AU,AG

Levenson, A. J. (1981). Ageism: A major deterrent to the introduction of curricula in aging. *Gerontology and Geriatrics Education, 1,* 161–162.

Reviews research suggesting that students in professional schools hold more positive attitudes toward the aged than do faculty and that their attitudes are more positive before they enter professional programs than after.

Kind	Recommendation	Readability	Audience
Editorial	**	2	SP

Lewis, M. I., & Butler, R. N. (1972). Why is women's lib ignoring old women? *Aging and Human Development, 3,* 223–231.

Notes the need for older women to be recognized in the women's movement, that they share problems of marital and family status, health care, economics, and self-concept. Further suggests that older women would bring new power and resources to the movement.

Kind	Recommendation	Readability	Audience
TA	**	1–2	GP,SP,AU,AG

Lillard, J. (1982). A double edged sword: Ageism and sexism. *Journal of Gerontological Nursing, 11,* 630–634.

Notes that care of chronically ill patients most often is the nurse's responsibility, requiring a consideration of ageism and sexism in nursing curricula. Suggests that older women may be grossly underserved in health care.

Kind	Recommendation	Readability	Audience
RA	**	1–2	SP

Minkler, M., & Stone, R. (1985). The feminization of poverty and older women. *The Gerontologist, 25,* 351–357.

Discusses the life course issues related to poverty among women, including lifelong dependency, education, and welfare policy issues.

Kind	Recommendation	Readability	Audience
RA	***	2	AU,AG

Nuessel, F. H. (1982). The language of ageism. *The Gerontologist, 22,* 273–276.

Notes the prevalence of ageist and sexist language which distorts, degrades, excludes, and subordinates the aged.

Kind	Recommendation	Readability	Audience
RA	**	2	GP,SP,AU

Nuessel, F. (1984, August–September). Old age needs a new name: But don't look for it in Webster's. *Aging,* pp. 4–6.

The author discusses the absence of positive terms for the aged in the dictionary and in popular language: common terms for the aged assign them bad habits, personality quirks, and other displeasing traits. Also examines the sexism included in most ageist language.

Kind	Recommendation	Readability	Audience
RA	**	1	GP

Nydegger, C. N. (1983). Family ties of the aged in cross-cultural perspective. *The Gerontologist, 23,* 26–32.

Examines current myths concerning family relations and historical and cross-cultural perspectives on the status of elders within the family.

Kind	Recommendation	Readability	Audience
RA	***	1–2	AU,AG

Palmore, E. B., & Manton, K. (1973). Ageism compared to racism and sexism. *Journal of Gerontology, 28,* 363–369.

Considers economic, educational, and occupational equality between racial, sex, and age groups. Finds age, sex, and race create a triple jeopardy in income and education.

Kind	*Recommendation*	*Readability*	*Audience*
EA	**	2–3	AU,AG

Patterson, S. L. (1981). Using naturalistic research on the elderly to change student attitudes and improve helping behavior. *Journal of Education for Social Work, 17*(2), 12–18.

Recommends the use in social work curricula of naturalistic research that involves the examination of the context and nature of aging, individual and social resources.

Kind	*Recommendation*	*Readability*	*Audience*
TA	*	1	SP

Payne, B., & Whittington, F. (1976). Older women: An examination of popular stereotypes and research evidence. *Social Problems, 23,* 488–504.

Examines research on older women and finds the most common stereotypes describe the old woman as sick, sexless, alone, and uninvolved except at church.

Kind	*Recommendation*	*Readability*	*Audience*
RA	**	2	AU,AG

Peacock, E. W., & Talley, W. M. (1984). Intergenerational contact: A way to counteract ageism. *Educational Gerontology, 10,* 13–24.

Examines age segregation and strategies and benefits of increased intergenerational contact, including a sense of community, a sense of the coherence of the life span, and historical knowledge.

Kind	*Recommendation*	*Readability*	*Audience*
TA	*	1–2	GP,SP

Peterson, D. A. (1985). Toward a definition of educational gerontology. In R. H. Sherron & D. B. Lumsden (Eds.), *Introduction to educational gerontology* (2nd ed; pp. 1–29). Washington, DC: Hemisphere.

Discusses the importance of education about the aging process as a corrective to the lack of attention in the media and general youth-oriented social values.

Kind	Recommendation	Readability	Audience
Handbook	**	2	SP,AU,AG

Peterson, D. A., & Karnes, E. L. (1976). Older people in adolescent literature. *The Gerontologist, 16,* 225–231.

Examined award-winning children's books from 1922 to 1975 and found portrayals of the aged to be diverse and generally positive. Women, however, were shown predominantly in home and family roles.

Kind	Recommendation	Readability	Audience
EA	**	2	AU,AG

Phillipson, C. (1982). *Capitalism and the construction of old age.* London: Macmillan Press.

Examines the social construction of old age in capitalist systems and the psychological and social justifications for treating the old poorly that are inherent in capitalism. The author suggests that the welfare system is inadequate because it fails to address the origins of the problems of the aged in capitalist ideology.

Kind	Recommendation	Readability	Audience
Book	***	2–3	AG

Pinkney, A. (1984). *The myth of black progress.* New York: Oxford University Press.

Examines the nature of policy issues related to the social status of blacks.

Kind	Recommendation	Readability	Audience
Book	**	2	AU,AG

Porcino, J. (1983). *Growing older, getting better.* **Reading, MA: Addison-Wesley.**

A guidebook for aging women, including discussions of economics, health, social policy, and discrimination in employment and medical care.

Kind	Recommendation	Readability	Audience
Book	***	1	GP

Ray, D., Raciti, M. A., & Ford, C. V. (1985). Ageism in psychiatrists: Associations with gender, certification, and theoretical orientation. *The Gerontologist, 25,* **496–500.**

Found that psychiatrists of all genders, theoretical orientations, and certification statuses discriminated against the aged in vignettes. Women, those with psychodynamic or psychoanalytic orientations, and board-certified psychiatrists discriminated the most.

Kind	Recommendation	Readability	Audience
EA	*	2	AU,AG

Richman, J. (1977). The foolishness and wisdom of age: Attitudes toward the elderly as reflected in jokes. *The Gerontologist, 17,* **210–219.**

Found negative attitudes in jokes more common toward the aged than toward children, and that the most derogatory jokes were made about the next older generation: parents or parent figures. Suggests that humor reveals ambivalence toward aging and an affirmation of potential and worth as long as life is lived fully.

Kind	Recommendation	Readability	Audience
EA	**	2	AU,AG

Riley, M. W., & Bond, K. (1983). Beyond ageism: Postponing the onset of disability. In M. W. Riley, B. B. Hess, & K. Bond (Eds.), *Aging in society: Selected reviews of recent research* **(pp. 243–252). Hillsdale, NJ: Erlbaum.**

Suggests gerontologists begin to build on knowledge to prevent or reverse disabilities among the old and to eliminate the remnants of ageism in the medical community and among the old themselves.

Kind	Recommendation	Readability	Audience
RC	**	2	SP,AU,AG

Rodeheaver, D. (1987a, March). All the experience of youth: Confessions of an ageist gerontologist. In D. Rodeheaver (Chair), *Ageism and sexism in gerontological and geriatric education: The power politics of the classroom and extension.* **Symposium presented at the meetings of the Association for Gerontology and Higher Education, Boston, MA.**

Examines the role of the expert on aging in perpetuating ageism and the reliance of that role on the powerlessness of the aged and a consequent legitimation of their diminished social status.

Kind	Recommendation	Readability	Audience
TA	**	1–2	SP,AU,AG

Rodeheaver, D. (1987b). When old age became a social problem, women were left behind. *The Gerontologist, 27,* **741–746.**

Examines the history of social policies for the aged and for women and suggests the absence of issues and values relevant to aging women.

Kind	Recommendation	Readability	Audience
TA	***	1–2	AU,AG

Rodin, J., & Langer, E. (1980). Aging labels: The decline of control and the fall of self-esteem. *Journal of Social Issues, 36(2),* **12–29.**

Social psychological perspective on self-perception, labeling, attribution, and issues of control in old age.

Kind	Recommendation	Readability	Audience
RA	**	2	SP,AU,AG

Roscoe, B. (1985). Social issues as social problems: Adolescents' perceptions. *Adolescence, 20,377–383.*

Examines adolescents' perceptions of what issues are social problems and the seriousness of those problems. Ageism was not considered a serious problem. The authors suggest that adolescent views derive from direct experience, developing idealism, and adult attitudes.

Kind	Recommendation	Readability	Audience
EA	*	2	AU,AG

Rosen, B., & Jerdee, T. H. (1976). The influence of age stereotypes on managerial decisions. *Journal of Applied Psychology,* **61, 428–432.**

Found that undergraduates in business courses held stereotypes about the aged with respect to physical, cognitive, and emotional characteristics.

Kind	Recommendation	Readability	Audience
EA	**	2	AU,AG

Rosow, I. (1974). *Socialization to old age.* **Berkeley: University of California Press.**

Classic discussion of the socialization of the aged to a normless, devalued age status. Suggests that insulation of the aged is an effective social solution to this problem.

Kind	Recommendation	Readability	Audience
Book	***	2	AU,AG

Salter, C. A., & Salter, C. (1976). Attitudes toward aging and behaviors toward the elderly among young people as a function of death anxiety. *The Gerontologist,* **16, 232–236.**

Found that attitudes toward the elderly were more positive as death anxiety increased.

Kind	Recommendation	Readability	Audience
EA	**	2	AU,AG

Schonfield, D. (1982). Who is stereotyping who and why? *The Gerontologist,* **22, 267–272.**

Clarifies the relationship between attitudes, prejudice, stereotypes, and beliefs. Suggests that ageism has been exaggerated, due in part to improper use of language, methodological problems, and the vested interest of gerontologists in old age policies and programs.

Kind	*Recommendation*	*Readability*	*Audience*
RA	**	2	SP,AU,AG

Schwab, D. P., & Heneman, H. G. (1978). Age stereotyping in performance appraisal. *Journal of Applied Psychology, 63,* 573–578.

An investigation of personnel specialists' evaluations of written performance reports on secretaries of varying ages. Older personnel specialists evaluated older secretaries more negatively.

Kind	*Recommendation*	*Readability*	*Audience*
E	*	2	AU,AG,SP

Seefeldt, C., Galper, A., Serock, K., & Jantz, R. K. (1978). The coming of age in children's literature. *Childhood Education, 54,* 118–122.

Found generally negative and passive portrayals of the aged in children's literature. Lists books that show the elderly in diverse roles, activities, and lifestyles and suggests volunteer programs and other forms of intergenerational contact.

Kind	*Recommendation*	*Readability*	*Audience*
EA	**	1	GP,SP,AU

Seefeldt, C., Jantz, R. K., Galper, A., & Serock, K. (1977). Children's attitudes toward the elderly: Educational implications. *Educational Gerontology, 2,* 301–310.

Research revealed children of all ages had little information about aging, although information is increasingly accurate as children age. Discusses the importance of knowledge, contact, and exposure to elderly in a variety of roles and activities, and with a variety of attributes.

Kind	*Recommendation*	*Readability*	*Audience*
EA	**	2	SP,AU,AG

Seltzer, M. M. (1977). Differential impact of various experiences on breaking down age stereotypes. *Educational Gerontology,* **2,** 183–189.

Found faculty attitudes and the learning environment of a college course more important in influencing perceptions of and attitudes about the aged than the content of the course or the course orientation.

Kind	*Recommendation*	*Readability*	*Audience*
EA	**	2	SP,AG

Seltzer, M. M., & Atchley, R. C. (1971). The concept of old: Changing attitudes and stereotypes. *The Gerontologist, 11,* 226–230.

Found attitudes and stereotypes in children's books from 1870 to 1960 less negative than anticipated. Suggest an oversensitivity on the part of gerontologists to anything that might be seen as ageism.

Kind	*Recommendation*	*Readability*	*Audience*
EA	**	2	AU,AG

Sigelman, L., & Sigelman, C. K. (1982). Sexism, racism, and ageism in voting behavior: An experimental analysis. *Social Psychology Quarterly, 45,* 263–269.

Simulated a mayoral election in which candidates varied by sex, age, and race. Ageism was more predominant than sexism or racism, especially among college-aged participants. All participants favored candidates most like themselves.

Kind	*Recommendation*	*Readability*	*Audience*
EA	**	2	AG

Silverman, M. (1977). The old man as woman: Detecting stereotypes of aged men with a femininity scale. *Perceptual and Motor Skills, 44,* 336–338.

Found that men over 65 and women generally were rated higher in femininity and that standards used to rate "men in general" were based on perceptions of young men.

Kind	*Recommendation*	*Readability*	*Audience*
EA	**	2	AG

Sohngen, M., & Smith, R. J. (1978). Images of old age in poetry. *The Gerontologist, 18,* 181–186.

Found that poetry about the aged focused largely on physical attributes, social and emotional losses, and the decline of emotional intensity.

Kind	Recommendation	Readability	Audience
EA	*	2	AU,AG

Sorgman, M. I., & Sorensen, M. (1984). Ageism: A course of study. *Theory into Practice, 23*(2), 117–123.

Presents a rationale and framework for developing curricula on ageism in schools.

Kind	Recommendation	Readability	Audience
TA	*	1	SP

Spicker, S. F., Woodward, K. M., & Van Tassel, D. D. (Eds.) (1978). *Aging and the elderly: Humanistic perspectives in gerontology.* **Atlantic Highlands, NJ: Humanities Press.**

Edited collection of essays on images of aging in literature, history, ethics, and politics.

Kind	Recommendation	Readability	Audience
Book	***	1–2	GP,SP,AU,AG

Steuer, J. L. (1982). Psychotherapy with older women: Ageism and sexism in traditional practice. *Psychotherapy: Theory, Research, and Practice, 19,* 429–436.

Sees sexism as a major component of neglect of the elderly in the mental health profession. Therapists foster traditional sex roles when they are no longer valid suggesting that therapy encourage sex-role deviance.

Kind	Recommendation	Readability	Audience
RA	**	2	SP,AU,AG

Tibbitts, C. (1979). Can we invalidate negative stereotypes of aging? *The Gerontologist, 19,* 10–20.

Discusses the historical context in which negative stereotypes of the aged emerged and suggests that emerging roles as workers, family members, and learners and knowledge and positive self-concepts will undermine these stereotypes.

Kind	*Recommendation*	*Readability*	*Audience*
TA	**	2	SP,AU,AG

Wanner, R. A., & McDonald, L. (1983). Ageism in the labor market: Estimating earnings discrimination against older workers. *Journal of Gerontology, 38,* 738–744.

Found lower earnings related to experience on the job, suggesting that employers assumed senior employees have lower productivity and fewer needs and, therefore, should be paid less.

Kind	*Recommendation*	*Readability*	*Audience*
EA	*	2–3	AU,AG

Wilhite, M. J., & Johnson, D. M. (1976). Changes in nursing students' stereotypic attitudes toward old people. *Nursing Research, 25,* 430–432.

Found changes in nursing students' attitudes most closely related to faculty attitudes toward the aged.

Kind	*Recommendation*	*Readability*	*Audience*
EA	**	1–2	SP,AG

Zinberg, N. E. (1976). Normal psychology of the aging process, revisited (I): Social learning and self-image in aging. *Journal of Geriatric Psychiatry, 9,* 131–150.

Suggests awareness of the way cultural stereotypes can produce self-fulfilling guidelines that inhibit personal growth among the aged.

Kind	*Recommendation*	*Readability*	*Audience*
RA	**	1–2	GP,SP,AU,AG

SUPPLEMENTAL MATERIAL
Group and Class Exercises/Discussion Topics

Exploring Attitudes and Beliefs

Many individuals are unaware that they hold different expectations for different age groups. An examination of ageism might begin with an examination of the nature of *age norms*—expectations for behavior that are based on a person's age—and *age constraints*—limitations on activities that are based on age. One excellent way of exploring these issues is the use of a projective technique, and an excellent picture created for this purpose is included in the book *Middle Age and Aging* (1968, The University of Chicago Press; p. 58), edited by Bernice Neugarten, and available in most university libraries. The picture shows a young woman, a young man, an older woman, and an older man. Alternatively, a picture from a magazine showing several people of different ages will work.

The group is shown the picture and given a few minutes to create a story explaining the picture. (Explain to the group that there are no right or wrong stories.) Then write on the blackboard the major themes in group members' stories. How is each character described and what is that character's role in the story? Are there assumptions made about the people in the picture that are based on their ages? For example, people frequently assume that there are two couples in the picture, but rarely do they suggest that the old woman and the young man form one of the couples. It is often assumed that this is a family discussion and one of the topics frequently mentioned is the possibility of putting the old woman in a nursing home. Rarely does anyone suggest that the old woman wants to return to school for her degree. That people so readily make assumptions based on age when they know nothing else about a character illustrates the prevalence of age norms. That some of those assumptions limit the opportunities of the people in the story—with whom they are coupled, what they are going to do—illustrates the impact of age constraints.

> *Alternative:* Ask members of the group to complete the following sentence: "At your age you should ____."
> Then ask them to complete the sentence as if they were speaking to a teenager; to someone who is 75.
> Record their answers in different columns and compare their expectations for people of different ages.

Exploring Images of Aging

Assign members of the group different sources of the image of aging in America: television (including commercials), magazines (including advertisements), greeting cards, literature, textbooks, and music. Have group members record the number of times an older character appears or is mentioned, the sex and race of that character, what the character says and does, what is said about or done to that character, the character's appearance and health. Use these to discuss the image of aging and group members' thoughts about the impact of those images.

Exploring Personal Attitudes

Recognizing ageism in others is one thing; recognizing it in ourselves is another. One way of measuring attitudes toward the aged is with a scale or questionnaire designed for that purpose. One example is Nathan Kogan's Attitudes Toward Old People Scale (*Journal of Abnormal and Social Psychology*, 1961, Vol. 62, pp. 44–54).

Alternative: There are a number of topics about which people hold strong opinions and that illustrate their attitudes toward the elderly. One such topic is the elderly driver. Another is financing social security. These topics will also frequently reveal erroneous beliefs and stereotypes about the aged.

Exploring Personal Beliefs

In addition to the previously mentioned discussion topics, Erdman Palmore has composed a short quiz to measure knowledge about aging ("Facts on Aging: A Short Quiz," *The Gerontologist*, 1977, Vol. 17, pp. 315–320; see also E. Palmore, "The Facts on Aging Quiz: A Review of Findings," *The Gerontologist*, 1980, Vol. 20, pp. 669–672; an alternative form is provided in E. Palmore, "The Facts on Aging Quiz: Part Two," *The Gerontologist*, 1981, Vol. 21, pp. 431–437.) A brief description of some of the most common misconceptions about aging is also provided by Robert Butler in his book *Why Survive?* (1975b) and provides basic material for presentation.

Exploring Age Discrimination

Virtually all age groups have met discrimination at some time. College students, for example, frequently experience discrimination in housing and employment. Young adults with children commonly meet discrimination in housing. Middle-aged women face discrimination in employment. Discuss the forms of discrimination group members have experienced. Does such discrimination constitute ageism? How does it compare to the discrimination experienced by the elderly?

Experiencing Old Age

It is possible to give group members some empathy for the experience of aging even though they may not be old themselves. The changes commonly experienced in vision and hearing, for example, are remarkably simulated in a slide/cassette kit entitled *Age Related Vision and Hearing Changes: An Empathetic Approach,* prepared by the Institute on Gerontology at the University of Michigan (1976). Many universities and colleges have copies of this kit in their media collections.

A unique approach was taken by Pat Moore, who disguised herself as an old woman and went undercover. Her experiences are recorded in her book *Disguised* (1985, Word Books).

An illustration of the value of life histories in understanding the experience of aging is provided by Barbara Myerhoff's book *Number Our Days* (1978, Touchstone). This can be used as a model for group members to collect life histories of family members.

In addition, there are a number of excellent literary accounts of aging. The following list is by no means exclusive:

Short stories	Fisher, M.F.K. (1964). *Sister age.* New York: Random House.
Personal essays	Macdonald, B., & Rich, C. (1983). *Look me in the eye.* San Francisco: Spinsters Ink. Cowley, M. (1980). *The view from 80.* New York: Penguin. (Original work published in 1976)
Novel	Sarton, M. (1973). *As we are now.* New York: Norton.
Personal journal	Scott-Maxwell, F. (1979). *The measure of my days.* New York: Penguin. (Original work published in 1968)
Autobiography	Jones, M. H. (1980). *The autobiography of Mother Jones* (rev. ed.). (M. F. Parton. Ed.). Chicago: Charles H. Kerr. (Original work published in 1925)

Steps Toward Change[1]

Assign group members the task of developing a project that will help alleviate ageism. The project may reflect the particular interests of the group. Some examples include integrating information about aging and ageism into the school curriculum; designing a non-ageist line of greeting cards; integrating naturalistic observation into social work, nursing, or medical school curricula; developing videotapes on the different ways of growing old in different cultures or subgroups; creating an "Age Game" that allows players to experience some of the events and decisions of aging.

---

[1] I am indebted to the students in my class, Adulthood and Aging, for the fall of 1986 for these ideas.

AUTHOR'S COMMENTS

Conceptual and Methodological Issues in the Study of Ageism

Although gerontologists have demonstrated that negative attitudes, stereotypes, and discrimination exist, questions have been raised about how pervasive ageism is and whether or not the evidence suggests a widespread prejudice against the aged. For example, while children do hold ambivalent and often negative attitudes toward the elderly, some studies find that they become increasingly accurate in their beliefs and more positive in their attitudes, especially among the white middle class (Ivester & King, 1977). And, although the aged themselves may exhibit some ageism, some studies find that they also see old age optimistically, as a time for happiness and adaptation (Borges & Dutton, 1976). Nor do the aged report personal experience with discrimination or ageism to be a common problem (Kahana, Liang, Fetton, Fairchild, & Harel, 1977).

Furthermore, images of the elderly are not exclusively negative. The elderly may be absent from children's television, but so is anyone over the age of 20 (Davis & Davis, 1985). And some studies of children's literature find positive portrayals of aging and the aged: Multidimensional characters are presented in a diversity of lifestyles and physical conditions, engaging in a variety of behaviors (Blue, 1978; Peterson & Karnes, 1976; Seltzer & Atchley, 1971). Why do these conflicting images of aging emerge?

The contradictions in gerontological research may reflect the real presence of both positive and negative attitudes and stereotypes, particularly among the aged themselves. Historians have noted that ambivalence has always characterized American images of the aged (Achenbaum, 1978). Brubaker and Powers (1976) suggest a psychological source of ambivalence, hypothesizing that, as objective personal indicators of old age increase (appearance, health, or whatever else an individual uses to define old age), self-definition as old also increases. If the individual's previous self-concept was positive, positive stereotypes and attitudes will be adopted. If the individual's previous self-concept was negative, negative stereotypes and attitudes about old age will be adopted. Such variations in stereotypes and attitudes would, presumably, be reflected in cultural images, too.

Other critics have suggested that the contradictory results reflect methodological and conceptual problems in the study of ageism. Kogan (1979) has reviewed studies attempting to change stereotypic beliefs and has noted that when within subjects designs are used (comparing the same subjects before and after some attempt to decrease ageism has taken place), stereotypes generally diminish. Kogan suggests that such change is virtually assured by the demand characteristics of the task: Comparing the attributes of different age groups before and after "treatment" is not a difficult task to decipher.

More problematic is the consistent confusion in gerontological research between attitudes—pro or con stances with regard to the elderly—and beliefs—statements of perceived facts. Nor has any clear relationship been established between attitudes and beliefs, or between attitudes, beliefs, and discriminatory behaviors (Kogan, 1979; Schonfield, 1982). This is especially problematic given the opinion of some social psychologists that attitudes are not easily measured or changed, that increasing knowledge does not necessarily change attitudes, and that changes in attitudes and beliefs do not necessarily change behavior (W. M. Smith, personal communication, August 5, 1987; Rodeheaver, 1987a). Schonfield attempted to clarify these conceptual issues:

> Ageism is an attitude with negative and more questionably positive features demonstrating prejudice against members of a chronological age group. The prejudgment is shown by behaving toward members of such a group according to its members' assumed characteristics and not in accord with the individual's own characteristics. Stereotypic behavior is found when the behavior is demonstrated toward all or most members of the group. A belief implies a potentially verifiable criterion concerning alleged knowledge. When the belief is false but is held by many individuals, it is called a myth. Stereotypic beliefs, or stereotypes "for short," are beliefs about qualities of all or almost all members of a group. [1982, p. 268]

The continual claim despite these methodological and conceptual problems that there is a pervasive prejudice against the aged has prompted some to suggest that gerontologists exaggerate the presence of ageism and are oversensitized to anything that could be considered ageism (Schonfield, 1982; Seltzer & Atchley, 1971). Others are less charitable, suggesting that gerontologists have contributed to ageism. Herrick (1983), for example, has noted that a preoccupation with biological and physiological sources of intellectual and personality change has meant that the learned behaviors of aging are often overlooked. This preoccupation is, he has suggested, akin to Spencer's science of racial differences: It reinforces ageism in those seeking reinforcement. The most vocal critics of the gerontological obsession with ageism have been Kalish (1979) and Kearl (1981–1982; Kearl, Moore, & Osberg, 1982). Both have noted the existence of a "new ageism" created by the research and assumptions not of an ageist public but of experts in the field of aging. The "new ageism" has three major characteristics:

1. *The stereotyping of new groups.* The claim that stereotypes about aging apply only to the least healthy, the least alert, and the least capable is accompanied by the claim that the aged are not all alike. These paradoxical claims encourage stereotyping of a subgroup of the aged.

2. *The emergence of a social-problem ideology regarding aging.* An emphasis on the need for services and programs of support and on a reliance on

federal intervention has emerged without consideration of the reduction in personal freedom and control such intervention might produce. At the very least, such an emphasis creates an image of the aged as helpless and dependent.

3. *Gerontologic patronization.* Gerontologists' blaming society and certain individuals within it for the unpleasant existence of the elderly suggests a patronizing belief that experts have all the answers. Yet, gerontological models, which Kalish (1979) calls the "failure models," may contribute to a sense of victimization and resignation among the elderly. For example, social critics who predict failure for the elderly in the absence of widespread social reform may be communicating a message that is internalized by the aged as personal incompetence (the Incompetence Model). Moreover, the common notion in gerontological practice that activity is the best way to adapt to old age is exclusionary since it is neither desired by nor desirable for all elders (the Geriactivist Model). Kearl (1981–1982) has suggested that the enthusiastic way gerontologists have embraced the need to eliminate ageism has led the possible relative advantages of ageism to be overlooked: "Facing collective downward mobility, disengagement, and deindividuation in an age-stratified society, *satisfactions are possibly gauged not against who one is but against who one is not*" (p. 280). That is, problem stereotypes can enhance individual life satisfaction among those perceiving themselves to be better off than those who really have problems. Furthermore, such negative stereotypes enhance participation in and support for political coalitions for the old.

While the arguments of critics of the new ageism do not necessarily persuade one that ageism is good, they do suggest that some attention must be paid to the role gerontologists have in shaping images of aging. Scientific knowledge is easily adapted to meet the needs of the media and scholars become image makers. Unwittingly, gerontologists may be contributing to the social problems they seek to resolve.

8
Aging, Work, and Retirement

Harvey L. Sterns
Ralph A. Alexander
Gerald V. Barrett
Lisa S. Schwartz
Nancy Kubitz Matheson

INTRODUCTION

We all work. For most people the primary purpose is to earn a living. Some people work out of the pure enjoyment of the activity and would pursue such activity whether or not they were paid. There are many other rewards in employment: opportunities to receive recognition, make friends, achievement, challenge of solving problems, and being a part of meaningful activities.

Many people spend 20 or more years getting ready to enter the world of work. Adults and older adults may spend as much as half of each day involved in work. Work provides an organizing force in our activities. Employment and retirement are a central factor in people's lives.

Workers are changing individuals in a changing environment. The workplace has been undergoing dynamic changes in the 1980s and will continue to change in the 1990s. Adult and older adult workers are imbedded in professional and job roles that may be rapidly changing due to economic, societal, and technological forces.

Industrial gerontological psychology is an interdisciplinary approach to the study of aging and draws from industrial and organizational psychology, developmental, and counseling psychology. There are thus many different types of issues embraced by this new area of psychology that addresses issues of aging and work.

Access to work opportunities may vary by age, sex, and social class. Educational background, interests, and experience all play a role in being hired. Industrial gerontology is the study of aging and work focusing on the employment and retirement issues of middle-aged and older workers. Major areas include social policy and law, stereotypes of the older worker, selection, job performance and appraisal, training and retraining, career progressions and development, motivational factors and organizational design, reentry workers, alternative work patterns, safety, plant closing, and layoff and retirement decisions (Sterns & Alexander, 1987).

There have been a number of important reviews and books that provide well-done summaries of past research and current issues (Birren, Robinson, & Livingston, 1986; Dennis, 1988; Doering, Rhodes, & Schuster, 1983; Rhodes, 1983, Robinson, Coberly, & Paul, 1985; Rosen & Jerdee, 1985; Stagner, 1985).

Over the past 25 years, adults 65 and over have grown from 8 to 12% of the U. S. population. In the next 35 years, people 65 and over may reach 17%, and by 2035, 20 to 25% of the American population will be 65 and over. These same trends are occurring in all developing countries. Many of these older people may choose to work beyond traditional retirement age. *Work-life extension* is a term referring to increasing the labor force participation of older adults through delayed retirements or labor force reentry by retirees.

There are many important issues that can be part of a presentation, unit, or course on industrial gerontological psychology. A major problem in the past was the lack of sufficient research and literature. In this introduction, we will present some of the current literature and emerging areas that we feel make this topic relevant to all audiences.

In Great Britain industrial gerontology began right after World War II to address issues in aging and work. This early research focused on the capability of older adult workers and on concerns regarding technological change and automation and their effects on the older worker. In the United States in the 1960s, the National Council on Aging stimulated consideration of issues surrounding middle-aged and older workers with conferences, reports, and curriculum materials.

SOCIAL POLICY AND LEGAL ISSUES

The continuation of such recent trends as changes in the age composition of the work force, improvements in the health and education of older adults, elimination of mandatory retirement, and major economic and technological changes requiring substantial organizational restructuring will become increasingly important to organizational staffing decisions involving older workers. Individual job performance plays a central role in staffing decisions such as hiring, training, promotion, retention, job assignment, career progression and planning, job design, layoff, and termination.

Although the research on job performance has been extensive over the past half-century, a number of issues take on particular importance in the context of the older employee. These generally involve the following topics: the perception that employers discriminate against older workers; potential age bias in performance appraisals; the question of whether or not there are reliable and systematic age differences and/or age changes in job performance; and age differences in other factors that may be related to job performance.

Perception of Age Bias

The first issue concerns perceived bias against older workers. A recent national work force survey reported that more than 80% of American workers believe that employers discriminate against older employees (U. S. House Select Committee on Aging, 1982). Much of the literature assumes or supports the notion that there is a generalized negative stereotype against older workers (Rhodes, 1983). This belief that older persons are at an unfair disadvantage in the work place has been a substantial factor for more than 20 years in both social and legal institutions that aim to eliminate such (perceived) discrimination. To the extent that the perception is accurate, steps are needed to remedy such practices even if they are unintentional. On the other hand, if this general perception is not accurate, the question becomes how can such a pervasive misperception be corrected? Age-related stereotyping has been reviewed by Rosen and Jerdee (1985). In one of their major studies age stereotypes were found to influence managerial decision regarding simulated managerial (administrative) problems. This investigation confirmed the hypothesis that stereotypes regarding the older employees' physical, cognitive, and emotional characteristics lead to discrimination against older workers.

The Age Discrimination in Employment Acts of 1967, 1978, and 1986 now define older workers as individuals 40 years old and above.

The Age Discrimination in Employment Act (ADEA) of 1967 (29 U.S.C. 623) specified protection of workers from age discrimination between the ages of 40 and 65 and promotion of employment opportunities for older workers capable of meeting job requirements. In 1974 the act was amended to include coverage of government employees at the local, state, and federal level. In 1978 it was amended to change coverage to age 70 and to abolish mandatory retirement altogether for federal employees. In 1986 the act was further amended to remove the maximum age limitation, with certain exceptions. It is a violation for employers to fail or refuse to hire, to discharge, or in other ways to discriminate against any individual with respect to compensation or other terms or conditions of employment because of age. Workers cannot be limited, segregated, or classified in a way that might deprive any individual of employment opportunities or adversely affect his or her status as an employee because of age.

From its inception the ADEA has allowed employers to consider an individual's age in employment decisions when the employer can show that age is a *bona fide occupational qualification* (BFOQ), reasonably necessary to the normal operations of a business. Such an exception is determined on the basis of all pertinent facts surrounding each situation. The establishment of this exception is difficult. Organizational practices such as the setting of maximum age limits on hiring must be substantiated with proof that age requirements are essential for the protection of the public or on the basis of some reasonable factors other than age, such as physical fitness. The employer may observe the terms of a bona fide seniority system or a bona fide employment benefit plan that is not a subterfuge to evade the purposes of the act. The act does not preclude the discharge or discipline of an older worker for good cause. Good general discussions of the ADEA are included in Edelman and Siegler (1978), Doering, Rhodes, and Schuster (1983), and Rosen and Jerdee (1985).

The issues in many cases involving BFOQs concern the question of whether there are age-related changes in the behavior of all or most individuals that would impair their adequate performance on a job beyond a certain chronological age.

HUMAN RESOURCE MANAGEMENT AND THE OLDER WORKER

Given the possibility of age discrimination in employment, the possibility of age-related bias in employee selection is a major concern. Two areas of primary interest with older workers are interviews and selection testing.

Interviews

The interview is the most widely used selection device; however, relatively little research has been done on age bias in the interview. Most of the research that has been done has been in laboratory settings rather than in actual organizations. Avolio and Barrett (1987) in a recent paper argue that the past laboratory research has been confounded, making it difficult to draw conclusions. They found that when these confounds are controlled, interview bias appears to be more a bias in favor of younger applicants rather than a negative bias against older people.

It is likely that the potential for bias and the perception of bias in interviews can be greatly reduced by assuring that the selection interviewer is well and carefully trained and that the interview is carefully designed to gather only that information that is clearly relevant to the applicant's future job performance (Avolio, Barrett, & Sterns, 1984).

Selection Testing

When ability or aptitude tests are used in selection, there is the possibility that such selection procedures may be biased against older job applicants. Such discussions are usually predicted on observations about average test scores and average job performance. Studies showing that older adults score, on average, lower than younger workers on selection tests with no average age differences in performance are often cited as evidence for potential age bias in selection tests (Doering et al, 1983). In some cases simple mean differences on tests as a function of age are deemed sufficient to suggest that selection tests are biased against older persons (Salthouse, 1986). Such analyses are both inadequate and inappropriate for assessing age discrimination in selection testing. The relevant question is whether or not the selection system predicts job performance as well for older workers as for younger workers (technically referred to as differential validity).

AGE DIFFERENCES AND JOB PERFORMANCE

Two major reviews of the research literature have appeared in an attempt to summarize what is known regarding age differences in job performance and age differences in the appraisal of job performance (Rhodes, 1983; Waldman & Avolio, 1986). These reviews appear to show very little consistent relationship between age and objective job performance evaluation. A more careful analysis of the research literature cited by these reviews, however, indicated that it really is not possible to draw any substantive conclusions from the available evidence.

Drawing conclusions regarding age changes in performance from performance differences between age groups is inappropriate. Such "cross-sectional" data is completely confounded by cohort effects. That is, there is no way of determining whether the observed differences are age related or are the result of the differential histories of the age cohorts. Little of the available data is based on longitudinal studies of behavioral or job performance change with age. In addition, none of the research to date has successfully separated the age/experience effects on performance. In most (if not all) occupations, age and experience are highly correlated. Seldom is an attempt made to control for this confound. This is particularly important not only for understanding the age–performance relationship but also for organizational decision making. If age–performance relationships are substantially moderated by either job experience or organizational tenure, this may have a significant impact on organizational selection and placement decisions for older workers.

There is a need to recognize that age–performance relationships may differ substantially as a function of occupation or of job requirements. The few studies that do exist cover a wide range of jobs, including clerical, professional, skilled trades, and blue collar.

JOB ATTITUDES

The extensive research history on attitudes toward work, organizational commitment, and job satisfaction consistently shows that such work-related attitudes are progressively more positive with increasing age (Rhodes, 1983). The difficulty with interpreting these findings is similar to the problems mentioned earlier of separating the effects of age and job experience that are highly correlated. The research to date has not succeeded in separating the effects on worker attitudes of age, experience, or what is more likely the combined effects of the two influences.

CAREER DEVELOPMENT

A life-span approach to career development emphasizes the fact that behavior change processes can occur at any point in the life course. Also, older adult workers have developed a knowledge and abilities base that continues to grow.

Older adult workers have experience-related strengths that can guide their own self-training. Depending on the level of work and worker, individuals can be continually developing and improving their work performance. Recent research and discussions of aging and expert cognition emphasize that individuals may show no decline in aspects of cognition that are fundamental to areas of lifetime specialization.

Career planning is the personal process of planning one's lifework. This includes evaluating abilities and interests, considering alternative career opportunities, establishing career goals, and planning practical developmental activities. In the past, career-planning activities were largely left up to the individual. In more recent years, however, organizations have begun to recognize that career-planning programs can contribute to the human resource management process. Such programs may aid in reducing turnover by clarifying career paths within the organization.

In summarizing major theories of career development Sterns and Patchett (1984) and Sterns (1986) emphasize that career development is one aspect of life-span development intimately intertwined with other aspects of life cycle. Occupational choice or assignment is not something that happens once in a lifetime. People and situations develop, and career decisions become a series of minidecisions. These minidecisions add up to a lifelong series of occupational choices.

Sterns and Patchett (1984) and Sterns (1986) have advanced a model of adult and older adult career development that is non-age-specific. The model assumes that transitions in work life may occur many times throughout a career (see Figure 1).

According to this model, the decision to change jobs or careers or to exit the system is directly influenced by attitudes toward mobility and success or failure in previous career-development activities. Numerous factors are hypothesized to affect mobility attitudes, such as employment, tenure or stage in career, growth need, fear of stagnation, marketability perceptions, job market conditions, and chance encounters. The decision to change jobs or careers also may affect one's attitude toward entering or reentering the work force.

TRAINING

Job change, promotion, prevention of obsolescence, and personal growth can be facilitated through well-designed training programs. Training programs for workers are designed to (a) improve self-awareness regarding one's role and responsibility in an organization, (b) increase job-related knowledge and skill, and (c) enhance motivation to perform the job well. Training is an important way to achieve productivity, job satisfaction, and organization revitalization.

The ability of individuals to learn and benefit from training and education at all points in the life span is increasingly emphasized in contemporary adult learning literature. Previous educational experience as well as the opportunity for continued growth as part of the work experience are important.

Sterns (1986) suggests that any training program might be successful if properly developed and that careful development of the entire training program is the most important parameter for successful training of the older adult worker, irrespective of the actual training technique used. Task analysis is an important component of training programs for older individuals performing in complex experimental and applied settings.

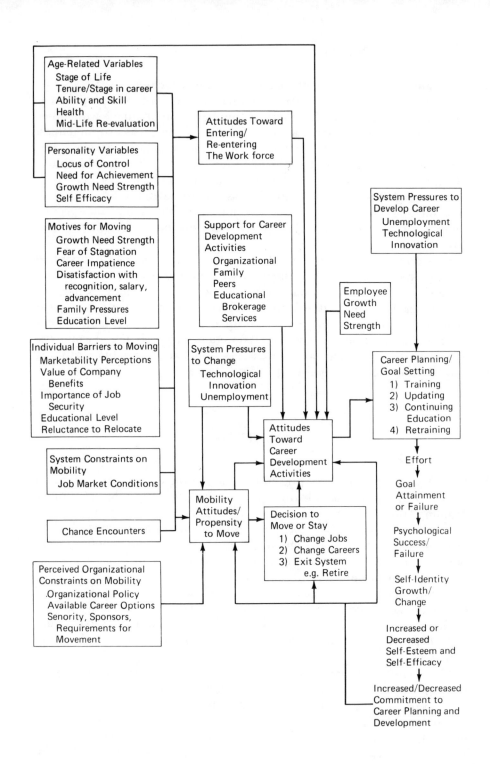

FIGURE 1.1 Career Progression in Middle and Later Adulthood.

TRAINING AND RETRAINING PROGRAM DESIGN

The adult and older adult training and retraining literature has documented a number of dimensions for successful training programs. Many of the recommendations in this section are principles of learning that apply to well-designed training at any age. However, special sensitivity may be needed in specific situations involving older adults. Five major areas emerge that should be considered when designing training programs: motivation, structure, familiarity, organization, and time (Sterns, 1986).

CONCLUSION

Middle-aged adult and older adult workers will play an increasing role in organizations as we move toward the year 2000 and beyond. Older adult workers have a great deal to offer organizations if given the opportunity. It is now possible to make firm recommendations on how to train, retrain, and develop the older worker. Older workers can learn, be trained, and demonstrate continuing career growth. Unwarranted negative attitudes on the part of supervisors may consciously or unconsciously exclude older workers. Effective training programs include consideration of motivation, structure, familiarity, organization, time, active participation, and learning strategies. Organizations must reward individuals for participation in training opportunities and provide workers with an opportunity to use these skills on the job. Training must be seen as an integral part of career development activities at all points in the working life span.

Extension of work life or early retirement should come about by choice on the part of the older adult worker. The value of an older worker should be judged on his or her merit, not by chronological age. Opportunities should be made available to older adult workers that are the same as for any other worker of similar competence, vigor, and ambition. Age-neutral policies need to be part of current personnel policies and will ensure that older persons who elect to continue working will have access to career opportunities consistent with their aspirations, abilities, and potential (Work in America Institute, Inc., 1980).

Decisions to change jobs or careers as well as decisions to engage in career development activities may come about as a result of changes within the individual, the environment, or a combination of both.

Comprehensive Outline

Content	References	Supplemental Material
I. Overview A. Definition of industrial gerontology and its content domain	Rosen, B., & Jerdee, T. H. (1985). *Older employees: New roles for valued resources*. Homewood, IL: Dow-Jones Irwin. Sterns, H. L., & Alexander, R. A. (1988). Industrial gerontology. The aging individual and work. In K. W. Schaie, *Annual review of gerontology and geriatrics* (Vol. 7, pp. 243–264). New York: Springer.	O'Toole, J. (1978). *Work, learning, and the American future*. San Francisco: Jossey-Bass. Stagner, R. (1985). Aging in industry. In J. E. Birren & K. W. Schaie (Eds.), *Handbook of the psychology of aging* (pp. 789–817). New York: Van Nostrand Reinhold.
B. Demographics and the changing work force	Johnston, W. B., & Packer, A. E. (Eds). (1987). *Workforce 2000: Work and workers for the twenty-first century*. Indianapolis, IN: Hudson Institute.	Work in America Institute, Inc. (1980). *The future of older workers in America*. Scarsdale, NY: Author. Humple, C. S., & Lyons, M. (1983). *Management and the older workforce: Policies and programs*. New York: American Management Association. Taeuber, C. (1984). Older workers: Force of the future? In P. K. Robinson, J. E. Livingston,

& J. E. Birren (Eds.), *Aging and technological advances* (pp. 75–89). New York: Plenum Press.

Office of Technology Assessment. (1985). *Technology and aging in America*. Washington, DC: U.S. Congress.

Humple, C. S., & Lyons, M. (1983). *Management and the older workforce: Policies and programs*. New York: American Management Association.

Sterns, H. L., & Pachett, M. (1984). Technology and the aging adult: Career development and training. In P. K. Robinson, J. E. Livingston, & J. E. Birren (Eds.), *Aging and technological advances* (pp. 261–278). New York: Plenum Press.

Skoglund, J. (1979). Work after retirement. *Aging and Work, 2*, 103–112.

Olbrich, E. (1986). Coping in old age. In J. E. Birren, P. K. Robinson, & J. E. Livingston (Eds.), *Age, health, and employment* (pp. 45–62). Englewood Cliffs, NJ: Prentice-Hall.

Sterns, H. L. (1986). Training and retraining adult and older adult workers. In J. E. Birren, P. K. Robinson, & J. E. Living-

Pallak, M. T., & Perloff, R. O. (Eds.). (1986). *Psychology and work: Productivity, change, and employment*. Washington, DC:

C. Technology and change in the workplace

D. Work-life extension

II. Careers and life-span development

A. Coping and adaptation at work
B. The life-span career process

Content	References	Supplemental Material
	ston (Eds.), *Age, health, and employment* (pp. 93–113). Englewood Cliffs, NJ: Prentice-Hall.	American Psychological Association.
	Sterns, H. L., & Patchett, M. (1984). Technology and the aging adult: Career development and training. In P. K. Robinson, J. E. Livingston, & J. E. Birren (Eds.), *Aging and technological advances.* New York: Plenum Press.	
	Neugarten, B. L. (1976). Adaptation and the life cycle. *The Counseling Psychologist, 6,* 16–20.	
C. Career counseling in adulthood	Brown, D. (1981). Emerging models of career development groups for persons at midlife. *The Vocational Guidance Quarterly, 29,* 332–340.	Schlossberg, N. K. (1976). The case for counseling adults. *The Counseling Psychologist, 6,* 33–36.
	Troll, L. E., & Nowak, C. (1976). "How old are you?"—The question of age bias in the counseling of adults. *The Counseling Psychologist, 6,* 41–43.	

III. Social policy and legal issues

A. Perception of age bias

Avolio, B. J., & Barrett, G. V. (1987). Effects of age stereotyping in a simulated interview. *Psychology and Aging, 24,* 56–63.

Rosen, B., & Jerdee, T. H. (1985). *Older employees: New roles for valued resources.* Homewood, IL: Dow Jones–Irwin.

Waldman, D. A., & Avolio, B. J. (1986). A meta-analysis of age differences in job performance. *Journal of Applied Psychology, 71*(1), 33–38.

Doering, M., Rhodes, S. K., & Schuster, M. (Eds.). (1983). *The aging worker: Research and recommendations.* Beverly Hills, CA: Sage.

B. The meaning of age

Avolio, B. J., Barrett, G. V., & Sterns, H. L. (1984). Alternatives to age for assessing occupational performance capacity. *Experimental Aging Research, 10,* 101–105.

Salthouse, T. A. (1986). Functional age: Examination of a concept. In J. E. Birren, P. K. Robinson, & J. E. Livingston (Eds.), *Age, health, and employment* (pp. 78–92). Englewood Cliffs, NJ: Prentice-Hall.

C. Age discrimination law

Rosen, B., & Jerdee, T. H. (1985). *Older employees: New roles for valued resources.* Homewood, IL: Dow Jones–Irwin.

Edelman, C. D., & Siegler, I. C. (1978). *Federal age discrimination in employment law: Slowing down the gold watch.* Charlottesville, VA: Michie.

Content	References	Supplemental Material
IV. Individual differences and the capabilities of older workers A. Slowing of behavior	Salthouse, T. A. (1985). Speed of behavior and its implications for cognition. In J. E. Birren & K. W. Schaie (Eds.), *Handbook of the psychology of aging* (pp. 400–426). New York: Van Nostrand Reinhold. Birren, J. E. (1974). Translation in gerontology—From lab to life: Psychophysiology and speed of response. *American Psychologist, 29,* 808–815	Botwinick, J. (1984). *Aging and behavior* (3rd ed.) (Chap. 13, pp. 229–248). New York: Springer. Slowness of behavior.
B. Well-practiced skills	Salthouse, T. A. (1984). Effects of age and skill in typing. *Journal of Experimental Psychology: General, 113,* 345–371.	
C. Perceptual changes and related behavior	Sterns, H. L., Barrett, G. V., & Alexander, R. A. (1985). Accidents and the aging individual. In J. E. Birren & K. W. Schaie (Eds.), *Handbook of the psychology of aging* (pp. 703–724). New York: Van Nostrand Reinhold.	Botwinick, J. (1984). *Aging and behavior* (3rd ed., pp. 229–248). New York: Springer.

Panek, P. E., Barrett, G. V., Sterns, H. L., & Alexander, R. A. (1977). A review of age changes in perceptual information processing ability with regard to driving. *Experimental Aging Research, 3,* 387–449.

V. Human resources management of the older worker
   A. Interviewing and selection

Haefner, J. E. (1977). Race, age, sex, and competence as factors on employer selection of the disadvantaged. *Journal of Applied Psychology, 62,* 199–202.

Britton, J. O., & Thomas, K. R. (1973). Age and sex as employment variables: View of employment service interviews. *Journal of Employment Counseling, 10,* 180–186.

Schwab, D. P., & Heneman, H. G., III. (1978). Age stereotyping in performance appraisal. *Journal of Applied Psychology, 63*(5), 573–578.

Sterns, H. L., & Alexander, R. A. (1988). Step 6: Use objec-

   B. Performance appraisal

Rhodes, S. R. (1983). Age-related differences in work attitudes and behavior: A review and conceptual analysis. *Psychological Bulletin, 93,* 328–367.

Waldman, D. A., & Avolio, B. J. (1986). A meta-analysis of age

Content	References	Supplemental Materials
	tive performance appraisals. In H. Dennis (Ed.), *Fourteen steps to managing an aging workforce* (pp. 171–190). Lexington, MA: Lexington Books.	differences in job perform-ance. *Journal of Applied Psychology, 71*(1), 33–38.
C. Job evaluation	Rosen, B., & Jerdee, T. H. (1985). *Older employees: New roles for valued resources.* Homewood, IL, Down Jones–Irwin.	
D. Training and retraining	Sterns, H. L., & Doverspike, D. (1988). Step 7: Offer well-designed retraining programs and encourage older workers to participate. In H. Dennis (Ed.), *Fourteen steps in managing an aging workforce* (pp. 97–110). Lexington, MA: Lexington Books.	Czaja, S. J., & Drury, C. G. (1981). Aging and pretraining in industrial inspection. *Human Factors, 23*, 485–494.
	Sterns, H. L. (1986). Training and retraining adult and older adult workers. In J. E. Birren, P. K. Robinson, & J. E. Livingston (Eds.), *Age, health, and employment* (pp. 93–113). Englewood Cliffs, NJ: Prentice-Hall.	Elias, P. K., Elias, M. F., Robbins, M. A., & Gage, P. (1987). Acquisition of word-processing skills by younger, middle-age, and older adults. *Psychology and Aging, 2*, 340–348.

VI. Attitudes toward work

Doering, M., Rhodes, S. R., & Schuster, M. (Eds.). (1983). *The aging worker: Research and recommendations.* Beverly Hills, CA: Sage.

A. Job satisfaction

Pond, S. B., & Geyer, P. D. (1987). Employee age as a moderator of the relation between perceived work alternatives and job satisfaction. *Journal of Applied Psychology, 72*(4), 552–557.

Rhodes, S. R. (1983). Age-related differences in work attitudes and behavior: A review and conceptual analysis. *Psychological Bulletin, 93*, 328–367.

B. Turnover and absenteeism

Mobley, W. J., Griffith, R. W., Hand, H. H., & Meglino, B. M. (1979). Review and conceptual analysis of the employee turnover process. *Psychological Bulletin, 86,* 593–622.

Rhodes, S. R. (1983). Age-related differences in work attitudes and behavior: A review and conceptual analysis. *Psychological Bulletin, 93*, 328–367.

C. Organizational commitment and job involvement

Steers, R. M. (1977). Antecedents and outcomes of organizational commitment. *Administrative Science Quarterly, 22*, 46–56.

Rhodes, S. R. (1983). Age-related differences in work attitudes and behavior: A review and conceptual analysis. *Psychological Bulletin, 93*, 328–367.

VII. Retirement

Robinson, P. K., Coblery, S., & Paul, C. (1985). Work and retirement. In R. H. Binstock & E. Shanas (Eds.), *Handbook of aging and the social sciences*

Content	References	Supplemental Material
A. Choice to retire and early retirement	(2nd ed.). New York: Van Nostrand Reinhold.	
	Morrison, M H. (1986). Work and retirement in an older society. In A. Pifer & L. Bronte (Eds.), *Our aging society* (pp. 341–365). New York: Norton.	
	Beck, S. H. (1985). Determinants of labor force activity among retired men. *Research on Aging, 7*, 251–280.	
B. Involuntary retirement	Jones, W. H. (1979). Grief and involuntary career change: Its implications for counseling. *The Vocational Guidance Quarterly, 27*, 196–201.	
C. Retirement and health finances	Maxwell, N. (1985). The retirement experience: Psychological and financial linkages to the labor market. *Social Science Quarterly, 66*, 22–23.	Newquist, D. D. (1986). Toward assessing health and functional capacity for policy development work-life extension. In J. E. Birren, P. K. Robinson & J. E. Livingston (Eds.), *Age, health, and employment*. Englewood Cliffs, NJ: Prentice-Hall.
D. Stages of retirement	Atchley, R. C. (1979). *Social forces*	Jacobsen, B. (1980). *Young*

E. Job design and alternative work patterns

and aging (pp. 178–205). Belmont, CA: Wardsworth.

programs for older workers. New York: Van Nostrand Reinhold.

Jacobsen, B. (1980). *Young programs for older workers.* New York: Van Nostrand Reinhold.

Humple, C. S., & Lyons, M. (1983). *Management and the older workforce: Policies and programs.* New York: American Management Association.

F. Accidents

Sterns, H. L., Barrett, G. V., & Alexander, R. A. (1985). Accidents and the aging individual. In J. E. Birren & K. W. Schaie (Eds.), *Handbook of the psychology of aging* (pp. 703–724). New York: Van Nostrand Reinhold.

ANNOTATED BIBLIOGRAPHY

Atchley, R. C. (1988). *Social forces and aging* (pp. 178–205). Belmont, CA: Wardsworth.

The author explores basic issues in retirement research. Attention is given to the variety of ways to define retirement as well as to different types of retirement. Further, Atchley diagrams and describes the factors affecting the decision to retire, the timing of retirement, individual situations brought on by retirement, determinants of retirement migration, the effects of retirement on couples, determinants of employer retirement policies, the effects of retirement work organizations, and the effects of retirement on communities and society, as well as pertinent research questions relating to each area.

Kind	Recommendation	Readability	Audience
TC	***	2	AU

Avolio, B. J., & Barrett, G. V. (1987). Effects of age stereotyping in a simulated interview. *Psychology and Aging, 2*, 56–63.

The effects of age stereotyping on subject ratings of interviewee potential was assessed. To correct past research inconsistencies and confounds, the authors controlled for variables such as nearness to retirement, unemployment status, and differential experience levels in their study of the relationship between job applicant age and participant ratings. Results indicated that participants gave higher overall interview ratings to younger interviewees even though they had the same qualifications as older interviewees. Ratings given to older interviewees were not significantly different from those given to interviewees whose age was not noted, however.

Kind	Recommendation	Readability	Audience
E	**	2	AG

Avolio, B. J., Barrett, G. V., & Sterns, H. L. (1984). Alternatives to age for assessing occupational performance capacity. *Experimental Aging Research, 10*, 101–105.

The concept of functional age as a basis for differentiation of individual performance levels has overlooked the intrinsic attributes related to job performance. The authors present a prediction model for assessing older worker performance that considers relevant performance on the job instead of chronological age. New techniques for predicting performance are generated as are expectancy tables that relate test scores to specific performance on a criterion task, resulting in an indicator of the probability of success. The authors suggest the use of intrinsic attributes as the basis for determination of the competence of older and younger workers and support their contention with research pertaining to aircraft flight proficiency.

Kind	Recommendation	Readability	Audience
TC	**	3	AG

Beck, S. H. (1985). Determinants of labor force activity among retired men. *Research on Aging,* **7, 251–280.**

This empirical article examines the impact of factors such as social/demographic, economic or financial, attitudes toward work and retirement, and health on work activity during retirement. Subjects included participants in the National Longitudinal Surveys of older men. The two factors found to be important indicates of postretirement employment include retirement income and health, although the negative relationship between retirement benefits and labor force activity is significant only at the lowest levels of the income distribution.

Kind	Recommendation	Readability	Audience
E	**	2	AG

Birren, J. E. (1974). Translation in gerontology—From lab to life: Psychophysiology and speed of response. *American Psychologist,* **29, 808–815.**

Older individuals show a tendency to slow in response which reflects a basic change in the speed with which the central nervous system processes information. The author discusses this age-related slowing with regard to perception, sensation, learning, and memory, and highlights changes in the peripheral and central nervous systems. Slowness in speed should be used as an explanatory independent variable when translating laboratory results to the real world.

Kind	Recommendation	Readability	Audience
TC	***	2	AU

Botwinick, J. (1984). *Aging and behavior* **(3rd ed.) (Chap. 13, pp. 229–248). New York: Springer.**

The author discusses two views of speeded performance, the consequence view and the determinant view, with respect to age-related slowing of behavior. Evidence for central slowing is presented as are models of speed loss. Cognitive processing time is explained through a discussion of actual studies and, finally, the traditional reaction time literature shows that response slowing with age is greatest at the most complex levels.

Kind	*Recommendation*	*Readability*	*Audience*
TC	**	2	AU

Britton, J. O., & Thomas, K. R. (1973). Age and sex as employment variables: Views of employment service interviewers. *Journal of Employment Counseling, 10,* 180–186.

This investigation measured perceptions of 56 employment interviewers regarding worker characteristics of males and females of varying ages. Results showed significant main effects due to age and sex. Older workers were found to be more difficult to place during a recession, most difficult to train, and least able to maintain production schedules. Younger workers were most likely to have accidents on the job and more absences from work. Women were absent from work more and had fewer skills that employers want. Prime age groups (25 to 35 years) were perceived as the most attractive. These results reveal attitudes toward employment problems of age and sex.

Kind	*Recommendation*	*Readability*	*Audience*
E	**	2	AG

Brown, D. (1981). Emerging models of career development groups for persons at midlife. *The Vocational Guidance Quarterly, 29,* 332–340.

The author presents emerging models of career development groups for persons at midlife. The first, a self-help model, assumes some help is better than no help. The interactive processes characterizing individual and group counseling are unnecessary to attain the knowledge and attitudes necessary to enhance the career development process. Brown criticizes this model as he does the informational model, which assumes that given accurate information about the work world, persons can make appropriate occupational choices. These models are not based on sound theories that have empirical support. The counselor, as stated by the author, is an essential factor as he or she offers multiple experiences to adults in midlife.

Kind	Recommendation	Readability	Audience
TC	**	1	GP

Czaja, S. J., & Drury, C. G. (1981). Aging and pretraining in industrial inspection. *Human Factors*, 23, 485–494.

Job training is discussed as a potential barrier to the older adult looking for employment. The existing stereotype that claims that older people are unable to learn new skills is presented with an emphasis on cognitive decline with age. The authors, through intervention research, show that the cognitive performance of older adults can be improved. The authors suggest that pretraining and the use of active training can improve the level of performance achieved and the durability of the skill, resulting in increased opportunities for employment for the older adult.

Kind	Recommendation	Readability	Audience
E	***	3	RG

Doering, M., Rhodes, S. R., & Schuster, M. (Eds.) (1983). *The aging worker: Research and recommendations*. Beverly Hills, CA: Sage.

This book provides an exhaustive review of the literature on aging and age-related differences in employees with regard to critical issues facing organizations. The book is structured into three parts. Part 1 discusses psychological characteristics and workplace behaviors of older workers. The specific studies pertaining to these characteristics and workplace behaviors are described in terms of population, age characteristics, n-size, and statistical results, when available. Part 2 focuses on organizational staffing activities as well as on career planning, training, and development. Part 3 addresses compensation, pensions, and retirement issues. Throughout the text, relevant research areas are summarized.

Kind	Recommendation	Readability	Audience
TB	***	3	AG

Edelman, C. D., & Siegler, I. C. (1978). *Federal age discrimination in employment law: Slowing down the gold watch*. Charlottesville, VA: Michie.

Although this book was written over a decade ago, it gives excellent background regarding the Age Discrimination in Employment Act. It discusses in depth many issues and provides examples of case law up until the time it was published. More recent sources will need to be consulted to provide information regarding the dates of the law effective January, 1987.

Kind	Recommendation	Readability	Audience
TC	***	2	AU

Elias, P. K., Elias, M. F., Robbins, M. A., & Gage, P. (1987). Acquisition of word-processing skills by younger, middle-age, and older adults. *Psychology and Aging, 2,* 340–348.

The authors investigated the existence of age differences in speed and performance levels achieved with a commercial word-processing training program. Results indicate that although all of the subjects mastered the requirements of word processing, the older group, as compared to younger and middle-aged groups, took longer to complete the training and evaluation procedures. This group also performed poorly on a review examination designed to test knowledge of word processing techniques. Recommendations are made for word-processing training protocols for older trainees. These include an explanation of hardware and software, the difference between typing and word-processing, and short training sessions.

Kind	Recommendation	Readability	Audience
E	**	2	AG

Haefner, J. E. (1977) Race, age, sex, and competence as factors on employer selection of the disadvantaged. *Journal of Applied Psychology, 62,* 199–202.

Interviews were conducted to determine assessments of hypothetical job candidates with varying characteristics. The objective of the study was to assess the current state of the employment market for individuals who might face discrimination in hiring due to race, sex, age, or competence. Results show that the race of a potential employee was not an important factor in hiring decisions but age, sex, and competence did affect decisions. Age discrimination against highly competent older workers clearly exists in employment settings for semiskilled jobs.

Kind	Recommendation	Readability	Audience
E	**	2	AG

Humple, C. S., & Lyons, M. (1983). *Management and the older workforce: Policies and programs.* New York: American Management Association.

The objectives of the briefing are threefold. They include the creation of a greater understanding of the relationship between an aging work force and societal changes, the understanding of unique management issues pertaining to older workers, and the translation of these awarenesses into improved company policy and planning. The briefing addresses major myths held concerning the older worker. Next, the interplay between the aging work force and societal and economic changes is described. Further, the interrelationship between technology, productivity, and alternative work arrangements, as they affect an older work force, is described. Case studies of older worker policies are reviewed as are techniques for training management in older worker issues. The briefing takes a product-oriented approach to older worker issues.

Kind	*Recommendation*	*Readability*	*Audience*
TB	***	2	GP

Jacobsen, B. (1980). *Young programs for older workers.* New York: Van Nostrand Reinhold.

This book, the result of a nationwide survey, outlines a variety of programs reflecting what companies are doing to hire, retrain, and provide new avenues of work for older employees. The book is organized into six sections each containing case examples ranging from banking to high technology to school systems and government. The sections include new work arrangements, reentry workers, secondary organizations, redeployment (involuntary movement of older workers), hiring older workers, and assessing and advising them. Approximately 70 examples of progressive policies currently being used are highlighted with emphasis on the needs of older workers in language for the layperson.

Kind	*Recommendation*	*Readability*	*Audience*
TB	***	1	GP

Johnston, W. B., & Packer, A. E. (Eds.). (1987). *Workforce 2000: Work and workers for the twenty-first century.* Indianapolis, IN: Hudson Institute.

The report provides basic information on the job market that can be , used in evaluating current public policies and, when inadequate, stimulating new policy initiatives. The forces shaping the American economy are discussed, including, among others, integration of goods to services. Projections concerning the development of the U.S. economy to the year 2000 are described as an aid in the evaluation of policy options. Demographic trends in the present and future work force are charted.

Kind	Recommendation	Readability	Audience
TB	**	2	GP

Jones, W. H. (1979). Grief and involuntary career change: Its implications for counseling. *The Vocational Guidance Quarterly,* **27, 196–201.**

The article discusses grief reactions to an involuntary career loss as well as the grief impact of this type of loss. The role of the counselor in aiding those who are experiencing grief reactions as a result of career loss is examined. Possible grief reactions exposed by Parkes (1984), Engel (1964), and Westberg (1971) are discussed, followed by ways in which a counselor can aid the client in working through the grief process in order to be free to explore new career options.

Kind	Recommendation	Readability	Audience
TC	**	1–2	SP

Maxwell, N. (1985). The retirement experience: Psychological and financial linkages to the labor market. *Social Science Quarterly,* **66, 22–33.**

The article examines the link between labor market activities and retirement income and life satisfaction after retirement. Further, it studies the influence of relative versus absolute income level on life satisfaction. The data were obtained from the older males cohort of the National Longitudinal Surveys of Work Experience. Results indicate that institutional factors, such as the industry in which one works, dominate the determination of retirement income. Further, life was related to the absolute level of retirement income and not to the comparison of retirement to preretirement income.

Kind	Recommendation	Readability	Audience
E	**	2–3	AG

Mobley, W. J., Griffith, R. W., Hand, H. H., & Meglino, B. M. (1979).

Review and conceptual analysis of the employee turnover process. *Psychological Bulletin, 86,* 593–622.

The authors present a conceptual model that pinpoints the need to distinguish between satisfaction (present oriented) and attraction/ expected utility (future oriented) for present and alternative roles. The present review, in agreement with the earlier reviews of Porter and Steers (1973) and Price (1977), found age to be consistently and negatively associated with turnover (as were tenure, overall job satisfaction, and reaction to job content). The authors point out, however, that since age is correlated with many other variables, it alone contributes little to the understanding of turnover behavior. It appears that intentions and commitment-attachment made a stronger contribution to turnover behavior than did satisfaction and demographic variables (including age). Considering the limited number of multivariate studies, the authors conclude that greater variance in turnover can be explained by using multiple variables.

Kind	Recommendation	Readability	Audience
RC	**	3	AG

Morrison, M. H. (1986). Work and retirement in an older society. In A. Pifer, & L. Bronte (Eds.), *Our aging society* (pp. 341–365). New York: Norton.

Employment and retirement policies have been used to secure balance in the work force so as to result in national economic objectives and diminished intergenerational tension. Retirement has both positive and negative consequences for the older population as outlined by the author. Alternative work options are discussed including phased retirement, annuitant pools, and retraining. The author expresses the need for a new value consensus regarding work and retirement, emphasizing the productivity potential of the older adult.

Kind	Recommendation	Readability	Audience
TC	**	3	AG

Neugarten, B. L. (1976). Adaptation and the life cycle. *The Counseling Psychologist, 6,* 16–20.

Every society is age graded and every society has a system of social expectations regarding age-appropriate behaviors. Age norms and age expectations operate as a system of social controls. The author discusses changes in the life cycle with respect to three dimensions of time: historical, chronological, and social. Women are having children later and are reentering the work force. Other changes include increased interiority, changed time perspective, and personalization of death. Changes in timing of the family cycle are outlined and discussed with respect to societal changes.

Kind	Recommendation	Readability	Audience
TC	**	2	GP

Newquist, D. D. (1986). Toward assessing health and functional capacity for policy development on work-life extension. In J. E. Birren, P. K. Robinson, and J. E. Livingston (Eds.), Age, health, and employment. Englewood Cliffs, NJ: Prentice-Hall.

The chapter discusses the importance of health as a factor influencing the work-life extension trend. The authors point out a variety of issues to consider when making statements about health and work capacity or disability among the older population. These factors include differences in and effectiveness of measures of health and/or disability, choice of central aspects of health to utilize when measuring disability, societal health standards, and finally, evaluation of health data.

Kind	Recommendation	Readability	Audience
HB	**	2	AG

Office of Technology Assessment (1985). *Technology and aging in America*. Washington, DC: U.S. Congress, OTA-BA-264

This book covers a broad range of topics specific to older adults. The explosion of workplace technologies has threatened the previously secure future of older workers. However, technology has been the major factor in the growth of the older population, improved health, and increased longevity. Chapter content includes health issues and health care costs, living environments, biotechnology, and workplace technology.

Kind	Recommendation	Readability	Audience
HB	***	2	GP

Olbrich, E. (1986). Coping in old age. In J. E. Birren, P. K. Robinson, & J. E. Livingston (Eds). *Age, health, and employment* (pp. 45–62). Englewood Cliffs, NJ: Prentice-Hall.

Coping refers to adaptive behavior and consists of a drastic change in behavior. The chapter summarizes well-known theories of adaptation and development and includes such theories as the psychoanalytic, cognitive conception, and cognitive-behavioral. Two hypotheses, the regression hypothesis and the growth hypothesis, are presented with specific attention paid to coping and aging. Longitudinal data from the Bonn Longitudinal Study on Aging show that older people meaningfully restructure their programs of adaptation and cope in order to restructure and reach a reequilibration of assimilative and accommodative processes.

Kind	Recommendation	Readability	Audience
TC	**	2	GP

O'Toole, J. (1978). *Work, learning, and the American future.* San Francisco: Jossey-Bass.

This book attacks traditional assumptions regarding work and the learning experience, and suggests that new perspectives will lead to improvements in the quality and quantity of jobs. The author suggests alternatives to current work and education processes. The book is divided into four parts: The first part identifies and defines the major problems of work and education; the second discusses the role of government in securing full employment and the roles of employers and unions; the third outlines alternative ways to address the future world of work with educational programs; and the fourth suggests policies to utilize the nation's human resources.

Kind	Recommendation	Readability	Audience
TB	**	2	GP

Pallak, M. T., & Perloff, R. O. (Eds.). (1986). *Psychology and work: Productivity, change, and employment.* Washington, DC: American Psychological Association.

This volume, derived from the Master Lecture presentations, provides a discussion of current issues regarding the individual in relation to the organization and the work system. "Work as a Human Context" examines the interrelationship between the impact of work and employment with the social context of work. In "Technological Change and the Structure of Work," computer-assisted technology is discussed with respect to the work force and training. Self-management systems that require a commitment to collective objectives are discussed in "The Psychology of Self-Management in Organizations" and a historical approach to career issues is examined in "Career Issues Through the Life Span." "Work, Family, and the Child" presents a discussion of the effects of the interaction between family dynamics and the workplace. Issues of importance including innovation and change, career patterns, and family systems are examined in detail.

Kind	Recommendation	Readability	Audience
TB	**	3	SP

Panek, P. E., Barrett, G. V., Sterns, H. L., & Alexander, R. A. (1977). A review of age changes in perceptual information processing ability with regard to driving. *Experimental Aging Research, 3*, 387–449.

The authors present a comprehensive review of age-related changes in hearing and vision in the context of driving behavior. Changes in information-processing abilities of selective attention, perceptual style, and perceptual motor reaction time are also included with emphasis on the ability changes that occur with regard to processing environmental information relevant to driving. Individual differences are mentioned as an explanatory variable, and training programs appropriately designed are recommended to teach compensatory strategies for what may be a declining set of information-processing skills.

Kind	Recommendation	Readability	Audience
RC	**	2	AG

Pond, S. B., & Geyer, P. D. (1987). Employee age as a moderator of the relation between perceived work alternatives and job satisfaction. *Journal of Applied Psychology, 72*(4), 552–557.

The literature suggests that the perception of the availability of work alternatives directly affects job satisfaction, and the authors suggest the employee age moderates the reaction between perceived alternatives and job satisfaction. A model of the adaptation cycle, specifically designed from the perspective of the older employee, is proposed to explain the weaker correlation between perceived work alternatives and job satisfaction that exists for older workers relative to younger workers. The study raises the issue that the effects of both psychosocial and biological aging in addition to work experience should be examined when studying the relation between perceived work alternatives and job satisfaction. The authors stress the importance of individual differences in perceptions. The model describes how employees consider a number of alternatives to adjust the dissatisfaction experienced.

Kind	Recommendation	Readability	Audience
E	**	2	AG

Robinson, P. K. (1986). Age, health, and job performance. In J. E. Birren, P. K. Robinson, & J. E. Livingston (Eds.), *Age, health, and employment*. Englewood Cliffs, NJ: Prentice-Hall.

The chapter discusses age-related changes in health among middle-aged and older workers and possible effects of these changes on work capacity and job performance. Workplace interventions such as reducing work hazards and promoting health in the workplace are discussed in terms of reducing the impact of aging on health. Finally, assessment, specific workplace accommodations, and retraining opportunities are proposed as a means of reducing the impact of age-related health changes in job performance.

Kind	Recommendation	Readability	Audience
HB	***	2	AG

Robinson, P. K., Coberly, S., & Paul, C. (1985). Work and retirement. In R. H. Binstock & E. Shanas (Eds.), *Handbook of aging and the social sciences* (2nd ed.). New York: Van Nostrand Reinhold.

The chapter views both macro and micro issues concerning work and retirement, in terms of macro issues such as labor force participation and micro issues such as the impact of work and retirement on the individual and the employer. The first part of the chapter describes current and projected labor force participation of selected population age groups and notes the changes in older adult employment patterns. Of major interest is the recent decline in labor force participation of males over the age of 55. The problems surrounding unemployed and discouraged older workers is also considered. The second part of the chapter deals with the place of leisure in the work and retirement stages of the life cycle, factors involved in the retirement decision, and the impact of retirement on the individual. Finally, the authors examine the role of the employer in determining the outcomes of individual aging as well as in contributing to national trends in labor force participation, unemployment, and retirement of the older population. Specific topics on concerns facing employers include skill shortages, functional assessment of individual performance productivity, and retirement age policy.

Kind	Recommendation	Readability	Audience
HB	***	2	AU

Rosen, B., & Jerdee, T. H. (1985). *Older employees: New roles for valued resources*. Homewood, IL: Dow Jones–Irwin.

This book, as its title suggests, offers a useful outlook for older adults with respect to employment possibilities and realities. Effective management of older employees includes a discussion of the age stereotypes pervasive in our culture along with the legal protection provided for older adults. Career planning, including midlife career change, and retraining to prevent obsolescence are considered from both individual and organizational viewpoints. Organizational strategies are offered for the management of older employees as are guidelines for change that emphasize early intervention so as to utilize fully the talents, experience, and commitment of older adult workers.

Kind	Recommendation	Readability	Audience
TB	***	2	GP

Salthouse, T. A. (1984). Effects of age and skill in typing. *Journal of Experimental Psychology: General, 113*, 345–371.

Time and accuracy of keystrokes in a variety of typinglike activities were investigated in this study. Typing has been shown to be similar to a series of choice reaction time tasks in which a subject is presented with a single visual stimulus and is instructed to rapidly press a particular button for each of the possible stimuli. Older typists were found to be slower in tapping rate and in choice reaction time but not in speed of typing. The significant effect of age on the eye-hand span suggests that one compensatory mechanism used to control the age-associated decline in perceptual–motor speed is more extensive anticipation of impending keystrokes. With compensatory strategies (i.e., looking four to five words ahead), the older adult can perform as well as younger adults.

Kind	Recommendation	Readability	Audience
E	***	3	AG

Salthouse, T. A. (1985). Speed of behavior and its implications for cognition. In J. E. Birren & K. W. Schaie (Eds.), *Handbook of the psychology of aging* (pp. 400–426). New York: Van Nostrand Reinhold.

The chapter reviews findings concerning the slowing-with-age phenomenon with a special emphasis on possible information-processing-related causes. The author assesses the magnitude and reliability of the slowing-with-age phenomenon via the magnitude of correlations between chronological age and time required to perform a given activity. In a review of over 50 correlations across a variety of speeded tasks, positive correlations were found with a median value of 45. The author tempers these results by indicating that health of the subject population, type of response needed for the task, and amount of practice at a task may influence the slowing-with-age findings. He also describes methodological problems that may hinder interpretation of these results. With these problems in mind, the author outlines six possible causes for the age-related slowing, in the context of information processing. These explanations include input and/or output rate, software differences, internal representation of control processes, capacity of working memory, concurrent processing demands, and hardware differences.

Kind	Recommendation	Readability	Audience
HB	**	3	AG

Salthouse, T. A. (1986). Functional age: Examination of a concept. In J. E. Birren, P. K. Robinson, & J. E. Livingston (Eds.), *Age, health, and employment* (pp. 78–92). Englewood Cliffs, NJ: Prentice-Hall.

Functional age has been used to extend knowledge about group trends to the individual level. Functional capabilities are more meaningful than chronological age for characterizing the status of the individual. However, there is no single correct definition of functional age. The author discusses three types of functional age (occupational, biomedical, and structural) and their respective purposes, variable selection procedures, validation criteria, and the roles of age. Failure to distinguish these three categories has led to much confusion and has hindered progress.

Kind	Recommendation	Readability	Audience
TC	**	2	AU

Schlossberg, N. K. (1976). The case for counseling adults. *The Counseling Psychologist, 6*, 33–36.

Role transformations are inevitable in adulthood and the counselor must be able to facilitate these changes and help clients to regain some control over their lives. Adult counseling requires attention to decision-making processes and an awareness of age bias. In addition, the counselor must be aware of adult development and look for situations left unsaid, called listening with the "third ear."

Kind	Recommendation	Readability	Audience
TC	**	2	SP

Schwab, D. P., & Heneman, H. G., III. (1978). Age stereotyping in performance appraisal. *Journal of Applied Psychology,* *63*(5), 573–578.

Personnel specialists were asked to evaluate written performance descriptions of secretaries on six dimensions; the fourth secretary profile lent itself to potential age bias. The authors found significant interactions between age of participants and age of target interaction. Older participants gave the older secretary *lower* evaluations and younger participants gave older secretaries *higher* evaluations. Results show that the amount of job experience does not have an impact on performance evaluations. Age stereotypes did not have as strong an impact as anticipated.

Kind	Recommendation	Readability	Audience
E	**	2	AG

Skoglund, J. (1979). Work after retirement. *Aging and work, 2,* 103–112.

This empirical study attempted to discover factors associated with work after retirement. Five hundred and thirty-four subjects between the ages of 60 to 75 were assessed on relevant demographic and attitudinal variables and the relationship between these variables and two factors: actual work past retirement age and attitudes toward retirement work. Results indicated that 66% of the respondents were positive toward continued work while only 40% had actually worked since retirement. Further, although females had a more work-oriented attitude, males and the well-educated of both sexes were more likely to work. Finally, attitudes common to both actual work and attitudes toward work include a work orientation, a reluctance to retire, and a positive perception of retirees.

Kind	Recommendation	Readability	Audience
E	**	2	AG

Stagner, R. (1985). Aging in industry. In J. E. Birren & K. W. Schaie (Eds.), *Handbook of the psychology of aging* **(pp. 789–817). New York: Van Nostrand Reinhold.**

This chapter addresses the issue of the aging worker in the industrial setting with an emphasis placed on the stereotype of the aging worker. Job performance is believed to decline, but the author points out problems regarding the performance approval process. Training and motivation are considered to be factors moderating this decline. Evidence is provided with respect to work and ability suggesting that the stereotyped view of the inefficient older worker is not justified. Recommendations are made for future research.

Kind	*Recommendation*	*Readability*	*Audience*
HB	**	2	AG

Steers, R. M. (1977). Antecedents and outcomes of organizational commitment. *Administrative Science Quarterly*, 22, 46–56.

A preliminary model concerning the antecedents and outcomes of organizational commitment was proposed and tested on 382 hospital employees and 119 scientists and engineers. Organizational commitment was defined as the relative strength of an individual's identification with and involvement in a particular organization. Age was found to be positively related to commitment when considering the hospital employee sample. Tenure was a competing variable. The author points out that more complex models must be developed and tested concerning the behavioral outcomes of employee commitment to organizations.

Kind	*Recommendation*	*Readability*	*Audience*
E	**	2	AG

Sterns, H. L. (1986). Training and retraining adult and older adult workers. In J. E. Birren, P. K. Robinson, & J. E. Livingston (Eds.), *Age, health, and employment* (pp. 93–113). Englewood Cliffs, NJ: Prentice-Hall.

The changing workplace brings with it the need for the individual to respond, change, and adapt to the changing environment. Older adult workers are required to change in response to innovations and must adopt new roles. Training is needed to build upon previous knowledge and experience and to prepare the older employee for challenges in the workplace. Moody's four-stage model for adult education is outlined and discussed as are specific areas necessary to be included in all retraining programs. Implications for training and retraining are discussed.

Kind	*Recommendation*	*Readability*	*Audience*
TC	**	2	GP

Sterns, H. L., & Alexander, R. A. (1987). Industrial gerontology. The aging individual and work. In K. W. Schaie (Ed.), *Annual review of gerontology and geriatrics*. (pp. 243–264). Vol. 7. New York: Springer.

The authors, in this chapter, focus on job-relevant training and older-adult-specific training. Major opportunities for career growth come from training and development, and particular attention is paid to individual developmental changes in a world of changing technology and economy. Because of the constantly changing work environment, job-relevant training is needed by all employees, especially older adults. The chapter also examines social policy and legal issues including the selection process, interviewing, age bias, and measurement of job performance. The Age Discrimination in Employment Act is discussed and its impact on organizational practice is addressed. Emphasis throughout the chapter is placed on a changing older adult worker in a changing employment environment.

Kind	*Recommendation*	*Readability*	*Audience*
RC	***	3	AG

Sterns, H. L., & Alexander, R. A. (1988). Step 6: Use objective performance appraisals. In H. Dennis (Ed.), *Fourteen Steps to Managing an Aging Workforce*. (pp. 171–190). Lexington, Mass.: D.C. Heath.

Performance appraisal use is discussed with specific attention placed on the impact on older workers. The authors suggest that the existing stereotypes regarding the older worker must be kept out of the appraisal process and instead the performance evaluation should be based upon actual job performance. Characteristics of a well-designed performance appraisal system are discussed with particular emphasis on a thoroughly and competently conducted job analysis. This assures that the performance evaluation encompasses all relevant aspects of job performance, and is not based on pre-existing beliefs about older workers.

Kind	*Recommendation*	*Readability*	*Audience*
TC	***	1	GP

Sterns, H. L., Barrett, G. V., & Alexander, R. A. (1985). Accidents and the aging individual. In J. E. Birren & K. W. Schaie (Eds.), *Hand-

book of the psychology of aging (pp. 703–724). New York: Van Nostrand Reinhold.

The chapter reviews the major areas of accident research with an emphasis on the relationship between aging and accidents. Models of accident-related behavior are examined as are the demographics of injuries and leading causes of death. Three major areas of accident research reviewed in the chapter include the highway environment, the home and community environment, and the workplace. Age-related data are examined concerning amount and type of accident involvement within the three major areas and research concerning predictors of accident involvement are explained. Finally, safety and injury prevention issues are viewed.

Kind	Recommendation	Readability	Audience
HB	**	2	AU

Sterns, H. L., & Doverspike, D. (1988). Step 7: Offer well-designed retraining programs and encourage older workers to participate. In H. Dennis (Ed.), *Fourteen steps in managing an aging workforce*. Lexington, MA: D.C. Heath.

The authors present a discussion of traditional topics regarding the training of older workers and more recent topics concerning the area of career development and management. Traditional topics include an overview of employment and training with an emphasis on designing an effective training program that includes a consideration of active participation, learning strategies, and transferring new skills to the job. Career development management includes research on career development and retirement planning. The authors offer five principles to ensure effective training and development of older workers.

Kind	Recommendation	Readability	Audience
TC	***	1	AP

Sterns, H. L., & Patchett, M. (1984). Technology and the aging adult: Career development and training. In P. K. Robinson, J. E. Livingston, & J. E. Birren (Eds.), *Aging and technological advances*. New York: Plenum Press.

The authors have attempted to develop a model of adult and older adult career development that is not age specific. According to their model, the decision to change jobs or careers or to exit the system is directly influenced by success or failure in previous career development activities as well as attitudes toward mobility. A number of factors are hypothesized to affect mobility attitudes. These include employment, tenure or stage in career, growth need, fear of stagnation, marketability perceptions, job market conditions, and chance encounters. Also, the decision to change job or career may affect one's attitudes toward entering or reentering the workforce. The authors note that these variables could be mediated by various personality variables. This model incorporates Hall's model of career growth (1971), which conceptualizes career planning from a goal-setting perspective.

Kind	Recommendation	Readability	Audience
TC	**	2	AU

Taeuber, C. (1984). Older workers: Force of the future? In P. K. Robinson, J. E. Livingston, & J. E. Birren (Eds.), *Aging and technological advances* (pp. 75–89). New York: Plenum Press.

Demographics regarding the elderly worker are provided along with a discussion of labor force participation rates. Industrial and occupational distributions, part-time employment, and unemployment statistics help to profile the older worker. The author examines the role of the older adult in the future labor market and concludes that with the employment of the baby boom generation, the labor force and the participation rates will be restructured in the face of inflexible work options and a sluggish economy.

Kind	Recommendation	Readability	Audience
RC	**	3	AG

Troll, L. E., & Nowak, C. (1976). "How old are you?"—The question of age bias in the counseling of adults. *The Counseling Psychologist, 6,* 41–43.

The authors discuss the possibility that counselors share the age stereotypes present in society. Definitions of appropriate behaviors vary by age of people under consideration and by the age of those who are stereotyping. Three kinds of age bias—age restrictiveness, age distortion, and ageism—are discussed with ramification for adult counseling. The counselor who asks a client's age is sure to assign age stereotypes to the client based on the answer, whether consciously or unconsciously. The authors recommend inquiring about more relevant characteristics.

Kind	Recommendation	Readability	Audience
TC	**	2	SP

Waldman, D. A., & Avolio, B. J. (1986). A meta-analysis of age differences in job performance. *Journal of Applied Psychology, 71*(1), 33–38.

A quantitative review was completed on data pertaining to the age–job performance relationship. Prior research reveals three types of performance measures that are often utilized: supervisory ratings, peer ratings, and individual ratings. Results of the meta-analysis indicated that the relationship between age and job performance was contingent upon the type of performance measure. Increase in performance was found at higher ages when performance was measured by productivity indices. Supervisory ratings, however, tended to be lower for older employees. Finally, moderator analysis revealed differences between professionals and nonprofessionals with performance ratings being more favorable with age for professionals, as compared to nonprofessionals.

Kind	Recommendation	Readability	Audience
E	***	3	AG

The future of older workers in America. **(1980). Scarsdale, NY: Work in America Institute, Inc.**

This policy study provides guidelines and recommendations to help all sectors respond constructively to the changing preferences of older workers. Knowledge about older workers and current progressive practices are summarized as are demographic and economic trends. Contents include present facts and projected trends concerning older workers. Age-neutral personnel policies include hiring, pay, training and development, and new options for an extended working life. Forty-six specific recommendations are included and discussed in the context of each chapter. These recommendations are directed primarily at employers and unions whose decisions set policies for the employees.

Kind	Recommendation	Readability	Audience
TB	**	3	GP

SUMMARY COMMENTS

The percentage of older adults in the workforce is declining. Projections about future patterns will depend on public policy regulations, economic conditions, workplace conditions, employer policies, technological change, and societal events and values. Even with the percentage decline of older workers, we are going to have an absolute increase in the number of older workers both full time and part time. It appears that there is a growing select group of older adults who are able and talented and who desire to work beyond traditional retirement age. Some older adults may be forced to continue to work out of economic necessity.

Adults make multiple career transitions throughout the life span. Career development and retirement education programs sensitize adult and older adult workers to potential options. Past discusison of aging and work has focused almost exclusively on the decision to retire.

Attitudes toward career development activities or the decision to retire are related to such factors as current employment, tenure or stage in career, need for achievement, and need for growth. In addition, fear of stagnation, marketability perceptions, job-market conditions, and chance encounters may play a role in decision making.

Technological innovation may have both positive and negative effects on the workplace. Quality of work life may be affected positively by the fact that new mechanization reduces or eliminates the tediousness of repetitive tasks or actual physical work. Quality of work life may be affected negatively by mass production or low-demand monitoring that may result in repetition and boredom. Machinery may make jobs faster paced, increasing the pressure to keep producing.

Negative consequences associated with technology-related change may be avoided or counteracted by careful job redesign, and a concern for social as well as technical programs is important to the career development of trainees at any age, in responding to changes in the workplace due to technological change.

Older workers must be given the opportunity for both short-term and long-term training opportunities. Negative attitudes on the part of supervisors may consciously or unconsciously exclude older workers.

Industrial gerontological psychology will be an important area for the future. Older adults of the 1990s and 2000s will need to continually update skills in a competitive working environment or accept employment in less demanding and low-paying jobs in the service area. Capable older workers should be able to successfully compete in the decades ahead.